WHEN PRIESTS BECOME PREDATORS

Profiles of Childhood Sexual Abuse Survivors

Thomas S. Neuberger

Thomas S. Neuberger
Publisher
Two East Seventh Street
Suite 302
Wilmington, Delaware 19801

Printed in the United States of America

ISBN 978-0-615-64824-8

This book is dedicated to the many survivors of childhood sexual crimes in Delaware who were brave enough to overcome their adversity and challenge their powerful church despite the overwhelming odds and forces they faced. Their words and the experiences related here seek to educate the reader and protect today's children.

CONTENTS

Introduction

On January 6, 2002, public awareness of the sexual crimes against children by Catholic priests, which had occurred for generations within the Roman Catholic Church, burst into the news starting in Boston, Massachusetts.[1] Expanded public awareness of the scandal swept through Iowa, Kentucky, San Diego, Los Angeles, Philadelphia and other major areas in the United States and abroad, including Ireland and Germany.[2] Governmental investigations followed, such as the September 2005[3] and January 2011 Grand Jury reports in Philadelphia[4] and four reports by the national Irish government from 1995 to 2011, ending with its most recent Cloyne Report.[5]

Through the heroic efforts of two Delaware State legislators, Senator Karen E. Peterson (Democrat) and Representative Deborah D. Hudson (Republican), the Delaware General Assembly unanimously enacted the Child Victim's Act of 2007. 10 *Del. C.* § 8145, which repealed the statute of limitations in civil suits relating to child abuse cases and provided a two year window in which victims could bring a civil action for personal injuries in cases previously barred by current law. Both before and after that remedial legislation, in the small state of Delaware alone, between January 2004 and July 2009, more than 160 separate lawsuits were filed in the state and federal courts arising from the crimes Catholic priests committed on children as far back as 1952 and as recently as 2006. Over 150 of those lawsuits involved the

Catholic Diocese of Wilmington, Inc. and Catholic religious orders of priests long active in Delaware, such as the Oblates of St. Francis de Sales, the Norbertines, and the Capuchins. The methods and tactics used by the church and its lawyers to discourage, intimidate and coerce the *survivors* of its crimes on children and youth are universal and are noted herein. (The victims of such childhood sexual crimes prefer to refer to themselves as *survivors* and not *victims*.)

The obstacles thrown up in Delaware by those who tried to prevent the restoration of these survivor's respect and dignity need to be understood by all our elected representatives, the media, and the voting public who can demand reform from their state legislators. One purpose of this book is to educate and motivate the citizenry at large to see that additional laws are passed to give survivors of childhood sexual abuse the opportunity to seek judicial relief in our courts nationwide. To that end, this work incorporates the actual words and experiences of these survivors as reported in existing court records.

Many other aspects of this crisis are poorly understood, if at all. For example, headlines and news stories fail to convey in detail the face of human suffering and the courage of those survivors of childhood sexual crimes who have come forward. Only attending a public trial or reviewing extensive video recordings of sworn testimony can provide some understanding of the magnitude of the personal anguish of survivors and their families, the tactics used by priest child abusers and their enabler bosses, the way religious dogma was perverted to enable these rogue priests to circumvent the family as a protective social institution for children, the mechanics of the psychological protective mechanisms of child victims, and the lifelong permanent emotional handicaps inflicted on survivors. These are all significant matters of public concern to our body politic, the public, and our legislators. Their political and social importance cannot be underestimated. Previously this vital information has been under-reported and unavailable in accessible and understandable formats.

The importance of the public's need to know the full and accurate particulars of little known aspects of the child abuse crisis within religious institutions, which are found in judicial records, falls within the parameters of the United States Supreme Court's 1975 decision in *Cox Broadcasting Corp. v. Cohn*: "In a society in which each individual has but *limited time and resources* with which to observe at first hand the operations of his government, he relies necessarily upon the press to bring to him in *convenient form the facts* of those operations. Great responsibility is accordingly placed upon the news media to report fully and accurately the proceedings of government, and *official records and documents open to the public are the best data* of government operations."[6] (Emphasis supplied)

And so, along with educating and motivating the public, another goal of this book is to act as the press and accurately and exactly republish the content of obscure multi-faceted judicial proceedings which are necessary to better inform us about matters of political and social importance which the courts and legislators of Delaware have addressed.[7] All these chapters are essentially fair and accurate verbatim reports of judicial trials, hearings and other proceedings taken directly from court records. At this time, the general public has no other convenient means of access to such material other than in book form since the media lacks the focus and the space for the task.

On another level it is hoped that this work will contribute to the professions of medicine, nursing, psychology, anthropology, sociology, law, criminal justice, and journalism, by presenting the actual phenomenological experiences of survivors of child abuse. Instead of presenting abstract quantitative studies of such individuals, it presents the lived experience of the persons in their own words, and is intended to deepen understanding of this phenomenon across academic and professional boundaries. It is hoped that this information will be invaluable for diagnostic and treatment purposes of adult victims of childhood sex crimes. Such victims rarely, if ever, tell a medical professional that they experienced a childhood sex crime which may be the source of their substance abuse, alcoholism, relational problems or other physical or emotional issues. With this information medical professionals may be assisted in making proper diagnoses and treatment alternatives may be enhanced. With the lived experiences related here, journalists and the media also will be better prepared to report on related crimes in other arenas, such as the 2011 Penn State University revelations of alleged child abuse by a football coach.

Moreover, this work presents the moral courage of ten survivors who publicly withstood all the opposition and dirty tricks which the Roman Catholic Church could muster. The individual chapters of this book stand as independent stories of the bravery and fortitude of the survivors under scrutiny and typify the experience of the universe of survivors from the Delaware sample. The narratives of these ten heroes appear in their own words as given in actual court proceedings, without paraphrase or interpretation. To assist the reader, and for ease of reading, when "questions" and "answers" from actual witness testimony are presented, the "Qs" and "As" from the actual transcripts have been removed so as to present a narrative exchange between the witness and the questioning attorney. In cases where the Q and A format is unnecessary to present the testimony, it is omitted altogether and the responses of the survivor are simply presented in his or her actual words as they occurred in court proceedings.

This book also fully documents the moral failures of the Diocese of Wilmington and two of its religious orders of priests, as found in their own business records. The decisions of many Delaware Bishops, the ultimate local authority in the Roman Catholic Church religious system, to employ priests despite repeated warnings such as, "be afraid to take a chance on him," also are explained. The code words and secret language used in church documents to record and identify which priests were child abusers are explained by a former priest who worked within the church medical and mental health system.

The consequences of this form of child abuse have gone unrecognized, or have been misunderstood and under-reported. Not only do sexually abused children suffer long into adulthood, their families suffer as well. Here, two leading psychiatrists and one preeminent psychologist testify to judges and juries about the delicate balance and wiring of a child's mind, the effects of trauma on it, the often subsequent protective amnesia imposed by the unconscious mind of a child, as well as the permanent destruction of the child's ability to form normal relationships with any human being for the rest of his or her life and the often inevitable substance abuse and addictions which follow.

The historic and unprecedented action of the United States Bankruptcy Court for the District of Delaware, a premier business court, also is presented. In August 2010 it allowed eight survivors to take the stand and recount their suffering in court and so to influence the ultimate resolution of the Diocese's dilatory bankruptcy proceedings which were designed to deny justice to all survivors.

The last half of this book presents the ultimate legal battle – the two month long trial of survivor John Vai. His trial included many victories, and one was the destruction on the witness stand of the key priest in the diocese, the right-hand man for four Bishops, who was involved with this local scandal for over thirty years. Like the jurors, readers will learn the evidence

against the church which was presented by John Vai's attorneys and the reader will be able to

reach his or her own conclusions about the general guilt or innocence of the Roman Catholic

Church and the justice of the claims of victims of its priests in Delaware.

Finally, this book is a contribution to the historic record. It exposes to public view the

universal tactics the church used against those survivors of sexual abuse by priests in Delaware

who were bold enough to stand up to the church. The documentary and oral history of the cover-

up by the diocese, the Oblates and the Norbertines are another part of this historic record, but are

not told here in a simple chronological fashion from 2004 through 2010. The straightjacket of a

chronology would detract from the profiles of the survivors contained herein. The historic record

reveals that the church made the business decisions to make the staffing of its institutions in a

time of personnel shortages more important than the protection of children. Taken together,

those decisions must lead any objective observer to conclude that the Roman Catholic Church

considered its role as a business entity more important than protecting the most helpless in our

society, children.

It is my hope that this book will provide the reader with a deeper understanding of the

many elements of this world-wide crisis, the search for justice by the once-innocent child victims

of the Roman Catholic Church and that it will lead to even more protections for today's children,

as well as justice for other survivors.

1

Douglas J. McClure, Sgt. U.S.M.C.

The sad exposition of the struggle for justice against the Roman Catholic Church in Delaware

begins with the funeral of Douglas McClure, who was the nicest person I have ever known.

Doug was a Marine veteran and his wake and burial honored him as a Marine. On April 30,

2009 a color guard of aged warriors marched in at the end of his wake and proudly carried his

battle flag, while taps resounded. The scarlet standard of the emblem found on the Marine Corps

Flag is rendered in gray and gold over that scarlet background. The motto ribbon flows from the

golden eagle's beak bears the words *Semper Fidelis*, "Always Faithful," with a flowing scroll

found below bearing the words *United States Marine Corps*. The eagle, globe and anchor

emblem found there has been part of Marine Corps iconography since 1868.[8]

Doug had tried to live according to the Marine Corps credo and now his life on this earth

had ended at age sixty-two. *Honor. Courage. Commitment.* Once a Marine, always a Marine.

These promises were for life. When he pledged his *Honor* he was held to the highest standards.

Respect for others was essential. He was expected to act responsibly and in a manner befitting

the title he had earned – Marine. *Courage* is not the absence of fear. It is the ability to face fear

and overcome it. It is the mental, moral and physical strength ingrained in every Marine. It steadied Doug in times of stress, carried him through every challenge and aided him in facing

new and unknown confrontations. His *Commitment* was to a spirit of determination and

dedication.[9] It was this lifelong pledge that gave Doug the ability to fight his second war after

Vietnam against the demons who came upon him the day when he read the Wilmington *News

Journal* story about John F. Dougherty and the fight John was waging against the Roman

Catholic Church and all the evil that priest Edward Carley had inflicted on him and many others

and that his church continued to cover-up.

 The room at the funeral home was filled with friends and family from over the years who

surveyed the photographs of Doug's life. He was most proud of those black and whites taken

during his service in Vietnam. There he was, strong and young again, bending over live

ordinance stacked under the wing of a fighter aircraft, bare-chested and determined in his combat

boots and fatigues, fulfilling the mission.

 I was honored that day to speak at Doug's funeral. Now a greying advocate, in 2003, I

had taken up another cause for what I always called "the little man."[10] My eulogy was based on

the sworn testimony Doug had given under grilling by church lawyers. I began –

 Doug McClure was twice a hero, once for our Country and again for our

community.

 At a time of great social turmoil during the Vietnam War he answered the call to

colors to defend our Country. He commanded eighty-six men in the war zone at Chu Lai

Marine airbase,[11] he served honorably and he was wounded permanently in both body

and spirit.

 Johnny Cash, in his 1971 song entitled the *Man In Black*, lamented the fact that "each week we lose a hundred fine young men"[12] to that war. We lost about 55,000 of our finest young men at that time who never had a chance at life, wounded or not. They paid the ultimate sacrifice for each of us. Doug survived, he served us all and for his entire life he carried his wounds, like his post traumatic stress disorder. But he never complained. Doug did not have to go. You see he was "1Y," he had a medical draft deferment. But in his own words – "Things were going on and I felt I had a responsibility."[13] So he enlisted on May 25, 1967 and served until May 25, 1971, four years.[14]

In Doug's own words here is what being a Marine meant to him:

To me the Marine Corps is it's like the greatest fraternal organization in the world. Nobody compares to that by any means. We go out, we're Marines. It's not something you become, it's something you are, you are born that way. And this is the outlook we have, this is the way we look at everything. We never give up, we never leave our men or any of that and that's the cockiness that you go around with. Sometimes they knock your teeth out, but you'll try.[15]

Doug worked on bombs for marine fighter jets, it was his specialty. That means the bombs, rockets, missiles, anything that is explosive on a plane. He very quickly advanced to corporal and sergeant and arrived in Vietnam in March 1968 for his tour of duty at Chu Lai, the Marine airbase which was the companion to DaNang further North.[16] Had he not left the Service, he would have been promoted to Master Sergeant in less than a month. He commanded eighty-six men at Chu Lai, and he serviced three Marine air groups, consisting of twelve squadrons of fighter jets.[17] On the airstrip he had to have everything ready each day for the air sorties, whatever the targets were going to be. In his words – *I had to be able to have everything ready for what they wanted and launch it on time.*[18]

This is how he described how he lived for twelve months over there: *I lived in a Conex box, big old metal box. Stayed out there by myself. Had a whole bunch of ammunition, a whole bunch of C rations. . . . I was in the middle of a runway and the runway was 13,000 feet and I was at the middle and it was a Conex box, you could stand up in it and all that. I'll tell you it's like the ones you see on the back of the tractor-trailers, but they're real small, the containers, one of them, and then that was mine and I had a little foxhole next door . . . .*[19] You see, it was the object of the enemy, the Viet-Cong, to get to that runway and destroy those planes and anyone in the way, like Doug.

Psalms 103:15-16 says:

As for man, his days are like grass,

he flourishes like a flower of the field;

the wind blows over it and it is gone,

and its place remembers it no more.[20]

Well, while in 125 years no one will remember any of us, let me recall some more of Doug's story.

Doug never thought he would live beyond age forty-two, so we had him with us for twenty more years after that. His biological father died at age forty-two, and his dear brother Dicky died of cancer at forty-two,[21] so Doug thought that is when the clock runs out and the game is over. He was wrong, and lived to age sixty-two.

He grew up in the Forty Acres of Wilmington, Delaware, in the Irish community. Elementary school friends included Peanuts Rykiel, Carl Agostini, Joe Butler, Brian Mann and many others.[22] He made friends very easily and we all are witnesses to that.[23]

The 1950s were a time of great turmoil in the world and when he was in public school he knew kids from Czechoslovakia, Hungary, and even Brazil.[24] At Wilmington High School he was a four-sport athlete – track where he ran the mile, cross country, swimming where he was the team captain his senior year, and golf.[25] A guy who tried out for the Olympics taught him how to dive. He would train at Canby Park Pool on the three meter board and at the YMCA on a one-meter board.[26] He continued running twenty mile runs after high school.[27] He played golf at all the Delaware clubs.[28]

And he was blessed with a mom, Natalie, who taught him how to dance at a young age and so he became a jitter-bug and had a leg up on most guys.[29] He was not always crippled needing that cane he had to use. Dancing was a passion with him. Doug was famous for a teenager back then. He had danced on TV on Dick Clark's original *American Bandstand* up in Philadelphia where he would go after cutting the last class at school.[30] He also danced at the Steel Pier, Grady & Hurst, the Starlight, and even in the Service when he was stationed in Jacksonville, Florida where he danced nightly. His favorite dances were the jitterbug, the strand and the cha-cha.[31] In high school for dancing he dressed in a Madras jacket, solid shirt, usually blue or pink, and slacks. Shoes from Flagg Brothers. In his own words again – *It was the whole deal.*[32] Doug did not always wear that worn Marine Corps jacket we saw on his shoulders.

Doug met his dear wife Nancy the week before Christmas in 1970 five months before he got out of the Service. He had a remarkable memory and told me that their first date was July 15, 1971, they dated for two years and married on October 26, 1973.[33] After that first date, in his own words – *right away* – they became exclusive. *She was a good person and I knew it*,[34] he said publicly and for the record. And he felt that way about her up to the very end. *She was a good person and I knew it.*

During their dating they went everywhere with her son Nicky who was about three, like the ski club on the Chesapeake, snow skiing in the Poconos.[35] He always loved Nicky and never missed any of his high school football games.[36] Their son Dougie was born three years after they married in 1976. And in his words, the birth of his son Dougie – *was a joyful experience* – for him.[37] He was just as proud of Dougie as he was of Nicky. He publicly bragged about Dougie's musical and singing abilities and the fact he can speak six languages. In Doug's own words – *He is just a phenomena to me and I asked him. I said Doug, you got to do something with this, you got to help people with this.*[38]

At work Doug was a Teamster and his union elected him shop steward.[39]

But from that marriage in 1973 until he blew his back out in 1987 Doug was fighting his demon, alcoholism. He drank all the time until October 28, 1987.[40] Nancy endured and stuck with him through very very hard times. And at Governor Bacon, he recovered and did not have another drink for twenty-two years until he died.[41] Then Doug was inspired by Kay Hernandez his quadriplegic vocational rehab counselor who challenged him to go back to school, and he did. In four years in 1994 he graduated from Del Tech, Phi Beta Kappa, Honor Society, a 3.72 grade average.[42] In his words – *I wanted to see if I could do it* – and he did![43] Doug mastered, math, physics, electronics, electricity. Not bad.

Doug was a smart man.

When he could not get a job because of his injuries, he enjoyed ham radio, calling all over the world, and looking up "scientific stuff and try[ing] to figure it out."[44] And don't forget the drag racing with his brothers Marty and Mark in Cecil County, N.Y., Virginia, N.C. and other places.[45]

Doug also gave back to this community unselfishly. That started when his brother Kevin drowned in the Brandywine in the 1950s which motivated Doug to become a strong swimmer. He taught water safety here and in the Marines to save others from drowning.[46] For thirty-five years he volunteered at the Wilmington Veterans Administration Nursing Home, where he drove disabled veterans. He was actively involved in AA for twenty-two years, where he served for some time as Chairman of Inner Group of Delaware. As a member of AA, he spoke to children and adults at various institutions, including Kirkwood Detox, Rockford Center, the Salvation Army, Delaware Psychiatric Center, and Delaware prisons. He was also a member of the local Marine Corps League, through which he volunteered at the Ronald McDonald House and the Veterans Administration hospital, sent supplies to servicemen and women overseas, and performed other charitable work. He tutored kids in math up to the end.

But Doug, unknown to all of us until 2005, also was called to fight another war which gravely wounded him in body and spirit, just as Vietnam had done. Doug was called to wrestle with the question of why and how there can be great evil in the world.

After he came back from the War and killing in Vietnam, Doug said it affected the practice of his religious faith. In his own words – *It didn't make a lot of sense to me, religion and killing. . . . I just don't get it. I don't see any happiness, I see sorrow.*[47]

The scriptures in the Book of *Job* tell of a successful wealthy married man with many children, respected in the community. Then he was confronted with evil and robbed of it all; he lost his children and wealth and was afflicted with great illness. He was urged to curse God and he argued with God. He complained contending that he had done nothing to deserve his misery. And he wrestled with the problem of how can there be evil in a world with a God. And Doug confronted that same problem which at one time or another has confronted all of us.

You see Doug was the victim of unspeakable evil at the tender age of eight. This evil so overwhelmed an eight year old that it rewired his brain as a defense mechanism for surviving the evil. That evil drove him to become an alcoholic at age thirteen as a means of self-medication to escape from it. And when he stopped drinking twenty-two years ago, depression then tried to overcome him. That evil also gave him amnesia, the total loss of memory of what had been done to him, so his little eight-year-old body could endure and survive. And survive he did, just like in Vietnam, in that Conex box on that 13,000 foot runway with jets taking off and landing everywhere. You see, Doug was tough.

How could an eight year old survive except through amnesia? No wonder Doug had a gripe with God, just like Job did. It did not make any sense. I would have had the same gripe with Almighty God. How could there be such evil in the world? Job and mankind have always had the same questions. We all have to find our own answer to that question about evil with which Doug wrestled.

In 2005 the long-lost memories of this evil flooded back into Doug's mind. Nightmarish shadows of an evil figure overwhelmed him. His VA doctors thought he was going crazy. Finally, he told Nancy what had been done to him. And they cried together. But instead of being consumed with hate, as I believe I would have been, he sought justice for himself and the other victims of such abuse. You see, Doug still was a hero.

The lawsuit that followed was never about the money. It was about exposing the truth and accountability for those who had permitted such evil. Almost as a foreshadowing, Doug told his lawyers that he was too old, he would never enjoy anything the court might award. It was for his family.

And so Doug became one of the three pioneers of the child abuse cases involving Roman Catholic priests in Delaware. When it was impossible to sue, Doug wanted to sue anyway. When no one in the community wanted to believe such evil existed, Doug cried out publicly in *The News Journal* that it did exist.[48] And our community listened and understood. Our elected officials responded to protect Doug and others like him. So did our courts.

In suing the Roman Catholic Church Doug challenged the most powerful institution in history and in the world. It never rolls over. It threw everything it had at Doug. And he did not bend. He was a Marine. It threw an army of lawyers against him, a ton of doctors and other hired gun experts to fight him, and it tried again and again to make him back off. But Doug was a Marine. He always accomplished his mission. He never left a man on the battlefield. And he was not going to leave any of the other abuse victims on the battlefield here in Delaware either.

Doug stood toe to toe with the most powerful institution in the entire world and it blinked and it gave up. It admitted in writing the immense evil Doug had suffered and it apologized to him. It also gave him just financial compensation which Doug wanted the world to know about, as an incentive to other victims, to encourage them to fight the good fight against that evil.

And so Doug was a second hero to me because of what he did for our community here in Delaware. He took the hill and raised the flag for the victims of priest abuse. And so Doug signed his last legal papers on Tuesday April 21st, the money was delivered from the coffers of the church and Doug went to rest along his beloved Chesapeake Bay.

While he was sitting there I like to think he and Jehovah God resolved their quarrel. Perhaps he heard the words Almighty God spoke out of the storm to Job.

Where were you when I laid the earth's foundation?

Have you given orders to the morning, or shown the dawn its place?

Have you comprehended the vast expanses of the earth?

Can you bring forth the constellations in their seasons?

Does the eagle soar at your command?

Would you discredit my justice?

Would you condemn me to justify yourself?

Everything under heaven belongs to me.[49]

And then Job understood and replied "Surely I spoke of things I did not understand."[50]

I think Doug, a very smart, tough and compassionate man figured it all out that night. I believe Doug got the answer to his question about evil. He then went home to paradise and we will see him on the other side where he awaits us, not in his worn out body but in a new healthy body, that young man again, the beebop dancer, swimmer, runner, athlete and hero.

* * *

Doug grew up at 1826 Shallcross Avenue, Wilmington, Delaware. The 1950s was a world far different from ours today. His was the supposedly safe world of the old black and white TV show – *Leave It To Beaver*. But a great, previously known danger had been carefully hidden from his parents by their church: – there was a real and present danger, if Doug as a child was left alone with a Roman Catholic priest, he could be sexually abused.

In Wilmington the Irish Catholic community was then and is still known as the Forty Acres. In 1861 at the time of the Civil War, a development opportunity presented itself and forty acres of the Shallcross Farm were sold for the purpose of plotting and selling building lots.[51] The area was especially promising for Irish immigrants who purchased lots in this new section of the city which would come to be occupied by many generations of their families.[52] The Forty Acres is bounded by Rockford Park on the north and west, Pennsylvania Avenue on the south, and the railroad tracks on the east. The first Roman Catholic Church for the community was St. James Chapel dedicated in 1869 but, when the first railroad tracks were laid too close, the parish relocated and in December 1887 the Church of St. Ann was dedicated at the corner of Gilpin Avenue and Union Street, where it stands to this day.[53]

Carefree children would run through the neighborhood. They would leave home in summer after breakfast and return for dinner. Kids played on the outdoor basketball court and baseball diamond with the athletic equipment priest Edward Carley used to entice them there. In the winter Carley provided ice skates to ensnare children. Carley was wealthy. That money gave him a big boat on the Sassafras River in nearby Maryland. He even entertained various classmates of Doug's in New York City at fancy restaurants where one, eventually a priest himself, got his first, big time, expensive hamburger.

Priests hung around on the street corners with kids. They were part of the gang. It was the 1950s.

Doug lived one block from the church on Shallcross Avenue. His parents put Doug in St. Ann's elementary school thinking he would be safe there, little knowing that a monster roamed its halls. Doug could step out into the street in front of his home and look down and see his church school. Eventually his parents caught on and got him out of there and into the public school system. But by then the damage had already been done to him.

St. Ann's school typically was very regimented and run by the drill-Sargent nuns. One of the greatest honors in school was for a boy to be chosen for training to be an altar boy. They dressed in red and white robes and assisted the priest in church services. Priests were considered to be just like God to an eight year old in the Roman Catholic Church at that time. Priests held the key to forgiveness of sins, and if you crossed them they could let you keep your sins in an unforgiven state which could send you to the fires of Hell forever. So you did what they told you. The priests and nuns ran the show, with no questions asked.

* * *

During his years-long battle with the Roman Catholic Church , Doug actually had to write down in his own words, and under oath, the nightmare of what had happened to him as a child. Here is some of what he said on January 23rd, 2009[54] or during a medical interview on May 30, 2008:[55]

When Father Carley was assigned to St. Ann's Church in 1954, I was about eight years old, in second grade.

I began training as an altar boy when I was eight years old at the sacristy at St. Ann's Church. Our goal was to be good Irish Catholic kids, go Notre Dame. With Carley it all started off as a joking, touching by him when he came to St. Ann's. This was before I had gone through puberty. I did not understand a lot. I remember when he first came to the parish. There was never a question about who a priest was. He was a representative of God.

A group of us would hang out in the neighborhood a block from St. Ann's church. Carley had everything we wanted in terms of equipment to play sports: bats, bases, hockey sticks, pucks, skates. We also went swimming at the YMCA on Washington Street and the Jewish YMCA on French Street. He took me to the Sassafras River, on his sailboat, on day trips to Ocean City, Maryland. As kids, back in those days, we just went out in the morning then came back in at night. No questions asked. Our parents did not think to ask questions. Carley would either be walking by, or driving by, in the neighborhood where we were playing. He would give a reason, for me to come with him, such as we need to go over and get something, or I need to see you.

The touching started in the sacristy and while we would be driving in the car. He touched my penis, fondled me, and would make me do the same to him. He would make me put his penis in my mouth and perform oral sex on him, and he would do the same to me. I experience the taste of his dick in my mouth to this day. He explained that this was what God wanted. In the car, he would recite passages from the *Bible*, while I was masturbating him, or he was masturbating me. Thinking back now, my neighbors included cops. But you just did not tell anyone. You did not do that.

His explanation was that this was what God wants. He is preparing you for Heaven, and these are heavenly sent sensations and feelings. It felt like I was required, by God, by this priest who was the equivalent of God in my life, and a representative of God on Earth, to participate in these activities, to let God's representative get some kind of pleasure out of me. At age eight I did not know any better and there was no one I could go to, to ask. I could not go to my parents. They would not believe me. At that time, it would be impossible to tell anyone what was going on.

Every day that I woke up, I would know something was going to happen if Carley wanted me . . . . I just did not know what.

He took me to his room in the rectory of St. Ann's. All the priests assigned to the church would see him take me frequently to his room where he had sex with me, such as the pastor monsignor [John J.] Bolen . . . .

I had to go up the stairs which were directly in front of the day room where all the priests gathered – it was their recreational area. There were two floors, and I had to go past this day room in order to go up the stairs to Carley's room. When other priests saw me going up there why didn't one of them stop him or stop me? I think if priests confessed to other priests, did one of them ever learn about me, and what he did to me, and keep quiet . . . or tell him it was okay and forgive him for it?

There wasn't much in his room: a writing table, drawer, a bed, a wooden crucifix, dramatized. It showed the nails and the blood of the Crucifixion.

In his room, he kept Vaseline in his drawer which he would use when he anally raped and sodomized me. He told me what he did to me, what he wanted me to do to him, was not an unholy thing. The conversation would begin as a *Bible* study and Carley would be praying or engaging me in spiritual discussions, such as explaining the mystery of the Eucharist or reading the *Bible* but quickly escalate to mutual touching, mutual oral sex, mutual anal sex. He would take my head, my hand, whatever he was in the mood for, and put it where he wanted – his erect penis, so he could cum wherever he wanted on that particular day, a little boy's mouth, a little boy's anus, a little boy's hand.

And that little boy was me. When I was just eight years old I became the receptacle for Carley's cum and base desires. The whole thing for him was the climax – I was just the ass or the mouth where he could do it. Even today, I can still taste his dick in my mouth. I can still hear the sound of him breathing before he was about to climax. I welcomed that sound, waited for it, because it meant that it would soon be over for the day.

When he took me into his room, it became my obligation to satisfy him in one way or the other, and the sooner I did it the better. He would tell me that everything he did he was entitled to do.

I knew it did not feel right. I knew there was something wrong with what I was made to do but it was at the direction of a priest, and it could not be, he was God's

representative on Earth, and that was the basis of the confusion that would eat me up,

haunt me, and destroy me for the years to come.

I swear, the biggest problem was . . . the confusion as to whether this was wrong

or right. And I couldn't ask anybody, I couldn't escape from this cage of confusion,

because it was unheard of, embarrassing, impossible, to try to get some outside advice

about what was going on, what was happening to me. So I've got to say that the caged,

isolated confusion was the absolute worst part of the entire experience. The loneliness,

the isolation, the confusion of a young boy who was doing as he was told by the Catholic

Diocese of Wilmington, Inc.'s representative of God on Earth.

He didn't care about my size, the fact that I was a little boy, and that when he bent

me over and stuck his dick in my anus that it hurt. He just did what he needed to do to

get off. Sometimes it would hurt so bad that I cried.[56]

He was very cold, always cut you short. There was no caring.[57] But the worst

was that I was so confused. That was the biggest, loneliest part of my life while the

abuse was taking place. I wanted to tell my parents from the very first day Carley

touched me but it was just impossible to think about telling them, it was unthinkable, a

priest, in those times, was not someone who you questioned. He never put out any signs.

It made me feel special to be so close with a priest. In those days a priest would just

show up at your house for dinner and it was an honor to the whole family. There was no

pathway out of the confusion. It was like a brick wall, and I could never break that

barrier to tell anyone.

We would be at the YMCA pool, both the Jewish YMCA the regular YMCA, we would be swimming naked, and Carley would come up behind me, he would grab my penis with his hands, or lean into me with an erect penis. And I could tell when he was doing that to another kid in the pool.

It happened approximately two to three times a week to me from ages eight to ten, for three years or at least 150 anal rapes and sodomy.

It was approximately 2005, I came back from Florida and I read about my buddy John Dougherty on delawareonline.com. John was a couple years older then me and we were in school together. The memories came flooding back to me. Then I told my wife Nancy about John, and then about me. She said she always had known something was wrong. Something I had always kept back, now she knew what it was.

I was taken out of St. Ann's school, in the middle of fifth grade and transferred to Highland elementary school. After that the contact with Carley ended. I guess in retrospect that my parents found out what was going on and that is why they left the church and put me in the public schools.

I remember right when I was taken out of school, I had to go to the psychiatrist's office across the street from St. Ann's. When I was sitting in the waiting room at the psychiatrist's office I could actually see Carley's room. I saw that psychiatrist many times, though I cannot remember his name.

Logically, now, I have made the connection: I suspect that my mother knew. I look back, now, as an adult, and that may be the reason she took me out of St. Ann's.

When it becomes a regular thing, it's just like you're a robot. The thing I am terrified about is not having control of myself. I never ever wanted to be out of control again as I was when I was a child, it terrifies me that would happen again. I still have nightmares of being in situations where I am not in control, losing control. I will not allow myself to be vulnerable. I even have a gun in my RV, just in case, for self defense. I have fifteen rounds of ammunition instead of the usual nine rounds.

I also cannot completely trust anyone. That was a big problem with my dear wife Nancy. I would not let her know me. And I think it is because I wasn't in control with Carley because I trusted him, so I let him control me. That would never happen again, will never happen again.

I do not grieve, not for my dad, mother, grandfather, or brother. I am incapable of grieving.

I don't know what a healthy sexual relationship is. I was always drunk when I would have sex. I started drinking when I was thirteen, which eventually led to either depression, anger, and alcoholism. So I never had intimacy, just the act of sex. At the time I did not care how the women felt, I just cared about me. Even with my wife that is how it started. I guess I wanted to be the one in control, the opposite of how it had been with Carley. That was an important thing missing from my life – shared, sexual intimacy. I wasn't able to have that, I did not know how. Carley took away any chance at normal development I had.

I don't believe in Heaven. I don't believe in Church. I have completely lost my faith. As children, we were called "lambs of God." It was the Church's obligation to teach us, raise us, and protect us. They didn't. I imagine the heads of the Catholic

Church sitting around every year and they sit at this big table, deciding where to spread out the pedophiles, like a shell game. The Pope himself started out as a parish priest. In the old days it was the same thing. This has been going on for ages. Their most precious possession – children – and they don't protect it. I get disgusted about the whole thing.

If there was a God, none of this would have happened. Especially not by his representative. That's the way that I look at it.

Talking about it now, thinking about it, makes me feel sick to my stomach. When I try to focus, my mind jumps here to there.

These are the things that I have to say now as a sixty-one year old man, and it is humiliating. The biggest thing I wonder, if I missed out on, is what could have been if my carefree childhood hadn't been taken from me. If nothing had interfered with my thought process when I was trying to learn.

It's like you are a possession, and once they have you, they keep you. It's like something was stolen from you, but you don't know what it is. I wasn't old enough to know. And when that time came in my life, it was already not functioning. I regret that. What was taken was something I've been looking for my whole life, the piece that makes everything as it should be.[58]

* * *

Of course, Doug's nightmare was not unique. Carley ran rampant through the children of the Forty Acres. Doug's lawyers found many of them who offered their own sworn evidence against the priestly enablers who allowed Carley to molest them at will.

In the same manner as with Doug, Carley also began to sexually abuse John F.

Dougherty, from ages ten to seventeen, from 1954 to 1961, in numerous locations, including in Carley's rectory bedroom at St. Ann's. Carley would take John into the rectory, through the first floor and up the stairs to Carley's second- floor lair. As Carley walked him through the rectory and up to his bedroom, young John was regularly seen by and had to greet pastor Msgr. John J. Bolen, associate pastor Paul Fallers and the rectory housekeeper who were on notice that he was being taken to the bedroom, but they never intervened or inquired as to why this was occurring.[59] Once there, Carley would take out his often-used large jar of Vaseline or other petroleum jelly, cover John with it and then anally rape and sodomize him. When he was finished, Carley would turn John over and urinate on him.[60]

Carley had first begun raping Doug while he was a little altar boy in training in the sacristy off the main altar of the St. Ann's church while supposedly teaching him the significance of the vestments and other religious symbols.[61] Carley's pattern also included sexually abusing at least two other young altar boys there. An anonymous witness fearing church retaliation, John Roe Number One, was sexually abused by Carley beginning in the sixth grade in 1958 when he was an eleven-year old altar boy and this continued for the next several years.[62] The first time Carley ever attacked him, he testified, was right in the sacristy, where Carley did it to him regularly.[63] In his words, "Carley would – fondle – him, do – mutual masturbation, and he tried to rape me one time. But that didn't work. It was attempted anal rape. There was oral type of sexual activity also. And it first started in the end of 1958 in the St. Ann's church sacristy, upstairs on the second floor where the altar boys would change into their church clothing."[64]

Retired *News Journal* editor and political commentator John Taylor also attended St.

Ann's from 1949 to 1957 where he too was an altar boy.[65] He recounted an incident in the 1955 to 1957 time frame, again in the sacristy when he was waiting to start a religious ceremony. Carley approached and grabbed him by "my balls," he recounted, and Taylor fought him off.[66] In later years, Taylor's mother also told him that she knew about Carley abusing boys,[67] because it was then common knowledge in that church community.

Amazingly and as the ultimate act of hypocracy, as Doug explained earlier, while sexually molesting Doug, Carley at the same time taught him religious dogma.[68] Carley did the same with John F. Dougherty.[69]

Carley raped Doug while on trips on his sailboat on the Sassafras River and to Ocean City, Maryland. Many other victims came forward to corroborate his testimony that Carley regularly took boys to places they otherwise would not have had the opportunity or the means to visit and where he would have the chance to use them for sex. Bob Rykiel who attended St. Ann's from 1955 to 1962 remembered Carley's sailboat in Maryland and his hotel room at the Stowaway Motel in Ocean City, Maryland. "Everyone knew that Carley was chasing boys," he said. "I used to run away from him after church," he declared. Students and members of the church would ask, "why is this man still employed at the church?"[70] John Taylor added that "Carley took boys on hundreds of trips to his boat on the Sassafras, New York City, Radio City Music Hall and stables outside of Wilmington." During trips across state lines and into Maryland, Carley would "grab boys" in his car.[71] John Roe Number One stated that Carley abused him while taking him on trips to visit old churches in Delaware and Maryland, and while on trips to seminaries.[72] John F. Dougherty recalled that Carley also took boys to the Stowaway and other motels, New York City, Vermont, Florida, Montreal, and Mexico where he always

-27-

molested them.[73] Dan Gerres explained that as a boy growing up in the Forty Acres, being invited by Carley to go on one of his trips was considered "one of the greatest things that could happen" and all the neighborhood boys would be waiting by their phones, hoping to be invited, but you always did have to swim naked.[74]

For Doug McClure, "the front seat of Carley's black Buick was a place of torment. There he would force me to sit in the middle bench seat and he would make me masturbate him as he drove or Carley would masturbate me."[75] Over seventy-five percent of all survivors in Delaware chose to file anonymously out of fear of retaliation by the church against their family members, embarrassment before their neighbors or because of mental health issues. John Roe Number Three was one of them. He explained the terror of that Buick Wildcat when Carley let him drive on a trip to Galena, Maryland: "Carley began fondling my genitals beneath my pants. He asked me to do the same to him but I refused. I was scared and shocked. As we neared Wilmington, Carley drove away from St. Ann's towards Montchanin, and said, 'I want to taste you.' Fortunately, we next had a minor auto collision, due to inattention no doubt."[76] Car buff John Roe Number One specifically recalled that it was indeed a black Buick, four door, with bench seating. This allowed Carley to have John Roe Number Three very close to him in the front seat. Carley would let him steer and later work the gas pedal, all while sexually abusing him with his hands down his pants.[77]

* * *

In his physician interviews, Doug also detailed some of the personal consequences for him from Carley's repeated rapes – survivor patterns and long term effects that are documented throughout this book, both by other survivors and also by medical experts. The scars from all this abuse were with Doug McClure for the rest of his life. Physicians explained the direct result of all this repeated oral sex, sodomy and anal sex on a second to fourth grader. Carol A. Tavani M.D. said that to "help with severe anxiety, with filling a void he felt, and with other depressive thoughts he began alcohol use at age thirteen which became regular alcohol abuse by age fifteen, and then for the next twenty-five years he abused alcohol, to age forty. He eventually drank 'a case of beer a day, sometimes with hard liquor in addition.' But after involvement and leadership in AA, he was sober for twenty years."[78]

Dr. Tavani's findings included a "significant history of depression, which goes back to childhood and clearly preceded the alcohol" abuse. Symptoms included thoughts "of dying. He recalls not having cared whether he died. . . . He would lie there, 'at eleven, twelve, thirteen years old . . .' He received psychiatric treatment after the fifth grade. He was treated as a child 'with Elavil™ (an older antidepressant) and Milltown™, used back then for anxiety and sleep.' The use of alcohol 'helped with' his depression, 'with the alcohol becoming 'my best friend.''' Regarding the temporal correlation between his depression and sexual abuse, Dr. Tavani reported Doug's statement that "It was there as a kid, before the alcohol."[79]

And there was Doug's failure to ever again trust anyone, failed relationships and sexual dysfunction. During high school Doug wondered if he were gay. Since he could never share intimacy or emotion this got in the way of his sexual performance. While he loved Nancy, and they married in 1973, they ended up having to lead separate lives to a great degree, for his libido was nearly nonexistent due to no fault of hers, just his.[80]

* * *

How could monsters, such as Carley and the many other priests found in subsequent chapters of this book, be allowed to roam the playing fields of childhood searching for their victims?

First, to the everlasting shame of the Diocese of Wilmington and its Bishops, Doug's lawyers found out that for Carley the red warning flags flew as early as his seminary training, long before he became an official priest. Both seminaries he attended expressed in writing multiple concerns about his character, abilities and other problems prior to the Diocese of Wilmington accepting him as a priest. These warning alarms included: "be afraid to take a chance on him;" "something strange about him;" "may create a problem;" "surprised we took him;" "sometimes unbalanced;" "temperament peculiar;" and there were concerns about his truthfulness because he lied and gave "a false address upon entering" the seminary.[81] He even was released from one seminary because of performance and health problems and he performed at a sub-par level at his second seminary, yet despite these problems, nevertheless he was hired by the diocese.[82]

Second, the diocese always put its business interests above its duty to protect the children entrusted to its care. Carley became a longtime problem priest of the diocese who, the diocese eventually admitted, had sexually abused young children while in its employ, including children at St. Ann's.[83] As was common in the diocese, Carley was only hired, qualified or not, due to a shortage of priests. Even at the very beginning of his employment, the Bishop of Wilmington conceded that he took a serious, conscious risk in hiring Carley. In a letter dated July 30, 1947, Bishop Edmond John FitzMaurice wrote about his analysis of whether to admit Carley to be a diocesan seminarian despite his red flags, "[p]rudence and the like tell me to pass up the applicant, but the heart and other considerations whisper me to take and give him a chance."[84]

Yet, even though the Bishop was cognizant that this was a risky decision, he knowingly undertook this danger because "more and more pastors are clamoring for assistants."[85] Several months later, FitzMaurice again acknowledged the risk, stating, "[t]here is, I realize, some risk entailed in my decision, but . . . I do not believe it is excessive, and I feel that the need for priests at this time in Wilmington is such to justify the venture."[86] The historian for the diocese is priest Thomas J. Peterman who testified as recently as November 8, 2010, at the trial of John Vai which is recounted in chapter five of this book. There he told a Delaware jury that as a result of his work as a historian, as well as his fifty-three years of experience as a priest in the diocese, since about 1957 there has been a shortage of priests in the Diocese of Wilmington. The shortage has gotten worse, not better since that date.[87]

As a key witness throughout the Child Victim's Act litigation, priest Clement Lemon, the longtime Diocesan Vicar of Clergy and Priests [personnel director], reluctantly had to admit, at the trial of John Vai which is presented in chapter five, that the diocese has faced a shortage of priests since at least the 1940's, if not before, a problem which continues to the present day.[88] This is confirmed by contemporaneously created documents by diocesan Chancellor Joseph Sweeney dated 1956 which note the "crucial lack of clergy in the diocese at present," that "[s]everal of the established parishes are greatly understaffed" and "the establishment of new parishes urgently needed has been postponed because of the lack of priests."[89] Donn Devine, the present diocesan archivist, also explained that "we've never had sufficient priests serve the number of people here . . . That's been true since the earliest days of the diocese."[90]

Third, the Diocese of Wilmington wilfully ignored the known danger that Roman Catholic priests presented to young children. It knew, for many years before Carley was ever hired, that Roman Catholic priests were a danger to children, but that most important fact was willfully kept hidden from the general public and church members found in the pews. Concerning this danger, the number two man in the diocese for many decades under multiple Bishops, priest Thomas Cini (thought by many to be the key man behind the decades-long cover-up by it with regard to child abuse) openly admitted in the Vai trial that "the Roman Catholic Church has recognized, since at least the 1800s, that it has an obligation to protect children from sexual abuse." And so the church instituted unpublicized customs or policies regarding the danger presented by its priests, "and these rules exist because the church authorities have recognized the possibility of priests sexually abusing children in their parishes." Cini freely admitted, specifically for Delaware, that from "the 1950s forward, the Diocese of Wilmington knew that there was a danger that some of its priests could sexually molest children."[91] Yet despite longtime notice of this "serious problem" from the 1940s to the 1970s, the diocese had no enforced formal rules or other policies intended either to detect or to prevent priest sexual abuse of children. Nor did the diocese institute any such protective measures until 1985.

Fourth, Bishops and other managers also had plenty of warning and actual notice about Carley himself once he started to work for them. For example, both John F. Dougherty and Doug McClure testified under oath that they were each brought into the rectory, through the first floor living area, past the many other priests who lived in the rectory on their way to Carley's bedroom lair.[92] John F. Dougherty specifically identified two priests – pastor John J. Bolen and associate pastor Paul Fallers, as well as the parish housekeeper, who saw them.[93] Both young boys had to respectfully greet these priests by name as they passed them as they were slowly ushered up to Carley's bedroom.[94]

Fifth, just as no "protective" measures were instituted until 1985 in the diocese and there were no rules or procedures to "detect" whether child abuse was happening, so the diocese never enforced any informal policies, customs or understandings which might have protected children from rogue priests – specifically no customs or understandings which said that no child was ever to be allowed in any priest's bedroom (the locus of much of the sexual abuse recounted throughout this book). Former Bishop Robert E. Mulvee explained here that since the 1950's, it has "always been the clear policy" to bar any child from spending the night in the rectory. They were "explicitly" barred from ever going upstairs in the rectory.[95] Now deceased, former Bishop Michael A. Saltarelli also noted the same.[96] But no such policy, custom or understanding was enforced.

The oldest living priest in the diocese, William Jennings, has served as a diocesan priest since 1940. He testified that he was Carley's immediate predecessor at St. Ann's, having lived and worked there from 1946 to 1954. He explained that "[i]n the 1950s, if a priest was taking a young boy up to his room on a regular basis . . . it would be a very bad mistake to let that go on. [I]t was wrong in '54 to take an eight or ten . . . year-old boy to a priest's bedroom on a regular basis . . . for any purpose."[97]

The current pastor of St. Ann's and number two in the diocese – Thomas Cini – agreed and testified before the John Vai trial jury that "a priest bringing a child up to his rectory bedroom is disturbing, red flag behavior." If that happened in the 1950s and 1960s, "and the associate pastor or one of the associate pastors or the pastor were aware of that and did nothing to stop that from happening . . . it would be a big mistake not to intervene." It has always been a rule of conduct within the diocese to prevent a child from visiting a priest in his bedroom. And that applies to the 1950s and the 1960s. To permit this "would be a very bad mistake,"[98] he concurred.

Distinguished Norbertine Abbott Emeritus E. Thomas DeWane testified under oath that for more than fifty years it was "standard procedure" and was "ingrained in us when I was a seminarian" that it is "very inappropriate" to have a child behind closed doors in a priest's bedroom.[99] Jennings also had explained that any priest who observed another priest taking a child up to his bedroom had a duty to look into it and "inquire what the reason was."[100]

However, this single practice – keeping children out of the bedroom of any priest – which could have protected children from some sexual abuse in the Diocese of Wilmington, was constantly ignored by bishops, pastors and colleagues of the child predators identified in this history.

Sixth, aside from actual knowledge by those priests who lived with Carley and were aware of his actions, his shameful reputation was known by the church community but was ignored to the peril of children. Eleven other eye witnesses also testified that Carley had a widely known reputation for inappropriate behavior with young parish boys. One of those boys was Bob Rykiel who attended St. Ann's from 1955 to 1962 and he compellingly described Carley's reputation in the community.

- [W]hen I attended St. Ann's elementary school everyone knew that Carley was chasing boys.

- I recall students at St. Ann's elementary school and parishioners at St. Ann's Roman Catholic Church asking why Carley was still employed at St. Ann's Church.

- I used to run away from Carley after mass.

- I got in trouble in about the Fall of 1963. My mother defended me in a meeting with a St. Ann's administrator. In that meeting, my mother made reference to Carley's behavior.[101]

Lloyd Seal, another student who attended St. Ann's from 1951 to 1958, testified that it was "common knowledge" not to get in a car with Carley. He even recalls hearing that John Dougherty's parents went to the parish pastor about Carley.[102] Donald Lenderman testified that in the time frame "between 1953 to 1956, it was common knowledge among my peers that Carley was homosexual." This is in addition to his personal knowledge about Carley trying to abuse him.[103] Donald Taylor attended St. Ann's from 1954 to 1959 and 1960 to 1962 and explained that he heard so many stories about Carley doing inappropriate things with boys that he "steer[ed] clear of Carley's path" and "avoided going to the confessional where Carley was stationed." He even told his mother about these things and she warned him "to make sure I was never alone with Carley and always have a friend" there.[104] Newspaperman John Taylor testified that "there were always suspicions that Carley was doing inappropriate things with young boys." His late mother shared the view that Carley was a child molester and recounted a story she heard about Carley offering to pay two young boys twenty dollars if he could give them blowjobs. This is in addition to Taylor's personal experience of Carley abusing him and grabbing at other young boys.[105] Another anonymous witness also testified that it was openly discussed among "the gang," his group of parish friends, that Carley sexually abused boys.[106] Nicholas Heesters attended St. Ann's from 1951 to 1959 and testified that he observed that a boy spent forty-five minutes alone with Carley and emerged with money, Carley's car [keys] and a motel reservation.

How the boy got these things was never discussed.[107] John Hahn attended St. Ann's from 1952 to 1959 and testified that he heard from altar boys that Carley "was sneaking feels." He also recalls hearing that the parents of one of the younger boys had complained to the Bishop about Carley.[108] Felix Cartagena attended St. Ann's from 1959 to 1962 and testified about all the parish boys being mysteriously pulled out of class, one by one, to be privately questioned by two priests about Carley.[109] Doug McClure himself even recalled that it was constantly discussed among the young parish boys that Carley touched them while on trips.[110]

Finally, St. Ann's Church also had direct knowledge of Carley's misconduct from another source. Its CYO football coach in the late 1950's, John Holmes Doherty, actually reported to the parish, but to no avail, that Carley had acted inappropriately with one of his players. He also regularly overheard his players talking about how something was going on with Carley, and based on what was said, he suspected it was sexual.[111]

One student's parents, Mrs. Carrie Agostini and her husband, learned in 1960 that Carley had tried to sexually abuse their son Carl. Her spouse immediately reported this personally to the Bishop, who lived a block or so away from their family, and who promised to take care of the matter. However, other than forcing Carley to come to the family home and apologize for his misconduct, nothing more was ever done to protect children from Carley.[112] And, despite this direct report to the Bishop himself, Carley still worked with children until 1993.

He served in at least eight parishes in his forty-five year career and was appointed to many positions of power, prestige and respect within the diocese including: Officialis of the Diocesan Tribunal for four years; a three year term as Pro-Synodal Judge; Associate Judge of the Diocesan Marriage Tribunal; two three year terms as Dean of the Eastern Shore Deanery; and an elevation from the rank of Reverend to Very Reverend.[113] As the Dean of the Eastern Shore

Deanery, Carley was the Bishop's personal representative to the numerous churches and parishes

in that geographic region. In 1993, after forty-five years as a priest of the Diocese of

Wilmington, Carley was allowed to retire as a priest in good standing, and he continued to

perform priestly functions in the area of Ocean City, Maryland and other places, with the

diocese's permission, authorization and blessing. He received retirement payments from the

diocese until his death in 1998.[114]

* * *

While Carley was long honored by his bosses, those who sought to expose him, like John

F. Dougherty and Douglas McClure, were attacked without mercy by the diocese for their

efforts. Under intense questioning by diocese lawyers, Doug related that after revelations began

to surface in 2002 about child abuse by priests in Boston, he heard another call to arms and his

Marine Corps training kicked in. When he became aware that his old neighbor John Dougherty

was lying there wounded on the battlefield, Doug the Marine saw that there was only one thing

he could do. "I had to come to the aid of my comrade, " he told me.

It was around January of 2005. I had seen an article in the paper and it was about

John being sexually abused by Carley. John was a couple years older than me. I knew

John and parts started coming back to me and so I called Beth Miller at the paper [*The

News Journal*] so she could get in touch with John to see if he wanted to get in touch

with me.[115]

I was at home in my bedroom looking at the news paper story about John on-line.

I cried. A few things started to come back to me. The memories were oral and anal. As the memory flooded in, I was in the third grade at school at St. Ann's.[116] And so I went to my wife Nancy in the living room. I was crying and she wanted to know what was wrong. I told her about what had happened and that John Dougherty's name was there and I wanted John to know that he wasn't alone.[117]

The reporter contacted John and within a couple of days John called me. He cried. I cried. We didn't discuss the particular circumstances of our abuse. It was how was he, how was he doing? He was worried about me and I was worried about him.[118] About a month later he cut it off. It was too painful for him.[119]

* * *

One of the substantial motivating factors that led directly to the enactment of the Child Victim's Act of 2007 is the life of John F. Dougherty, another survivor of priest Edward Carley. A year after the Boston revelations of 2002 rattled the church establishment, John wrote a remarkable six-page, single-spaced email dated February 5, 2003, and he embarked on a mission to disseminate it as widely as possible within the church and to the media. In what could be described as a cry from the depths of his soul, he recounted almost ten years of personal sexual torment by Carley, beginning when John was only ten years old in 1954. Part of John's pain was caused by the pain of his little brother and other friends at St. Ann's church who were comrades in suffering. After thirty years of psychiatric care and therapy, the source of John's anguish and the wreckage of his adult emotional life were determined to have been caused by the sexual abuse he suffered and which his conscious mind had long buried through the protective mechanism of amnesia.[120]

As just one example, he recounted how "Carley led me to his room where he proceeded to remove my clothes and cover my lower body with Vaseline from an oversized jar [which Doug McClure also had described]. He then placed me on his bed and sodomized me and when he was finished he turned me over to face him and urinated on me while [I was] still on the bed."[121] The email also describes Carley's trips with other young boys, all of which were motivated by Carley's appetite for sex. John movingly concludes with a recitation of his own permanent injuries and suffering.

> *Where am I today? . . . I can't address my wife [Jean] by her first name. I can't depend on my thinking accurately and every day is different as to how I feel. Some days I'm despondent and I never experience joy and some days just go by unnoticed. I get by . . . I've contacted some of my boyhood friends who were abused and they won't deal with it. I have had terrible problems over the past five years with suicidal thoughts. I don't trust anyone. I can't trust anyone. I feel like I'm totally alone with no recourse. "The News Journal" newspaper in Wilmington DE. won't print my story because I can't corroborate it. I never wanted to use the abuse issue as an "excuse" for my failures but therapy has allowed me to see that the abuse is a very real reason for my aberrant behavior throughout my life. My inability to sleep regularly or to hold down a job or to be consistent in my life has been so damaging. We've always been poor and in debt because of my inability to handle money. The rage that is inside of me almost destroyed me. How could anyone rape a little kid like Carley raped me? I was only ten years old. He was a priest! How could so many of us kids been so molested so many times and have no one know? Why hasn't someone else come forward?[122]*

Eventually, *The News Journal* did find the corroboration it needed to write about the church scandal. On November 21, 2005 the details which John F. Dougherty had recounted in his email were reported and John became for the public one of its vivid images of how the church's crimes affect children, to those who would listen and who were not afraid of the truth.[123] After playing his part in a long 2005 expose by *The News Journal* detailing the cover-up of priest sex abuse in Delaware, John's suffering directly influenced Delaware legislators seeking to assist survivors seeking access to justice. His willingness to go public contributed to the enactment of the Child Victim's Act of 2007. Two years later, John filed a successful lawsuit against St. Ann's church were Carley was employed when he raped John. On April 12, 2010, John received a written letter of apology from the pastor of St. Ann's Church who made a public statement expressing "deep sorrow for the sexual abuse that Mr. Dougherty and the other boys of St. Ann's Church suffered as children at the hands of Edward Carley, and also for the suffering of their families as a result of such abuse."[124] John died after a very long bout with cancer on March 12, 2011. His obituary acknowledged his renown as an accomplished professional musician and guitarist, and noted his "public revelation of his childhood abuse by a priest of the Diocese of Wilmington, Edward Carley, [which] helped lead to the passage of the child sexual abuse statute in Delaware that lifted the statute of limitations on claims against the church and clergy. It also paved the way for other victims of abuse to be able to speak out and seek help after years of fear and pain."[125]

* * *

Doug's reactions to the revelations by John Dougherty led to a bout with depression. He wrestled with snippets of long lost memories of childhood sexual abuse which started to return to his consciousness.

With the return of the memories of my childhood trauma at the hands of Carley, the severe depression came. With that I literally thought I was going nuts, and they were getting ready to commit me at the VA, so I took off to Florida.[126] It was just you get down in a hole and everything is flashing in front of you, you can't get any clear thoughts and, again, it was the humiliation of what had happened, trying to justify things, but you had no idea. Trying to look for answers. There were none. As I tried to figure it out the best I could it just got worse and worse so I just took off. I called my wife and said I'm going to Florida.[127]

I was hearing things, seeing things. It was terrifying to me. I would hear voices, but it was never enough that I could hear – I could recognize anything that was being said. I would see things and as I tried to look at it it would be gone and it would be over here. So, I would look over here and I could never focus on anything.[128]

I was having a terrible time myself and I just never stopped. I would go to the point of exhaustion and then try to sleep and then I would be up and gone. I never hung around, I never went sightseeing. I would just drive and drive and drive.[129]

Eventually Doug came out of it. John Dougherty had been criticized for publicly exposing the diocese and Carley. And so, Doug wanted to let the community know that John Dougherty was not alone. Doug then went to speak with a newspaper reporter.[130] As a consequence, in November 2005 *The News Journal* ran a story exposing priests Edward Carley and John Lind. John Dougherty, Douglas McClure and Joseph Curry were identified as serial victims of the diocese and Carley. But Doug told the paper that despite the depression and all his other problems arising from Carley, "this is not over. It's not over for the rest of the people who are still living with this."[131] John Dougherty was no longer alone on the battlefield and the many others who had lost their childhoods at the hands of diocese priests had to know that help was on the way. The Marines had landed, for Doug.

So in December 2006 Doug filed the third lawsuit against the diocese in Delaware charging it with responsibility for his rapes and the rapes of many others. Eventually, after the Delaware Child Victim's Act became law in July 2007, almost 145 additional lawsuits followed. Carley had died in 1998 and was buried with honors from the diocese. But Doug contended that the diocese and St. Ann's church never did anything to protect him or others from Carley. Doug declared that "I am just one of many victims, but I encourage others who have suffered in silence for so long also to come forward."[132]

For two and a half years Doug then faced the full fury of the Roman Catholic Church and its army of lawyers, psychiatrists, psychologists and many other defenders. He endured days of relentless grilling, directed not to justice, but to the church's attempt to escape accountability, at whatever the cost. For two days, church medical professionals set out on the same mission. Doug suffered greatly and his health deteriorated.

Finally, in December 2008 two attorneys for the diocese and even priest Thomas Cini, its number two man, admitted and acknowledged on behalf of the Diocese of Wilmington that Doug McClure had been a victim of childhood sexual abuse by Carley. They even said they sincerely apologized for the sexual abuse inflicted by Carley.[133] Doug was relieved. He felt like a great burden had been lifted off of his shoulders and he could go forward with the long, painful process of treatment and healing.[134] At the same time, it appears that the diocese hoped that Doug would drop his court case, quietly go away and accept their mere words, or that he would settle cheaply with the diocese. When he refused, another battle broke out again just one month later. At that point Doug was accused of being just a liar who was making the entire thing up. He was accused of "lapses in reality" and "hallucinatory" perceptions and an "impaired ability to accurately report his experiences."[135]

His public trial was set to begin on April 13, 2009.

Doug did not believe that he would live through the several-week-long hell of a trial and thought that it would kill him. The constant attacks on him and his failing health were taking their toll. He then had a premonition of his death. After he died, I publicly stated my non-medical opinion that the Bishop's hardball tactics killed Doug.

So Doug directed his lawyers to push as hard as they could to settle for as much money as they could and to refuse all demands to keep the settlement amount confidential, as had happened with the two cases against the diocese that started before his. Those confidential settlements had lead to false rumors in the survivor community that both cases were failures and did not financially punish the diocese and its other enablers. But Doug wanted to hit them hard in the court of public opinion and also where it hurt, in the pocketbook, as an example for John Dougherty and the 145 others who eventually followed him. He hoped that, knowing his example, they would never give up and, in his terms, they would take the hill held by the enemy.

On April 8, 2009 Doug announced that he had settled his Delaware Superior Court lawsuit against the Diocese of Wilmington and St. Ann's Parish for the sum of $1,525,000 and compassionate letters of apology.[136] But the letters of apology were never delivered. Six months later, in October 2009, his widow, his beloved Nancy, had to go to court to get them.[137] It was claimed that they had been overlooked at the bottom of a pile of paper. From this behavior, it appears that the letters of apology just were not important to the diocese. Nor had the lost childhoods of hundreds of children in Delaware been important either.

In addition to the settlement payment, and the promised compassionate letters of apology from Bishop Francis Malooly on behalf of the diocese, and from pastor Thomas Cini on behalf of St. Ann's, the diocese released the following statements:

The diocese and St. Ann's Church acknowledge that Mr. McClure is a human being, and apologize to him, his family, and to the people of the Diocese of Wilmington for the actions of former diocesan priest Edward Carley. . . . The diocese and St. Ann's are deeply ashamed of Carley's abusive misconduct, and that Carley betrayed his mission to give healing and the love of God.

Doug issued this statement –

When I first came forward, my goal was simple. I wanted my fellow survivors of Carley to know that they were not alone and I wanted to expose what everyone knew was going on at St. Ann's in the 1950s. It has been a long and difficult journey, but my goal is now done, my mission is complete.

Getting this behind me is a bigger deal to me than coming home from Vietnam. I hope that my sharing the horrors which were done to me will somehow give strength to Carley's many other victims to come forward and face their fears. You cannot get a do-over with your life, but by coming forward, you can seize control and take back the power he took from you so long ago. I am living proof.

I want to thank my wife and family for standing by my side through all of this. I also want to thank Judge Calvin L. Scott Jr. and the Delaware General Assembly. Without them, I never would have had the opportunity to seek fairness and justice in a court of law. I am forever grateful. I now look forward to continuing with my volunteer work with those in AA and at the Rockford Center.[138]

A few weeks passed, the legal papers were signed, and on April 21st Doug came in to say good-bye to his lawyers and pick up his settlement check. He then drove his RV down to the Eastern Shore of Maryland where he sat down outside and gazed out on the beautiful sunset and his beloved Chesapeake Bay.

Honor. Courage. Commitment. In those last moments, his sacred Marine Corp oath probably ran through his mind. Doug had accomplished the mission and left no one lying behind on the battlefield. He had made the struggle for justice for many survivors much easier. He closed his eyes and went to sleep.

2

Commander Kenneth J. Whitwell, U.S.N.

At the time of his trial Naval Commander Kenneth J. Whitwell was a thirty-nine year old professional warrior, medical officer, and fighter pilot. At six feet four inches tall, with an athletic build, he is always wired for battle, has the attitude of Tom Cruise in the 1986 movie *Top Gun,* and is an Alpha male. But privately he has lived with his opposite dark side. Ken readily states that it was the discipline he found in the Navy which saved him from a ruined life and gave him the courage to face up to his nightmarish past. It enabled him to survive professionally, while privately off the base he was a total wreck.

The damages trial for Ken in federal court in Wilmington, Delaware began on March 29, 2007. It was meant to be a symbol for all those hesitant, fearful survivors elsewhere in Delaware to demonstrate that justice can be obtained if they too have the courage to step forward and face their tormentors. One such victim was Robert Quill who sat silently in the audience throughout Ken's trial, anonymous and alone, but growing in courage through observing Ken's example in baring his soul to the judge, jury, and the public. Contemporaneously, that very spring Rob then led the charge for enactment of the Child Victim's Act of 2007 which gave all survivors in Delaware the right to sue their tormenters and their institutional bosses for justice. Rob testified four times before the Delaware State legislature that year, and his determination, eloquence and powerful testimony terrified the church, the insurance industry and their lawyers as to what was to come, and he substantially contributed to the passage of that historic law. Rob was their worst nightmare come to life, an articulate, educated survivor unafraid of them and relentless in causing the dam of injustice, which for too long had denied survivors their day in court, to collapse and send a torrent of justice down to flood the valley below which included the courts of Delaware.

With similar courage, Ken had sued Norbertine priest Edward J. Smith, who in defiant response then deliberately had refused to reply and instead had defaulted in the lawsuit brought against him, which resulted in a legal judgment being entered against Smith.[139] All that remained was for an eight-person Delaware federal jury to decide upon what actually had happened to young Kenny as a child and to determine the appropriate punishment for Smith.

Then, after doing its work, as reported by *The News Journal*, on March 30, 2007, the jury awarded forty-one million dollars in damages to Ken, six million dollars as compensation for his injuries, and thirty-five million dollars in punitive damages,[140] to send a message to the community at large that sexual abuse of children will not be tolerated in Delaware.[141] This was the first jury award ever in Delaware to a victim of childhood sexual abuse by a Roman Catholic priest.[142]

Beginning at age fourteen young Kenny was orally and anally raped by Smith more than 230 times over the course of thirty-three months. As reported, "Whitwell covered his face in his hands and wiped tears away when the final verdict was read, turned and embraced his wife, Amy, and they wept together."[143] He later told the press, "the jury spoke out very loudly that all Delaware officials must do everything in their power to hold these persons accountable for their past crimes." He thanked the judge and jury "for allowing me to expose the truth about matters which have been hidden away for far too long, and for seeing that justice was done not only for me, but also for all the many other victims who have been denied their day in court by armies of lawyers and church bureaucrats who are more interested in a cover-up than in protecting innocent children and revealing the truth of what happens behind closed doors in their church."[144] As to the large monetary award, Ken eventually collected only about $61,000 from Smith who pled poverty.

* * *

At trial Ken's mother Joyce Casey painted part of the picture of how predator priests typically cut their prey out of the pack. She first showed the jury an old color photo of fourteen-year-old Kenny and herself with a pet racoon they were saving.[145] She sobbed throughout as she explained that Ken was not always that steadfast naval officer sitting before them in his service dress blue uniform with his ribbons. She began her sworn testimony by explaining to the jury that twenty-five years ago, when he was a boy:

> [D]uring his freshman year in high school Kenny was shy, quiet, a good boy and a good student, who had three other brothers.[146]. . . I was having marital problems at that time and my husband and I eventually divorced. During this period of vulnerability, along came Smith, who was one of Ken's freshman teachers, to cut him out of the pack. Smith was a very charismatic man. Most of the time he was very unpriestly. He seemed to be

very interested in the family and how everybody was doing.[147] . . . He was a teacher, a priest. We trusted him. That was where they were going to school.[148]

He dressed very unpriestly. I mean, he wore very expensive clothing, jewelry, watch. He always looked – it was just – you were surprised to see someone. And he always had a new car.[149] . . . He wore imported Italian leather shoes from South Philly. The whole house would just take on the odor of his cologne. And he would drive a new car and boast he came from money. He would say, I get money that was left for me and so it's just not a problem.[150]

So eventually he began spending time with my family. He kind of got to know everybody. Kenney just didn't get gifts. He would bring, you know, ski sweaters for everybody or jackets for everybody. And he became – our family knew him. When my father was ill, he drove me up to New Jersey to the hospital. When my niece got married, she and her fiancé thought he was just so much fun. Do you think he'd marry them at Villanova? And when my niece was born, he did the christening. He attended family barbecues and even did the Catholic mass in our home.[151] . . . He always seemed interested in everybody and even brought his mom down from South Philly to visit.[152]

I never had any problem with Smith spending time with Kenny when he was a freshman in high school. I knew where Kenny was and he was safe.[153] . . . When Kenny spent time at the school where the priests lived, called the priory, he was safe there being with all the priests at the priory.[154]

As far as the amount of time he was spending with Smith, when he wasn't at sports team practices or studying or things like that, Smith always just assured me that he was with a good group, meaning the other priests where they lived in the priory. They were doing fun things. They were just going to be safe. He didn't need to go to the parties other students threw.[155]

And then Smith dropped out of my life. I don't know the exact date, but he had taken Ken's younger brother Michael up to South Philly and Michael came home quite late and he said Smith, between giving him stuff to drink, showing movies, did inappropriate grabbing of him and he punched him and left. But he drove home from South Philly, because Michael was sixteen at the time. So the next day, Smith called to ask if Michael got home and I said yes. I said, you owe him and us an apology, which we didn't get, and that was the end of the conversation. And he never asked for forgiveness from me or from Michael.[156] . . . Then after that call I asked Kenny if he had ever been abused but he told me "No."[157]

But after college in Philadelphia, despite the fact that he had a scholarship here, Ken went to Oregon for professional school. I always felt like Ken was running. I thought maybe it was from the family, the fact that his father and I were divorced. I never knew.[158] . . . But years later, in November of 2004 Ken came up from Florida. That's when he told me that he had been molested by Smith. I cried that night and so did Ken.[159]

* * *

Next Ken's wife, Amy Whitwell, then age thirty-eight and married to Ken for ten years,[160] explained for more than an hour how she thought she had married a prince charming, but her naval officer husband was no prince. Amy illustrated how damaged a survivor really is if you get behind the false front which many of them present. Once thought to be her prince

charming, Ken's wife learned, as do all wives married to survivors, that instead he was a Dr.

Jekyll and Mr. Hyde, living with a split personality.

Amy explained that she –

was a Navy nurse and I thought I had found my prince charming, a tall handsome Naval

officer who I married with the full ceremony, the Navy Service Dress White Uniform,

referred to as "choker whites" because of the gold buttons all the way up the neck, white

gloves, full-size medals on his chest, a sword hanging from his side and all that went with

that.[161]. . . But we immediately led two lives, Ken was with it, thriving and in command

when on duty and he was a bottled up volcanic angry nightmare at home. One evening in

a screaming argument in our bedroom, I yelled at him that "You can't hate me this bad.

You haven't known me this long."[162] What was wrong with our relationship? He was

curled up in a fetal position. Like a little child, a light seemed to go on in his head, he

made some connection of time and events, and he said, "Could it have been because a

priest abused me when I was young?"[163] Well, I was a psychiatric nurse on a lock-down

psychiatric floor for two years.[164] All of a sudden relief flowed over me. It was not me,

he did not hate me, something else had severely damaged my prince charming long ago.

That explains everything. That explains why you're so angry. It explains it's not me

that's the problem. You need help. I backed off.[165]

We had first met when Ken and I were both stationed at the Naval Hospital at

Groton, Connecticut. Ken was one of the six to eight single officers at the hospital and

we all kind of hung out and did things together. Many of the other people at the hospital were married and had families, so that left the six to eight of us to go hiking and we would play on the volleyball team together and softball team, and did a lot of fun things like that.[166]. . . I would listen to him talk about how he thought he would never be in a relationship, that no one would accept him the way he was. Several of the girls were chasing him. My best friend, Heidi, claimed him. But Ken wasn't responding to any of those signals from the women chasing him.[167]

Basically, from the moment I met Ken, I loved him, so I broke off an earlier relationship, hoping to get to know Ken better, hoping that maybe if I wasn't in a relationship with someone else, he'd want to get to know me a little bit better. And it didn't quite go as planned. Ken didn't ask me out. I tried to get his attention by baking muffins and I took them to his clinic, and the corpsmen would say, "Dr. Whitwell, Lieutenant Farrell is here with muffins again."[168]. . . I was pretty forward in a demure way, but to no avail. He didn't respond to my signals at all. Eventually, since he hadn't responded to me, one evening it was after we had gone to mass together actually, that we went back to my apartment to watch hockey, that I asked him if possibly he was gay. The Navy's policy was "don't ask, don't tell." And I thought that maybe he didn't have anybody to talk to about it. And maybe he would like to, you know, vent to me, maybe, or say things that he hadn't been comfortable to say in front of anybody else. As a psych duty nurse I was a pretty good listener.[169] He fidgeted and said, "no, no," he was always attracted to women. But that he had been in counseling in Oregon when he was in optometry school for poor interpersonal relationships and poor self-esteem.[170]

Once I even followed him home from a party and asked him to give me a hug because I was feeling bad, and he did. He gave me a hug, our only hug.[171] . . . He never

asked me out. We had never been on a date. We hadn't held hands. We had never

kissed. We hugged once when I asked him to hug me. It was pretty sophomoric for a

twenty-seven-year-old man, I thought. It was strikingly like he was thirteen. You know,

a thirteen-year-old boy just learning the ropes. But I went over to Ken's one evening and

I asked to talk to him, and he said, sure. And I told him that I – you know, wake up

dreaming about kissing him, that I really would like to know how he felt about me

because I really had feelings for him. And he said to me, Amy, my mom always told me

that there would be another, Amy. So it's at that time that I realized that he did feel about

me the way I felt about him.[172] . . . And we went on our first date the next day, married

about six months later and were then stationed in New York City.[173]

And as far as the physical relationship part of it, he didn't seem comfortable and if

I would initiate something, sometimes we'd make love and sometimes we wouldn't, and

even if we did, it wouldn't be satisfying to him and it certainly wasn't satisfying to me at

that point.[174] . . . He wasn't there in some physical ways, but he certainly wasn't there in

any emotional way.[175] . . . He had never given me a kiss on the cheek. He never tried to

hold my hand.[176]

And we had a doorman in our thirty-six story building and the doorman saw me

leaving crying many mornings and coming home from work crying sometimes. And

there were many arguments. His grandfather's funeral, we argued in front of his family.

Skiing in Vermont, we argued in front of his family. We went with his brothers to State

College, Pennsylvania, where most of his brothers had graduated college, to revisit their old family friends, and we got into an argument there that I actually ended up at my sister's home. She lives in State College as well. And I was going to take the bus back to New York and he came to me and apologized for the argument. But I went to his brothers and said, "Why is he acting this way? Why is he treating me this way?" And they said, "that's just Ken. He'll be different tomorrow." So I felt pretty lonely and almost tricked by it all because I wasn't married to prince charming and I had nobody to discuss it with.[177]

The arguments and – I called it the chip on his shoulder. He didn't seem to be able to hear what I was saying. I would say something to him that was what I thought was a very concerned and an open-ended question, that maybe he would talk to me a little bit, and what he would hear had to be different than what I said because what would come out of him was an argumentative, defensive, angry, sometimes resentful person.[178]

Now his professional life was always great. He ended up graduating top of his class in the MBA program the Navy had placed him in and ended up getting a fellowship award for the best fellowship project. The night of the ceremony for his fellowship project, there was a party at Tavern on the Green to honor the nominees and the award winners and I told him I couldn't go with him because I couldn't stand beside him and be a smiling wife when he wasn't putting the work into being a husband. I didn't think he deserved to have a wife on his arm because he wasn't being a husband.[179]

He channeled the energy of his considerable anger into his professional life to help him succeed. He even started running marathons, adventure racing on a mountain bike at night down mountains, he would run around Central Park in New York City, and when that was not enough he filled his backpack full of bocci balls and then do the run

again. He would run up the twenty-two flights of stairs to our apartment.[180] . . . Next set

of orders, Ken got selected for flight school. He had done the things his mentors in the

Navy had wanted him to do and done really well in those and this was his tour that he

would get to do something in the Navy that he felt was fun. He wanted to do the aviation

thing even though he was a medical officer, not a fighter pilot.[181]

It all continued at our next duty station in Aberdeen, Maryland.[182] . . . We tried

living as friends, no stress of being a married couple. The pressure for physical relations

was off.[183] . . . I wanted to have a baby.[184] . . . The arguments continued, the more demands

on him I placed, and it wasn't just physical demands. At this point, he was so saddened

that I was lonely and so saddened that he couldn't make a difference, couldn't – I would

come to him with my needs of any sort and he would get defensive and disappear,

physically and emotionally. He would go away for two days, work long hours, wait until

I was asleep before he came to bed, not look at me. He would leave notes. When he

would finally come around to realizing where I was, or maybe what I had said, it made it

through to him. So I would read these notes and realize he was my Kenny, and I would

charge ahead and we'd try to work things out again.[185]

When he testified later in the trial, Ken recognized how awful all this was for Amy. He

told the jury that –

I can't imagine the hell I put Amy through the last ten years and what she has had to deal

with and put up with and the fact that she's still here. Quite frankly, I don't know why

except that there's a reason for why I met her and why she hunted me down and made me marry her. I'm so grateful for that.[186]

[Amy continued.]

And so it was in one argument that we were both emotional and crying. The baby had been born and I wasn't sleeping a lot. I was – and I had taken a part-time job there. So I was working. And we had some stress back in our lives. And it's just when the stress is even at all present that anything that wasn't Ken's first nature would disappear. So in this argument, I said to him, and when I said it, he was already, curled up in a ball in the corner of the bedroom, and I said, "what did somebody do to you that makes you act this way?" And that's when he looked at me and said, "Could it have been because a priest abused me when I was young."[187]

Well, the psych nurse took over for a minute and said, of course, it could be because of that. And I was so relieved as his wife because it wasn't me that was, I guess, repulsive I suppose is what I felt I was at that time.[188] . . . All of a sudden some of his quirks made sense to me. Remember the smell of cologne throughout the house that Ken's mother told us reeked from Smith? Well, the cologne thing. I gave him cologne for one of our first Valentine's Days together and he didn't wear it and I couldn't figure out why. And it was almost – and instead of gently letting me down or, you know, explaining something to me in a sensitive way, he would get angry about it. So the cologne thing became something not to be mentioned.[189]

He had nightmares for the first three years we were married that were so bad that I would sleep very lightly because he would thrash and hit and kick so hard that I would have bruises. And one night I woke up in time to catch his arm before it came right down on my head. And I would wake him and say, "Kenny, you're dreaming. What are you dreaming about?" And he would wake up and not know, but he would be in a full sweat. And those weren't the worst ones. The worst ones is when I would wake up to this noise and it was him crying in his sleep and he was whimpering and he couldn't tell me what those dreams were either when he would wake up. He wouldn't know. He would just continue to whimper for another couple minutes.

Also, to this day, he still dresses in another room and doesn't come in when I'm dressing. I joined him once in the shower thinking that's what I've seen in the movies on TV and that would be a fun thing to do and he was so embarrassed and almost angry that I did that, that I wouldn't do that again.[190]

Well eventually Ken got comfortable enough in his command that he could find maybe a counselor, psychiatrist that he could trust or talk to, and that was Captain William A. McDonald who saved our marriage. The fact is that he asked Ken, or challenged Ken to go back and face Smith and that Ken should tell his family. To that point, I was the only one who knew about his past, so we would have arguments or have family expectations on us, and I would either be disagreeing in front of his family or we wouldn't be able to participate in the family functions because we didn't have the energy to do it and I didn't have the energy, once again, to be the happy wife on his arm. And Captain McDonald said, You need to let your family in on this, too, which was a huge burden of relief for me, because I could tell somebody else and cry with his mom and talk to her and have her understand finally where I was coming from.[191]

At first Ken was reluctant to go back and confront Smith, who had allowed all this to happen. He told me, first, the reasons why he thought maybe he couldn't or shouldn't, the embarrassment, the not being able to go back to his alma mater for homecomings, the separation it would cause between he and his brothers because his brothers had graduated from there and maybe his brothers wouldn't feel comfortable to go back to their alma mater. And then he said, "You know, there's a reason this has happened to me." And somewhere along the line, he got promoted enough, and somewhere along the line, he accomplished enough in his own life that he could face his past.

And he said, "I am going to make sure that this doesn't happen to other children, that this won't happen to our sons." And he went back and came – I mean, came here and went to the school and told his mom and his brothers and his dad.[192]

Now, looking back, with Ken, what you see is not what you get. He looks like Ken of the Ken and Barbie Dolls, and I heard that a lot when we were first got married. Oh, you did marry a Ken. But he acted then very much like somebody that the whole world had just dumped on. And to this day, I know everybody has stress in their life. Ken has a layer of stress in his life that just never seems to go away. And, unfortunately, it's about the fun things. It's about the anniversaries and the holidays and Valentine's Day. It's about getting together and just having fun. It's about making love as a married couple. Those are the first things to go in him when he's stressed.

That's not a natural thing for him and he has told me that it won't ever be natural, that that is just not the way he's wired now. And I grieve for him because I know deep down, we are professionals. We're educated. We're bright and we're healthy. And the reality we live in is good, but because we've accepted the reality we have, that has been chosen for us, and where we dreamed of being is not where we are. And I know a lot of people are not where they dreamed of being, but it's hard when we have the same dream and he has worked so hard to meet me even halfway and he can't. So we've kind of adapted our life that I will only work part-time, that I will have our home in order, that I will have our boys in a safe place, that at least I will be involved in the schools until he can be involved himself. And I can go more than halfway when we need us to. And that's our reality.

When we got married in 1997, I never thought ten years later a courtroom is where I would be. But knowing everything I know, and knowing Ken, I would have to say this is the best place to be. If this is our path, and if this is the direction victims need to go so they have a voice, people who can't speak out for themselves, people who, for whatever reason, chose to abuse other things, so be it. So if he can be a spokesperson for the people who can't speak, this is the best place to be.[193]

* * *

Next, for over two hours the Commander himself testified in his *Top Gun* form. Throughout the trial he was dressed in his service dress blues (the black, double breasted suit and tie, with gold rank insignia on the sleeve at the wrist, with ribbons). His gold naval aviator wings were proudly pinned to the left side of his chest along with his personal decorations, medals and campaign ribbons. Eventually he told the jury why he had finished flight school and received his wings in January 2003.

I had to prove myself and become a fighter pilot because the Top Gun Marine fighter pilots I treated medically cannot relate to you if you are not really one of them. If you don't wear gold wings and wear brown shoes in the Navy, Marine Corps aviation, you are a doctor to them who happens to wear a uniform. Once you earn gold wings and wear brown shoes, you are now one of them. You are part of them. You are under the umbrella and you are now a naval officer who happens to also be their doctor. So I became a pilot and won my wings so they would open up to me medically.[194] I tried to ignore the fact that twice during flight training I had thrown my guts up into my gloves and I did not understand why until my military psychiatrist pointed out that the pilots on those days were wearing powerful cologne, just like Smith wore when he sexually abused me as a teenager.[195]

Ken placed his white cover, "hat" to a civilian, on the witness stand and then his hand on the *Bible*, stood foursquare and took the oath "to tell the truth, the whole truth, and nothing but the truth, so help me God." That oath reminded him of the oath he took to become a commissioned officer in the Armed Forces where he pledged to "bear true, faith, and allegiance to the . . . Constitution of the United States,"[196] in whose court he now appeared. As a naval officer the three core values, the bedrock principals, are Honor, Courage and Commitment.[197] His obligation to honor the uniform was directly involved with his testimony that day. As an officer in uniform that meant that he had to "be honest and truthful in our dealings . . . with those outside the Navy . . . Abide by an uncompromising code of integrity . . . Fulfill or exceed our legal and ethical responsibilities in our public and personal lives twenty-four hours a day. Illegal or improper behavior or even the appearance of such behavior will not be tolerated. We are accountable for our professional and personal behavior."[198]

After the preliminaries, he first explained how as a young teenager he was a vulnerable victim. Ken told the jury that:

I was a young early teenager when I first met Smith. My parents got separated three times before they finally got divorced. The first time I remember a separation I was twelve and my older brother David was fourteen, and we both knew they were separated. We kept it from the two younger ones, but we both knew it and they were separated two other times after that, before they were finally divorced when I was – I guess nineteen when they were finally divorced.[199]. . . Sometimes there's not enough parent to go around, especially for active boys. So that had an effect upon me. My dad and I were never close. He was never home very much. He worked very hard and worked very long. But even when he was home, you could tell he really didn't want to be there, that that wasn't the thing that most interested him. So we were not very close at all.

I was a shy fourteen-year-old kid. Awkward, very insecure about myself. I stuttered a lot as a young boy and that always made me very socially, very uneasy and very unsure of myself. So I tended to, in the classroom, sit in the back of the classroom. Didn't want to get called upon. Didn't want to get singled out. So it was kind of awkward, but I guess I survived because I was pretty good at sports. But as far as anything else, socially, I would not feel myself very comfortable at all.[200]

* * *

He then moved on to explain the dangerous environment that was part of the Norbertine priests' culture at his school. Archmere Academy was not the safe haven parents thought they had found for their children, where they would be protected from the dangers of the outside

-61-

world.

Ken testified that he –

was raised a Roman Catholic and its Norbertine religious order ran my high school.[201] . . .

Religious order priests answer to a superior, here an abbott, who answers eventually to

the Pope in Rome. The Norbertines are found all over the United States and the world.[202]

They are found in Philadelphia, Chicago, Albuquerque, Missouri, California, Wisconsin,

just to name a few of the places I know.[203] . . . They live in communities or groups in a

residential building called a priory. The priory at Archmere Academy, my high school in

Claymont, Delaware, was called the Patio. It was their residence and was right on the

Archmere grounds right between the soccer fields and tennis courts. All the priests who

worked at Archmere at that time lived there, so there were a couple dozen. I saw them, I

saw where they lived. Smith always showed me his room as well as some of the other

priests' rooms. I saw their common rooms, where they watched TV, where they had

meetings, their kitchen, library over there. They had a bowling alley in the basement. I

got the full tour when I was there.[204]

Smith and I did some of our drinking at the priory. We did not drink alone but

with the other priests, despite the fact I was an underage minor. When we were at the

priory, some of the other priests we drank with, if we were in his room watching a movie,

again, in 1982, cable was new, so – so the priory had cable. So if we were watching a

movie on HBO or something like that, there would be a couple priests in, either in his

room or in the common room. The common room is where they had their refrigerator

that was fully stocked with all the alcohol and whatever you wanted. Whatever kind of beer, wine, and then the bar was right next to it. Happy hour is a social function at their priory, so that was – they were always stocked for that. Smith liked Tanqueray and tonic. In the summertime it was always frozen Pina Coladas.[205]

When I was drinking with Smith at the priory there were several priests around. Michael Collins, the assistant prefect of discipline, was there, Timothy Mullin, an eventual headmaster at Archmere, was there, James Bagnato, and John Logan. [Mullin is discussed in chapter four as a participant in gang rapes of several boys.] Those are priests who usually ended up in his room [and who] I drank with personally in Smith's room. But the other priests that were there, Salvatore H. Cuccia, Thomas Hagendorf, the librarian and college counselor, all of them saw me going in and out of the common room where the alcohol was kept and they never questioned when I went in, or came out with a handful of beer or wine and went back to Smith's room. There was never a question from anyone. And they were all teachers at my school but Logan. Some of them were actually – one was my English teacher, one was the guidance counselor. One was the class counselor. So if I didn't drink with them, they saw that I had alcohol and I was there around alcohol with them.[206]

The drinking at the priory was always on a Friday or Saturday evening. As I say, happy hour was a function there, so it would be in the early evening hours. If we were watching a movie, a little bit later in the evening. And drinking was involved, then it would be later in the evening. But it was only on Friday or Saturday evening.

I know I was coming out of there at 10:00, 11:00, 12:00 o'clock, 1:00 o'clock in the morning. So that was not uncommon. When I was coming out of there from being with Smith at 10:00, 11:00, 12:00, 1:00 a.m. in the morning, without a doubt, during my three-year relationship with Smith there, I ran into every priest that lived there at one time or another after ten, eleven pm or midnight. I mean every single one I remember. In particular, the first time, that really jogged my memory, I ran into Joseph McLaughlin our Headmaster. It was 11:30 at night, Friday night. I'm coming out of Smith's room, down the stairs and out the door to get in Smith's car so he can drive me home and there's McLaughlin walking in the front door. I knew for a fact I was going to get called into his office on Monday or he was going to call my mom and tell her – I figured something bad was going to happen. He's our Headmaster. He's a priest. He lives there. He saw me coming out at 11:30 at night. But nothing happened.[207]

Smith always had pornographic movies in his room also. But the priory also had cable TV. Early on when I was still a freshman and fourteen we were in his room once, just Smith and Collins, and me. We were watching, it was an HBO special. I just remember that it was something to do with sex or sexuality or something, just because I was uncomfortable sitting here with two priests watching a show that dissected and talked about human sexuality and, you know, there were naked women on the screen. It was just uncomfortable for me. But it was even more uncomfortable when you hear your Dean of Students, Collins, make the comment that he thought women were more sexy and sexually attractive with their clothes on versus their clothes off. And as you watch a topless woman go by the screen, that that kind of stuck with me, that kind of made me feel like I didn't know what was going on. I was very uncomfortable. But, again, like I'm not going to say anything. I'm not going to do anything. If it was wrong, I would have assumed that someone would do something about it.[208]

All three summers, Smith and a couple of his closer friend priests also rented a house, so there was a house full of three or four priests that got together and rented down the Jersey Shore, near Avalon, Stone Harbor. It was usually for two or so weeks. I did not sleep on the couch but instead in Smith's room. Each of the priests had one room and I slept in Smith's room in his bed with him. None of the other priests in the beach house ever questioned that.[209]

After the passage of the Child Victim's Act of 2007, Ken then sued the Norbertines and Archmere Academy for their role in his injuries and their gross negligence in supervising Smith. Ken's lawyers here discovered for him much more about Norbertine priests which he did not have the opportunity to present to the jury at his earlier damages trial. Ken learned that Smith was known to be a criminal child abuser several years before Smith started on Ken but the Norbertines still did not remove him from access to young males. For instance, as explained under oath by Smith's religious boss in 2007, priest James Bagnato, the Norbertines also operated St. John Neumann High School in Philadelphia, Pennsylvania. There in the fall of 1980 Smith was elevated to the job of school principal, before his later assignment to Archmere, despite concern with "an over familiarity with a number of students."[210] But while Smith became principal in September of 1980, just four short months later, by January of 1981 he was gone "because of sexual allegations" raised "by more than one student."[211] Bagnato also freely admits that "Smith was involved with incidents with young boys at Neumann."[212] He confesses that it appears from Norbertine records that the senior student council president at Neumann raised accusations that Smith had made homosexual advances against him at Neumann in the fall of 1980 leading to his removal in January of 1981.[213] On May 21, 2002 the *Philadelphia Daily News* also reported accusations against Smith back at this time involving sexual abuse by him of a freshman and two other teenagers at that school.[214] After his removal from Philadelphia, Smith then was hidden out as a parish priest in Salisbury, Maryland for a year before he was sent to Archmere Academy in 1982 and took up his criminal ways with Ken.[215]

The long-time Norbertine Dean of Students at Archmere, and once even its headmaster for a short time, priest Michael Collins,[216] known by some as Mr. Archmere, also admitted under oath that while Smith was at Archmere, Collins was aware that Smith had been removed as principal at Neumann High School several years before because one student accused him of making homosexual advances.[217] He could not contest that it appears from Norbertine business records that at least the senior student council president at Neumann raised accusations that Smith had made homosexual advances against him at Neumann in the fall of 1980 which ended up with Smith's being removed.[218] Despite this fact, the Collins still recommended that Smith be made the campus minister at Archmere, which did in fact happen, thus giving Smith access to Ken and to the entire student population.[219] Collins made this recommendation despite the fact that he knew Smith also was undergoing psychiatric treatment after his removal from Neumann.[220]

And then even more red warning flags went up. Collins also admits that while Ken was at Archmere he thought that "Smith was more or less unprofessional in the attention that he paid" to Ken, and that his attention "was excessive."[221] But these forewarnings did nothing to deliver this student from Smith's criminal influence. The Norbertine recklessness in protecting Ken, one of the students entrusted to them by his parents for an education in a safe environment, is revealed by Collins' own sworn testimony.

Q. Okay. And now I am saying during Kenny Whitwell's sophomore year, when you were seeing this excessive attention being paid to Kenny Whitwell, I am asking you if you questioned Smith about it, and you told me no?

A. No. That's correct.

Q. Okay. And my next question is: Well, knowing that there were these accusations at Neumann High School, did you sit him down and say, "Is something going on here?"

A. No.

Q. Okay. Knowing that Abbot John Neitzel had sent him for some – to see a medical professional after the St. John Neumann experience, did you at this time, because he was having excessive attention to Kenny Whitwell, did you sit him down and ask him whether anything was going on?

A. No.

Q. Okay. And I think you are saying that you didn't bring any of this to [headmaster Joseph] McLaughlin's direct attention?

A. No.[222]

In June 1983, Ken's sophomore year, Norbertine priest Joseph McLaughlin began his initial thirteen year term as headmaster. In 2008 he again was headmaster and he gave the following testimony at that time.[223] McLaughlin knew that Smith had been removed from Neumann. He was an official in the Norbertine community there at that time.[224] He never was advised that Smith had been cleared of the sexual offense-charges which resulted in his removal from Philadelphia.[225] But he still did nothing to protect anyone from Smith when he took over at Archmere. He freely admits that he cannot recall ever checking with Smith's boss in the Norbertine chain of command to see if Smith allegedly was safe to be around Ken or others.[226] But showing where his true values were placed, he later did see that Smith was removed from the Archmere faculty after he discovered that Smith was involved in financial mismanagement of money from a 50/50 raffle he was running for the school.[227] From this it appears that an individual can lose a position in the Norbertines if money is involved but that same person will suffer no negative consequences if there is a danger that he might commit sexual crimes against children.

Last there is the testimony of the very high American Norbertine official, Thomas deWane, an ordained priest since 1958.[228] Concerning the overriding loyalty and protection Norbertine priests give to each other and which subordinates any duty to protect children from child abusers, he first explained that in the Wisconsin Norbertine jurisdiction the priests there once "reacted negatively toward" the possibility of abandoning one of their fellow priests despite the fact of "a priest sexually abusing a minor child."[229] This lead to some shocking admissions concerning the duty to protect children and where Norbertine priorities lie.

> MR. STEPHEN NEUBERGER: Q. Is that one of the reasons why Father Smith was not kicked out of the Immaculate Conception Priory in 2002?
>
> WITNESS: A. I can't say that, because this happened at St. Norbert Abbey. I don't know – I can't say that that's what they were basing it on. But I think that there was kind of an understanding that way, yes.[230]

. . .

Q. Now, is there ever an act that a priest can commit which would, in your opinion, drawing on your many years of distinguished experience with the Norbertines, is there ever an act that a priest can commit where he would be expelled or where the order would petition the Abbot General in Rome to petition the Pope to remove him from the priesthood?

A. Well, I'm going to have to use my imagination. Is that what you are asking me to do?

Yes.

A serial killer.

So there is, like, a hierarchy of serious offenses, then?

There are always, I think, immoral issues, there is a hierarchy of offenses.

So killing a lot of people is higher in the hierarchy of bad – moral offenses than –

Well, I would think that the individual who would be in the community, he might kill somebody in the community.

I'm sorry?

He might kill somebody in the community. I mean, you are asking me to – for an imaginary thing, and –

You're saying that the serial killer might kill one of the priests in the Norbertine community?

Might kill the administrator.

Might kill the administrator?

Yeah.

But is the administrator in a better position to protect himself from being sexually abused by the priest than would be a young child in a school?

Surely.

And does that factor in?

So far as what we should do about it?

Yes. So far as the fact that one crime would be directed against the order itself versus another crime being directed against a child?

Well, if your object is to prevent him from committing the crime again, which is the object, I'm just saying that if it was a serial killer, it might be of such a state of mind that the guy is crazy and, therefore, something should be done about it immediately.[231]

To their shame, Norbertine priorities appear to have planned to protect themselves from threats of physical harm to their persons, but they did not give the same level of protection to young children.

* * *

Returning to Ken's trial testimony on day one, it eventually swung to the absent defiant priest, Edward J. Smith.

When I started my freshman year in the fall of 1982 as a fourteen-year-old, Smith was my religion teacher.[232]. . . He was a younger guy. So he got the name as being the young, hip, cool priest, because he was younger than the rest of them and he acted younger than the rest of them as well. He immediately stood out from the other priests. As I said, he was the hip cool guy. He dressed differently. He chose not to wear the traditional collar. He would instead wear $200 ski sweaters that were very bright, very colorful, very ostentatious. I mean, he stood out just from the way he dressed. He had a very expensive watch. It was a gold watch and it had diamond dust covering the entire watch. You don't meet him and shake his hand and not take notice of that. He wore gold chains, smelled very heavily of Polo cologne. That is one of the first things that you take from him when you meet him, is he smelled of cologne. He was dressed more like he was going to a disco rather than as a priest.

He also drove a different car from the other priests. No box on wheels for him. First he had a white Oldsmobile Cutlass and then he started driving a silver Mercury Cougar, two-door kind of much more sporty sedan.[233] . . . So the impression you got from him immediately is this guy is different. This guy is a different priest than the other priests. He certainly looked it. He talked that way. The young girls thought he was really cool because he knew how to dance. He was from South Philadelphia. That was his whole persona. That was him. As a result, he's very charismatic. People respond to that. Kids, fourteen and fifteen-year-old kids are going to respond to a priest, respond to a teacher who talks like them, acts like them, knows what they're going through, just like he's one of us. So his – his office was always very crowded because there was always kids hanging around.[234]

Smith then singled me out. He started paying attention to me. He asked me to meet him in his office after class, during my free period, help him move a box, help him do something and we would be hanging out when the other kids came by as well. And he built me up in front of my fellow students. So immediately he began separating me from my classmates as being someone different, someone who was gaining his attention.[235]

Then, he progressed from, "hey, can you help me out setting up chairs for the school

assembly during school hours. Hey, come by the office. I need help doing this." It

started with a group of boys. It was always boys and there would have been three or four

of us helping him out. He would move to it was just me then helping him out. And then

that moved to off-school hours, after school. So he began having me help him do things

at the priory or moving something from the school over to the priory. And as a token of

his appreciation, he would offer to take us to – get something to eat, go out to dinner, just

something quick, not that big of a deal. But then, as I say, it stopped being a group thing

and started being just a Ken thing and so I began doing things with him after school

along those lines, helping him do something.[236]

And then if I missed my ride home, he'd offer to take me home. And so that's

how he arrived in our house. He arrived in our house because it was a Friday afternoon, I

had to help him do something after soccer practice and my brother went home. So he

offered to take me home and he did. And that's how he met our family. So he

immediately – you know, he immediately engaged our family. And, again, he's there

because I brought him home. So that made me feel special in my own family. He was a

teacher, but not only a teacher, but he was a teacher and a priest. Even that, that's one

notch above just a coach coming by. It's the coach that happens to be the priest. That

was just the start. Now that became a regular occurrence. He was at our house probably

two, three days a week from that day out. He would either bring me home for something

or find a reason to stop by.[237] . . . So he would stay for dinner. He would keep my mom

company. My mom never had any adult conversation, so to speak, after dinner. And so he would be over all the time. If he wasn't bringing me home. He was stopping by and when he stopped by, he stayed.[238]

I'm fourteen years old. Any child that gets any kind of attention from an adult is going to respond to that. That's just human nature. Then you add on to that an adult who is a teacher, who is an official at the school, someone who is important, someone in authority that even makes you feel even better. And on top of that, he's a priest. So what could be better than bringing home a priest and having a priest think that you are something special.[239] . . . He was a priest – at that time I truly believed that, a priest, we were taught, is basically God's representative here on earth. They are, you know – in so many words, they're God's right-hand man. And God communicates to us through priests. Priests are chosen. This is their vocation. They are chosen by God to do this special thing here on earth. So when you put that into context, that's how you taught – that's how you respond to priests.[240]

Smith then began giving me and my brothers lots and lots of gifts. First professional football jerseys, sweat pants, ski equipment, heavy jackets, for me a better stereo set than the equipment that my parents even had, and a snowmobile. Mom stopped him when I was sixteen from buying me a car.[241]

* * *

Eventually, the difficult subject of how Smith had used young Kenny as his sexual plaything had to be addressed for the jury to comprehend the magnitude of the harm Kenny endured. Ken here explained that –

the first time he touched me in a sexual way was December of 1982. Smith needed my

-73-

help wrapping Christmas presents. He gave his friends these figurines, Hummels they're called, I guess, and they're a couple hundred dollars apiece. And he had a trunk full of them that he wanted me to help wrap and give to his friends. He had thirty or forty of them on display in different places in his room. I didn't know that they were that expensive until he gave one to my mom and my mom told me, what an expensive gift. Do you know how much they are? I said, I have no idea. She said, they start at a hundred dollars. I said, that's kind of strange, because we just got done wrapping fifty to sixty of them, and she couldn't believe that. So we were wrapping gifts in his room, his private room. Most of the priests had a sitting room and then a bedroom, so we were in his sitting room and we were wrapping presents. I had my back to him and I was just going along, wrapping presents.

And there was a show on TV and there was a commercial. The commercial had some women in bathing suits. I stopped what I was doing. I was fourteen. I wasn't going to not look. So I went ahead and looked, and as I was looking, I then felt Smith reach around and grab my crotch. And before I could turn around and say, what are you doing, he asked me if I had a hard-on or not. And, again, I didn't know how to respond. I was turning to him and always I – as I turned to him, he then put his hand into my pants and began rubbing my genitals. And he rubbed – he continued to rub. I didn't move. I didn't know what to think, what to say. He continued to rub them until – until he made me ejaculate in my pants. And that's when I started to move the first time, I started to shake, because I was so scared. I didn't know what happened. And Smith had – Smith told me that it was okay, it wasn't my fault, I didn't do anything wrong, because – maybe

-74-

that's why I was shaking like I was. I thought maybe I did something wrong.[242]. . . And

that's when he explained to me that everything was okay and that what happened was

normal and it was fine. And that began the explanation of physical contact, sex and

relationships and intimacy, that night was my first night, was my first night of education

from Smith about what happened and about sex and sexuality.[243]. . . I was obviously

stunned. My face must have looked like a deer caught in the headlights, because I didn't

blink. I didn't know what to say. I didn't know what to do and so I just began shaking

uncontrollably because it – something wasn't right. But by the end of his explanation, I

stopped shaking. I had stopped – I had calmed down and that's how it all started.[244]

He told me that this was God's expression of love to me, that I was chosen for

that, and how lucky I was. And he convinced me that I was – I was fortunate because I

was going to receive God's love and he was the – it was going to be through him. And he

was going to educate me on sex and sexuality because I didn't know anything at that

point in time. And that began my education. The equation of God's love and a sexual act

and that it was okay and that it was normal, that it was fine.

You know, he's a priest. He's a good counselor. He certainly knows what to say.

He counsels young teenage boys and girls all the time, so his delivery, his manner,

everything he said, it made sense to me. Of course, at that point in time, I'm looking for

something to make sense because I'm scared to death when this thing first happened. So

his explanation, again, while it sounds somewhat hollow now, was perfectly fine, was

perfectly acceptable and made a lot of sense to an immature fourteen year old boy.[245]

Now I did not tell anybody about what he did. His argument was a pretty good one to a fourteen year old boy who didn't know about sex. He was educating me. From then on for the next few years, any time I questioned or asked him a question about it, it was an opportunity to get educated about sex and sexuality and about intimacy and what intimacy really is and what it means. He basically told me, everybody knows that, Ken. I'm just bringing you up to speed basically because you're a nice boy, but you're a little uneducated about these things and how lucky you were to find me to help you through these things. He used my awkwardness and my shyness and my ease of embarrassment against me because he said, if you do tell anyone, the only one that's going to be embarrassed is going to be you because they already know it's okay. They know this is normal. They know this is healthy. They know it's fine. If you bring it up to anyone, it's just going to be you that's going to be embarrassed because he knew if he told that to me that I would never risk public embarrassment, especially about the topic of sex.[246]

Now a fourteen year old still does have some conscience, whether undeveloped or not, so there was a lot of anxiety inside of me. There was this incredible dichotomy that swirled inside of me. The sexual acts that I was being forced to perform or being forced upon me created a tremendous amount of anxiety inside of me. Made it a tremendous amount of guilt, a tremendous amount – I mean, the feelings of something not being correct, it just made me feel really bad. On top of feeling bad about the actual physical act, Smith made me feel guilty about questioning it. You know, he would not only convince me with his long diatribes about explaining to me, but he started writing me these long, long letters, these epistles, I called them, thesis, that he would only let me read in the priory about explaining exactly why it was okay and how people should act if

-76-

they love each other and, you know, so if I didn't get it verbally, I got it in the written word as well. And every time I questioned him, every time I read one of those letters, I walked away feeling more and more guilty because I'm refusing God – look at me. Who am I? I'm refusing God's love. I'm questioning God's love. I'm questioning his messenger here on earth. I mean, I felt awful because I felt awful about the situation. And I was questioning it and I was not feeling right about it. I really thought something was wrong with me because I felt bad about something that I should be feeling good about. At least that's what I was told I should feel good about.[247]

If I hadn't been so focused on my sports and my school studies, I mean, thank God I went to a school that made me do four hours of homework a night because the hours I didn't spend with Smith I spent either studying or playing sports. I didn't have time to focus on those competing forces inside my body, inside my head, because if I stopped for a moment and thought about it, I couldn't understand it. I couldn't make sense of it. And not making sense of your world, you just start down a very, very quick spiral. It's a very quick slippery slope off that edge into nothingness. So I'm grateful for still being here.[248]

He also would always warn me that girls were bad news. Look at the kids in my class. Suzie Q. and Johnny were getting into a fight about this and that. Aren't you glad I'm protecting you from those things? Aren't you glad you don't have to go through that. Aren't you glad you're getting real love and a real situation from someone who cares for you. Those people don't care for each other and you don't need that and I'm protecting you from that. Smith knew everything about what all the other kids were doing because they wanted to tell him. They wanted to be his buddy. But then he would use all that information against me because he would say look at all this crap that your classmates are going through. And he would call that. He would call the fourteen and fifteen year old crushes and things that normal boys and girls were doing, and he would convince me that what I was doing was so much better, so much safer, was so much more out of love and that – so my point is, in a very sick and twisted way, I trusted Smith more when these things happened because, again, he was saying and it was happening. He was saying and it was happening. He was unfolding these events for me, perfectly orchestrating the world which I knew.[249]

The following weeks after the first incident, starting in December of '82, a sexual act occurred every time I was with him. It started off with we always ended up in his room some way, somehow. He always had an excuse to go to his room. And he would go to give me a hug goodbye, saying, okay, thanks very much for helping him. He'd always end up with his hand on my genitals outside my pants. And he would then quickly move them inside my pants and do the same exact thing again. He would rub me until I ejaculated in my pants, and that was how the first couple of weeks, the first couple of months went. He started off with just my pants were always on and for the next couple of weeks, couple of months, that's how it always went. And then he took the next step and pushed me forward and he – whenever he introduced something new, he would always, again, he would sense my unease about it and he would always be ready with the explanations. So we progressed on to other things.[250]

He had pornography in his room and he would show it to me as a joke. He would be making fun of particular genitalia of the individuals and he would – you know, he would sort of dehumanize it and sort of make it, you know, push it off to the side. And then he switched very quickly and very abruptly to, doesn't that look good, doesn't that look nice. I bet that feels really good. And let me show you how that feels and let me show you what that is. And so that's how I ended up with him removing my pants and having him performing sex upon me with those videos. My resistance to that went back and forth and then he finally made me comfortable enough with it to allow him to do it, even though I would always say "No." I'd say, "No" "not right now" and I would always try to avoid it, but whenever you went out with Smith, we always ended up in his room some way, somehow.[251]. . . And that was what I was forced to do if I was going to be allowed to go home. I wanted to go home. It was one o'clock in the morning. I'm still only fourteen. But he would never let me unless he was able to perform those sexual acts upon me. So he moved to forcing himself upon me and then he slowly moved to force me to do it upon him. That's over a course of several months. That is not a one-snapshot deal.[252]

He would make me grab his genitals and he would force me to perform oral sex upon him. He would force me to watch him masturbate or anything he was doing sexually. When I just turned sixteen he anally raped me at the Jersey Shore at one of his friends house. And we were staying in the apartment above the garage. It was just a one room apartment, fold-out couch. So we went to bed, and this was not the first time I was forced to share a bed with him. This was – this is par for the course when you are in bed with Smith. I would always go off to the far side of the bed as far as I possibly could just to avoid contact with him, but he would always make his way over to the bed, always make his way over to where you were, start rubbing himself on your body. His pants were always on, as were mine. He would always rub my back, rub my leg. I pretended to be asleep because if I could avoid it, obviously, that would be better. But he wouldn't let me go to sleep. And it got to the point that I had to exchange sex for sleep. And so I always tried to resist, though, and he would always be persistent. He would always then reach over and remove my pants and then perform the acts upon me. And the problem with that is from following every night there's a morning, so every morning you can't get out of bed until something happens again. So there's always the anxiety of just wanting to go to sleep, always then gets skipped because now once you're asleep, now you have to wait to figure out what's going to happen the next day, the next morning. So that particular evening, when he inched his way and wormed his way over to my side of the bed, he wasn't wearing any pants. And he quickly removed mine and rolled me over onto my stomach and then he anally raped me. When he finished, and he rolled off of me, bragged to me, said, "There, that's what it's like to be fucked." And I just remember putting my pants back on, curling up on the side of the bed, hoped that I wouldn't be fucked again in the morning.[253] I'm a heterosexual man. Being forced to grab the penis of another man either with your hand or with your mouth is disgusting. Absolutely revolting. Being raped anally was an awful thing, too, and then being basically made fun of for it or being bragged about having it done to you was salt into the wound.[254]

The sexual crimes continued for the next three years, in 1983, 1984 and 1985 in Delaware, Pennsylvania, New Jersey, Wisconsin, and even Vermont on ski trips.[255] . . .

For example, after he had finished with me, by typically performing oral sex on me, he would force me to watch him masturbate.[256]. . . Despite my resistance, by January of 1985 he had forced me to perform oral sex on him also.[257] . . . While my classmates on a typical weekend would go to parties, my typical weekend during my high school years was being sexually molested is pretty much how I felt.[258]

It all ended in late summer of 1985 at the Jersey Shore when I was seventeen. My family had rented a beach house in Ocean City. My brothers and I began to attract the attention of several female lifeguards on the beach and began hanging out with them at the beach. One evening we planned on going out and that's good. Then Smith showed up later that afternoon and told me he was taking me to Wildwood and that was it. I said I had plans, but ok. I told my brothers who were like, "whoa, whoa, whoa, Ken. You can't ditch us, man. The girls are coming because you're coming. If you don't come, they're going to drop us. You can't go." So I told Smith, "No. I wasn't going." He screamed and yelled and said "That's it." He threatened me that "it's over, you're cut off. You're out." And I kept walking. I turned my back and I kept walking. He continued shouting until he started to draw the attention of others. So he turned around and got in his car and left. And it ended.[259]. . . After thirty-three months, from December of 1982 to when it ended in 1985, conservatively Smith had committed sexual acts on me on 234 occasions.[260]

* * *

The testimony ended with Ken describing how, on the advice of his medical officer, he decided to confront the Norbertine culture and Smith himself. Ken said –

after I grew up, finished medical school, became a Naval officer, acknowledged my demons and eventually received psychiatric treatment in the Navy, as I had promised Amy, in 2004 I decided to confront my tormentors.[261] . . . My psychiatrist, Captain McDonald had told me that one of the things that is very, very helpful with my kind of anger is to go and face your past, and he convinced me, and he was right, that it's necessary, it's part of your therapy, it's part of your treatment. I told him, I said, "Well, I'll be happy to do that, but I'm not telling my mother." I didn't want to do that. I know that would crush her. Come to find out that she needs to heal too and she needs to know about it first. So he convinced me that's what I needed to do and so I did.[262]

I needed to step forward and do what is the right thing and to protect other children. I – having two small boys, just want to protect them. There's evil out there that you just – if someone knew about a predator in my neighborhood, I'd want them to tell me, and yet I knew about one and I wasn't telling anybody else. So now I had to either be a hypocrite and teach my children to do what I say, not what I do, or I need to step up and actually do that stuff and actually do that. So I don't want to teach them that you don't do something just because it's hard and coming forward I knew it was going to be really hard.[263] There's no honor in knowing the right thing to do and then not doing it just because it's hard, because it would be difficult, because it could be expensive, because it could take too much out of you. That is not the lesson I wanted to teach my children. I really hope some day that they read the transcript and are proud of me because I did the right thing even though it was real hard. And – because there's no other way that we're going to protect these children unless they know that these predators are out there. So I had to – I had to get up the courage. I mean, this is a hard thing to do. It's not a simple

thing to do. It is not a simple process. But once you decide you're going to do

something, again, you commit to the end of it, you get there no matter what the obstacle,

because no matter what pitfall you might find.[264]

And so in November of 2004 at age thirty-six I went to Archmere Academy. I

met with the Headmaster of Archmere at that time and Collins, the Dean of Students,

who was also the Dean of Students and my history teacher back then, still doing the same

thing twenty some years later. Collins was the one I was drinking and watching naked

women with.[265] . . . As a result of the meeting, the school accepted no responsibility

whatsoever for what had happened.[266] They washed their hands, like the Roman

procurator Pontius Pilate when he sentenced Jesus to death, and said that Smith didn't

work there any more. He wasn't there. So they felt as if Smith wasn't a problem any

more.[267]

Next I tracked Smith down thirty miles to the south in Middletown, Delaware

where he was living in another Norbertine priory near lots of playgrounds, ball fields,

running trails, basketball courts and places where kids are found.[268] . . . Unannounced I

asked to meet with James Bagnato the religious boss at that location who I had hung

around drinking with as a fourteen year old. First, I got a tour of the place from a retired

priest and learned they wanted to bring in school groups, kids, school age children for

religious events.[269] . . . Then while I was there in the waiting room, dressed in my

uniform, Smith came down the hallway. He was way down at the end of the hallway.

But he was wearing Polo cologne. So I could smell him down the end of the hallway.

He kind of looked funny at me. As he approached closer to me, I had my name tag on, so he said, "Kenny, is that you?" I said, "Yes, Ed, it's me." He said, "It didn't look like you. You look so different." I said, "Well, I've aged. I wear new clothes now. I have a uniform now." He goes, "Oh, wow, okay." We had a little chit-chat like that for just thirty seconds or so. And then Smith stopped what he was saying and he got real serious looking and he leaned in real close to me and whispered to me, "So we're okay with what happened between you and I; right? We're okay with that; right? That was all right?" I pulled back and said obviously, "NO! Absolutely not." I mean it was a disgusting thought that gave me that visceral response. Again, I felt like I was going to throw up and choked that down. I couldn't believe that's what he would say. I said "Absolutely not. I'm not okay with that. I'm not okay." He said, "Oh, no, really? Oh, man." Then he started to speak to me again.[270] "Oh, really? Are you sure?" I just cut him off. I said "I'm here to talk to Bagnato. If you want to talk to me, you can do so afterwards, that's fine." And then I went into a, like a ten-minute dissertation on the weather, 95 traffic, whatever it was. Just started letting go, just talking about anything, just so he would not. And he went white. He stared at me just without moving. Started to sweat. And then he re-engaged and kind of went back to being Ed and chatted with me back and forth and then Bagnato came and I left. And I went and talked to Bagnato.[271] . . . Smith never apologized to me in that hall.[272]

I then spoke with Bagnato for about forty-five minutes to an hour in private. I told him I was a victim of sexual abuse at the hands of Smith. I described the types of sexual abuse, the length, the period, the more disgusting acts, and I let him have it.[273] . . . I wanted to reduce Smith's power in the Norbertines, strip him of the ability to portray himself as a priest, his position. He looked at me like, I can't do that. I don't have the power to do that. I said, 'You're the head of the Order here. Of course, you can." He just kind of shook his head. He kind of gave me that kind of look.[274] Amazingly, as the head of the Delaware Norbertines he never apologized on their behalf.[275] . . . He was just as irresponsible at the Norbertines at Archmere. And so I left there knowing full and well that I had to expose him, the Norbertine Order and the things that happened at their school.[276] . . . I had to expose this evil to try to protect those children in those sub-developments that I drove past, all those playgrounds, the children that were at risk if I wasn't willing to go forward because it was too hard. So here I was. I was going forward.[277] . . . No one took any responsibility for the actions that happened to me. No one felt guilty. No one felt bad. There was no – there was no blame being taken by anyone and I left there, you know, just completely resolved that I was going to do something.[278]

And now it has been twenty-five years since my sexual abuse began. My journey from a shy, scared fourteen year old to a naval commander has been a long one. It has been a hard one. It has been something I never imagined I would have to do in my life. I – you know, my life. God, it's just – I don't get a do-over in my life. I don't get to go back and live my innocence and my childhood, live a normal, like a normal teenager would. I don't get any of that back. There's nothing I can do about that. Nothing anyone can do about that. And I didn't get a chance to choose that. I didn't get a chance to be normal. And I have to live with that every day.

The only thing I can do is try to go forward with what I have right now, pick up the pieces of what I have and try to go forward and do the best I can. And that includes coming forward and speaking in public about this, to try to protect children. I mean, there's no way. No one is going to know about these things unless someone talks about it and tells them about it. And I wish Smith would have shown up today. I still in the back of my mind wish he would have to sit over there and listen to what happened to me, that he'd have to look in my wife's eyes and my mother's eyes and know the pain that we went through and still go through. He doesn't – he won't even give me that courtesy.

[Ken ended, looked at the eight jurors, spoke for all survivors, and said] I've – the only thing a victim ever wants is a chance for justice, the chance to come forward and get his day in court. And I woke up many nights and I couldn't go back to sleep because I would dream about that day, about this day, right here, right now. And what I would say to him, to people who would listen, to people who would judge me, and get a real apology, a real apology from him.[279]. . . If he's sorry, why is he not here convincing you that he's sorry? You're going to tell us how much that's worth. He wouldn't do that, so I don't think he's sorry. I don't believe that for a minute, that he's sorry. And that kind of anger has got to go away sometime and I know that anger is starting to be released today because I'm here today, and I'm here today and able to say it despite how hard it is, how embarrassing it is, to have you here, with these things. But I'm grateful for it. I love serving this country and I'm grateful for days like today it serves me back and gives me its chance. I am grateful for you sitting here and providing that service to me.[280]

* * *

And so the first day of the trial concluded with Ken's moving testimony. The following trial day was devoted to educating the jury and the general public for the first time about the permanent medical and emotional traumas suffered by survivors of childhood sexual abuse. In the eventual trial of survivor John Vai, held three and a half years later, and recounted in chapter five, a team of two physicians and one psychologist painted the complete picture of the "walking wounded" whose souls were murdered when they were children. Here just one physician assumed this task.

On day two, I first explained to the Court that I was calling to the witness stand expert psychiatrist, Dr. Carol A. Tavani. "But I don't think it's therapeutic for my client to sit through this clinical analysis, so I would ask, with the Court's permission, that he be excused and he'll be allowed to sit outside the courtroom while I call Carol A. Tavani, M.D." To which the Court replied, "Absolutely."[281] I then walked out of the well of the court and swung open the gate between the public seating and the courtroom, as the diminutive four-foot ten-inch witness entered and was escorted by me to the witness stand where she took the oath.

Dr. Tavani began by explaining that she is –

a board-certified neuropsychiatrist. A psychiatrist is a physician who deals with psychiatric disorders, mental health issues and a neuropsychiatrist is much more medically oriented. It's sort of an interface between neurology and psychiatry and the relationship between the brain and the body.[282]

I'm in private practice. I do a couple of different things, but the bulk of my life is spent in the hospital. I started the psychiatric consultation service twenty years ago at Christiana Hospital, which is the premier medical facility here in Delaware. There wasn't really a psychiatrist who went there to see the patients who were medically surgically admitted and who would deal with that interface between the medical and the psychiatric issues. My background is in emergency medicine, internal medicine, and then I also trained in psychiatry. I went back and trained. I was an E.R. doctor for seven years. So I was kind of uniquely suited to that interface. It filled a niche, so I started that service and it has kind of grown to be rather large.

At Christiana base, I would say I do at least 2,000 consults a year. It's a pretty big service. And now I also go over to Riverside Hospital, which is their extended-care facility. I do four or five a week there, so I do well over 2,000 consults a year.

So if someone is at Christiana and has psychiatric complications, we would get that consultation, and it could be – it could really run the gamut of anything from depression or upset or anxiety to delirium, if somebody has a bypass surgery and they get confused and agitated and delirious, for example, I'm the one that comes and figures that out and fixes it and determines what medicines we can give you that will be safe. And also I look at, very carefully at the drug interactions and what's compatible. Could this be a medication that's doing this? It's very medically oriented. I also see patients in my office.

As far as my educational degrees go, I have a Bachelor of Science in biology and chemistry. I have a Master of Science in biology, specifically nutritional deficiencies. And then I have an M.D. In 1979 I graduated from Thomas Jefferson medical school in Philadelphia. I then did my first year of residency at Jefferson. I was invited to work in the E.R. and so then I became an attending in the Department of Emergency Medicine. I went back to Jefferson in the daytime and did the psychiatry residency, and that's a four-year residency, and then came back to – well, it was then the Medical Center of Delaware, but it's now Christiana Care. And essentially in the mid-1980s started the psychiatric consultation services I mentioned before.

And I became very involved in – on a national level, really, and on a state level. I've been a delegate to the American Medical Association for many years. I have been President of the State Psychiatric Society and also Chief of Staff at Christiana, first woman for both of those positions. Chief of staff, is over the entire medical, surgical and dental staff, elected by the entire physician and surgical and dental body. Well over a thousand physicians. I believe that was 1997 to '99 into 2000. I was President of the State Medical Society as well, and I'm still very active in various regards there. I've been going to the A.M.A. since 1992. I served as an alternate delegate and then a delegate from the State Medical Society. And now that I've rotated off that, actually, I've – I have become the representative of Christiana Care, of all of Christiana Care to the American Medical Association, to the Organized Medical Staff Section. And I'm also State Chair of that at the A.M.A. now. Also, there is something called the Organization of State Medical Society Presidents. That's a small body. The only people who belong to it are physicians who are or have been Presidents of the State Medical Societies. And I'm actually on the governing board of that. That is just twelve people nationwide that have that distinction. I've been its president.

[Dr. Tavani also explained that she is also the doctor for physicians, judges and even lawyers in Delaware.] I also have been deeply involved with the Physicians Health

Committee. A special interest of mine is helping our brethren, other professionals, and it's actually twenty years, it's just about my whole professional career, I have chaired the Physicians Health Committee. It deals with doctors who have problems of various kinds. Depression, litigation stress, substance abuse. It could be anything. Bipolar. You know, they're people, too. And kind of as a derivative of that, I was asked to be the physician member of the Delaware Bar Association's Professional Guidance Committee, which is their committee that does the same thing for attorneys. I also consult in that capacity to Office of Disciplinary Counsel, because when a lawyer comes before the Office of Disciplinary Counsel, for example, and they have taken their mail and stuffed it in a drawer for three months and haven't renewed their CLEs or whatever, you know, it sort of becomes apparent that something is the matter with this person. They are procrastinating or they're so depressed, they can't see straight. So I will be asked to evaluate that person by the Office of Disciplinary Counsel and get them whatever help they need and then re-evaluate them over time to make sure that they are safe to practice.

I also lecture. In fact, I just gave the Delaware Bar Association's CLE on stress in the professions and I've been asked to do something called a bench and bar in June, which is a big lecture on essentially the same topic. But I lecture in medicine, of course, a lot all over the country.

I have acted as an expert witness in many courts and I have never been rejected as an expert witness by any court." (The Court then ruled that Dr. Tavani was qualified to give her opinion as to the psychological and emotional injuries suffered by Ken in his case.)

[After shifting gears from her credentials to her examination and evaluation of Ken, the doctor explained that] I spent about half a day conducting a psychiatric evaluation of Commander Kenneth Whitwell. Mr. Neuberger asked me to evaluate him and to determine if he had a psychiatric diagnosis and what was the genesis of it if he did and, if so, what was his state at this point in time, what I thought his prognosis would be, and what recommendations I might have for treatment. I didn't really have a lot of [his] medical records. He's otherwise fairly healthy, but I had a four-page letter from Captain McDonald his Naval psychiatrist.

First, I conducted an interview, a comprehensive, thorough interview. To begin with, first of all, you like to know what the person's understanding is of why they're here today and what we're here to find out. My sequence, then, is I go through a detailed medical history. Now, in this case, we don't have a lot of – a lot of medical issues. But it's important to know that because there are many medical things that can affect your mental status, like if somebody has had a stroke, or if somebody has a thyroid problem, your thyroid is sluggish, it can make you depressed, so you can give somebody all the anti-depressant in the world. If you don't fix the thyroid problem, you are not going to get where you want to go. And that's my specialty, so I really hone in carefully on that.

Then we go through the psychiatric history. What have they had formally and even if they haven't had any treatment formally, because, unfortunately, most people in the world who have psychiatric problems have never gotten any treatment and if they've gotten it, only about one-fourth of them have been adequate. It's really kind of sad.

Then I go through social history. Where did they grow up? What did your parents do for a living? What was childhood like for you? Did anything happen in childhood? What are all the formative things who make you – What are all the things that make you the sum total of who you are today. You want to get an idea of an educational history, how did somebody do in school, and then not only academically, but how were your social relationships. Did you have friends? When did you start to date? What was that like? Did you get into any trouble with the law? What is your empathy level? You know, were you kind to other people? Were you mean to other people, that sort of thing. You try to get a flavor of who this person is from their social history. And then what their work history was. How did they do professionally in addition to their relationships. All of those things are important in looking at somebody.

And then you go into the mental status examination, and that really starts when you greet the patient in the waiting room. How do they look? How are they groomed? Are they looking at you? How do they walk into the room? Are they standing straight up or are they all hunched over like they're scared to death? Just a general idea of somebody's appearance and behavior. You look at what their mood is. You look at if how they are behaving matches their mood, matches what they're saying. You listen to their speech. Is it slow? Is it gunfire rapid, like they're manic? Is it coherent? Are they answering what you're asking them? What is their fund of vocabulary? Do they seem intelligent? Do they seem maybe marginally intelligent? All of those things are important.

And then you look carefully at their cognitive status. What's their memory like?

What's their long-term memory like? What is their short-term memory like? Do they have any insight into that they have a problem or if they have a problem, do they have an understanding of why they have the problem? Their degrees of insight. And then if they understand that, do they have some idea of what they might do about it and then the final level of insight is are they doing it. And then their judgment. Are they behaving appropriately to circumstance? Are they doing things that show poor judgment? Are they – to take an unrelated example, if somebody is diabetic, are they not taking their medicine? What's their judgment like in relation to their problems. Are they still doing things they know they shouldn't be doing or are they really trying to help themselves. You get an idea of their judgment.

So you take all of those things and you try to we've them together into an integrated gestalt or picture of what this person is about, and from that, you come up with a diagnostic formulation. Do they have a psychiatric diagnosis? There's a, sort of a Bible of psychiatry. It's called the DSM-IV, and that gives all the psychiatric diagnoses that the American Psychiatric Association recognizes. It's a book that's constantly in flux because it gets updated and with different cultural things, we have to look at different – different matters and every few years they come out with another one. So you make your diagnoses in that terminology. And it has five axis.

I did all those things. It takes a long time. If you are going to do that right and really put it together, thoroughly, you have to really sit there with a person for several hours. But you come up with a diagnostic formulation and then some recommendations for what might be helpful to that person. That day I met with him and then afterwards for a little more than an hour I also met with his wife, Amy.

As a result of everything I think I got a handle on what kind of a person he is and what makes him tick. But before I get into that I need to explain that I also am familiar with medical issues that are related to victims of childhood sexual abuse. As I said before, my area is the interface between medicine and psychiatry, the mind, the brain, the body connection. So that sort of an issue is right where this falls. In the hospital, when I go in to see somebody, frequently, I get called when something is the matter with somebody and they can't quite figure out what it is. Nobody can put their finger on it. A good example would be, you know, a woman comes in with abdominal pain and she gets a million dollar work up. Nobody can figure out what this abdominal pain is and she keeps coming in. It's a revolving door. I have pain, I have pain. You get CAT scans, you get MRIs, you get every lab test in the book and you start to think, something else is going on. Just because you can't find it doesn't mean it doesn't exist. And frequently, when somebody has been abused, when a woman has been abused, one thing that they frequently get that I have found out over the years is unexplained abdominal or pelvic pain.

So that has become a red flag for me, that when somebody is complaining of this and nobody can figure out what it is, that's a question that needs to be asked. And sometimes questions about abuse get skirted in medicine because people are uncomfortable and, you know, they don't want to bring it up and they think it's maybe prying or it's not appropriate, but that can often be at the heart of the matter. And it's really a favor to ask that question, because you can't start healing until you nail that and call it what it is. It's just sort of an unrelated example. You know, people will get a rash over a strange area of their body and you can't figure it out. And then you ask that question and when you find out if they've been abused, what has been done to them, darned if it isn't right where that rash is cropping up. It's amazing. The relationship between the mind and the brain and the body is truly amazing. The mind is so powerful.

And the other thing that happens is – and I hope we're going to get to this – but sort of blocking out information. There are different, I will call them coping mechanisms, which the victims of childhood sexual abuse use to live through the abuse. First of all, when a child is undergoing abuse, particularly a sexual abuse, what the kid's mind does is it takes – it takes itself somewhere else. It sort of divorces, you know, the mental process, what's going on physically. It's the mind's defense. If something is too traumatic for you to handle, it kind of divorces itself and it goes on a sort of auto pilot. And that is, I guess, even life-saving. It's adaptive at the moment. But then, since they get so good at that, because it's protective, it's a protective mechanism, it takes on a life of its own. So later on in life, it does this disassociating. When the person starts to get upset, they disassociate like that and maybe then it's not so productive. Maybe it's counter-productive. But that's what the mind has learned to do as a coping mechanism.

There is a coping mechanism called memory repression. The memories are so painful, that the mind sort of stuffs it and repression, unlike suppression, is not really a conscious thing. The mind does it. You don't say to yourself consciously, this is so painful, that I'm going to not think about it. That's trying to suppress something. In repression, the mind does it automatically. You just block it out. And a tipoff to that is when you are talking to somebody and you're getting this social history that I went through, and somebody will say, you know, I don't remember anything before the age of eight or eleven. You think to yourself, hmm. Normally, they say, you know, people don't remember maybe before the age of two, although some people do. But, you know, when somebody doesn't remember their life before eight or eleven or whatever it is, something happened. And that's another red flag because why don't they remember. So then you want to delve into that.

Then there is another coping mechanism called denial. It's another way that the mind shields one's self from things that are painful. You don't make connections. You don't connect the dots between what happened and the reason for behaviors or circumstances later on.

Also, just going back to memory repression, there is a term known as traumatic amnesia. And that goes back to repression. You really don't remember. The mind has truly blocked it out. Well, you can have amnesia for a lot of different reasons. You could have a head injury and get amnesia. A so-called traumatic amnesia is really more that the mind has blocked things out that are too painful. You know, the mind tries to protect you from what's too painful to look at right then and there. And that's true traumatic amnesia or repression.

These kinds of coping mechanisms help the survivor shield or remove themselves from the immediate pain of the sexual abuse as it's going on. Again, it's so upsetting that what the mind does is it basically removes itself from what's going on physically in the here and now. So it shields you from what's too traumatic to look at or to deal with.

Now, let me add that these victims of childhood sexual abuse suffer every day. You see, these things leave scars. They're pervasive. Not that they don't go on and have a life, but it affects you. It colors how you see the world. Usually, or oftentimes, people are abused by individuals they're supposed to be able to trust. So if you can't trust the people that you were supposed to be able to put trust in, then the world becomes a rather unsafe place in one's mind. And then who can you trust? So the ripple effect is that it affects your relationships, especially your close relationships. Again, people that you are supposed to be able to trust. It affects your ability to trust anybody. It makes you afraid for not only yourself, but the people you love, and it puts a wall around one's self.

And so now we can discuss my diagnosis of the Commander under the DSM-IV five categories or axis. Axis one is your primary psychiatric disorder. It could be major depression. It could be schizophrenia, whatever your diagnosis. It could be alcohol dependence, whatever your diagnoses are. And you can have more than one.

For Ken Whitwell, at the very least, he has a mood disorder with anxious and depressed features secondary to what happened to him. Really, you could make a case here too for a post-traumatic stress disorder. Post-traumatic stress disorder is a condition which tends to become chronic if it's not treated. And it's characterized by a number of symptoms and those – and it happens in response to a traumatic, obviously, event that was either life-threatening or some sort of serious injury was threatened. So he had these experiences and has just about all of the primary symptoms.

He's got nightmares that cause him to wake up screaming in a sweat. He gets flashbacks of fragments of what happened. And that's how things usually come back, by the way. Something usually triggers, some precipitant triggers a recall of something that is long buried and then it starts to come back in fragments, like a jigsaw puzzle, and then the pieces start to come together. And that's pretty upsetting when that happens. But he's got nightmares. He's got flashbacks. He's got intrusive recollections of what happened. He basically sees the world as an unsafe place. One of the criteria for post-traumatic are seeing yourself as having sort of a foreshortened future, like something will happen to you. Now, that's why it gets a little arguable, because if you want to stick to the letter of DSM-IV, and this will probably be revised in the next iteration, DSM-IV is talking about something physical, like you're going to die prematurely. In his case, it's more the sense of his professional career being foreshortened. So that's why I'm saying he may not technically fit the diagnosis, but I can tell you, if you were treating this guy in your chair in your office, you would be treating him for post-traumatic stress disorder. So he's got many, many – they have trouble with trust again, with relationships. He's got many, many criteria, really enough to fit the diagnosis, in my opinion.

Now I mentioned anxiety features and depression. Several, several features. He tends, and the other thing is there's – there's this confusion sort of between what should be pleasurable in life, like an intimate relationship, and this anxiety, because any hint of an intimate relationship trying to happen or going forward, and he gets very uncomfortable. He gets guilty. He gets tense. It becomes not pleasurable and he cannot carry forward with it. So it's impacting his life.

On Axis II, that refers to what's called a personality disorder. He has no such condition. A personality disorder refers more to not a state, like depression or anxiety, but it's a chronic pervasive pattern of how you behave in life that's not very adaptive. A good example would be like a sociopath or what's called an antisocial personality disorder. This is your garden variety criminal who steals and robs and beats people up and has no remorse for anything and it's all about them. That's an antisocial personality disorder. Ken on the other hand is a kind person who has a lot of empathy for others.

And then there is Axis III which is any medical diagnoses, and he's pretty healthy. He has had a surgery or two along the way, but he's healthy.

Axis IV refers to your stress source in life and you just characterize them as mild, moderate or severe. And in some regards, his are severe to moderate in some arenas. He has some parts of his life that are really good.

And last there is Axis V which is called a Global Assessment of Functioning. And it's a little bit arbitrary, but it's a scale that goes from zero to a hundred. Now, a hundred is perfect, which means that you have absolutely no issues that interfere with anything. Now, nobody is a hundred. You're not a hundred. I'm not a hundred. Her Honor is not a hundred. Nobody is a hundred. Maybe ninety-nine if you're a very highly functioning person and you're really wrapped tight. Zero would be like curled up in a ball, vegetative state. Most of us are somewhere in between there. And as I said before, he has some really good parts of his life, because he has excelled academically. He's very intelligent. He has done really well professionally. He has had a lot of distinctions. He's very well thought of. You know, I put him as at least a ninety professionally. But what's interesting here is that there's this other whole aspect of his life, which is a mess, and I wouldn't give him more than a sixty, and a sixty means if you go by the little definitions of the – it goes in increments of ten. A sixty means serious impairment in one or more areas of your life.

So just to review, I found that he has a mood disorder with several anxiety and depressive features. He did not have any pre-existing emotional or psychiatric issues. Ken also exhibits areas of moderate and even severe stress. Severe in the arenas of his personal relationships and the – the after-effects of the abuse. And then in the Global Assessment of Functioning, he's at the top of his game in his professional life. But in his personal life, he's no more than a sixty and his personal life, he's suffering serious impairment.

All these problems are caused by the years of childhood sexual abuse he experienced. It all goes back to that. It's absolutely referable to that. And it all fits together nicely, too. He also experiences these problems on a daily basis. I can say all of this with a reasonable degree of medical certainty, that the years of sexual abuse he experienced are the cause of his current problems.

To be a little more specific. His ability to form relationships has been affected permanently. When you look at his life, as I said, he did very well academically. Professionally channeled everything into that. He was good at that. It was not an emotionally charged area. That part was great. It wasn't really until he got married that this began to become apparent. His wife – even in their courtship, as I understand it, always had to be the prime mover. She made all the first moves. When they got married, she would always have to initiate any kind of intimacy and much, if not most of the time, he really wouldn't even respond to that. And she really became convinced the guy was

gay, because she felt he wasn't even attracted to her. He couldn't – he can't, now, say, I

love you. He would never tell her she looked pretty. She would try to foster that and it

just was not forthcoming. And as I said, it really fits, because if you look back to some

of the things that were said to him by this individual, he was – he was discouraged

from dating. This all happened in his teens. And he really wasn't allowed, if you will, to

date by this individual, and he would be told, girls are bad news. They do nothing but get

you in trouble. He never bought his wife flowers. And then we come to find out he was

told, they want flowers. You know, there are so many connections here. I mean, it just

fits together. And then he was threatened with if he did go out with a girl, that – the

threat was one of social ostracism, and this really fit in, because if you remember what I

said before, he was self-conscious. It had its roots in the stuttering. So he never really

felt like he fit in on some level, although he overcame that, captain of the team and all

that. But that was kind of a chink in the armor. And I think that this person knew that or

gathered it somehow and that was – that was the stick, you know, that was the threat, that

he wasn't going to fit in if this came out. And it really kept him from doing so

successfully for a long time, until he, at one point, just mustered up all his basically, and

it was very brave of him, because he was scared stiff, and he went out with a girl, and

actually, it was after that that the relationship ended.

      To loop back again to his Global Assessment of Functioning, and my distinction

in how people live their professional and their private lives. This goes to knowing a little

bit how we as professionals function. Most professional people are highly intelligent.

They cope largely by intellectualization. They really identify themselves strongly with what they do. How do I identify myself? I'm a doctor. It's not a job. It's a mission. Many people in the professions feel that way. And he said this to me. His mission is kind of make the world a better place and to help people. Your heart is in it. It's a core part of your identity. And because of that, we will hang onto that almost to the exclusion of everything else. A professional can be wildly successful, but if you scratch the surface of what's going on in their personal lives and you're just blown away because their personal life is going down in flames and it's not even showing, at least yet, professionally. When somebody in the professions is having a problem, their professional functionality is the last thing to go. So they will hang onto that.

And if you look at this case right here, I mean, the guy is doing great in his profession, but his marriage and his family life is a sham. It's a mess. And it's still a mess. Now, he finally was able to identify, because things started to come back, what was the root of this. And, you know, hopefully, that can be the beginning of some progress.

He also is experiencing tremendous fear, on multiple counts. When his wife makes these overtures and he can't respond, that's – that's largely fear-driven. There's such confusion in his mind between what's pleasurable and what he has to feel guilty about, because you know, as a kid, if somebody – if somebody touches you physically, there's a certain physical reflection. It's pleasurable on one count, but it's so terrifying and traumatic that any time later on that you start to get that physical feeling, it goes back to all the upset and it gets all jumbled up and you can't function then. But he's also –

remember when I said that the world becomes an unsafe place, and you can't trust people that you are supposed to be able to trust. Well, he's so afraid for his children in the world, he can barely let them out of his sight. I mean, he talks about giving up his career early so that he can be home with them all the time and be there their soccer coach and their whatever coach, because he's afraid to let them be entrusted to anyone else even for a little while. I mean, he feels that he has to be there 24/7, which is not even possible. I mean, they have to go to school and whatnot, to protect his kids and he's willing to give up his career because he's so frightened that the same thing is going to happen to his children. So when you ask me is this pervasive and does he suffer from this every day, he can't relate to his wife, his kids aren't going to be safe anywhere. And I will tell you something, even if he was with them 24/7, it would not be enough, because this is internal by now. This is a scar.

He even wants to leave the service early although this will have an economic impact on him. I asked him that and it seems to take such a second seat to what's fear-driven, that it's – it's very – it just becomes very secondary. But the pity is that it wouldn't solve his problem even if he did that. Even after he leaves the service and is spending more time with his children, he's still going to be having to deal with problems. There's this obsessional quality to it. You know, it's almost like somebody with an obsessive/compulsive disorder that has to check something twenty times. But even after you check it twenty times, in five minutes, there it is again haunting you. And that is the way this is fear-driven. It's not going to go away by itself like that. And just quitting the service and staying there with his kids is not going to allay his fear. This fear is in here by now.

Some of these coping mechanisms, like denial and things like that which I mentioned, they helped him at the moment, but, boy, has it had a backlash later. Abuse sets things in motion internally in you that rewires you. The brain in trauma, and this has been studied in sexual abuse, it has been studied in the Vietnam war, in post-traumatic stress disorder that's from combat. The brain actually seems to get re-hard-wired and, in fact, it's also interesting that some of the treatments for post-traumatic, like EMDR, actually involve re-hard-wiring the brain in one way or another.

These conditions are permanent. They leave scars.

To try to wrap this up, let me talk about trying to get better. Weekly therapy by a very experienced and trained person would be of help to Ken Whitwell. He's pretty impaired interpersonally. I mean, he isn't relating to his – to his life partner well. As I said, he's in fear for his kids. It's very pervasive. And I think he needs to address this, however painful that would be, pretty intensively. So I would – I would want him to be seeing a skilled person, who understands post-traumatic, and who really gets it, and who understands the fear and would challenge him, but not more than he can tolerate, so that he'll get so scared and buck. And possibly with a combination of medications, at least for now, to get a handle on this anxiety and some of the depressive elements and the nightmares and whatnot. Something to help him sleep better. I think that combination would be – would be optimal. But weekly, because it would have to be reasonably intensive. Just talking about it once a month is not going to cut it. But it is not terribly easy to find such a person, and he is in the military on top of that going all around the world. In seven years, if he retired at age forty-six and returned home, he could find

someone here or in Virginia. But I grimace to think that he would have to wait seven

years for treatment. It makes me ill to think that, because these people, not just him, but

his wife, these people are suffering and, in my humble opinion, the sooner, the better. It's

already overdue.

   If he was able to get that kind of treatment, combination of medicines, intense

therapy with a skilled person, some improvement would be made in mitigating some of

the damage that has been done to him. I think it could be mitigated. I think his quality of

life would improve. I think his ability to relate to his wife could improve. And I really

think he wants it to underneath this all. He just doesn't know how. And I think he might

not be so deathly afraid for his children that it drives these irrational decisions he's

describing. The odds are that he will need therapy indefinitely, and the other dimension

is, really, there should be some couples therapy mixed with this, with him and his wife or

maybe with his wife sitting in on some of the sessions, because we need her perspective,

too.

And then Ken ended and I rested his case. After a short recess my closing argument was

presented to the jury.

* * *

And after its deliberations, "the jury spoke out loudly" and awarded forty-one million

dollars in damages to the Commander, six million dollars as compensation for his injuries, and

thirty-five million dollars in punitive damages[283] to send a message to the community at large

that sexual abuse of children will not be tolerated in Delaware.[284] This verdict directly affected the enactment of the Child Victim's Act of 2007 in July, only a few months later, and put the fear of financial punishment foremost in the minds of the enablers in the church hierarchy who, to preserve their prestige and power, had protected the criminals within their priesthood instead of helpless children. A day of reckoning was undoubtedly coming in Delaware, if other survivors would take up the justice of their own cause and seek accountability from those responsible for their lost lives.

3

James Sheehan

The Oblates of St. Francis de Sales are a world-wide Roman Catholic order of priests operating

in Delaware.[285] Since 1903 they have managed Salesianum School, a high school for boys in

Wilmington, Delaware.[286] Their treatment of James Sheehan's quest for accountability and

justice exemplifies the brutal tactics used by the Roman Catholic Church to prevent survivors

from ever achieving some degree of justice and restoring their dignity and humanity. Every

weapon in the church's arsenal was used against Sheehan to deter and humiliate him – and any

others who would be so bold as to challenge it. What happened to Jimmy could easily happen to

others who seek judicial relief against the church's authority.

    An editorial in *The News Journal* on November 26, 2006 observed that "the pompous

arrogance of the Oblates of St. Francis de Sales – who run Salesianum School – exemplifies the

worst of the Catholic Church's handling of its sexual abuse scandals."[287] Three weeks later, *The

News Journal* aptly described the cover-ups and moral failures of the Oblates:

> Oblates of St. Francis Keep Their Guilty Secret while Public Trust
> Dies
>
> Some time ago, a crime may have been committed. The public doesn't know

when, where or what exactly happened.

The public also doesn't know who the victim was. But it probably was a male high school student, a boy placed in the hands of the priests and brothers who ran his school. He most likely was placed there by parents who implicitly trusted those priests and brothers.

Now the public really doesn't need to know when the crime happened, or who the victim was. The victim and his family have suffered enough. But we do know the boy was molested and his life most likely was scarred.

The public does have a need to know who the suspected criminal was and the nature of the evidence against him, because he was one of those priests and brothers. By his position, he came into contact with hundreds, perhaps thousands, of other boys over the years. Their families also implicitly trusted those priests and brothers, and they are left to wonder if they were wrong to do so.

Even though the public suspects a crime took place, the perpetrator – the man who shattered the boy's life – cannot technically be called a criminal because through a fluke of the law, the statute of limitations has expired.

The victim's fear and shame aided the perpetrator in his crime. So did a history of trust in the school, and the cynical connivance of the perpetrator's superiors and colleagues.

Worse, the public does not know if there was one victim or many. It does not know if the school harbored one perpetrator or many. And because the public doesn't know who is guilty, the rest of those priests and brothers, the ones who dedicated their lives to building up the trust in the school, are under suspicion.

The school is Salesianum, one of Delaware's proudest institutions. And the order protecting those dark secrets is the Oblates of St. Francis de Sales.

The public does know that members of the order have been accused. The Catholic Diocese of Wilmington has acknowledged that. But it is up to the Oblates to come clean, as the diocese and other orders have.

Yet the Oblates have refused to name the members of their order who have been accused, or the nature of the accusations. They also have been silent about their own investigations into the allegations. Considering how institutions have behaved over the centuries, you could be sure that if the allegations had been found to be without merit, that fact would have been trumpeted throughout the state.

Any hope that this scandal will disappear is a wasted one. The only thing that is disappearing is trust.[288]

The Oblates' treatment of one of their 1964 graduates, James Sheehan, does indeed show the Oblates and the church at their worst.

But not until after Sheehan's and forty-one other cases were filed with the courts on August 4, 2011 were the Oblates forced to release a list of twelve of their known priests and all their prior assignments in response to demands from the media.[289] Four were still alive and allegedly were "living in monitored locations, after having been removed from ministry." All twelve priests had "admitted or substantiated allegations" against them.[290] What is remarkable about the information released and admitted about these twelve dangerous priests is that historically such men predominantly gathered in groups at Salesianum. So, to answer the question asked in the above-quoted *News Journal* editorial, the Oblates "harbored" many perpetrators, not just one, and thus they multiplied the danger to the 1,200 students at Salesianum School who had been entrusted to their care. While it appears that children elsewhere in the diocese may have been subject to the criminal actions of just one priest in their local churches or schools, at Salesianum, from 1982 to 1985, Richard N. Grant, John Heckle, Dennis W. Killion, Jack McDevitt, Francis L. Norris and James W. O'Neill, six priests in all, roamed the halls of the school searching for boys.[291] Earlier, from 1977 to 1986, there were always four and even five abuser priests working with children, including Robert Drelich.[292] From 1961 to 1969, the list included three or four priests at the same time: Richard Grant, John Heckle, Francis L. Norris, Henry Paul, Harold J. McGovern, Harold Hermley, Jack McDevitt, and John X. Harvey.[293] The 1945 to 1946 and 1990 to 1992 eras included two priests at the same time, and 1971 to 1974 just one.[294]

From this data it does appear that at Salesianum there was a protected group of priest child-molesters seeking their prey. And for the Oblates the words of Jesus of Nazareth, who boldly exposed the religious leaders of his day, still ring true.

> Woe to you, teachers of the law and Pharisees, you hypocrites! You are like whitewashed tombs, which look beautiful on the outside but on the inside are full of dead men's bones and everything unclean. In the same way, on the outside you appear to people as righteous but on the inside you are full of hypocrisy and wickedness.[295]. . .

> You snakes! You brood of vipers! How will you escape being condemned to hell?[296]

Jesus spoke quite directly to the fate after this life of those who have led children into sin. "And whoever welcomes a little child like this in my name welcomes me. But if anyone causes one of these little ones who believe in me to sin, it would be better for him to have a large millstone hung around his neck and to be drowned in the depths of the sea."[297] The analogy of a nest of snakes or vipers aptly describes the Oblates living in Delaware. A similar secular condemnation of all priests who use children for their sexual gratification is found in the work of the Italian epic poet Dante Alighieri in *The Inferno*. There Dante reserved the eighth of the nine descending circles of Hell, just above the ninth circle which contains the pit where Satan is bound, for sexual seducers who eternally march to the constant whip of punishing demons.[298] Today this appears to be the place reserved for those who – like the Oblates – wore priestly garments but sexually abused young James Sheehan and other boys entrusted to their care, all while lying to these boys that their deliberately aberrant behavior was the will of God. For liars and their present day defenders another eighth circle punishment also seems appropriate, for that is where liars and false witnesses as a consequence endure an afflicting eternal loathsome disease.[299]

* * *

The conduct of Oblate priest Francis L. Norris is typical of the above-mentioned Oblates who victimized young students from the 1940s to the present day. The misconduct of the Oblates who shielded him and endangered thousands of students at Salesianum and elsewhere was called "the cynical connivance of the perpetrator's superiors and colleagues" by the editorial board of *The News Journal*, quoted earlier. After lengthy and exhaustive legal due process, this knowing misbehavior also was recorded by the Delaware Supreme Court. After examining all the evidence against the Oblates which resulted in a jury verdict against them, these respected justices concluded that the Oblates knew full well that Norris was a grave danger to youth, but they protected him anyway. Chief Justice Myron T. Steele ruled here that – "There is abundant evidence – including the Oblates' own records demonstrating prior knowledge of Norris' sexual abuse of children and his many other problems."[300] Yet, as was typically done for decades throughout this diocese, Norris was allowed to operate as a priest for years after his managers had actual knowledge that he was sexually abusing children.

James Sheehan's seven-day jury trial[301] began on November 16, 2009. By the end of the trial, the jury learned from Jimmy himself that in April 1962 he had lost his innocence at the hands of priest Francis L. Norris. But before Jimmy was called to testify, the jury heard from Norris' fellow Oblates that Norris was an out-of- control alcoholic, unable to restrain his own actions. In December 1960, the middle of the school year and his assignment at an Oblate school in Lockport, New York, Norris was suddenly transferred to Salesianum School in Wilmington, Delaware, hundreds of miles away.[302] At trial Oblate priest John DiFillipo, who worked with Norris in New York prior to his abrupt transfer, testified that Norris was "a heavy drinker" and "everybody knew it."[303] Priest, and eventual Oblate CEO or Provincial, Daniel Gambet, who lived with Norris at Salesianum, confirmed that Norris had "a drinking problem" and was "a problem drinker."[304] William Keech, another priest who worked with Norris, also added that he was an "alcoholic."[305] And, in his own handwriting, before his swift reassignment, Norris himself lamented and confessed to his superiors about his drinking: – "What is wrong with me. I know that I shouldn't do these things and I do them. I cannot help myself."[306] Clearly his out-of-control drinking was well known to his superiors.[307]

The jury also learned that Norris had attempted suicide. On December 6, 1960 his site supervisor reported to the Oblate Provincial that "Norris informed me that he had deliberately withheld his insulin from himself with the idea of inducing diabetic coma or shock. [But] this did not happen."[308] In addition, the evidence presented at trial established that Norris had serious mental health issues relating to the sexual abuse of children which required his immediate psychiatric hospitalization. Indeed, he had long suffered from mental health problems so serious that in November, shortly before his sudden transfer, Oblate doctors recommended immediate inpatient psychiatric hospitalization for him at Seton Psychiatric Institute in Baltimore. One had warned that Norris "is in need of psychiatric care. He feels that we [meaning the Oblates] will have a condition that will grow more serious as time goes on if it is not given attention,"[309] reported an Oblate on-site manager.

In 1960 the Seton Institute was a well-known facility where pedophile priests and other clergy were treated.[310] At trial, one health care professional who worked at Seton explained that it was not a facility for priests whose problem was alcohol. In fact, it had no alcohol abuse program.[311] Instead, it was the premier facility for treating priests with what then were referred to as "mental health problems."[312] Upon review of the Oblate business records, the only conclusion reached by two medical professionals who testified at trial was that Norris was referred to Seton because of his history of sexual abuse of minors.[313] "Given the nature and the phrasing of how that referral was made in the letter, it's doubtful that it had to do with anything other than sexual abuse of a minor, " testified psychiatrist David Springer, M.D., a physician experienced in treating priest child abusers.[314]

Furthermore, the trial evidence showed that in an August 1959 letter from Norris to his supervisor, Norris acknowledged receiving a "letter of admonition" for causing a "scandal" at his

Lockport teaching assignment.[315] The jury then learned that the word "scandal" had been a frequently used "code word" for sexual abuse of minor children.[316] Other code words frequently used to protect pedophile priests from exposure included "health" problems, "depression," "nervous breakdown" and "alcoholism," all of which were used extensively at the time to imply sexual abuse of a child.[317] The term "pedophilia" was not yet in use at that time.[318] David Springer, previously the medical director at St. John Vianney Center, a psychiatric facility operated by the Archdiocese of Philadelphia, and devoted exclusively to treating clergy,[319] also explained why he believed the scandal referred to in this 1959 record could not have been alcoholism. Because of the widespread problem of alcoholism in religious communities of priests at the time, "it wasn't really considered . . . a matter of stigma or shame,"[320] he stated.

Documents presented at trial also proved that Norris later wrote about his sexual crimes. His personnel file contains several self-serving letters he wrote to his superiors in which he discusses a horrible wrong which supposedly gave him nightmares and made him sick. In a May 18, 1965 letter to the Provincial, Norris wrote, "I am far from being perfect, Father, and I know what is expected of me. I promised you I would do nothing that would cause talk or embarrassment to the Oblates. *Whenever I look back and see the wrong I did, I get sick. I hope this will not be held against me and follow me wherever I go.*[321](emphasis added). Two years later, on September 11, 1967, in a handwritten note to the Provincial, Norris again wrote that, "I want to start a clean slate. I hope it will not be necessary to tell Fr. Langan about the *problems I had in the past.* I don't have them today and I will not have them again. *I know I will never forget what the past was. It still haunts me. Many a night I wake out of a nightmare and I find myself shaking. I know I can't rub the slate clean of the past*, but I know I will keep it clean for the future."[322] (emphasis added). In response, in order to protect Norris the Provincial agreed not to tell his new supervisor "about the past."[323] And so, once again the Oblates covered-up a known danger and put children at risk.

The jury at Jimmy Sheehan's trial learned that Norris' survivor victims were many. Michael Jordan, another 1964 graduate of Salesianum, testified that he also had been sexually abused by Norris when he was a fifteen year old sophomore in the spring of 1962:[324] Norris would –

> come over [to] the house, visit with my parents. And he used to come over there and drink and stuff with several other priests. [Once] he was supposed to be tutoring me in English. My parents were home at the time. They came downstairs – we were sitting in the living room on the couch, had a coffee table there. He brought over this great big tape recorder and the paper that I was supposed to be reading and he was taping it. My parents came downstairs. I remember my mother asking me how was I doing. He said, "Oh, he's doing good," and everything. Anyway, so my parents went out, and it was just me and him there.
>
> A short time after my parents left – he was sitting to my right and he moved over closer to me, put his left arm across the top of my shoulders and his right hand on my knee and said, "Michael" – I remember that distinctly. He said, "I've been hearing some stories about you and young girls," which at that period in my life was totally false. I was completely innocent at that young age. He said, "You know you can get in trouble with girls if they get pregnant and everything."
>
> Meanwhile, he's sliding his hand – sliding his hand down my leg and he grabbed

my penis and started stroking it. And then he said – he was asking me how good it felt and everything. So I said – he asked me, "Does it feel good?" And I said, "No," thinking that if I said no, he'd stop. But he didn't stop. What he did was he reached up for my zipper on my trousers. When he reached up for my zipper, I pushed his hand away and I said, "Get the F away from me." And I moved down to the other end of the coffee table and stood up. I was standing – we lived in a row house, and I was standing in the little archway between the living room and the dining room. I was just standing there, staring at him. I was just – I mean, everything I'd been taught all my life had just went right down the drain about priests were supposed to be God's messengers on earth, they could do no wrong. You know, they make you go in a box and tell them your sins and they forgive your sins. I mean, my head was just spinning. He said – he said, "Well, Michael, it's getting late, I'm going to go upstairs and say good night to your little brother."[325]

John Doe Number Seven was another victim. He too testified at Jimmy's trial that he had been sexually abused by Norris, and once again even in the context of counseling. In his words, in the spring of 1962 when he was twelve or thirteen years old, he confessed a personal sexual problem to Norris, who was then one of his teachers. So –

Norris asked me if I'd be willing to discuss it outside the confessional. I said, "I suppose." So we met outside the confessional. . . . He said "there was someone else who had the same problem and that if we could get together, it should help me.". . . But one day after school – probably that same day, but it could have been another one – he took me to some room backstage or band room – he blindfolded me and said he was going to take me to a back room. He led me to some place, sat me down, and said he had to go get someone else and came back. And he told me it was another child. He came back and placed the child down beside me – who he said was another child beside me and he said, "Okay, I'm going to be leaving now, I'll be back in a little bit." I said, "Okay." At that point I heard a zipper go down. And it was around that time that he pulled mine down also. I didn't. He did. My head was forced down on his penis repeatedly. And I could smell the stench of stale tobacco, cigars and I could feel the robe. It was pretty obvious it was either Norris or one of his henchmen. Around that time he started massaging me, I suppose, at which point I started getting sick. I believe I vomited. I couldn't stop spitting for months. And it got quiet. Norris came back and led me out, still blindfolded. That was pretty much it for that day.

It may have been the next day. It was for sure within a week. He asked me if it helped any, if the session helped any, reminding me, now, remember – and he told me this before, too. "Remember, this is God's work, there's no sin involved here, this is all God's work." And I said, "No, I don't think it helped me at all." And he said, "Well, I think you need another session." I said, "Well, I think I'm okay right now, no thank you." And he said, "Well, okay, but just keep in mind now, remember" – and he kept repeating that it wasn't a sin. And then maybe a week, a couple weeks later the same thing. "How are you doing?" "Oh, I'm doing great, thanks a lot." And I refused to spend any further time with him.[326]

* * *

Despite their own extensive business records about Norris' history of sexual crime in Lockport and the current personal knowledge of many long-time Oblate officials about his alcoholism and other disorders, as well as the temporal corroboration of Jimmy Sheehan's claims by three other living victims of Norris at Salesianum who had come forward before trial, two of whom took the witness stand at trial, the Oblates insisted on putting Jimmy through the personal hell on earth known as trial by jury, which is nothing more than a substitute for the brutal medieval trial by combat to the death between opponents who had a legal dispute.[327] From the beginning the Oblates denied that Jimmy was ever even the victim of a sexual crime. Before the jury their lawyer repeatedly phrased Jimmy's claims in a way that implied he was not telling the truth: "*if* Frank Norris did" this, or "*if* the abuse occurred."[328] The Oblate implication was that Jimmy was just a lying[329] opportunist who was "recruited"[330] by unscrupulous lawyers to make trumped-up claims against an innocent and honorable priest. The church raised the same defense during the trial of John Vai which is found in chapter five.

The fact is that in 2009 the Oblate leadership knew of Jimmy's many grave health issues. At the time of his seven-day trial, he had survived several heart attacks and quadruple bypass surgery. He also suffered from congestive heart failure, COPD (Chronic Obstructive Pulmonary Disease), atrial fibrillation, diabetes mellitus and hypertension. Years before he had a dual chamber defibrillator implanted to combat paroxysmal atrial fibrillation, ineffective pumping of blood to the heart, but the problem continued.[331] During his lawsuit, Jimmy was hospitalized more than seven times. At trial, he was on oxygen therapy to treat his congestive heart failure and COPD. Metal cylinders of compressed oxygen were kept at his seat in the courtroom, delivering oxygen to him through a nasal cannula. Throughout his trial Jimmy was short of breath, wheezing at times, and at his table his lawyers always heard his labored breathing. He also took thirteen medications daily.[332]

Because he could not drive, a secretary would pick him up and drive him to the courthouse entrance each day. He had to bring his oxygen cylinders in a carry-on, so he had enough air for the day. At breaks or lunch he would change these tanks. He was extremely fatigued throughout his trial and his prolonged testimony left him ashen faced answering the question of whether Norris was an Oblate saint or *"if"* he was the devil Jimmy allegedly falsely claimed. Sometimes Jimmy could not keep his eyes open, and would have to be nudged awake. He ate mints and candy to try to keep energized. The seven days of his trial were long days for him, but he never complained about how he felt or about anything else. He just wanted the lies to stop and the truth to be told, in order to protect others, in Delaware and elsewhere.

But, as a standard tactic from their church's game plan, the Oblate leadership in 2009 deliberately placed him in mortal danger due to the stress of trial. As explained in chapter one, Doug McClure – after a premonition of his impending death, caused by his failing health – settled his claims against the Diocese of Wilmington. He died just weeks thereafter. Jimmy faced a similar fate. But if there was one thing Jimmy Sheehan and Doug McClure both had, it was guts. Jimmy had been a co-captain of the University of North Carolina football team in college. He was no quitter. Still, the human body can only take so much.

* * *

Deep in the trial after all the evidence described above had been presented, Jimmy walked slowly to the witness stand and took the oath. He testified that he was raised as a devout Catholic and regularly served as an altar boy for Bishops Cartwright and Hyle and for many other priests.[333] Former Oblate provincial Daniel Gambet reluctantly was forced to confirm that Jimmy "was a good Catholic kid," since he had been one of Jimmy's teachers.[334]

Now a sixty-three year old witness, Jimmy testified that around Holy Week in April of 1962, when he was just fifteen –

we were playing basketball in the gymnasium, a group of my friends and I, which we normally did most nights.[335] This particular night it was a little earlier than usual. This man was standing in the doorway, looking at us playing basketball. I sort of recognized him, but I wasn't sure because I didn't know him that well. But it ended up being Frank Norris. And he said, "Okay, guys, it's time to go . . . you got to get out of here." And he started shutting the lights off. And I remember we all balked at him, "Wait a minute . . . wait a minute . . . we usually stay till a little bit later." We all had curfews, so we knew what time we had to leave. And he said, "Oh, no, I got to get you out of here now . . . turn the lights off, get ready and I'll give you all a ride home." Well, some of them said – a couple guys lived real close. "Oh, no, no, I can't let you walk." So he – it's hard – I can for sure remember one of the guys. There were five or six of us. We piled into the car and he was taking us home. Well, he took one or two home. He drove right by my house or close to my house where I said I would jump out. I was one of the closer ones. I said, "I live here." He said, "Oh, I'll get you on the way back . . . you'll get home." So we took a couple other guys home. Then Norris started talking gibberish. I remember feeling uncomfortable.[336]

I thought he was drunk. Then he started talking about, did you guys know – I don't know how many of us were still left in the car, but there were a few. He said, "Do you guys know that these whores hang out" – he used the word "whores" – "hang out up at the Scottish Rite Cathedral," which is up by the old Sears up where the unemployment office is now, on Lea Boulevard. You know, "No." And my friend he starts saying, "Oh, really . . . let's go see them . . . let's drive by there." And I wanted to hit him. I want to go home, . . . shut up. You know, he was – we never did go by, which I don't believe that ever existed anyway. So I said, "Let's go home." Then he dropped my friend off who lived a good ten blocks from my house. I think that was the last one he dropped off. Now we're alone. My house was south, but we headed north and we ended up by P.S. DuPont High School at the time. I said, Father, "I don't live" – I knew he didn't know exactly where I lived. I said, "I don't live here." He goes, "I know . . . I need to talk to you." I'm thinking did I do something wrong? He pulls over in a very secluded area between P.S. DuPont's football field and – there were some row houses. I guess it was 10:00 at night, somewhere in that area. I know I was coming close to my curfew. He pulled over and started talking to me. And, again, it seemed very convoluted.[337]

[Jimmy explained that Norris told him that] "God wants me to give you a message . . . God needs to talk to you. God wants what is going to happen tonight to happen . . . I want you to trust in God." It was all "God, God, God. . . . you believe in God." Yeah. Fleetingly, I was like, God wants to talk to me. I can remember – you're looking at an old man now, but I was just a baby then. I'm thinking, Man, God wants to talk to me. So he started, you know, saying, "Now, whatever happens, you understand that this is God's will." And at that point he started reaching over and he started feeling my thigh. I was sitting in the front seat from the beginning on. You know, all of a sudden it's – I mean, I felt uncomfortable. I didn't really know what to do. And as he started moving closer to my genitals, I said, "Father, what" – "Just trust me". . . "let this go" . . .

"God wants this to happen and you will know in good time why." And in the back of my head somewhere, even though I knew it was wrong or I felt uncomfortable with it, I also thought, you know, maybe God is telling me something. This is God's representative. Anyway, he got close to my groin and I jumped out of the car. I said, "I can't do this." I said, "I'll go home . . . I'll get home." And it was quite a distance from my house now, maybe a couple miles, plus I'm right on my curfew, which my father was very strict about. So I started walking. I remember walking down a couple blocks. And Harlan School is the middle school for P.S. DuPont at that time. I got along that school, and he was following me at the same time and he had the window down. "Jimmy, come here . . . now get back in this car . . . I need to explain this . . . you have to hear this." And to be honest with you, I was surprised I jumped out the first time, that I had the courage to do it, looking back at how I was in those days. I often wondered, well, you did do – you got out. But I got back in because I wanted to go home and he's saying nothing. So I got back in. And as soon as we got back in and started moving down the road again, he reached over again for my thigh and I jumped right back out. And he said, "No, no, no . . . wait . . . nothing will happen . . . don't worry about it . . . I won't touch you, but God does have this message for you." I thought, Well, as long as you don't touch me, you can tell me what God has for me.[338]

[In Jimmy's words, he then got back into the car after Norris twice had groped him] because I didn't think he was going to do it again. I don't know why. I don't. You know, I don't know why. I think the "God" thing had something to do with it. Maybe I was afraid I was going to get in trouble not doing what he said. I can't tell you why I got back in the car. So he went close to my house, which he didn't know where it was. I told

him the address and so forth. We got within a block and I said, "I want to just go home."

He rode right by my house and continued on back to Salesianum. At that point he drove

into the school and – it was the practice football field and the gym, that entrance, which

was the far end of the school. He drove around back. And you saw the picture of some

of the alcoves back there between the gym and the auditorium. It forms a U behind the

school, which is a very secluded, dark area. There were never any cars parked back there

or anything unless there was an event going on. He pulled over and he started groping

me again, went immediately for my genitals and went for my zipper.[339]

I just remember being almost catatonic. I was almost paralyzed. I don't know

why it happened. I always felt – and I think that's part of it. You feel guilty. He said

"this is God's will and it will come to you all in time . . . you will understand . . . I

promise you this." So he pulled my zipper down, pulled my penis out and started

fondling it. And I had an erection, which over the years I was always so embarrassed to

even talk about. You know, you think, even then I got an erection; what's wrong with

me? And at the same point, he took my hand and he took my – and I didn't realize it at

the time, but his penis was out and he put my hand, two fingers, on his penis, which I

don't know if that would matter – you talk about describing it. It was extremely tiny.

And he put two fingers on it. And almost immediately I felt a wetness, that he had

ejaculated, I guess I felt nauseous, confused. Almost just blanked it all out. I mean, it

was like – you know, knowing that God wasn't in that car. As soon as he was released –

which I didn't even understand then. Over the years I know what happened. He pulled

-123-

his zipper up and said, "Okay, we'll get you home." And we pulled out of the parking lot, went right to my house.[340]

Now, I'm even worried – this happened and now my father is going to be mad at me because I think 10:30 was the curfew, or somewhere around there, and I knew I was late. So we got there and I just got out of the car – he parked right in front of my house – and walked up the steps. And I saw my father standing in the front doorway, which wasn't good. The next thing I know, he's right behind me. I said, "Where are you going?" He said, "I'm going to explain to your father what happened." And again I'm like, "You are?" My father opened the door and said, "Where you been, and who the hell are you?" Because he had a sweatshirt on and I remember him being dirty. I remember he was fat. We called him Humpty Dumpty. He said, "I'm Father Norris, Mr. Sheehan." He said, "I'm sorry . . . Jimmy told me he had a curfew and you'd be angry." He said, "He was helping me with the stage crew over in the auditorium, moving some things around, and I really appreciated his help . . . time got away from us, so I thought I'd bring him home and explain to you why he was late." "Oh, okay." And then my father was disarmed immediately. I was shocked. And then my father invited him in. "Come on in, Father." I remember my father said, "Oh, would you like a drink?" And my father always had a bottle of whiskey out on the table and some beers. He had been relaxing. So they went out to the kitchen, and I went right up the steps. And I didn't – I'm sort of like listening, and they're laughing and talking. "Oh, what would you like?" And I'm just getting – I got so nauseated. I remember just going right in the bathroom and puking. And I remember going to bed, just laying there, and I could hear them laughing

-124-

for like the next hour in their conversation. And I knew my father was very happy. You know, he had such a reverence and respect for the priests. This was – you know, here is a priest coming into my home. I think he was honored. He ended up leaving. But I didn't sleep that night.[341]

[Jimmy explained that about fourteen years later, in the mid-1970s, he told his brother-in-law, and family that he had been a victim.[342] In the 1960s he also had told one of his classmates about it.[343] Before then he never advised anyone what had happened to him. In his words] –

I was ashamed. . . .[344] I think my father would have believed me. But I couldn't. First of all, I was ashamed – you know, at that point I didn't know if I did anything wrong. And, also, I know that my father would have killed him. I mean it. I know my father would have – if I told my father – at that point I saw how mad he was at me for being late. If anybody was messing with his kids, he would have been. He was a big man, 300-pound butcher. So I didn't. I couldn't tell him. And, God forbid, I would never tell my mother – well, that's later on down the line. But my mother, it would have crushed her. She was so devout and so innocent and just – especially when she got to know him. I could never. She was so proud to have a priest visit our house, you know, because he came over after that. So I couldn't tell them. I couldn't. Even years later.[345]

[Norris stalked Jimmy for the next few years until he graduated.] My parents were naive and happy that they had this priest come in – and honored that this priest came into our house. They could tell, "Yeah, Father was over today." And my mother would cook him something. My brother used to tell me – and I never saw it myself. But my brother would say he used to sing songs to my mother – it would upset me. I would

leave. The minute I saw him, I'd leave the house. So this went on for the next three

years – till I graduated. He would come over maybe once a week, four times a month.

Maybe two of those times were in the day when my mother was there, and the other

times my father was home and they would – you know, he would have some drinks with

my father. And I was out of there. I would leave. And my mother even made the

statement to me – she goes, "You're not very nice to him . . . you know, you could stay

and talk for a while." I said I just – I took off."[346]

* * *

[Jimmy's life changed immediately. It was clear that he lost his innocence that

night.] I was probably a little more jaded and I didn't trust people as much.[347] I always

wanted a confessor my whole life, somebody that – you know, particularly being a

Catholic, a priest or somebody to talk to and to talk out problems or just to talk. I just

never trusted anybody that way. And I do have a – I have a fear of people in authority, a

fear that people are going to let me down.[348] My mother used to say I was moody after

that. She'd always go, "Boy, you're moody." And I would get into, you know, solemn

moods. "Sullen," I guess, is the word. To this day a lot of people don't know who I am.

I always put up a pretty good facade. But I would play sports. I would bury myself in

practice.[349] Something happened to me that day, I always had my bed to come home to

and pull those covers up over my head, and the world would go away. That's how I felt.

And I felt safe in my home and in my bed, with my family.[350]

Jimmy explained that his life of alcoholism began immediately after the three sexual assaults that evening. Alcohol became a compensating mechanism, just as it had been for young

Doug McClure who was an alcoholic by age twelve after being used as Edward Carley's sexual

release for three years –

   The 1962 professional baseball season started that same year and I became a

drunk. We went to a Phillies game, a bunch of friends and I, bought a bottle of gin on

the way up, which I had never – I had drank – my father would give me a beer over at the

house. Irish Catholic family, there was certainly plenty of beer around. But he would

give me a beer once in a while. I never drank too much. But then we got a bottle and I

got a little loaded. We went to a Phillies game in the old Connie Mack Stadium and I put

the bottle of gin down. I remember doing chin-ups off of the center field bleachers. And

I remember the P.A. announcer saying, "Would that gentleman please get back in the

stands." Coming home on the train, I was climbing out the train to go up on a ladder to

get up on the roof, and then all of a sudden, before I got out there, I saw a telephone pole

go by. I went, "Wow, that could have been me hitting that pole." I can remember

distinctly that was probably the first time I ever drank for effect. And then the drinking

all began.[351]

   During the course of my life I was not generally able to have just one drink. I

never wanted one or two. . . . But I would – a six-pack or more.[352] I found out when I

drank it was a way of forgetting. . . . I was a disciplined drinker. I always got my day

done before I – even when I got older. And I remember in college I wouldn't drink

during football season.[353] I like beer, but I had drank bourbon, Seven and Seven – I drank

everything at one point or another. . . . So as I went through high school, especially in the summers in high school and the summers at North Carolina, I would drink heavily every

day. Binge drinking. . . . I like drinking out. I'd drink at taverns and parties or out.[354]

* * *

The Oblates fought hard against Jimmy Sheehan and succeeded in confounding the jury.

On November 24, 2009 nine women and three men returned a confused verdict against the

Oblates and for Jimmy, declaring that "yes" the Oblates were liable to Jimmy under the Child

Victim's Act because as a minor he had been sexually abused by their employee and they had

been grossly negligent in fulfilling their duty to protect a student entrusted to their care.[355]

However, as reported by two jurors to the media, the jury also mistakenly believed that the law

did not allow them to make an award of money to James Sheehan.[356] The jubilant Oblates and

their lawyers "hugged in the hallway outside the courtroom" celebrating their temporary success

in bewildering the jury.[357] But despite his disappointment, Jimmy thanked Judge Calvin L. Scott

Jr. for a fair trial and "giving me the chance to publicly expose what was done to me and to so

many other boys." He noted that the lawsuit was "never about the money, it was about getting

out the truth."[358] "This has been a long journey" he said, adding that "the survivor movement for

victims of sexual assault by Catholic priests is about revealing the truth in a public forum, and

we did that for all to see. This has been about getting the truth out about the recklessness of the

Oblates and their failure to protect children from a zone of danger created by alcoholic and

suicidal priests."[359]

Jimmy's lawyers stated that "the jury was obviously confused on the matter of

appropriate damages for three unchallenged sexual assaults that evening, included being forced

to masturbate a priest. Of course, there has to be injury for having to endure a forced masturbation and other abuse."[360] And so to correct this mistake they would appeal to a higher court, they declared.

The Oblates were encouraged and emboldened by their success in so confusing the jury that it had denied financial relief to survivors of sexual abuse by Oblate priests. And so they set out through their own independent and separate appeal of this nominal jury verdict against them to deny relief to any other survivor of any of the many other predator priests located in Delaware over the past fifty years. They decided to seek to have the Supreme Court of Delaware strike down the entire Child Victim's Act of 2007 which was allowing challenges to their longstanding immunity from accountability under the civil laws that historically should have been protecting children. The Oblates appeared to declare an all-out war against *all* survivors by using the example of Jimmy's case to strike down the entire Child Victim's Act.

* * *

It is likely that they undertook an appeal because the heat of bad publicity was becoming too intense. Their earlier experience with survivor Eric Eden, who on January 8, 2004 had filed the first Delaware lawsuit against the Oblates and the Diocese of Wilmington, led to the first torrent of negative publicity for the Oblates.[361] That lawsuit and the dozens of others filed against the Oblates after the Child Victim's Act was enacted in July 2007, coupled with the truth that came out during Jimmy's public trial, caused the Oblates to try to stop any further public disclosures of the dirty secrets of the Roman Catholic Church in the Diocese of Wilmington.

The torrent of bad publicity began when Eric Eden courageously stepped forward almost two years to the day after revelations about predator priests in the Archdiocese of Boston rocked the American public. As reported by *The Philadelphia Inquirer*, thirty-five year old Eric Eden bravely filed a lawsuit against the Oblates, Salesianum and the Diocese charging that James W. O'Neill, the principal of that school, had molested him for nine years starting when Eden was an eight year old schoolboy, the same age when young Doug McClure entered his own personal hell. Sometimes the sexual abuse even occurred in the principal's office.[362] This was the same James W. O'Neill who the Oblates in 2011 finally and reluctantly admitted roamed the halls of Salesianum School, from 1982 to 1985, along with Richard N. Grant, John Heckle, Dennis W. Killion, Jack McDevitt and Francis L. Norris, all searching for boys.[363] But in 2004 the Oblates denied all but one last incident lodged against them by Eric and instead entered their usual cover-up mode.[364] Fourteen months later, in March 2005, speaking to Judge Calvin L. Scott Jr., in open court, their lawyer tried to explain O'Neill's behavior as a one-night-only mistake by a drunken priest. He said, "Your Honor, this whole mountain out of a mole hill has now become the Rocky Mountains out of a mole hill. The investigation went like this, as best we can conclude: Father O'Neill had been reported to have been acting in a rambunctious way following a night of wine, following a night of too much intake, too much alcohol."[365]

Unrepentant, the Oblates then moved O'Neill out of the country, where amazingly he was assigned to work with little children. As they unashamedly reported on their website at the time, before they hid the information and related pictures from public view, O'Neill became the director of their Chablais Mission Fund. As its director he reported that in February 2006 he spent three weeks in India with five-and six-year-old children – about six in all – in an Indian orphanage, and even provided on-line some of the pictures of these small children who were exposed to him overseas.[366] But when it came time in Eric's court case for the Oblates to present O'Neill for sworn examination under oath by Eric's lawyers, O'Neill had been hidden away in

Africa.

As reported by *The News Journal*, O'Neill did not show up for his May 2007 deposition because he was in the nation of South Africa where the Oblates had secreted him.[367] At the time there was no Child Victim's Act in South Africa, or in India for that matter. Children were fair game in both. Judge Calvin L. Scott Jr. of the Delaware Superior Court was given a copy of the Indian web page in court, including the photos of the boys endangered by O'Neill's presence overseas. Eric's lawyer Thomas Crumplar then wryly stated, "You don't have a recovering alcoholic running a bar,"[368] an ironic comment on the danger presented by O'Neill's proximity to small children. The Oblates then were ordered by Judge Scott to make O'Neill return to face Eric and his lawyers for questioning under oath.[369]

When O'Neill finally did face Eric, as reported by the media, he refused to answer questions over 190 times. O'Neill claimed he had a constitutional right not to incriminate himself by admitting any wrongdoing even though Eric's was not a criminal case.[370] So it was back to court again, where Judge Scott patiently dealt with this further delay. The judge allowed O'Neill to keep silent about his actions in Pennsylvania, Maryland, Virginia and North Carolina where he also had endangered children, but he ordered him to answer questions about what he had done to children in Delaware and New Jersey.[371]

The questioning of O'Neill was supposed to continue, but instead of appearing to face questions posed by Eric's lawyers in December 2007 as ordered, O'Neill fled Delaware again, proudly wearing his Notre Dame University "Fighting Irish" jacket, perhaps trying to send some type of misguided subliminal message that the civil laws did not apply to a Catholic priest.[372] However, after an emergency hearing before Judge Scott, O'Neill was ordered to show up in court at 2:30 pm that same December day, or else. So, under the threat of jail time, he reluctantly returned that day from another state and walked into court wearing his Notre Dame jacket. O'Neill then was marched over to Eric's lawyers' offices to face Eric and answer the questions he strove so hard to avoid. "Court orders need to be obeyed. My client appreciates Judge Scott enforcing the law and not giving special treatment to someone just because he's a priest," stated Eric's lawyer.[373] Trial was set for the following October 2008.

The Associated Press later reported what happened when O'Neill testified that December day after all his efforts to avoid being deposed. "O'Neill admitted his wrongdoing," and "Defendant O'Neill has admitted molesting plaintiff, " the article stated. But despite this confession, the Oblates perversely continued to deny any wrongdoing on their part, just as they always had for Eric and even for Jimmy Sheehan.[374] Later in 2011 The Associated Press provided even more detail:

- First, that O'Neill had "admitted to another priest that, while drunk and visiting Eden's home, he tried to put his hand underneath the boy's shirt in an attempt at sexual gratification."[375]

- Second, "that O'Neill acknowledged having inappropriate sexual contact with Eden for several years beginning in the early 1980s. The admitted contact involved numerous instances of hugging and caressing Eric to a point of sexual gratification for O'Neill."[376] In an affidavit that Eric submitted, the media also reported that he "said the abuse he suffered included sitting on O'Neill's lap while the priest put his hands down Eden's pants and fondled him until O'Neill ejaculated."[377]

-132-

- Third, "O'Neill reportedly testified that he acknowledged, when confronted by two other priests in April 2002, similar instances of touching Eden over several years."[378]

Despite all this, the Oblates still carried forward with a version of what they also argued in the Jimmy Sheehan case. As reported by *The Associated Press*, the Oblates felt that there was abundant evidence that Eric Eden "is a fabricating, exaggerating, and manipulative individual who is 'shamelessly motivated by money.'"[379] Such tactics are another page from the universal script the Roman Catholic Church uses in seeking to destroy the character of survivors. The intent of such falsehoods is to discourage survivors from going public on the theory that no one would want to endure a personal onslaught by church lawyers.

* * *

The Oblates hoped their appeal would put an end to all the negative publicity and also conserve Oblate financial resources which otherwise might be awarded to survivors who succeeded against them in court. So the appeal began and the story of Delaware's state court judges comes to the fore. Judge Calvin L. Scott Jr. of the Delaware Superior Court, and others, distinguished themselves and the Delaware judiciary throughout.

In January 2004 Judge Scott had been assigned responsibility for the initial case filed by Eric Eden. Later Judge Scott was given the task of managing the cascade of subsequent similar survivor child abuse cases filed in the Delaware state courts. He was a likely hero. A patient humble man, he believes in the constitutional right to trial by jury of legal disputes and the corresponding wisdom of twelve average citizens in deciding the truth of a dispute. He does not let his ego become an additional player in the courtroom. Always fair, he is obedient to the law and he is not a judicial activist. Nor will this judge countenance unneeded delays in getting a case before a jury, once an ironclad date has been set for trial. To borrow the description of the Hollywood portrayal of another respected jurist, Judge Scott always "did a good job – ruling succinctly. He set boundaries. He wasn't a jerk, but he was in control of his courtroom and kept things going."[380] Judge Scott had the perfect unflappable judicial temperament necessary for the boiling emotional caldron which is a trial of any priest and his powerful bosses.

Long before the passage of the Child Victim's Act in 2007, Judge Scott opened the Delaware Courts to any childhood sexual abuse victim who had lost his ability to file a claim due to traumatic amnesia.[381] According to Eric Eden's lawsuit, that type of amnesia had caused him to repress the memories of repeated molestation between 1976 and the public revelations of the Boston scandal in 2002 which finally ended with Boston's Roman Catholic Cardinal Bernard Law fleeing to Rome.[382] Eric filed a legal claim within twenty-four months of recovering the memories of what had been done to him by school principal O'Neill. The normal legal rule in Delaware then was that all such claims must be filed within twenty-four months of when the event happened. So for Eric, according to the Oblates, the clock ran out in 1987, which was two years after the last sexual act upon his person. The Oblates argued that a claim filed in 2004 was seventeen years out of date and should be dismissed immediately by the courts. Obviously, the Oblates jumped at this chance to deny justice to Eric by raising a statute-of-limitations defense.

But, because of Eric's amnesia Judge Scott found that a long-established and well accepted exception to the statute of limitations applied. On December 4, 2006 Judge Scott opened the doors of the temple of justice for Eric and similar survivors when he ruled that "the statute of limitations does not apply to the 900 incidents that allegedly occurred prior to the last incident" which Eric had reported in 1985.[383] The judge held that plainly and fairly, Eric

"suffered from memory suppression that disabled him from relaying memories of the sexual

abuse he allegedly suffered as a child. Plaintiff argues that he 'had complete *amnesia* of the

other nine years worth of sexual abuse' prior to the 1985 incident" and so Eric's case would

proceed, Judge Scott decided.[384] By placing the law on the side of fairness, justice and equity for

survivors, Judge Scott also sent a clear message that the courts were open to hear these

survivor's claims. They stood on an equal footing with the powerful in these matters and their

cases would be heard by the Delaware courts. With this ruling in 2006, it was clear that priest

child rapists and their protectors in Delaware could be held accountable by the legal system.

Even-handed and fair judicial rulings continued by Judge Scott and other members of the

Delaware Superior Court as the tide of court cases filed by survivors rose ever higher and higher.

Of course the Oblates hunkered down and did their best to destroy Eric Eden and Jimmy

Sheehan. They were convinced that the confused jury verdict at the end of Jimmy Sheehan's

trial increased their chances of having the Delaware Supreme Court step in and place its finger

on the scales of justice against each and every injured tormented individual and on the side of the

powerful. It now was time to try every other remaining tactic and appeal to that Court to save

them from accountability and so to end about 150 child sex abuse cases against the Roman

Catholic Church which sought justice for helpless little people. But their pleas fell on deaf ears.

Initially, the diocese itself, which was not even a party to the Sheehan case, in a friend of

the court legal filing reminded the Supreme Court that the church operated throughout Delaware

and the Eastern Shore of Maryland and it faced purported significant disabling consequences

from the Child Victim's Act. The diocese was suffering from at least 136 cases against it already, and it had tried to seek the protection of the federal bankruptcy laws to deal with the alleged financial consequences facing the church.[385] The plight of the diocese also was alleged to be affecting the insurance industry because it "creates insurability problems for both for-profit and non-profit institutions,"[386] meaning businesses as well as churches. In sweeping language, the Court was reminded that "institutions, and their insurers and lenders," meaning banks, were affected by the claims of survivors.[387] Since the Child Victim's Act applied even-handedly to all types of business entities, such as churches, businesses, public, private and religious schools, with no exceptions for the powerful, public or private, five public school districts then weighed in but eventually failed in crying wolf for the public school system against whom lawsuits by survivors also had been filed.[388] The Oblates even brought in additional legal firepower for the appeal to argue their case, the capable and professional former general counsel for the U.S. Conference of Catholic Bishops.[389]

But this formidable array of influential interests first had to overpower the lead attorney opposing them in the appeal, Stephen J. Neuberger. Aside from being a relentless terror to hostile witnesses in the courtroom,[390] akin to a Clarence Darrow,[391] Stephen was the powerful legal intellect behind the success of all survivors who filed court cases in Delaware. A graduate of Temple University's Beasley School of Law in Philadelphia, Stephen embodies the goal of Temple lawyers which is not to serve powerful moneyed interests but instead to serve the downtrodden in society, "to shape the law in service to the lives" it touches and to use "the power of law to change lives."[392] His conduct throughout the eight-year battle against a mighty religious enterprise reflected this commitment to using the law to help the less fortunate. His work ethic was prodigious. Stephen was the then unknown, behind-the-scenes, legal mind answering all legal objections raised by the church, business and insurance interests who lobbied intensely against the enactment of the Child Victim's Act by the Delaware General Assembly. Whenever this powerful trio raised alleged legal objections to legislative relief for survivors, overnight Stephen checkmated their false claims and his work product then was used by the supporters of survivors in their counter lobbying efforts. For eight years Stephen's exceptional legal skills and unwavering effort also resulted in every legal success in court for the survivors. He set all the legal precedents, such as the amnesia ruling before Judge Scott and the right of the federal courts to hear cases under the Child Victim's Act.[393] He also forced predator priests to answer questions about their actions and defeated their attempts to hide behind the Fifth Amendment.[394] And twice he successfully upheld before two lower court state judges the authority of the Delaware State legislature to enact the Child Victim's Act.[395]

As is noted in chapter five below, along with his co-counsel in all the Delaware Child Victim's Act cases, Thomas C. Crumplar, Stephen also represented abuse survivor John M.Vai in his late 2010 trial against priest Francis DeLuca and St. Elizabeth's Roman Catholic Church. Victory there resulted in the first jury verdict ever that held accountable an individual parish anywhere in the world, and not just its parent diocese corporation, for its long cover up of the sexual abuse of its young parishioners by its parish priests.

And so the stage was set before the Delaware Supreme Court. There victims faced the combined interests of banks, insurance companies, big business and influential, politically connected churches.

Delaware has a reputation as a business haven. Indeed, while it has a notable Bill of Rights found in Article I of its Constitution of 1897, how many other states also can boast of including an entirely separate constitutional article enshrining business corporations, namely Article IX of the Delaware Constitution? Because of this business friendly reputation, unyielding business, insurance and church interests believed that crying "wolf" in Delaware would lead to the rights of survivors of childhood crimes by dominant social institutions either being denied or severely confined by the courts. That was thought to be the – "Delaware Way" – promoting and protecting business interests at all costs over human rights. After all, Delaware should not appear inhospitable to any economic interests and, indeed, the rights of a mere handful of flesh and blood individuals who had been injured should be subordinate to business as usual, which meant practical immunity from accountability by the church in this instance.

Historically, it can be said that the reputation of the Delaware Courts is a very positive one from the viewpoint of great business interests. The U.S. Chamber of Commerce constantly ranks Delaware's courts first in the nation for a fair, reasonable and efficient litigation environment in the areas of personal injury and contracts lawsuits. In 2010 the Chamber's *State Liability Systems Ranking Study* once again placed Delaware first out of fifty states, a ranking of the best and the worst, in doing the best job of creating a fair and reasonable environment for civil court cases of interest to the business community, in particular personal injury lawsuits of importance to over 1,482 in-house general counsel, senior litigators or attorneys, and other senior business executives at companies with annual revenues of at least $100 million.[396] California, in contrast, ranked 46th, or among the worst states. And so it appeared that the Oblates and their companions had a good chance of success with their pleas to the Delaware Supreme Court to protect the interests of institutions, banks and insurance companies over the 150 or so merely damaged claimants presently before the courts.

They were wrong. On February 22, 2011, two months after the resounding John Vai verdict by a Delaware jury described in chapter five, the Delaware Supreme Court unanimously upheld the landmark Delaware Child Victim's Act of 2007 over a constitutional due process challenge by the Roman Catholic Church. In a twenty-four page Opinion written by learned and respected Chief Judge Myron T. Steele, the Court, sitting with all of its judges present, unanimously rejected the claim by the Oblates that the Act violated the due process protections of the Delaware and United States Constitutions. When you think of Chief Judge Steele, think of Spencer Tracy as Chief Judge Dan Haywood delivering the decision of the Court on the Nazis in the 1961 film *Judgment at Nuremberg*.[397] And remember that judge condemning *"Conscious participation in a . . . system of cruelty and injustice in violation of every moral and legal principle known to all civilized nations."* Then apply that judgment to the church in Delaware and remember Chief Judge Steele upholding the Child Victim's Act which allowed the courts and juries to condemn the conscious participation of the bosses in the Roman Catholic Church who cooperated in another system of cruelty and injustice to children – one that violated every moral and legal principle known to every civilized nation. And also remember the ultimate judgment of the courts and the people of Delaware in enacting the Child Victim's Act. Again, in the words of Spencer Tracy as Chief Judge Haywood, *"Let it now be noted that here, in our decision, this is what we stand for: justice, truth, and the value of a single human being."*[398] To its everlasting honor, that was the result of the Jimmy Sheehan ruling by the Delaware Supreme Court. It stood for justice for survivors. It affirmed that the truth of the crimes against them would continue to be told. And finally, it affirmed the value of a single human being, over the interests of business and the powerful who had once confused and mislead a jury.

The Delaware Supreme Court observed that at least since 1945 the United States

Supreme Court has found that laws such as the Child Victim's Act [CVA] do not violate due

process. "As a matter of constitutional law, statutes of limitations go to matters of remedy, not

destruction of fundamental rights," it stated,[399] thereby rejecting Oblate claims that by being held

accountable they were being denied rights so fundamental to organized society as to be like

freedom of speech, freedom of the press, trial by jury or even the freedom to assemble and

petition government for the redress of grievances. "Under Delaware law, the CVA can be

applied retroactively because it affects matters of procedure and remedies, not substantive or

vested rights," said the Court in reply.[400] The Court also observed that "we do not sit as an

uberlegislature to eviscerate proper legislative enactments. It is beyond the province of courts to

question the policy or wisdom of an otherwise valid law," any changes are the responsibility of

the legislature it declared.[401]

The Delaware Supreme Court also rejected the Oblates' claims of unfair prejudice due to

the passage of time, noting the "abundant evidence – including the Oblates' own records

demonstrating prior knowledge of Norris' sexual abuse of children and his many other

problems."[402] The Court also ordered a new trial on damages against the Oblates to correct the

mistaken premise that resulted in the Sheehan jury thinking that it could not award money to

Jimmy, finding that the Oblates had created an error here on "the most critical issue in the

case,"[403] found at its "very heart."[404]

For the third time Stephen Neuberger had successfully defended the authority of the

legislature to act to relieve human suffering. In a press release following victory in the Sheehan

case he stated: "This is a tremendous victory for all survivors of childhood sexual abuse in

Delaware. Jimmy thanks the Delaware Supreme Court for its thoughtful consideration of these complex issues and for unanimously ensuring that the courthouse doors remain open to all abuse survivors. He also thanks the Delaware General Assembly for giving him the chance to expose the Oblates' decades long cover up of Father Norris' despicable crimes that he inflicted on so many innocent boys at Salesianum."[405] Echoing the words of respected and influential former U.S. Supreme Court Justice Louis Brandeis, Stephen added that, "Sunlight is the best disinfectant and Delaware children today are safer when the cover ups end and the sins of the past are finally exposed to the bright light of public scrutiny."[406] In so saying he echoed Justice Brandeis' statement, "Publicity is justly commended as a remedy for social and industrial diseases. Sunlight is said to be the best of disinfectants; electric light the most efficient policeman."[407] With its affirmation of human rights over business interests, the Delaware Supreme Court had ensured that the truth about the horrors of child abuse by priests within the Roman Catholic Church, a prominent but morally corrupt religious institution, would continue to come out. The quest for justice for all survivors would continue and the horrible truth would be further revealed in the courts of the State of Delaware. In time the church might even be disinfected now that the sunlight of truth had begun to shine on crimes and policies long hidden from public review.

4

The DeLuca Eight in Delaware Bankruptcy Court

Learned and respected President (also Chief) Judge James T. Vaughn, Jr. of the Delaware

Superior Court had been assigned the trials of twenty-two cases of survivors who had been the

victims of unrepentant diocesan priest Francis DeLuca. In early October 2009, there had been

several days of grueling hearings in which fresh teams of eight or more diocesan lawyers and

their staff were opposed only by two or three attorneys. Church lawyers presented forty-two

motions consisting of one worthless legal argument after another, all designed to prevent any

trial from beginning.[408] Ever patient, President Judge Vaughn then ruled that the separate trials

of eight victims, known as the DeLuca Eight, would begin on October 19, 2009 before juries in

Kent County, Delaware, one after the other, until justice had been rendered for each of these

survivors and the truth was told about this priest and his cohorts. The corporate defendants in

seven of these eight cases consisted of the diocese and three of its individual parish churches

together with the living remorseless predator, DeLuca himself.[409]

President Judge Vaughn also had ruled that there was sufficient evidence of gross

negligence in the supervision of priests by the individual parish churches for a reasonable jury to

return a verdict against the diocese and each of its three parish entities separately. He also had decided that there was enough evidence for judgments to be returned against the three parishes

for fraud against the parents of these children and the same fraud by the diocese in hiding

DeLuca's dangerousness from parents.[410] More important, the judge had found that the conduct

of the individual parishes separately, or the conduct of the diocese alone was sufficiently

reckless, intentional and malicious so that a jury could return a verdict for punitive damages

against each of them to punish them for their deliberate misconduct and to send a message to the

community at large.[411] Since it appeared that the total assets of the diocese and its fifty-seven

separately incorporated parish churches exceeded $1.7 billion dollars, the future looked bleak for

the Diocese of Wilmington if juries were allowed to award fair and adequate compensation to

members of the DeLuca Eight, and eventually to all of the remaining victims of all the predator

diocesan priests, as well as also to punish them for malicious misconduct.

Immediately, the diocese then tried to change the legal forum for the more than 136

lawsuits filed by survivors which it faced. Like the Oblates who sought to strike down the Child

Victim's Act and wipe out the cases of all survivors who had challenged the church by appealing

to the business instinct of the Delaware state court system, the diocese tried a variant of that

tactic. But since it had been losing constantly before the state courts and justice was advancing

slowly but surely for all survivors in that venue, the diocese sought to change the battleground

by removing all of the cases it faced to the premier federal business court in Delaware found

within the national legal system – the United States Bankruptcy Court for the District of

Delaware. The Bishop's mistake here was his misplaced belief that the United States' business

courts would subordinate the interests and dignity of survivors to those of corporations, treat

these forever impaired survivors as a business commodity, and ignore the scope of their humanity and suffering. But, if Judge Calvin Scott and Chief Justice Myron Steele were the bane of the diocese in the state court system, it quickly learned that bankruptcy Judge Christopher S. Sontchi was their equal. Highly intelligent, experienced and hard working, he was neither biased, impatient, rude, nor arrogant. His impartiality was without question and he was no one's fool. He knew how to keep control of his courtroom and, with a sense of humor, he was able to defuse highly emotional situations. Nor was he reluctant to dispense equity and justice in his courtroom, despite its foundations in the business universe. Moreover, to the disappointment of the Bishop, justice was indeed blind in Sontchi's courtroom and so there the little man stood on an equal footing with the rich and mighty.

The Bishop reacted to these state court courtroom defeats and, as reported by *The Philadelphia Inquirer*, the diocese late one Sunday night "filed for bankruptcy protection just hours before eight clergy sex-abuse trials were set to begin" the next morning on Monday October 19, 2009.[412] Thus it became the seventh diocese in the United States to use such a trick against survivors to prevent the church's dirty linen from being aired at a public trial.[413] *The Associated Press* noted that the "bankruptcy filing automatically delays the first of eight consecutive abuse trials scheduled in Delaware."[414] *The Washington Post* reported that one attorney for the survivors "described the bankruptcy filing as a 'desperate effort to hide the truth from the public and conceal thousands of pages of scandalous documents' from being made public in court."[415] He added that – "This filing is the latest, sad chapter in the diocese's decades long 'cover-up' of these despicable crimes, to maintain the secrecy surrounding its responsibility and complicity in the sexual abuse of hundreds of Catholic children."[416] The *New York Times* reported that the filing was an "outrage" to some.[417] Niall Stange, writing in *The Irish Times* noted that the survivors' attorneys met the bankruptcy filing device "with scorn," and that there were "five or six people who are dying and they are going to lose their trial dates as a result of this. The longer the church hierarchy delay, the more people will die."[418]

The prior Bishop, Michael A. Saltarelli, was quite unique in the church hierarchy because he had sought to fairly compensate survivors and to avoid using protracted court fights to add to their suffering. So in their own press release, attorneys for the survivors stated that the new Bishop of the diocese, W. Francis Malooly, now fourteen months into office, sought to reverse "the compassionate and fair policies of his predecessor and to introduce the slash and burn, take no prisoners policies of the national Roman Catholic Church. Again and again he has abandoned the conciliatory policies of his predecessor [they said]. He uses the national Roman Catholic Church play book and not the one of the prior Bishop who tried to follow the teaching of the carpenter from Galilee, who said bring the little children to me and let no one harm them. Instead, the Bishop repudiates those teachings and wants these child victims to suffer still more and to be denied justice."[419] Public condemnation of his callous action and of the continuing cover-up of the unflattering truth by Bishop Malooly was best expressed in a remarkable editorial by *The Philadelphia Inquirer.*

Breaking Faith

The best way for Wilmington's Roman Catholic Bishop W. Francis Malooly to demonstrate his stated concern for "all victims of sexual abuse by priests of our diocese" would be to give those victims their day in court.

Instead, Malooly's eleventh hour decision Sunday to file for bankruptcy protection effectively halted the first of eight clergy sex abuse trials set to start the next day. That will have the net effect to further delay or perhaps thwart many victims' long quest for justice.

The Bishop wrote to the diocese's 230,000 faithful that the "painful decision" to file for bankruptcy was intended to ensure that funds are available so that all of the victims get a fair settlement.

In other words, the Bishop claims he doesn't want one big verdict to deplete the church coffers and leave nothing for the other victims.

Puh-leeze.

Malooly denied that church leaders were trying "to dodge responsibility for past criminal misconduct by clergy – or for mistakes made by Diocesan authorities."

If true, it's a welcome change from a church hierarchy that for decades has shielded predator priests by moving them from parish to parish. But an idiom recited by the many fine nuns in parish schools comes to mind: Actions speak louder than words.

Given the real world impact of the bankruptcy claim, there's no way around the perception that Delaware church officials have ducked for cover – in what one attorney for an abuse case plaintiff called "scandal prevention."

Indeed, the first trial in a civil damages lawsuit brought by a former altar boy, John M. Vai, 57, would have revealed chilling testimony about violent sex acts by a priest from 1966 to 1970, according to Vai's attorneys.

Now, those embarrassing allegations and many others won't be aired in open court for months and months, if at all. Nor will the public hear any details of church leaders' efforts to cover for predator priests.

As time goes on, it becomes increasingly difficult to mount legal claims like these because they rely heavily on victims' testimony about long ago abuse. So the danger is that justice delayed will mean justice denied.

The diocese's move represents a stunning rebuke to Delaware state lawmakers, who, in 2007, voted to clear the air on the state's clergy sex-abuse scandal.

Dover lawmakers open[ed] a two year window permitting civil suits by adult victims of sex abuse, even though the alleged assaults occurred years ago and the statute of limitations had lapsed.

Patterned after a California law, the measure put the First State in the forefront to give abuse victims their day in court. It gave hope to victims' advocates in Pennsylvania, who have been stymied in their push for similar legislation in Harrisburg. That effort is opposed by the Archdiocese of Philadelphia, the state Catholic Conference, and others.

In Philadelphia alone, hundreds of abuse victims have been awaiting justice since a scathing grand jury report in 2005. The report concluded that 63 archdiocesan priests had sexually abused children and that top church leaders helped cover for some.

But church officials across the nation continue to fight statute moratoriums with specious claims that victim' lawsuits will lead to parish closing, and several dioceses have resorted to the dubious bankruptcy claim.

If nothing else, the Delaware bankruptcy filing appears premature. After all, diocesan officials won't even know the full scope of their financial liability until the abuse cases go to trial.

Legal experts said the diocese – which is a separate entity from Wilmington parishes and church schools – could have awaited the outcome of the trials before claiming it is broke.

Had Wilmington church officials allowed the civil cases to go forward, they would have avoided the perception that the cover-up continues.[420]

That Judge Sontchi was not going to treat the survivors as expendable commodities or faceless unnamed creditors was revealed just three days later when the survivors' lawyers first appeared before him and began to lay the foundation for his personal understanding of the survivors' humanity.

MR. THOMAS NEUBERGER: There have been accusations made that we are somehow selling out some clients for the benefit of other clients and therefore there's a need for a fair and equitable process here, meaning everybody gets the same recovery. And I think the Court can understand, just conceptually, that if you've been anally raped a hundred times versus someone who was maybe masturbated one time, the lifelong damages could be different.

THE COURT: I understand.

MR. NEUBERGER: Okay. And the point is they're not fungible. Each person is particularized.

THE COURT: Oh, *absolutely. Every person is unique.*

MR. NEUBERGER: Yes. And that would factor into whatever process we put in place.

THE COURT: Understood. (emphasis added).[421]

For the next two years the diocese sought to stop any public trial from ever occurring against any of its fifty-seven separate parishes, even though they had not sought the protection of the federal bankruptcy laws, despite being separate business corporations under Delaware law. To that end it continued to deny the personhood of the individuals whose lives were being affected in this business court. Then, just twelve days after filing the October bankruptcy, on November 2nd, in countering this effort, the diocese lost round one of the legal battle which was being waged before Judge Sontchi. In an action without precedent in the federal bankruptcy courts anywhere, Judge Sontchi allowed a brief ninety-second video to be viewed by a packed courtroom audience. It movingly portrayed in flesh and blood the individuality and suffering of all survivors, as exemplified by survivor Michael Schulte being cross-examined by a church lawyer in a video-taped survivor deposition. The printed page fails to capture the emotion and truth of Mike's narrative, as he paused, gasped for breadth, and wept in describing his face-down anal rape by DeLuca who held Mike's arms up, behind his back so he could not escape. At that point it was clear that this was not to be the normal business bankruptcy proceeding that the diocese envisioned. No survivors would be prevented from telling their individual stories of personal suffering, and the diocese would not cram down the throats of the victims its miserly plans about compensating them. Then I said to the Court – "Your Honor, for the record, we will prove that the individual survivors who have lived up to the present – and my eight clients will be grievously injured by the loss of their right at this time to take the stand and unburden themselves of the nightmare that's been haunting them for fifty years."[422]

Michael Schulte's riveting testimony unfolded as follows. Acting on behalf of all the survivors, co-counsel Robert Jacobs began questioning medical expert witness Carol A. Tavani, M.D.:

BY MR. ROBERT JACOBS: Q. Now, Doctor, did you see a video of Mr. Michael Schulte?

CAROL A. TAVANI, M.D.: A. I did.

Q. How does that impact your testimony that you are about to give?

A. I think it, if anything, strengthens my opinions as to the effect of the abuse on the victims.

MR. JACOBS: Your Honor, could we show that video now?

(Whereupon at 1:01 p.m., the hearing in this matter proceeded with the following video testimony of Michael Schulte:)

DIOCESE LAWYER. Q. The hotel room in Philadelphia, and you described the room for us, and I had asked you about the bag you told me your mother had packed. You went to bed that night?

MR. MICHAEL SCHULTE. A. Yes.

Q. And you were in a separate bed from DeLuca?

A. Yes. I had the bed that as you walked into the room was on the left. It was in between the bathroom and the far right bed.

Q. And you were clothed fully in your brother's pajamas?

A. Yes. Top and bottom, matching.

Q. I'm going to ask you to tell me what happened that night. What you remember.

A. I remember being face down in bed. I remember being very, very tired at bed.

I remember having difficulty breathing, and I was again face down with my arms up. I remember again having trouble breathing and it was because there was a weight on my back.

I tried to roll over. I tried to roll over! But I couldn't get this person off my back! There was somebody feeling close to me, skin to skin, sweating on me, and I remember they were aligned with my body.

So, his hips were about the same area as my hips, and again, I think my most – I couldn't wake up. And it's not the way it was when I was younger. I could usually wake right up.

I couldn't get this person off of me! And it seemed like the more I resisted, I couldn't get him off, but the person would stop and then I would feel a movement.

I just couldn't get this person off of me, and I couldn't wake up. It was very frustrating for me. I'm sorry, I hope that answered your question.

(The video had concluded.)[423]

* * *

For the next ten months the diocese used the bankruptcy to continue its cover-up of the horrors committed on the children entrusted to its care and preventing the start of any trials against any of its parish churches or its living predator priests where the truth would be presented for all the world to see. Only seven of the original DeLuca Eight cases involved parishes and so in bankruptcy court the Deluca Eight eventually became Seven. But the legal maneuvering finally ended in a dramatic two-day hearing on August 12 and 13, 2010 where Judge Sontchi allowed seven more survivors to take the stand to prove why justice demanded that they be allowed to continue with their cases in the state courts against both individual parish churches and living predator priests. His actions in hearing from actual victims that day were without precedent in any bankruptcy court in the land, and so the courtroom was packed with survivors and the media.[424] A second, even larger, overflow courtroom also was filled and the court proceedings were beamed in a closed circuit video feed to large video screens so the proceedings could be followed by the spill-over public crowd consisting mostly of other survivors, their friends and the media.

The lead counsel for ninety-nine survivors began –

THE COURT: Mr. Neuberger, opening statement?

MR. THOMAS. NEUBERGER: Yes, Your Honor. . . . On October 19th, the trials for my eight DeLuca clients were set to begin. Twelve hours beforehand the diocese filed this Chapter 11 proceeding and those trials were stopped. Simultaneous with their petition, they filed an adversary action – on October 19th, the next day, they filed the adversary action to extend the stay to the parishes who Judge Vaughn had said were still going to go to trial. And we had day one of two days of hearings before this Court, and you took testimony.

At that early stage, we agreed to a stay with a definite expiration in exchange for two vital things. Number one, the long withheld personnel files of all the perpetrators of the debtor, who Bishop Saltarelli, in his compassion, years ago, admitted were serial pedophiles. Those files had been withheld again and again, and it is very important to the survivor community that the truth found in those documents be obtained. My eight plaintiffs were willing to forego their rights at that hearing in exchange for that information. Secondly, all the insurance information on the parishes was to be turned over. And both of these were to be done expeditiously.

Unfortunately, they weren't done expeditiously and they dribbled out to us. And to this day, for example, the medical records of the perpetrators are withheld, despite the fact that Judge [Sue] Robinson, in the United States District Court, Judge [Calvin] Scott and another one of our state court judges, Judge [Robert] Young, have ordered that there are no privileges under Delaware law for perpetrators of sexual abuse on children.

Those records are where the damning information is found, because a medical report to the Bishop will say so-and-so admitted he abused John Vai, or any of my other clients. So they never lived up to the deal, and we have not, to this date, pursued that issue with Your Honor in the effort of not consuming court time inefficiently. It was agreed as a prelude to the mediation, in front of both the mediators, that those documents would be turned over the next day. Guess what? They still have not been turned over. So that's the record of how we agreed to the deal.

We flowed into mediation. It's now August. And my request in this hearing in response to their motion is a very simple one. Lift the stay for all the cases and allow us to go to the state court trial judges for scheduling conferences to obtain a trial date. None of these trial dates will be before October 1st. In all likelihood they will be in the year 2011 and beyond. No activity would be allowed in the stayed cases prior to October 1st, besides the scheduling conferences. So we can walk and chew gum at the same time.

That gives them plenty of time to be continuing with the mediation. We've had five days of it, and it's been unsuccessful thus far. We will be there. Now, today, they are seeking to extend the stay.

I think that sets the stage. Okay? We're here to present evidence, to contest their application for a stay, an injunction against Barry Lamb who's dying, an extension of the stay, with reference to Raymond Donahue who is dying and the DeLuca Eight and all the others. And we will meet the legal test. We will show the present psychiatric injuries that are being caused by the diocese treating my clients like ping-pong balls and ignoring the fact that they are human beings and have a psyche and emotions. And we will address the public interest. And we know that the Court will consider all the evidence and apply the law and make a just decision.

That's my opening.

THE COURT: Thank you, Mr. Neuberger.[425]

Stephen Neuberger then took over and that day won perhaps the most important legal battle of the entire bankruptcy through his questioning of seven survivor witnesses. They explained what these priests had done to them, their injuries and their need to confront their tormentors in open court before a jury of twelve ordinary citizens and one impartial judge.

John Doe Number Three

The lead witness, who preferred to remain anonymous to protect his family and children from retaliation, was a driven man, severely damaged, who had lived four years hiding out in his own basement away from his family. He had run a business, was highly intelligent, with good analytical and critical skills and was very goal oriented. He rarely missed a court proceeding during the bankruptcy and had dedicated himself to keeping pressure on all parties in order to successfully conclude the bankruptcy for the benefit of all survivors. After he was sworn to tell the truth, Stephen Neuberger established his background.

Your Honor, Mr. Doe Number Three is a survivor of priest Francis DeLuca. He was abused from 1962 to 1965. He is one of the DeLuca Eight that the Court has heard so much about, whose trial was set to begin back in October, and is currently rescheduled for this October. From the medical report of Dr. [David] Springer, which is one of the exhibits, Your Honor, he suffers from post traumatic stress disorder – and the Court will hear from Dr. Springer later – he suffers from post traumatic stress disorder, personality disorders, chronic memories, flashbacks, things of that nature. His Global Assessment of Functioning is at a fifty-five on a scale of one to 100. His recommended treatment from Dr. Springer is weekly psychotherapy combined with some type medication. And just as Dr. Springer indicated in his expert report, which is in the record, DeLuca's abuse ripped apart his self esteem as a child and threw him into a state of confusion and self-doubt, which has lasted his whole life. He'll touch on that somewhat during his testimony about his injuries.

MR. STEPHEN NEUBERGER: Mr. Doe, did you grow up Catholic?

THE WITNESS: Yes, I did.

Okay. Actually, before we get into that, how old are you today?

Fifty-nine, approaching sixty.

What kinds of things have you done for a living during your life?

I've worked as a garbage man. I've worked as a waiter. I've worked as an advertising and marketing consultant. I've owned my own businesses. I've – and worked for others.

Now, when you were growing up, was religion something that was important to your family?

Very much so. Well, on my mother's side of the family, one of our great aunts was a nun. On my father's side of the family, my mother – his mother was a member of the Altar Society. We were the type of family that ate fish on Friday and went to confession on Saturday and mass every Sunday. I was an altar boy, became a mass commentator, and practiced my faith rather religiously, as did my father, my mother, his parents.

Could you please tell the Court how you came in contact with priest DeLuca?

Well, he conducted my altar boy training to begin with. That was one way. There were several ways that I came in contact with him. The one that I remember most was in the fifth grade. I had occasion to bring flowers to one of the – a Sister – the nun who was teaching me, because she was ill. And there – as a token of gratitude, they allowed me to take the empty bottles – soda bottles from the convent. And there were three cases of them or so, and as I was working with them, DeLuca approached me and asked me if he could drive me down to the gas station on Kirkwood Highway. He would help me, you know, return the bottles and get the money.

Okay. Was he also a parish priest at St. John the Beloved when you were there?

Yes, he was. And he happened to teach religion in that fifth grade class.

Did there come a time when he began to sexually abuse you?

Yes, sir, he did.

Okay. Could you please tell the Court what happened?

Well, the abuse lasted over three years or so. It started in fifth grade when I was about ten and a half years old. It stopped some time after my eighth grade.

And just briefly, could you tell the Court what happened?

Well, it – the abuse started simple enough. I was – after DeLuca took me to get the soda bottles returned, I was scheduled for early morning mass as an altar boy. After that early morning mass, he asked me if I wanted to go back to the rectory and take a nap. And, you know, I didn't see any reason why not to do that. I wouldn't normally go home. And when we went up to his bedroom, I lay down on his bed, and he began to rub my genitals and abuse me. Things progressed from that point on. And the – my abuse kind of grew into overnight stays at the rectory, where – I mean, he would eventually – I don't understand how – what type of explanation you're looking for here. I mean –

I'll just rephrase – what types of things would he do to you? I'm not trying to get into the graphic details, but just –

JUDGE SONTCHI: Well, let me just make a note.

MR. S. NEUBERGER: Sure.

THE COURT: It is what it is. The Court is not afraid.

THE WITNESS: Okay.

THE COURT: And you're not going to offend the sensibilities of the Court if you speak frankly about what occurred.

THE WITNESS: Thank you. Also, I wanted to just say thank you for letting me talk about this today.

-157-

Some of the things that DeLuca would do to me were intense French kissing that would be of a very prolonged nature. He would disrobe me. He would masturbate me. He would force me to masturbate him. He would force me to masturbate ourselves together. And he would try to hump me, for lack of a better term, until he achieved orgasm. And he would do this repeatedly and repeatedly and repeatedly over this three-year period.

Now, Mr. Doe, from the time – you mentioned that some of the abuse took place in the rectory. Were there any other locations where such abuse took place?

Yes. They took place in the basement of the rectory, in his bedroom in the rectory. They took place in the school – in the teachers' lounge, in his car, at the drive-in movie. They took place in hotel rooms. It also took place in front of other boys – there were other boys present when this happened. And I believe that covers all the locations.

Okay. You said in hotel rooms. Was that in hotel rooms in Delaware, or was it elsewhere?

Hotel rooms both in New York City and Philadelphia.

Was he taking you on a trip there? Was that how you ended up there, or how did you end up there?

Yes. He would take us – take me and, as I mentioned, other individuals, for overnight visits, sometimes lasting two days. While we were there, he would take us to shows, take us to Radio City Music Hall, movies and out to eat, that type of thing.

Now, when you mentioned the rectory, were there any other priests around when these kinds of things would happen, generally?

Yes.

Okay. And did they see you or did you see them? Or how did –

Yes. Not only did other priests see me, but other people affiliated, which I thought with the parish, saw me.

And these priests that saw you, were they employed by St. John the Beloved, or did they work at St. John the Beloved?

Yes. Yes, they did.

Okay. Did you ever tell anyone about the abuse?

While it was going on, no. I did tell other people about it as I got older. I was having difficulty at the University of Delaware. And I sought counseling help from a counselor there. And after several meetings, when I began to feel comfortable with talking with this individual, I brought up the fact of my abuse. I've told my wife. I've told my children. I've told other counselors.

Why didn't you tell someone when you were a child?

You know, I've gone over that over and over in my head. And I don't know. I was – it was a confusing thing. I didn't know whether – I didn't really know – I was a ten-year-old boy – what was going on.

What did a priest mean to you when you were ten?

He was an authority figure. I mean, if – not only was he an authority figure, he was someone that who you looked up to. I mean, he – you know, not just DeLuca, but other priests, you held in reverence. And –

Okay. Now, could you describe to the Court a little bit the impact that the abuse has had on your life, from then until today.

From then? It's destroyed my life. I've – as a young kid growing up, I mean, there are friends in my class that started – bullying is not the right word – but were – and teasing's not strong enough – that would – brought up my association with DeLuca in his bedroom. I got in fights in my high school where I was called names specifically, derogatory names. It forced me to leave that high school. As I got older, the problems got worse. I had problems relating to people. I can't stand people to invade my space. I cringe when my own son puts his arm around me. Imagine that. One time, when I was seeking counseling, I brought the subject up with my psychiatrist. After meeting with him for an extended period of time, I felt comfortable talking to him about it.

But the discussion about what happened to me initiated such an emotional crisis with me personally, I spent roughly four years in my basement, cut myself off from everybody. I cut myself off from my family, my children, employment, everything.

I suffer from chronic flashbacks, as you referenced. There's a variety of triggers that will bring these things on. The – I suffer from these anxiety attacks. They tell me I'm bipolar. I suffer from depression. I went through one marriage. Fortunately I'm married now. But I have intimacy issues. I have sexual dysfunction issues. I have issues regarding sexual identity. And I believe this is all traced back to what happened to me starting from a young boy, over and over and over again.

Now, Mr. Doe, could I ask you, why did you eventually come forward and file your lawsuit?

I was looking for some kind of way to reconcile and relieve all the things that happened to me and continue to happen to me. I was looking for some relief from the chronic attacks and the feelings of depression and anxiety, the tightness in my stomach. You know, just this constant cloud, if you will. And I wanted – I was hoping that this finally would create a path to achieve that – I mean, to put it behind me so I can move on with my life.

Was it an easy or difficult decision deciding to come forward this way?

It was the most difficult decision I ever had to make. Because you're talking about things that I've guarded, I've never told anybody. And I knew what was going to happen. Or I suspected. I'd have to tell the story over and over and over again, and sit in front of a room full of people who I don't even know and talk about this.

Why did you file anonymously?

I didn't want my past to come out and affect my children.

Now, were you aware that your trial was originally scheduled for October of 2009, before President Judge Vaughn, down in Dover?

Yes.

Was your trial date important to you?

Absolutely.

How come?

It represented what I assumed to be a process that would lead me to achieving some kind of relief and reconciliation, if you will, resolve of what happened to me.

Now, when the diocese filed for bankruptcy, the – twelve and a half hours before the first trial was set to begin, how did that make you feel?

I thought it was going to drive me around the bend. I'm nervous about being up here on the stand. I guard this information carefully. I don't want to admit to anyone what I've suffered and what I've done. And to convince myself that I should do that was very difficult.

Could you explain to the Court how every day for the last approximately ten months since the diocese filed for bankruptcy, what that's been like for you?

My – it's been terrible. My attacks have – my panic attacks continue to happen. I've been depressed. I'm beginning to withdraw, you know, shut people out. And I spend days just sitting in my room not wanting to go out of my house. And it affects me. I'm self-employed, and that means I don't make any money. So that – you know, and this – to your point, how it affects me, it just doesn't affect me, it affects my family. It affects my wife. I've been angry. I've been snapping at people – my children and her for things I wouldn't normally do. And most importantly, what this has done now is added an extra layer to all the things that bothered me. Now, I feel worthless, as if I don't matter. And it's compounded, because, you know, it just – I'll just leave it as I just feel worthless now.

Just, are you aware that President Judge Vaughn has rescheduled your trial date for October of this year?

Yes, I have.

Okay. And is that something that you're looking forward to?

Very much so.

For all the reasons you've just discussed?

All the reasons I have just discussed.

Okay.

But I'm concerned that – I mean, this stopping and going, it just continues to – to drive me into, you know, continued depression.

Okay. Now, did you hear what I said a little bit earlier about how one of the things that Dr. Springer thought you needed was some kind of treatment on a certain basis –

Oh, yeah.

– of medication and things like that?

Yeah.

Have you been getting that kind of treatment?

No.

How come?

The last time – the last time I did that it didn't go very well. I do not want to go through that again at this point in time. And I'm afraid of that.

Is closure something that is important to you?

Yes. It is. I would like to find closure. You know, to me it represents a way to mitigate the attacks I go through, the deep depression, the flashbacks and the nightmares.

Now, you think the trial with Judge Vaughn would give you that closure that you need to start to make progress?

I believe so. That's why I decided to file the lawsuit.

MR. S. NEUBERGER: Your Honor, I have no further questions.

THE COURT: All right. Thank you, Mr. Doe. You may step down."[426]

Mary Dougherty

The next survivor to be called was a woman. Intense. Passionate. Strong. Ready to walk to hell and back to get justice for survivors. A spitfire. A street fighter. Angry. What you saw is what you got with Mary Dougherty. As a child she had threatened to kill the priest who molested her if he also went after her younger sister.

MR. STEPHEN NEUBERGER: Your Honor, the abuse survivors call Ms. Mary Dougherty. If I could request, could she affirm rather than swear upon the *Bible*?

THE COURT: Everyone affirms in my court.

S. NEUBERGER: Oh. I apologize.

THE COURT: That's all right.

S. NEUBERGER: Your Honor, just, briefly, Ms. Dougherty is a survivor of priest Leonard Mackiewicz. She was sexually abused in the summer of 1966. Her trial date is actually this month, August 30th of 2010, before Judge [T. Henley] Graves down in Georgetown. From the expert medical report, which, I believe, is found at Defense Exhibit 5.2, from Dr. [Carol] Tavani, she suffers from depressive disorder, chronic post-traumatic stress disorder and a lot of other things that are in the report. The recommended treatment includes weekly therapy with a counselor as well as psychiatric treatment with a psychiatrist. As Dr. Tavani wrote in her report, Ms. Dougherty is haunted by a sense of guilt about what did I do, why did this happen, and it's against her personal beliefs to hate, but she is unable to divest herself of the anger and hatred which consumes her over what happened to her.

Now, Mary, if you don't mind my asking, how old are you?

THE WITNESS: Fifty-seven.

Okay. And did you grow up Catholic?

Yes.

What kinds of things have you done for a living during the course of your life?

I was a proof operator for a bank, a teller for a bank. I've been a waitress, a day childcare giver, assembly line work, assessment work for the county, real estate work, about fifteen or twenty different –

Okay. When you were a child, though, what did a priest mean to you?

Everything. It was God. It was – a Catholic priest named me. My uncle was a Catholic priest. I had two aunts that were nuns. They – that – utmost respect was demanded that be given to them. They were God's soldiers, his representatives to us as children. And as adults. My parents felt that way.

Could you please tell the Court how you came to come in contact with Mackiewicz?

He was our parish priest. I was a thirteen year old. That summer of 1966, when you got out of eighth grade you were allowed to join CYO. Join, that was, like, a big deal. And, because then you knew you could go places, and your parents would let you go because you were safe because the priests were the chaperones, and he was one of our chaperones at the different activities that we were allowed to participate in.

Did there come a time when Mackiewicz began to abuse you?

Yes. Well, the first time I didn't know that he was abusing me. I was, I mean, we were given a CYO room in the basement of the church, because CYO was pretty new at that time. It was a new thing. And I was hanging a poster. I would get there early, and I was very active in it from the get go, and I was hanging a poster up and he came up behind me, and he was a big fat drunk thing, and he pushed me up against the wall with his body weight, and he was telling me, and there was – he was poking something in my back. And I thought it was his belt or, maybe, the cross thing from their robe and telling me that 'this is power!' 'This is power!' And then we could hear the other kids coming in and, you know, so he backed off and went and let, you know, went about his business like nothing ever happened, and, then, a couple of days later I was telling some of the guys that what he did, and they told me that, you know, oh, he had a hard-on. And I didn't know what that was. So they explained it to me, but then they said No, because priests didn't – couldn't do that. And we, you know, we were thirteen. We didn't know that it was even humanly possible for a priest to have an erection.

Did the abuse ever escalate beyond that?

Yes. Through that whole summer everywhere we went, any CYO activity, if we were in a pool he'd do his beach whale thing, his whale thing, and he'd swim up underneath and he'd grab you by the crotch. Or, you know, forward, grab you by the breasts. It got to the point where the, you know, it was – he would get in the pool and the girls would scatter. And, then, when I was in the shower after one of the pool parties one time that was at my community pool, and he came in and just stood there holding his crotch and telling me that he had the power. This is – he would say 'This is power!' 'This is power!' And then one of the boys came in and he just walked away like nothing

-166-

ever – oh, sorry. Didn't know you were in there. Someone was in there.

And then it would – it was constant verbal. I had – I'm one of eight children, we were all born very close in age, that he would walk up to, in a group, and, now, like he was talk, you know, just having a conversation, and he would lick his lips. And he would ask – how's Tom? How's Pat? How's little Colleen? How's little Carol? And it was constant, the, or he'd lean over when we'd be doing something, and 'I have the power! I have the power!'

Did there come a time when the CYO took a trip to the Indian River Inlet down in Sussex County?

Yes.

Could you please describe to the Court what happened there?

I'm – don't know how to swim. I'm afraid of water, and I – everybody was hanging out in water listening to music, and I took a walk, and I [was] walking on the beach, and the next thing I knew I was on the ground and Mackiewicz was on top of me. And he had me by the throat and he was banging my head in the sand. And he was humping me and – and pushing on me and telling me 'this is power, bitch!' 'This is power, bitch!' And the – he was – he just keep banging my head so hard into the sand that I could – got to the point that I couldn't hear him. But I couldn't get my legs back together to get him off of me, to make it stop. And I knew he was going to kill me. He had this look in his eyes and that disgusting whiskey/cigar smell. And he was just telling me 'I have the power, bitch! I have the power, bitch!' And then priest [Leonard] Kempski, out of nowhere, came and tackled him off of me and told me to run. And that's what I did. I ran. And, then, and I just stayed away from him the rest of the day.

Did you ever tell anybody about what happened?

I went home and I told my mother, and my mother smacked me on the side of my head and said that no priest would ever do that to a human being. So my girl – I went to my girlfriend's house, and her mother cleaned me up, and she was very kind and very gentle, and she told me to never speak of this again to anyone. To never, ever, say what happened, but to never, ever be alone with that man.

Now, after that time, did you ever run into Mackiewicz again?

Yes. We were at the school dance, and the bathrooms were upstairs, and I was coming downstairs, and he asked me how my little sister – he grabbed his crotch and licked his lips and said 'how's Carol. How's little Carol?' 'She's so sweet and quiet' or something like that. So I knew I had to do something, because I knew he was going to go after – start on them. And that was a Friday dance. So Saturday I waited in church for him, and when he went into the confessional, and I opened the door, and I told him if he ever came near me or any of my brothers or sisters I'd kill him. And I meant it, and he knew I meant it.

Now, so Mackiewicz was still a priest in the church where priest Kempski caught him doing that to you?

Yes.

Mary, just to change gears a little bit, could you please describe to the Court the impact that the abuse has had on your life?

I missed out on the sexual revolution because of I was afraid to, you know, to

-168-

have anyone touch me. I started drinking. I spent, probably, after that, until I was in my early twenties, trying to be the perfect daughter because that – I figured there was something wrong with me. I mean, God, that a priest would do that to me, that I had to be, there had to be something very evil about me. So I spent all those years trying to be just so fake and perfect and doing everything the right way and being the good Catholic girl. And then I – around twenty-one I found alcohol, and it kind of numbed the pain. So I pretty much drank and experimented with drugs up until I was twenty-six and met my ex-husband.

And did the abuse impact your relationship with your now ex-husband?

Of course. It's pretty hard to have a healthy sexual relationship when you can't – [Mary began to cry] –

Just take your time.

When you can't stand someone being on top of you or touching you or, you know, can't have them drinking or even enjoy a cigar because the smell of whiskey or the smell of a cigar makes you sick and crazy. And still that, even after I sobered up and had my children it was difficult for them, to try to teach your children how sacred and holy and precious that they are when you don't even believe that about yourself. You lead by example. And my example was to have a nicotine addiction and a food addiction. So in that regard I deeply feel for my daughters –

Now Mary, even aside from the relationship with your daughters and with your now ex-husband, since you came forward has there been any other impact on the relationship with your family?

Sure, that family I described with a priest and two nuns in it, my family are still very devout Catholics and believe that this is a conspiracy to bring the Catholic church down, and by coming public I have tainted their name.

Now, did you hear me read some of the things that Dr. Tavani said that you suffer from? PTSD, depression, things of that nature? Do you think you suffer from those kinds of things?

Yes, I do.

And, also, do you recall what Dr. Tavani said about you having some anger, some serious concerns with anger?

Yes. But I'm getting it under control. I've been – I'm in counseling. I'm getting it under control. I'm –

Okay.

The church is still standing, so.

Are you Catholic any longer?

No, no, no, no, no, no! I had to leave when I found out. I always thought I was the only one. I couldn't imagine that there were others that this would even have ever been – there would be other people, and when I found out that – it kind of – kind of made me feel good that I wasn't alone, that I wasn't the freak in the world that the priest, that, then, there were others. So, and but that they knew it, and they did what they did. Then I – I couldn't hide. I – no could – I couldn't raise my daughters or bring myself to go back.

Now, was coming forward an easy or a difficult decision?

It's been a very difficult, very, very difficult decision.

Now, were you aware that your trial date was originally scheduled for August

30th of this year before Judge Graves down in Georgetown?

Yes.

Was that date important to you?

It was extremely important. Validation. Justice. Justice. Justice not for myself,

but for every victim. For everyone's that been – this has – [or] is afraid to come forward.

For every – every child that wanted to know what they did to deserve this, what – that I

want all of them to know, and if I have to be the voice – that we didn't do a thing wrong.

That these men that used the name of God, the sanctity of Christ, to abuse us and then to

treat us like trash and discard us, are the ones that have done repeatedly, repeatedly and

continue every time that they pull this nonsense and to keep us out of court and to keep

people from knowing what really happened. They are the ones that need to confess their

sins and stand up and take responsibility and do the Christly thing.

Now, Mary, what was your reaction when the diocese filed for bankruptcy last

year?

It made me sick. It just made me sick. I mean physically sick. Physically sick,

Stephen. I – I started smoking again after a heart attack. It's constant stress. I don't sleep.

I'm on medication for sleep. I'm on medication for my nerves. I have to go to counseling

every week. Always, not, and I'm not paranoid, but I'm just wondering, always

wondering, what the next thing they're going to do to demean us. I mean, how much

further can they demean – how much – how much more can we take?

What was your reaction to learning that you were probably going to lose your trial date against the parish, against Holy Rosary?

Extreme, extreme sadness and depression. Anger, a lot of anger. I'm really angry.

And just to keep moving things along a little bit, the feelings that you've been experiencing, are they similar to the feelings which you've previously been describing?

Oh, yeah.

Now, Mary, in Dr. Tavani's expert report she indicated the kinds of counseling, and you just, sort of, mentioned those things. Are you making progress in counseling while all this is going on?

No. I've been in counseling since I was twenty-five years old. I'm still there.

So you think the counseling's working?

It's keeping me under control.

Are you making forward progress?

Forward, no, but not backwards, and I don't – I'm sober. I've remained sober for seventeen years, so that's a good thing, but to move forward no, it's, you know, like, opening the door and banging your head and opening the door and you're banging your head and you open the door and you're banging your head. That's what it is.

Mary, is closure something that you are looking for?

Yes.

Does your trial date before Judge Graves relate to that?

Of course it does.

How come?

Because, again, back to the validation that it wasn't me, that I wasn't the evil dirty little girl that, the little bitch that deserved what he did.

Is it important to you to hear a jury say that to you?

Yes.

To wrap it up Mary, do you have a lot of faith in the mediation process with the

Diocese?

No – I have none. I am – was a member of the committee [of unsecured creditors

in this bankruptcy proceeding]. I was there for all five days of the mediation process.

That is my foundation for saying I don't have a lot of faith in the process if we do not get

our jury trials to bring pressure on the Diocese to get serious with us survivors.

MR. S. NEUBERGER: No further questions, Your Honor.

THE COURT: All right. You may step down.

THE WITNESS: Okay. Thank you, Your Honor.[427]

After listening to just two survivor witnesses, the Court and the public had learned a great

deal about the devastating short and long term effects on survivors of childhood sexual abuse

and the relapses they were suffering directly due to the delay-at-all-costs strategy of the Roman

Catholic Church. In addition to learning that John Doe Number Three had spent four years

living and hiding out in his basement from his own family and Mary Dougherty had become

physically sick and had started smoking again after a heart attack which followed the bankruptcy

filing, the court also heard detailed medical evidence on the permanent injuries suffered by

survivors from two prominent medical psychiatric professionals. Then the survivors sought to

show Judge Sontchi actual admissions concerning the grievous harms they suffered which the

previous – and now deceased – Bishop of the Diocese, Michael A. Saltarelli, had made when questioned under oath by Thomas Neuberger. The diocese lawyers tried to stop this damning evidence from being presented, but Judge Sontchi overruled their objections.

When previously deposed, Bishop Saltarelli had admitted that the multiple injuries caused by the sexual abuse of minors is absolutely devastating and long-lasting for each of them.[428] In his words, they suffer terrible enormous pain, anger and confusion.[429] He agreed that no words can ever describe the pain and suffering inflicted on a child abused by a priest.[430] He also agreed that the effects of such crimes can reverberate through a child's life and extend into adulthood.[431] For him the victims of sexual abuse by priests "are the walking wounded."[432] To him, the many consequences of childhood sexual abuse can include, alcohol abuse, drug use, suicide, confusion over sexual identity, divorce, inability to maintain a stable marital relationship or relationships with others, guilt, anger, grief, feelings of worthlessness, loss of faith and loss of trust in God.[433] And finally, because of the unique role of the priest in Roman Catholic culture, because members are taught from childhood on that priests are direct intermediaries between God and a child, Saltarelli admitted that it would have been very difficult back then for any abused child to ever to have attempted to report wrongful conduct of a priest to anyone at all.[434] The diocese tried everything to keep Judge Sontchi from learning these truths.

> THE COURT: Why don't I hear from you first, because it's your objection?
>
> BISHOP'S LAWYER: Yes. Exhibit number seven is the deposition testimony of Bishop Saltarelli. I don't know what relevance that would have.[435]
>
> MR. THOMAS NEUBERGER: Exhibit seven is a list of designations from the deposition of Bishop Saltarelli, corroborating the general causation testimony of medical experts of our clients that abuse of children causes them grievous harm, causes them

lifelong harm, causes them to have problems with relationships, alcohol abuse, substance abuse.[436]

BISHOP'S LAWYER: On Exhibit number seven, Your Honor, they're purportedly being offered to show Bishop Saltarelli concurring with medical experts about the effect of the abuse on the victims. Bishop Saltarelli is not a doctor, was not a doctor, does not have, did not have medical training – so it would not be appropriate to introduce those documents for that purpose.

THE COURT: All right. I'm going to overrule the objection and document seven is admitted into evidence.[437]

John Vai

Stephen Neuberger proceeded relentlessly. The third witness was John Vai who in the end succeeded in obtaining the permission of the court for his trial to begin just two months later before President Judge Vaughn. Always stoic about the cards which fate had dealt him, John was an untiring soldier capable of enduring the endless hand to hand combat with the diocese. Along with Mary Dougherty, he served as one of the seven survivors on the official committee of unsecured creditors for the diocese bankruptcy. Brilliant and courageous, John had the capacity to see beyond tactics and to understand the entire unfolding battlefield strategy against the church and its foot soldiers, so necessary for the final victory for all survivors affected by the bankruptcy.

MR. S. NEUBERGER: Your Honor, John Vai is a survivor of priest DeLuca. He was sexually abused from 1966 to 1970. His trial date was set to begin in October of

2009, and it has currently been rescheduled by President Judge [James] Vaughn for 25

October of 2010. From the medical report by Dr. Tavani, which is, I believe, Defense

Exhibit 1.2, among other things he suffers from post-traumatic stress disorder, chronic,

long-lasting depression, a host of other things. His recommended treatment includes

psychiatric and psychological counseling combined with medication. Also from the

medical report, he grieves the segment of his life that is gone. By facing the horrors of

his youth he risks his sanity. He feels like a captive in his own body. And, lastly, page

thirty-two, "Somebody stole something I'm never going to get back, my innocence." I

believe that's a quote that he gave to Dr. Tavani.

[After the witness was sworn] MR. S. NEUBERGER: Now, John, how old are

you today?

THE WITNESS: Fifty-eight.

And what do you do for a living?

Construction manager.

Did you grow up Catholic?

Yes, I did.

Was religion important to your family?

Yes. Three brothers, a mother and father, all St. Elizabeth's parish. We were

staunch Catholics. Every Sunday church. Saturday is confession. The weddings,

everything was associated with our parish. We were St. Elizabeth's parish participants.

And, as a child, what did a priest symbolize to you?

Basically, authoritarian figure. Prior to DeLuca a – a somebody you could trust.

A friend. Somebody you could go to. If you had problems with your family, you didn't want to tell your mother something, you would feel comfortable going to a priest.

Were they a God-like figure to you?

Absolutely. They were everything. They were the equivalent of an elected official that you looked up to. You would seek advice. Hard to believe in this world, but that's the way we looked at it back in the sixties.

And could you tell the Court how you came into contact priest DeLuca initially.

I was the only child of four that stayed at St. Elizabeth's from first grade to twelfth. My other three brothers migrated out of the Catholic school to public school at the end of eighth grade, which was the end of grade school back then. I believe DeLuca came into the parish at the end of my eighth grade and stayed there till the end of my junior year in high school. He was a religion teacher. He was the mentor of the altar boys. He went so far as to associate very closely with my mother and father. He came to our house on Sundays. We broke bread. He was a friend of the family. He was somebody that my parents thought was a very good influence on me. As one of four boys they assumed that one of us, because we were staunch Catholics, would end up in the priesthood. A great honor in my parents' eyes. Something that I looked up to. And this was the beginning of the relationship I had with Francis DeLuca.

Now, did there come a time when DeLuca began to sexually abuse you?

DeLuca had this unbelievable ability to establish a friendship first. As an authoritarian figure, as a mentor, as the altar boy foreman, as a religious person, when he picked you out of the class to answer a question, when he assigned you from fifty altar boys to serve on Christmas mass or Easter, great honor. I was one of a handful that was picked to go to these special occurrences, and it brought me closer to him. And the closer we got the stranger the relationship got. Now, realize I was thirteen, fourteen, fifteen, in that period, and I thought that this was a mentoring program.

It started with uncomfortable touching. Touch the shoulder while you're – even at my parents' house he'd rub my knee, and I don't think any of us took it beyond he's a friendly guy. It migrated into taking me right down the street from this court where the Saville Apartments are. There used to be Mullen's Haberdashery. It was the premier men's store, like a Wright and Simon's. DeLuca, I assume with his own money, bought me my first suit. Shoes, socks, underwear, pants, a tie, two shirts, button-down Oxford shirts. In a family of low middle class this was off-the-wall. My parents didn't know how to take it. I was adamant that Father DeLuca was my new best friend and let me hang out with him. Things like that.

It progressively got closer and closer. He was – if this was a male/female relationship he was courting me. He was entertaining me. He was in love with me, in my view. And the relationship got way out of hand. From a friendly touch to a hand in my crotch to a kiss on the ear. This isn't at my parents' house. This is at other places. It just got worse and worse, to the point where he started groping. Then he started humping. Then it got to the point in different locations clothes came off. Masturbation. Mutual masturbation. Oral sex. Anal sex.

I don't want to shock the Court. I mean, it's – it's not easy to bring up this constant turmoil in my past, as a child that I was raped by a priest, somebody that I

-178-

thought was a friend. It was a two-edged sword. He was the religious teacher. He was

the – everything that I thought I was doing to move up and to identify myself as better

than my brothers, where there was a lot of – there was a lot of challenge between us.

Who was the best in this and the best in that? I was trying to identify myself that I had a

priest, a well respected priest at St. Elizabeth's, as my best friend.

Now, John, you mentioned that there were various locations where DeLuca did

these things to you. Could you please describe to the Court what those locations were?

The first and most awkward location was at the Americana Hotel in New York

City for a weekend trip. Musical, Statue of Liberty, things like that. There was, I

believe, two other, possibly three other, students, other altar boys, and what I recall was

either the first night or the second night I was laying in bed. I was closest to the window.

It was – lights were out. I remember the light in the bathroom going on, and DeLuca

came over around the side of the bed and he started masturbating me. At that point in my

life, it's not like the kids today. I didn't have any concept of erection, ejaculation,

man-to-man stuff or man-to-boy stuff. It was just off-the-wall. He humped my leg. I

was frozen in time. I couldn't move. I was scared that the – my friend who was sleeping

next to me would wake up and think that there was something bizarre about me, least

alone about the priest. That was the worst time it happened and the first time.

From that point on it was a constant interaction with DeLuca. He'd call my

mother and say can John come up to the church? We've got some special altar boy thing.

He needs to do this. We'd go back to the rectory. This sounds like a broken story, but

he'd take you up to his room. He'd do the same thing. He was a – his passion was to dry hump you, to ejaculate on you. He'd touch you and grope you.

I've been to Rehoboth Beach. I've been to beaches in New Jersey with him. I've been in his car. I drove his car. As a sixteen year old to have a priest say here's the keys. Drive my car. It was just, it was a setup. He was, basically, breaking me down to the point where I would be scared to say something, and, at the time same, he was enjoying the, in his view, the sexual part of it. It was horrible.

All right, John. You mentioned being taken up into the rectory. Where there other priests around when he was doing this?

At St. Elizabeth's, unlike it is today, was a busy place back in the sixties. I believe there was three, maybe four, maybe even five priests in and out of there. There was a housekeeper. I don't believe she lived there. She might have. I wasn't checking the – see who was there, but there was a lot of people moving in and out. A lot of Roman collar people. In the rectory I saw other kids coming in there. By kids, kids two years younger than me, kids a year older than me, but you, kind of, like, knew something strange was going on, and you didn't say much because you were part of the – the whole scenario, like, DeLuca, the one that you respect, and he's taking you up to his room. This has got to be a great honor.

I was abused over a three-year period, and in order to identify – I don't know if I could stand giving the full version, mentally or physically, but it would take days, if not weeks. If I wanted to expose my soul again and say everything that was – everything that happened, I don't think we'd – you and I would have the time, Your Honor. It would take weeks.

Now, John, could you describe to the Court a little bit the impact that the abuse has had on your life from then until now?

Well, once I got out of high school I basically disassociated myself in total with St. Elizabeth's. I attended zero functions. I'm never going back for a reunion. Anything that has to do with St. Elizabeth's, St. Elizabeth's church, organized religion, it's completely off the menu. To say I sleep well at night is an understatement. I guess you'd call me a card-carrying insomniac. If I get three hours of sleep a night that's a long night. It just migrates.

I don't trust authority. It was very hard for me to go to this legal firm and say I was abused.

Basically, I can't hold a job for more than four or five years. Knowing that I had to come here today, for the last six or seven weeks, or as short a period it may have been, or whenever, I'm on the verge of getting fired every day that I go in, because I'm this close to telling my boss, who I should respect and follow his lead, he is the one paying my bills and helping me pay my kids through school, just to screw off. I just don't trust anybody that is an authoritarian figure at all.

John, was coming forward an easy or a difficult thing?

It's near impossible. Unless something is done with this system and this church recognizes that this is a major problem, I'm afraid that other victims that are maybe not as courageous, and I don't want to paint myself as a courageous person, but unless they have the gall to step up and say look, I was abused, I'm not afraid to use my name, this is just going to continue on.

Now, John, whose trial was set to begin twelve and a half hours after the bankruptcy was filed?

Mine.

And was your trial date important to you?

It absolutely was important for me. I had harbored all this horror for forty years. I endured three plus years of abuse, on and off. I lived with that. I'm here to tell you I'm still alive. Maybe I'm half the person I could have been, but unless I can come to some kind of conclusion and end this in a fashion that somebody lets me face DeLuca, somebody lets me face his handlers, and somebody explains to me how they let him run rampant from church to church to church, I'm never going to be satisfied. There's no closure until somebody in charge tells me I really screwed up and end it right there.

John, what have the last ten months of individual twenty-four hour days while this bankruptcy has been going on, what have they been like for you?

Once I got over the sadness that I wasn't going to get my day in court – I didn't realize that bankruptcy, at least this bankruptcy, would take, in my view, forever. I thought, maybe, again, naive, three months, six months. Now we're into ten months, and two, and I wear two hats. I'm on the committee, and I'm also a victim. It's like I'm on a lazy Susan. Day in and day out. Try to deal with my family life. Try to deal with my children. Try to stay employed so I can pay for my mortgage. And, yet, I'm trying to deal with my responsibility as a committee member and trying to put all this minutiae of all this anger that I've got somewhere. I don't know how I deal with it. I really don't.

Now, John, are you aware that President Judge Vaughn has rescheduled your trial against the parish for October 25th of this year?

Yes, I am.

Are you looking forward to that date?

Well, I'm looking forward to it, but, at the same time, if this gets postponed again, how many times do I have to steel up, do I have to put my helmet on, do I have to get ready to tell my story, the full story? Not twenty minutes of, you know, this happened to me. I don't know if I'm excited or traumatized again. If this doesn't go forward I don't think I can come up for, you know, from drowning water three times. I don't know who would.

Now, John, even just a parish trial. Would that help you start the healing process or getting this stuff out?

To get my story out, to face the monster, to face his handlers, yes, that is what I need. Me, personally, I need to face DeLuca. I need to face who's in charge, and I'm really not sure who's in charge anymore. And I want somebody to tell me I screwed up or I didn't screw up or John, it was your fault. Let's just put all the cards on the table and let the judicial system play it out. I don't know what everybody's trying to hide from.

Do you trust the diocese to do the right thing?

No. Since being a committee member and seeing all of the meetings and all the internal information and it's just – it's a giant circus of how many times can we hide behind the wall is the way I see it.

And, John, do you trust the diocese to do the right thing in the mediation?

I was at the mediation every minute that it was open. Sunup, sundown, we were even there on July 4th in that 100 degree temperature outside. And I didn't see, I wasn't privy to anything that would give me any kind of hope that we are heading into some kind of settlement.

Now, John, you mentioned closure a couple of times. Is it fair to say that's something that you're looking for?

That's all, personally, that I'm looking for.

And would a trial against St. Elizabeth's and DeLuca help you with that?

Yes. Win, lose or draw, I want my story out on the table in front of a jury of twelve.

MR. S. NEUBERGER: I have no further questions, Your Honor.

THE COURT: Thank you. Mr. Vai, you may step down.

THE WITNESS: Thank you, Your Honor.[438]

John Doe Number One/Felix Flanigan

Felix is a former Marine and never afraid of a fight. Here as a last resort he was fighting in the bankruptcy court. And then, when provoked beyond endurance by the tricks and delays of the diocese, Felix proved himself the most powerful witness of the day. A Vietnam combat veteran, Felix had guts, plus the diocese had crossed him one time too many. Initially he had filed his lawsuit as an anonymous plaintiff, John Doe Number One, to protect his family from retaliation and for health reasons. But as his dramatic testimony below electrified the courtroom, he proudly stood up in the witness stand, leaned on the cane he used to hobble around in court, tossed his anonymity aside and directly challenged the power of the diocese.

MR. S. NEUBERGER: Your Honor, the abuse survivors call John Doe Number One.

[Using his cane, Felix walked slowly forward from his seat in the public section of the courtroom, up to the wooden rail and through the swinging gate separating the court and the lawyers from the public, turned left and slowly stepped up to the witness stand.]

THE COURT: All right. Mr. Doe. You may be seated, sir, if you wish. All right.

(Witness sworn)

THE CLERK: Please state and spell your name for the record.

UNIDENTIFIED SPEAKER: John Doe Number One.

THE COURT: It's okay. Thank you. Please be seated, sir, and make sure you're close to the microphone.

THE WITNESS: Thank you, Your Honor.

THE COURT: You're welcome.

MR. S. NEUBERGER: Your Honor, John Doe Number One is also a survivor of priest DeLuca. He was sexually abused from 1961 until 1964. He also had an October of 2009 trial date, which is current – which has been rescheduled against the parish and DeLuca for October of 2010. From the medical report of Dr. Springer, who I'll hear from in a few minutes his diagnosis includes post-traumatic stress disorder, bipolar disorder, various ongoing memories of the abuse, and his Global Assessment of Functioning is at a level of fifty-five. His recommended treatment is ongoing counseling and psychiatric

-185-

treatment for the rest of his life.

Just a couple of quotes from Defense Exhibit 1.5, which is Dr. Springer's report. "Mr. Doe is haunted with memories of the sexual abuse and sometimes gets flashbacks to particular incidents. He carries with him enormous amounts of shame and guilt. He feels guilty to this day, 'believing that I allowed others to be subjected to DeLuca's perversions, and my own cowardly actions still haunt.'" Then page 24. "It is not an understatement to say that Mr. Doe has lived a psychological nightmare due to the actions of DeLuca."

MR. S. NEUBERGER: Now, Mr. Doe, how old are you?

THE WITNESS: I am sixty years old.

And, just briefly, what kinds of jobs have you done for a living during your adult life?

During my adult life I started as a paperboy when I was nine. Then I was a janitor. I worked for the post office while I was in high school. Then I joined the Marine Corps and served in Vietnam. From that point on I worked in a lumberyard. I worked for a flying company, in sales. I worked, again, for another lumber company, and I worked for the State of Delaware, a federal job, to try to find disabled vets jobs.

Now, did you grow up Catholic?

Yes, I did.

And, briefly, was religion important to your family as a whole?

Religion was our family. That was the cornerstone of the family. I have an aunt and an uncle. One was an Oblate priest. The other is still a Benedictine nun.

I was very, very religious.

Could you tell the Court about the day that that all ended?

Yeah. The day that all ended was on a Sunday evening. I believe it was in the fall. I was invited by DeLuca to come help count the collection of the Sunday receipts at the church. And I remember being excited, to the point where I was wondering if any of my friends were going to be there to help me with the process. It was around 7 o'clock at night. I got to the rectory, and I was the only one there besides DeLuca. I did my job. I counted the collection. He made all the thing – bank statement and everything, and then we went upstairs, and he offered me a bowl of ice cream, which I gladly took. At that point he said would you like to see my room. I went upstairs and saw his room, and being from a family of eight and three boys living in a room ten by ten, I thought this was magnificent. He had a nice big room, a sitting room. He had books. A bookcase on the wall. Television set. Nice easy chair. And then off of that room was the bedroom. And in, basically, in the bedroom he had a little night stand, a couple of religious pictures on the wall, a crucifix, a lamp and a bed.

We proceeded to watch television for about an hour or so, and then I said, "I have to go home. I have a paper route." You know, responsibilities in the morning to deliver papers. He said "No, it's too late. I already asked your mom if you could stay the night." I said "oh, okay." I said, "I don't have any pajamas or anything," and he goes "oh, you can – you can wear a pair of mine." I remember putting the pajamas on and they were about ten sizes too big, of course, being twelve years old or whatever I was at the time. And I said, "is there another room that I can -- I am going to sleep in?" He

-187-

goes "no, you're sleeping in here." And I go – I felt very uncomfortable at the time. So I got in bed and I started to go to sleep, but I was really having troubles with it because I was wondering what I had gotten myself into.

The next thing I know, I don't know whether it was two minutes, ten minutes or an hour, he was on my – at my back with an erection. He then reached around and grabbed me and pretty much screwed me up for the rest of my life. [Emotion began to come over Felix's face and he began to struggle to contain his emotions.]

Were you abused in the rectory more than once?

Yes, I was.

During any of the times were there ever any other priests around?

Yes, there was.

Okay. And, John, just – Mr. Doe? John Doe.

THE WITNESS: Excuse me, Steve. [He turned to his left facing Judge Sontchi who sat at the center of the courtroom against the back wall.] Is it all right, Your Honor, if I change from John Doe Number One to use my real name?

THE COURT: I'd like you to consult with your attorney, but it is your decision.

MR. S. NEUBERGER: It's his decision, Your Honor.

THE COURT: Very good.

[Both courtrooms erupted with cheers and emotion from the public galleries packed with survivors, in both the closed circuit video courtroom and also where Judge Sontchi and the witness spoke.[439] The Judge allowed the spirited acclamation to subside. And then he declared gently.]

THE COURT: I understand the emotion that is involved in this case, but, please, let's not have any more outbursts like that. It's inappropriate in the courtroom.

Will you please provide your name for the record and spell your last name? You can remain seated, if you wish.

[John Doe started to rise from his seat, pushing on his cane. He brought himself up, Marine ramrod straight and tall.]

THE WITNESS: Yes. [He turned to his right, looked across the courtroom to the far side where the bishop and his army of lawyers were sitting and he stated very slowly, staring them down for each and every survivor who they previously had intimidated, and sending a clear message that they were men and women with dignity who feared them no longer.]   My name is Flanigan. [And he spelled it out slowly.] F-E-L-I-X F-L-A-N-I-G-A-N.

THE COURT: Thank you, sir.

THE WITNESS: You're welcome. Thank you, Your Honor.

S. NEUBERGER: Now, Felix, did you ever tell anyone about the abuse?

No, I did not.

Did you ever tell any priests about the abuse?

Yes, I did, in confession.

Many years later when you were an adult, sometime around 2002 or 2004, did you ever meet with priest Thomas Cini to talk about the abuse?

Yes, I did.

What did Cini say to you during that meeting?

I believe the meeting was around an hour and a half. He showed considerable sorrow for the fact that I was abused when I was younger, and he explained to me the reasoning behind it was that's how they did it back then, and it was a "cover-up" by the diocese. They just moved the priests around.

Did he say what happened to DeLuca?

Yeah, he said he was transferred to St. Elizabeth's.

Did he say what DeLuca was doing now?

I asked, specifically, of the monsignor if he had been defrocked. And he had not been defrocked.

Okay. Now just to change gears a little bit, Felix, can you describe to the Court the impact that the abuse has had on your life?

It changed me completely from the day of the first abuse. I don't know exactly how many. I know there was more than ten times that I was abused but there's a lot of stuff that I've compartmentalized. I've forgotten but I became very angry. I became very cautious of everyone. I have a lot of trust issues. And I've had a lot of depressive episodes. And I've also showed anger a lot of times of things that I really shouldn't have been angry about. This is just the short version.

Now Felix, why did you file your lawsuit?

I filed my lawsuit to bring justice to all the abuse victims, mainly for myself and what my family's had to go through these past forty or fifty years.

Now, you originally filed the lawsuit as a John Doe. Why did you do that?

I have a very large family. I have eight brothers and sisters. I have an uncle who is an Oblate priest. I have an aunt who is now a Benedictine nun, has served in the diocese for over fifty years. And I have two sons. I did not think that those people should have to answer questions about my name being out there. And I also had a mother that was still alive that I didn't think should have to answer questions in the parish that she still belonged to and still frequented.

Now, you were aware that your trial date was originally set for October of 2009, right?

Yes.

How did it feel when the bankruptcy was filed the night before the first trial was set to begin, the trial at which you were going to testify as a witness, testify as a plaintiff in your own case?

Like the rug was pulled out from under me.

And could you please describe to the Court what the last ten months – how the last ten months have been to you – for you?

I've been in treatment. I believe if we look back on the record, it was probably every two weeks – psychotherapy. And I'm on – currently on medication, which I have been for about eight months and I'm not sleeping well. I just don't see an end – don't see an end to this. It's been one thing after another. I read the excerpts. I go to the – talk to my attorneys. I talk to everyone and it just doesn't seem like there's an end. Everything gets pushed back. I just can't – I can't see an end to this. It seems like a charade to me. I just don't understand it.

Okay. Now even just a trial against the parish and against DeLuca, can that help you start the healing process?

Yes. That could be on the – I could be on the road to recovery as long as I was able to express in Court exactly what happened to me. The long version.

Is closure something that's important to you?

I'm not sure I really like that word closure. I'm more of the fact that I need to recover from all the things that happened and all the mistrust that the public has out there on what the victims have really gone through. And I think that it would be – I would be well on my road to recovery if justice could be done.

Is it important for you to stand before a jury of your peers and tell your story?

Absolutely.

THE COURT: All right. Thank you, Mr. Flanigan. You may step down.

THE WITNESS: Thank you. Thank you very much, Judge.[440]

John Doe Number Four

A man of few words. Shy. Injured even more than the others. A survivor taken by DeLuca to Rome itself where DeLuca perpetrated sexual crimes on his person, after DeLuca had had an audience with the Pope himself. Tall but reluctant, almost twenty years younger than the other witnesses, but with an inner fortitude which enabled him to find the courage to take the stand as a careful combatant.

MR. S. NEUBERGER: Your Honor, the abuse survivors call John Doe Number Four.

(Witness sworn)

Your Honor, Mr. Doe Number Four is a survivor of DeLuca. His sexual abuse that he experienced began in 1979. He also, like the other DeLuca victims you've heard from today, their trial dates were set to begin last October. They've been rescheduled for this October. From the medical report prepared by Dr. Springer, who the Court just heard from, among other things, his diagnosis includes post-traumatic stress disorder, major depressive disorder, lots of other disorders, intrusive thoughts about the abuse, guilt regarding not fighting back, guilt over his mother's reaction to eventually learning about it. And his Global Assessment of Functioning is only at a level of forty-five. The recommended treatment includes weekly psychotherapy sessions and medications from a psychiatrist just to begin to address his many problems. He concludes that "Mr. Doe has long buried his emotional reaction to the abuse and the strong emotions concerning it, have only recently begun to surface. He has recurrent, intrusive thoughts about the abuse which disturb his sleep, his work and his social functioning. And he's wracked with guilt and shame and remorse and will have to live with not only his embarrassment about being a sexual abuse victim but will have to live with his mother's pain and sorrow over not having stopped her son from being abused by DeLuca."

MR. S. NEUBERGER: Now, Mr. Doe, how old are you today?

THE WITNESS: Forty-two.

Okay. And what do you do for a living?

Right now, I'm a self-employed contractor.

And as a child, can you describe for the Court what a priest meant to you or what a priest symbolized?

-193-

Basically, the priest was everything. I mean, the word hit – what they said, went and it just – what they said, went. I mean, it was very high.

Was your family actively involved in church life at St. Matthew's?

Very. My mother ran the social hall, bingo. My father was president of Men's Guild. We basically lived at the church and the hall.

And did there come a time when eventually DeLuca began to sexually abuse you?

Yes, somewhere around age eleven. Like I said, my mom ran bingo. DeLuca came over and sold the last bingo special and at the end of the night they would put a moneybag together. The rectory was right around the corner, actually, right through the backyard of the bingo hall. I would, basically, run the bingo bag over. They'd ask me to come in. Started out as coming in to chat and it proceeded from there.

What kinds of things would he do to you?

Groping, kissing, dry humping, ejaculating on me.

And where in the rectory did DeLuca abuse you?

He had a, basically, a second floor suite that consisted of the living room, a bathroom and his bedroom.

Were there any other priests around when he would take you up there?

I greeted other priests regularly. Every time I visited.

Did he ever abuse you in any other locations other than in the rectory?

Yeah. There was a trip to Italy and Rome, a trip to New York.

When was the first time you ever told someone about the abuse?

Not till my later years. It goes back to seeing articles in the paper about DeLuca and I guess I was about thirty-nine.

Now, are you someone that likes to talk?

No.

Okay. And you like talking about your feelings?

No.

All right. To paraphrase The Duke, John Wayne, it's a sign of weakness?

Yeah. Definitely a sign of weakness.

The story that you've mentioned here today, is that the full version of the story?

No. You can't tell an *eleven-year* story over twenty minutes.

Can you describe to the best of your ability and comfort level the impact that the abuse has had on your life? And I do realize you've already given an extensive deposition about this.

Anywhere from no sleep at night, anger issues. As far as moving my family to twelve acres in Smyrna just to put us in solitude and confinement, I'll say, mostly my teenage boys take a lot of the brunt of it. I didn't let them go places. Wouldn't let them spend the night anywhere. Really hard on them.

Are you trying to avoid having happen to them what happened to you? Is that part of it?

Definitely.

I think you mentioned your sleep patterns and if they have been affected at all?

If you consider a couple hours of no sleep a sleeping pattern, yeah.

Okay. You heard me read from the diagnosis from Dr. Springer's report a little earlier about the major depressive disorder and things of that nature and the Global Assessment of Functioning of level forty-five. Do you agree that you suffer from those kinds of things?

Sure, if not more.

Why did you come forward and file your lawsuit?

Again, it goes back to seeing some of the stuff that came out in the papers originally about DeLuca. At first, I thought it was just me and I [saw] more and more that came forward. I, basically, wanted to put my name into the situation to, basically, put him through what I've been put through as far as the tension and the stress. I just figured the more that we were involved the more pressure we'd put on him.

Why was your October of 2009 trial date important to you?

More to look him in the eye than anything.

And when the diocese filed for bankruptcy the night before John Vai's trial was set to begin, how did that make you feel?

That whole – the whole process made me feel like a yo-yo. It's up, down, up, down. All the delays. The bankruptcy thing. Everything.

And how would you feel if you lost your new trial date the same way you lost the one last year?

It just be another knockout.

Okay. Is it important to you to be told that it wasn't your fault?

Sure.

Okay. Have you begun seeking some kind of, you know, counseling or the types of treatment that Dr. Springer had said might be helpful to you to start to try to come to grips with everything?

No, I haven't. I just – I just feel that there's going to be no way to heal it until something comes about of it.

MR. S. NEUBERGER: No further questions, Your Honor.

THE COURT: Thank you, sir. You may step down.[441]

Michael Sowden

Mike Sowden lives as a recluse, a hermit. He views human sexuality as barbaric. But he impresses you as a classic gentlemen, white haired and distinguished, always conducting himself in a respectful and deferential manner. He is always courteous and polite, despite his misfortune of being the victim of both an Oblate and also a diocesan priest. Fearlessly, he served as a public face for the survivor movement throughout the struggle with the church, always making himself available for press conferences or other events as a representative survivor face and voice.

MR. S. NEUBERGER: Your Honor, the abuse survivors call Mr. Michael Sowden.

THE COURT: Okay.

(Witness sworn)

MR. S. NEUBERGER: Your Honor, Mr. Sowden is also a survivor of DeLuca. He was sexually abused from 1961 to 1962. He was also one of the DeLuca Eight, with their trial dates in October 2009. It's rescheduled for October 2010 now. He was seen by Dr. Tavani whose diagnosis included chronic post-traumatic stress disorder, depressive disorder, several other disorders and he has a Global Assessment of Functioning of fifty which includes significant impairment in some areas of his life and the report goes on to list some of those areas. The recommended treatment includes weekly psychological counseling sessions, monthly psychiatric counseling sessions, psychiatric medications all for the remainder of his life. And the report – Dr. Tavani's report says for example, "That since coming forward and bringing this lawsuit, he's unable to suppress the memories of the abuse and how it – and it affects his daily life as he goes through his daily life." And then it also says that "There's a major impairment in the ability to form and sustain a relationship. He sees sexuality as barbaric." And it gets into that in some detail.

MR. S. NEUBERGER: Now, Mike, how old are you today?

THE WITNESS: Sixty-two.

And what kinds of things have you done for a living?

Well, I was a funeral director all my life. I retired. And now I deliver flowers.

As a child in the early 1960's, would you please describe to the Court what a – the significance of a priest?

He was just like God.

Okay. Could you please tell the Court how you eventually came in contact with priest DeLuca?

I was an altar boy there and another friend and I – excuse me – we hung around together and we sort of became DeLuca's pet. He would come to our houses at night, he would call first, and take us to Howard Johnson's for hamburgers, things like this that we would do regularly; maybe once a week.

Did there come a time when DeLuca eventually began to sexually abuse you?

When I was around eleven, he had asked this other friend and I, my parents, if we could go to New York to see *My Fair Lady*. So, we went for the weekend. In a hotel, sometime during the night, the hand came across me, across my body. It was his hand going down my pajamas. The next thing I knew, he was humping me until he ejaculated. I did not move a muscle. And then it was done.

Did he ever try to sexually abuse you any other times that you can presently remember?

Well, he wanted to go to Philadelphia to pick out vestments, the clothes they wear to say mass. We stayed in the Bellevue-Stratford. We no sooner got in the room and he was chasing me. He ended up on top of me on the bed. I fought him off as best I could and then the next thing I know he's gone and I was there for hours. He did come back. Didn't say anything but –

And did he ever try to sexually abuse that you can presently remember again?

I can't remember. He could have but I cannot swear to anything.

Do you recall DeLuca's deposition on how many times he said he sexually abused you?

Yes.

And how many times was that?

More than ten.

More than ten. Okay. Now, I just ran through and asked you these questions sort of in a bit of an abbreviated fashion. Is there more of the story to tell? The details, the specifics about –

Oh yes. Yes.

The things that were covered in your deposition, for example?

I covered them, yes.

Okay. Did you ever tell anybody about the abuse?

I was fifty-five when I first told somebody.

And who did you tell?

I told a good friend of mine.

Can you describe to the Court, please, the impact that the sexual abuse has had on your life?

I live as a recluse. I do have two girls. They don't live in Wilmington so that's not a problem. I cannot hold a relationship at all. I hate to have someone touch me. Hate it. I've had to say to women, and this is embarrassing after a while, please just keep your hands to yourself. I can't handle it. And I ended them. And I live alone and I can – that's how I deal with it.

For example, do you have, like, nightmares or flashbacks or trouble sleeping or things of that nature?

Trouble sleeping but not the nightmares.

Trouble sleeping, okay. Are you still a religious person the way you were when you were a child?

No.

Why did you file your lawsuit?

My children said I needed to do it. I fought them. I was afraid.

And did your children think it would be a good – a positive step for you?

A positive step to – I don't think they used the word "closure" but I needed to do it.

Okay. Was it –

I mean it was months before I called you.

Okay. Okay. Was that an easy or difficult decision to pick up that phone and call us and eventually –

Difficult.

Difficult. Okay. How come?

I don't want people to know this happened to me. It's embarrassing.

Are you aware that Judge Vaughn had rescheduled your trial?

Yes.

Okay. And was that something you were looking forward to, to help with that – with that therapy?

Yes.

Do you think that your trial could help that healing process, that process of facing your fears, facing your demons?

Yes.

Okay. Do you trust the diocese?

Not with all the things that they've pulled, no.

Okay. Do you trust the Diocese of Wilmington to do the right thing by you and by the other survivors?

No.

Do you trust the Diocese of Wilmington to do the right thing in mediation?

No.

Is it important for you to sit on the witness stand and tell your story to a jury?

Yes. I think they need to be accountable. All the delays is like we're trying to wiggle out of it.

And how long have you been waiting for them to be held accountable for their actions, specifically regarding DeLuca?

You want to go back to grade school? '61, '62; '60 or '61.

Okay. So, almost fifty years or –

I can't add and subtract.

MR. S. NEUBERGER: Okay. Your Honor, I have no further questions.

THE COURT: Okay. Thank you, Mr. Schulte (sic). You may step down.[442]

Michael Schulte

The last witness of the day was Michael Schulte. His ninety-second video description of his childhood violent anal rape by DeLuca which was shown in open court in the first two weeks of the bankruptcy had transformed the survivors from nameless individuals into suffering human beings who were before the Court fighting for justice. Relentless, determined, with a quiet intensity and steadfast, for decades Mike had pursued DeLuca within the halls of the diocese seeking to out him and to have some bishop step in to protect vulnerable children from him.

Unfortunately, his decades of pleas were always met with deception and lies, and DeLuca without remorse continued to use children for his sexual gratification, ultimately ending up in jail in New York after abusing his own grand nephew and another boy, all while still a priest of the Diocese of Wilmington. So Mike took matters into his own hands and went to the press, and along with John F. Dougherty and others their stories became the foundation in the media for the groundswell which eventually lead to enactment by the Delaware State legislature of the Child Victim's Act of 2007.

MR. S. NEUBERGER: Your Honor, the abuse survivors last call Mr. Michael Schulte.

THE COURT: Oh, I'm sorry.

MR. S. NEUBERGER: That was Mr. Sowden.

THE COURT: Oh. I apologize.

MR. S. NEUBERGER: You're the judge, though, Your Honor. It could have been worse.

THE COURT: I don't think so. I apologize, Mr. Sowden, for getting your name wrong.

(Witness sworn)

MR. S. NEUBERGER: Your Honor, Michael Schulte is a survivor of DeLuca. He was sexually abused in 1961 and 1962. He was one of the original members and a current member of the DeLuca Eight set for trial last year and he's currently looking forward to his trial this year. He was seen by Dr. Springer and his diagnosis included among other things post-traumatic stress disorder, major depressive disorder, panic disorder, several disorders I can't even pronounce. And he has a Global Assessment of Functioning of fifty-five. The recommended treatment from Dr. Springer included weekly psychiatric treatment including the possibility of psychiatric medications to help them deal with things. In Dr. Springer's report he talks about how the core of Mr. Schulte's problems is his sense of self-doubt and low self-esteem brought about by DeLuca's acts of forced sexual behavior. It talks about how Mr. Schulte has often used alcohol to numb himself to those feelings. And how he has spent his shattered life dealing with the consequences of having his life destroyed by the abuse of DeLuca and the abusive response displayed by the Diocese of Wilmington for approximately forty years specifically regarding Mr. Schulte.

MR. S. NEUBERGER: Now, Mike, how old are you today?

THE WITNESS: I'm sixty-two.

And what was your profession before you retired?

Before I retired. I worked for General Motors for approximately forty years and I retired four years ago.

Okay. And could you in your own words, what did a priest mean to you as a young Catholic growing up in a large devout Catholic family?

Well, he was held in highest esteem as everybody else has said. Some people called him a God. But he was definitely a plateau of authority, unquestionable authority.

Did there come a time when DeLuca eventually began to sexually abuse you?

I'm not sure when it started but if you're interested in the first assault, I can tell you – I was in seventh grade. It was one of these trips; it was to Philadelphia. So, it started somewhere in Delaware. I guess, you know, the touching, whatever. Regardless, we went to see the movie the *King of Kings* at the Boyd Theater and thanks to somebody else I now know which hotel I stayed at. I had a question with that. Regardless, we stayed at a fancy hotel. We had a large meal just before that and, basically, reflecting on that whole event, I now am convinced that I was somehow given an alcoholic beverage or something to sedate me and it was a room in a high floor. It was, like, maybe the eighteenth or twentieth floor or something like that.

Regardless, there was two beds in the room and I remember waking up in the middle of the night and I was an individual that I usually arouse very easily and I was usually in control of my faculties in a very short time line. I couldn't get awake. I knew somebody was on my back. I knew there was skin to skin contact and I knew he was – I couldn't get him off. [Mike began to weep.] Excuse me.

It's okay.

Regardless, that was the first molestation.

And I'm sorry to ask that, but what do you think was done to you that night?

Oh, I think there was anal penetration and some other things. And I think, when we go to court, I think all that will come out.

And was that the only time that DeLuca ever sexually abused you?

No. The second trip was to Richmond, Virginia and it was under the – he needed to get envelopes for the Sunday collection. And, again, it was an overnight deal again. And, sorry, I can't remember too much. I thought he was going to kill me and I passed out. That's the second molestation.

Okay. We can move on. After that happened, did you ever tell anyone about the abuse?

Well, actually, I told my brother; right after this happened. And it was sort of like a Wally Cleaver, Beaver thing, you know. Don't tell anybody anything. So, I listened to my older brother. But it wasn't until I saw – and I thought I was the only one.

First of all, I didn't do anything wrong, but I saw somebody in my mind being molested. When the door was open at the rectory where DeLuca lived with the other priests. I could see. I saw a youth with his pants down and DeLuca in the room. And that's when I realized that I wasn't the only one. And at that point, I told my parents. And we got a hold of the proper authorities and Bishop Hyle. And he sent a priest to investigate.

And who is the priest that he sent to investigate?

Douglas Dempster.

Could you explain to the Court what that investigation consisted of?

He told us, after we gave him all the information, that we were forbidden to tell anybody. And it was basically an implication that you'd be excommunicated. And, again, we're all Catholic so we were coerced into a situation where we couldn't say anything to anybody. The assumption was that they'd take care of the matter.

And that was at some point in the 1960's, correct?

Correct.

Okay. And did there come a time approximately thirty years later when you reported DeLuca's sexual abuse of you to the diocese again?

-206-

I had to. My mother, again, she's in the situation here where she tells me to call this John Doe, who is not here, and just to talk to him. And I realize the phone number is out of state. And I called and he was molested. And I says, [sic] "Well, I don't understand it. You were, like, a couple years younger than I." And we got to talking and I says, "Well, how did he molest you?" And he went through this scenario. And I said, "Well, that doesn't sound like anything he did." And he said, "Well, I don't understand." He says, "That's the way Dempster was." I said, "Who said anything about Dempster?" It was Dempster who molested him!

So, at that time I said "What the heck? They sent a guy to investigate me that's also a pedophile or whatever you want to call him." So, that's when I got a hold of monsignor [Clement] Lemon and told him the story.

Monsignor Lemon is higher up in the Diocese of Wilmington?

Yes. He told me he would get back with me but he didn't get back with me. And I would imagine that's the time frame that he was questioned and released to Syracuse, New York. Allowed to take an early retirement.

And then did there come a time approximately ten years later when you learned that DeLuca was still spending time with children?

Yes.

Could you just explain to the Court what you knew then or how you came to –

I had strong suspicion and it was somebody that told me that he was seeing somebody and that he had children and – this is where I think I failed. I failed as a parent.   He was still out there. He was still molesting.

-207-

I'd been to Attorney General Jane Brady. I'd been to the news media. I'd been to quite a few different people trying to tell them DeLuca is a pedophile. He needs to be watched. And it didn't happen. And can we mention his great-nephew Mike Dingle? That's the same time frame.

Yes. Sure. And you mentioned that – did you come forward – you mentioned the AG's Office, you mentioned the news media and, for example, there were some feature stories about you in the newspaper in the 2000 range, in the 2000's at some point, right?

That's correct.

Talking about this story, right?

That's correct.

And this was long before the Child Victim's Act was enacted, correct?

Yes.

And did you ever report the abuse again to the diocese in the 2000 time frame?

Yes. And there was a matter of credibility.

Well, who did you report it to?

Well, I talked on the phone to Monsignor Cini. And again I thought it was a matter of credibility.

Why did you think it was a matter of credibility?

There was [sic] so many different things that led me to assume that he was still doing his molestations and that I needed to follow up with it myself as a parent. I needed to have a little more tenacity than I had in the past.

Okay. So, what did you do?

In regards to that? First of all, as a matter of credibility, I decided, hey, if you don't believe me, I said you have psychiatric evaluations; I'll subject myself to that. If you want to give me sodium pentothal, whatever, I'll tell you exactly what happened and how it happened and so I did have a few sessions with the Catholic Charities.

Well, how did you get the impression that you weren't being believed?

I thought it was more of a hostile scenario and there was a couple times that – and I felt like I was set up. They asked me a very loaded question. They said – Catholic Charities. And they asked me a loaded question. They said "What would you do if you knew he was still molesting?" And I said, "Well, I'd put a cap in him." And she says, "I got to report you." She says, "That's – I've got to – it's my job. I got to report you." And so, they apparently reported it to the Wilmington Police and they tried contacting me. They wanted to talk to me and this and that. And I was, like, I'm glad I never followed up with it. They didn't – nothing really came of it but –

But they called the cops on you?

Oh, yeah. Yeah.

Did they ever call the cops about DeLuca?

No.

Did Cini ever tell he was going to call the police on DeLuca?

No.

Right. Mike, could you describe to the Court some of the impact that the abuse you suffered at that young age? That that abuse has had on your life?

I'll make this as terse as possible because I know we've heard of others. Failed marriages, plural, the self-esteem, that's an obvious, the authority figure. It goes on and on and on. The relationship with my children.

I think you – did you hear me talk about some of these diagnoses from Dr. Springer about the various depressive disorders, post-traumatic stress disorder, thinks like that?

Yes.

Do you generally agree that you suffer from those kinds of things?

Well, I've heard somebody say this morning, they said, boy, I slept good last night. And I said, "Well, thank goodness for you."

Okay. And is having trouble sleeping a regular occurrence with you?

There's a cadence to it. Anytime there's anything to do with a church here or I get something from a law office or whatever, it could be a week or two weeks, it seems like there's a peak to it. There's a definite cadence to it. So, there are times that it's better than others but there's other times that, you know, here it is, 3 o'clock in the morning, you know. Might as well get up.

Given that you had reported the abuse in the 60's, in '93, sometime in the early 2000's, you went to the paper, you went to the Attorney General's Office, you went to everybody you could find, what made you finally file a lawsuit?

I think there's a window of opportunity with the legal system and I thought maybe I could have some closure with this. There was a possibility.

Was it an easy or a difficult decision for you to finally decide to bring a lawsuit?

Nothing's easy. It was hard.

And how did learning that they had filed for bankruptcy and putting a hold on the trials, how did that make you feel?

I think I need to give you an analogy. I've got a scar on my hand right here. I don't know if Your Honor can see it or not. It's got about six stitches. It happened when I was a child. It's still there. I don't feel it. I can't remember the pain associated with it. But that's my physical side. I think I got a mental side similar to it. I'm always going to have a scar. That scar's still there but every time they jerk us around, the Catholic Church, it's either somebody festers that wound or throws salt in it or something. Whether it's bankruptcy or the court date's changed or something. So, every time we change something, my wound is still open. They're still hurting me.

Could you describe for the Court what the – what every day for the last ten months has been like for you, specifically, about the abuse and things like that?

I wish I could say it's getting easier. It's not getting easier. There's got to be closure to this. We got to get the train back on the tracks. We got to get these things resolved. It's not just the people in the courtroom here. There's a lot of other people that need to have some sort of closure to this. We need to do it.

And you've never sat in a courtroom where you're a party and faced DeLuca, right?

Oh, I – that I was looking at him?

Yes.

I went to Syracuse. I saw the sentence up there. And that was when he was being criminally prosecuted for sexually abusing his great nephew Mike Dingle who is also one of the DeLuca Eight. And I saw the delay, delay and postponement and all this – they're very consistent, the church, in these matters. They really are.

All right. Does it matter to you that the trial you seek would just be DeLuca and representatives of St. John the Beloved Parish?

I think it would be in good faith and it's in the right direction.

And is the right direction somewhere towards the idea of closure?

Yes. That's what I want. I want closure. I'm sixty-two years old. I need to put this behind me.

Okay. You trust the Diocese of Wilmington?

I think the church and the Diocese of Wilmington are big business and I don't trust big business.

Do you trust the Diocese of Wilmington to do the right thing by you?

By me? No. I see myself as a threat and they'll have to take me as a business proposition, you know.

No further questions, Your Honor.

THE COURT: Thank you, sir. You may step down.

MR. THOMAS. NEUBERGER: Your Honor, we have no further witnesses to present and we rest our opposition.[443]

* * *

On the following day, August 13th, the court heard final arguments from the lawyers before announcing its decision. In part, I argued –

I have proven that the harm to my survivor clients is continuing, is grave and is irreparable. For the second time in ten months, my clients – my seven DeLuca clients – are steeling themselves mentally and physically for the endurance course they would have to run at a trial knowing full well they'll be vigorously cross-examined by parish counsel who will deny they were ever touched. There'll be medical experts who will heap calumny on their heads, who will deny they were ever injured. But these brave individuals have testified they want their day in court and that they need that day in court to begin to heal.

They want to confront DeLuca himself who is still alive and tell the jury what a monster he was, that he murdered their souls and how their local pastors and the associate priests situated with them enabled those crimes to occur. They want a jury, as the medical experts have pointed out and as they testified, to validate their histories, reject the defense theories and restore their human dignity. They want the truth to be told, the misdeeds of these remaining parishes exposed to the light of day.

But for its own tactical reasons, the diocese thinks these survivors are ping pong balls. It challenges their dignity and their human emotions. The first bounce was the abuse. The second was their refusal to believe their reports, Monsignor Cini's very recently, in the 2000s, challenging Michael Schulte or Catholic Charities calling the police on him. The third bounce was their lost October trials. The fourth bounce was the failed five-day long two-week mediation process. And the fifth bounce would be the loss of their October 25th trial dates.

They've risen to the occasion once, twice and, if the diocese has its way, who knows how many other times in the future. They're trying to roll the boulder up the hill, like Sisyphus, seeking truth, release and vindication. And they're calling on our justice system to protect them.[444]

Later that day Judge Sontchi issued his decision from the bench in open court.

THE CLERK: All rise.

THE COURT: Please be seated. I apologize for the delay. I was finalizing my thoughts. All right, what we're going to do is I'm going to make my ruling. I'm going to answer any questions of counsel. In addition I've asked my staff to have available a written version of my ruling that will be made available to the extent anyone would like it in writing during the recess.

. . .

The issue before the Court is whether to extend the previously consensual injunction preventing the abuse plaintiffs from proceeding with litigation against non-debtor parties, i.e. individuals and parishes. The automatic stay only applies to the debtor. However, the Court may extend the scope of that stay where allowing actions against non-debtors to proceed may harm the debtor's reorganization efforts. This is extraordinary relief and the defendant must meet the traditional injunction standards to prevail. One, likelihood of success on the merits; two, irreparable harm; three, balance of harms favors entering the injunction and four, the public interest favors the injunction.

. . .

The Court agrees for the most part with the plaintiffs and committee and will grant the motion in part and deny the motion in part as follows. First some comments by the Court.

-214-

One, for those unfamiliar with our bankruptcy system it may seem surprising that the debtor is still in bankruptcy approximately ten months after the case was filed. Those of us who live these cases everyday of our professional lives may in turn be surprised by their surprise. The reality is that while some cases, even large and complicated cases, proceed quite quickly, it is not surprising whatsoever that a case such as this is still in bankruptcy nor is it the fault of any party. These cases take time. Some mass tort cases take years and years to resolve. I certainly hope that will not be the case here and I will [do] what I can to expedite a resolution. But this bankruptcy will not resolve itself overnight even if the mediation on August 30 and September 1 is successful.

Two, the Court strongly supports mediation both generally and in this case. With some exceptions, I've entered an order generally staying all litigation and the bankruptcy case in general to allow the mediation to occur and to increase the likelihood of its success. Nonetheless, the case cannot be held in abeyance forever nor should it be held in abeyance at all in connection with matters that will not have an effect on the mediation.   . . .

Now my ruling. The Court finds based on the evidence on the record that one, allowing the trials and the pretrial preparations to continue in the DeLuca seven cases, i.e. those involving John Doe's Number Two, Three and Four, and Mr.'s Vai, Schulte, Sowden and Flanigan as well as the case of Mr. [Joseph] Curry will not adversely affect the mediation nor the likelihood of the mediation being successful.

Two, similarly, allowing Ms. Dougherty's case to proceed with regard to scheduling only will not adversely effect the mediation.

Three, there is a significant risk of irreparable harm to the DeLuca seven, Mr. Curry and Ms. Dougherty by a further extension of the stay.

Four, the balance of harms in the public interest favor allowing these trials and in the case of Ms. Dougherty the scheduling of her trial to go forward.

. . .

I direct debtor's counsel to prepare an order circulated among counsel and submitted under certification of counsel. In the meantime the ruling is so ordered as set forth on the record today.

Are there any questions?

MR. THOMAS NEUBERGER: On behalf of the plaintiffs, no, Your Honor.

BISHOP'S LAWYER: No questions, Your Honor.

THE COURT: Very good. Copies of this will be made available shortly. We'll take a recess.[445]

With this Judge Sontchi concluded that the "significant risk of irreparable harm" to these survivors, coupled with the public interest, dictated a rejection of the bishop's attempt to further cover-up the misdeeds of the diocese, its churches and its priests. The trials then began with John Vai whose eventual December 2010 multi-million dollar verdict rocked the premier parish in the diocese, St. Elizabeth's, and exposed the misdeeds of multiple enabling priests who assisted DeLuca in his wrongdoing.

The victory that day for all survivors was sweet. *The News Journal's* front page headline was "'DELUCA SEVEN' CAN GO TO TRIAL: Ruling raises stakes in priest abuse cases."[446] But the story was told in two simple front page pictures, one the day of the ruling by Judge Sontchi and one the day before. In one, taken on the first day of the hearings, Mary Dougherty,

-216-

Mike Schulte and Mike Sowden, along with their lawyer Stephen Neuberger, are seen

approaching the courthouse, in a heavy rain storm. Several golf umbrellas are raised high to

protect them from the elements. Mike Schulte's head is down; he is looking at his feet. Mary

looks grave, serious and concerned. Mike Sowden's look is determined.[447] In the second, taken

at the end of the next day, the sun is shining as Mary bursts out of the front courthouse door onto

the public square. One of her young daughters is behind her left shoulder holding the glass door

open for another female supporter. Mary's lawyer Tom Neuberger, looking a foot-and-a-half

taller than Mary, grey haired and rumpled, but with a wide smile, is besides her patting her on

her back. And Mary has her head cocked to the right, her arms held high pumping her fists in

the air in victory, as if she has just crossed the goal line with the winning touchdown. Her smile

is broad and triumphant. Tears are in her eyes.[448] Her message is clear. We beat them! This is

not China or Iran. This is America. With all their power, money and lawyers, we beat them! As

reported in the media, her lawyers declared that "The cover-up is over. The truth about these

crimes will be told to a jury."[449] And they soon were presented to a jury, with a resounding

result, as described in the next chapter which recounts the trial of John Vai and which the reader

can review as a juror and see the evidence against the Roman Catholic Church which the diocese

unsuccessfully sought to keep from the public.

* * *

A remarkable hidden treasure trove of evidence, which previously had been covered-up

by the church through its bankruptcy filing, was placed in the public court record for that two

day hearing before Judge Sontchi.[450]

First are three pages of church records on priest Walter D. Power, who the diocese

ordained in 1952. In a 1970 memorandum to Bishop Thomas Mardaga it was reported that in

1957 Power was stationed at St. Helena's church north of Wilmington and that at least one family had gone to the Delaware State Police to have Powers arrested on a "morals charge." A state trooper then warned coadjutor Bishop H. James Cartwright of the pending arrest and the trooper "suggested that unless immediate transfer out of State took place, Fr. Power would be served a warrant." Cartwright then "went immediately to St. Helena's and ordered Fr. Power out of State. He left at once" and was hidden out in Maryland assignments for the rest of his career until his eventual death in 1998. This document is noteworthy because it assesses whether it was safe in 1970 to return Power to the State of Delaware where he still might be subject to arrest. Here a cynical recommendation to the bishop concludes that "the likelihood of action against Fr. Power in Delaware is remote. The boys then involved would all be over 21 at this time (some 13 years later than the incident). They would hardly open the issue themselves [obviously out of fear of being attacked by the church] and their families could not do so for them since they are no longer minors."[451]

Other secret documents revealed that Power continued to be a danger to children in the church's Maryland hideouts for him. In 1964, to her credit, one nun spoke directly with Bishop Michael Hyle about her "'suspicions'" regarding Father Power." This forced the bishop to make a confidential inquiry. Doing all he could to put the situation in a light most favorable to Power, Hyle stated that "according to his testimony, Father Power disclaimed doing anything more than hugging the boys or squeezing their arms. He admits that, in view of his past history, this was improper and, to a certain extent, dangerous for him."[452] Echos of the assertion made against boys in the John Vai trial found in chapter five, that they are at fault because they present a sexual temptation to priests, also are found here. In the words of Bishop Hyle, "We must not be too ready to condemn a man because of his past; and if he is really striving to overcome a weakness of his nature, we should give him every encouragement. But on the other hand, we must help him to avoid occasions that would be dangerous to his spiritual welfare " meaning the temptations children present to helpless priests.[453]

The fact that Bishop Hyle was very active in the 1960s dealing with the cover-up of numerous priests like Power and Francis DeLuca, is revealed in another church record regarding Leonard J. Mackiewicz, who was ordained by the diocese in 1957 and died in 1994. In May of 1967 Hyle received a written plea for help from priest Edward M. Leinheiser, the pastor of Holy Rosary Church, to try to put a stop to Mackiewicz. But this plea to the bishop fell on deaf ears since Mackiewicz is the same Holy Rosary priest who tried to rape Mary Dougherty, later that summer, as she testified from the stand in Judge Sontchi's courtroom.

"Most Rev. And Dear Bishop," Leinheiser wrote,

> . . . It is my duty to inform you of a situation here that has gotten beyond my control.

> Father Mackiewicz is openly defying me and my position as pastor . . .

> Last night he took a layman up to his room on the third floor, telling me that he wanted him to help him move something, which was a lie. Tonight, while I was saying the Rosary at a Wake, he took a young high school boy up to his room. I had told him some time ago that you do not approve taking laymen to our rooms.

> You may say, why not talk it over with him. That is impossible and would end up in a fight. Father Mackiewicz absolutely hates me and everything that I stand for.

> . . . So, I turn to you for help.[454]

But help never came, and Mary Dougherty, Raymond Donahue and many others suffered a lifetime of torment as a direct result.

One of the most revealing records concerning the operation of the diocese at this time and the conduct of the priests staffing it also saw the light of day in bankruptcy court. Here priest John A. Lind was ordained by the diocese in 1960 and actually removed from his job in 1966. Church records reveal that he also was on Bishop Hyle's radar screen. An August 2, 1965, ten-page, typewritten document was presented to Judge Sontchi from church business records marked "*Confidential* to be opened only by Most Rev. Ordinary or Vicar General," [the Bishop or his chief deputy].[455] The unidentified author, obviously another diocese priest, here recounts events involving Lind from his seminary days in 1958 through 1965. They include the following incidents.

- In 1958 Lind was involved on a daily basis with sex with another male seminary student. When the anonymous author reported this to a superior he was told that he "ought not to jeopardize my position in the seminary by denouncing him as he would almost certainly retaliate."[456]

- Lind was involved sexually with two outside employees during summer vacation.

- Lind claimed that it was his confessor priest who actually started him in homosexuality on a full-time basis.

- Lind bragged that "he had successfully seduced a couple of minor seminarians."[457]

- In 1960 the author of this confidential document, after reporting Lind to another superior, again was warned not to expose him.[458]

- After Lind was ordained in 1960, the anonymous author learned from Lind "that he was seducing a number of young boys in [his first] parish" and he also was having "sex with some of the young men in the parish." Lind also took two

-220-

young boys, "his pets," to Canada on vacation with him.[459]

- In 1962 the Chancellor of the diocese himself was told directly about how dangerous Lind was but all that happened was that a few weeks later he was simply moved to another church.[460]

- After that transfer to another parish, Lind then bragged "that he was now involved sexually with boys in his new parish."[461]

- In 1963 he reported that Lind's "sex appetite seemed to be insatiable, that he had not even the trace of moral remorse," and he "spoke of having sex at least three times a day." Lind would have sex with four boys at once in his rectory bedroom, he would keep them overnight with him for sex in the rectory, and he would go to Salisbury Maryland for sex with boys also.[462]

- Lind bragged of a cot he kept in the parish school "which he used whenever he needed a more convenient place for sex play."[463]

- The writer also confessed to having sex himself with one of the boys Lind provided.[464]

- Lind then was transferred to St. Elizabeth's [a subject presented more fully in chapter five], where Lind pointed the author to his car to "check over a 'real dream' in the back seat. The reference was to a 13 year old blond lad from the parish, one of three boys in the car at the time."[465]

- He concluded his top secret document by pointing out that again a superior had prevented him from denouncing Lind and so "his depravity has continued unabated."[466]

Yet another of the diocese's secrets involved the sworn deposition testimony of survivor

Barry Lamb, taken in November 2009, which had been kept out of the public record.[467] Lamb reported victimization in gang rapes by diocesan and Norbertine priests, two student suicides resulting there from, and that a key witness in the upcoming John Vai trial had looked the other way while Barry was on his way to being sexually assaulted by another diocesan priest.

Priest Edward Dudzinski was ordained by the diocese in 1978 and he was removed in 1985. Barry Lamb was an altar boy at St. Mary Magdalen church when Dudzinski was an associate priest working there under priest Thomas Peterman,[468] the pastor there and also a key witness in the John Vai trial described in chapter five.

Barry described how in 1984 he was taken to a motel room on route 13 south of Wilmington, where on two separate occasions he and young Kevin Heaney and up to three other young boys were anally and orally gang-raped by Dudzinski, priest Timothy Mullin (a Norbertine stationed at Archmere Academy), and two other men. Kevin Heaney and one of the other boys both later committed suicide.[469] Mullin in 1997 became the sixth headmaster at Archmere Academy for the Norbertines[470] who are discussed more fully in chapter two. Ironically, Mullin is now deceased and a building at Archmere is named in his memory.

Priest Peterman, who previously served as the assistant pastor at St. Elizabeth's, was the principal of its high school and a key witness in the subsequent John Vai trial where he denied all knowledge that young John was a repeated victim of Francis DeLuca in the very rectory where Peterman also lived. This behavior is consistent with Barry Lamb's memory of Peterman turning away when he saw Dudzinski leading Lamb up the rectory stairs to his second floor bedroom, where three other priests lived and where Barry was often sexually abused by Dudzinski.[471]

Concerning prior diocese business records on Dudzinski, they warned years earlier of the danger he posed. One 1976 evaluation of him by his priest supervisor, while he was a priest-in-training for the diocese, reported that "Ed had stayed up late, having the teenage president of the C.Y.O. stay over in the rectory."[472] A 1977 report on him also warned of a strong complaint by a mother about Dudzinski's "relationship with her son" and that "the woman was feeling pressured by Ed." An overnight fishing trip with another young boy also was reported and the supervisor concluded that "I see a pattern in Ed's ministry where he has a need to be with young boys and has often given me seemingly legitimate reasons for being with them. While gut feelings are difficult to document, I find that this incident allows me to recommend that Ed seek counsel from Dr. Lugar."[473] When it came time in August 1977 to determine whether Dudzinski should be ordained a priest of the diocese, his pastor and supervisor "who has been working closely with Dudzinski, is not prepared to make a positive recommendation."[474] None of this protected Barry Lamb and other survivors of Dudzinski for he still was ordained in this diocese, which had an historic manpower shortage of priests, to the detriment of his many victims.

Regarding the never ending cover-up, as Judge Sontchi would later succinctly observe, the key questions to be answered were, "what happened, what did the Church hierarchy know and when did they know it, and, finally, what did the Church do about it? The answer was too often that they knew much and did little – all of it in secret."[475]

* * *

Things only got worse for the Bishop and his lawyers in the bankruptcy proceedings after the August hearings. Judge Sontchi was clearly on to them and their devices and steadfastly refused to place his thumb on the scales of justice unfairly in the favor of the Bishop or to approve unreasonable delays.

Despite the fact that a settlement was reached in February 2011 after the Vai trial victory, matters dragged on and on. Finally, on May 20, 2011 in open court, Judge Sontchi made it clear that his patience with the unnecessary and hurtful delays had come to an end. Survivor attorney Robert Jacobs had pleaded that "it is imperative for the survivors that this come to an end. Some had died already without an apology from the diocese, some are sick and others – their widows are still waiting for an apology. . . . my clients are out there in limbo and I think it is unfair."[476] Judge Sontchi responded:

> THE COURT: Well, in Bankruptcy Court, a week equals about three months in the real world. And we're all used to operating at a breakneck pace. Usually that is because there are business realities that are driving a case and, as a result, speed is often necessary. The Catholic Diocese of Wilmington isn't, for really anybody's understanding, a business. With that said, there are other equities in play here as to having this case reach confirmation *as soon as possible.*
>
> First of all, it was filed in 2009, October 2009, and we're not that far away from the second year anniversary of the case. Also, you have a large constituency here which is the abuse survivors who – many of whom are older, many of whom suffered abuse in the 60s, the 70s and had to – or these people on their behalf had to lobby in order to get the statute of limitations expanded, had to go through the process of filing complaints, many had to go through the process of litigation and in these cases – some have come to trial and some are on the verge of trial as of the time the case was filed.
>
> And I think it is not at all insignificant that *every day is important in connection with getting this thing resolved* (emphasis supplied).[477]

Despite this clear message to conclude having been delivered in judicially appropriate language, the Bishop in the weeks that followed still sought further delay by attempting to secure

-224-

the right, when he eventually exited the supervision, confines and strictures of the bankruptcy court, to pay pensions or other monies to living predator priests to make life easier for them. He also attempted to punish the lead attorneys for the survivors who had fought him so hard over the years by denying them certain protections found in the bankruptcy laws, unless they recanted and withdrew various court papers which had pointed out some of the more notorious and embarrassing misbehavior of the church.

Judge Sontchi slammed down these efforts in strong judicial language twice finding that the diocese was acting in "bad faith," which in bankruptcy court was the equivalent of dropping a hydrogen bomb on their legal camp. Because of these bad faith findings, the survivors could have demanded that the entire bankruptcy be dismissed as the fraud that it actually was. The next step would have been obtaining multi-million dollar state court judgments against diocese and parish assets, eventually resulting in the sale of their vast land holdings and other treasures. I was ready to take this step.

As far as providing pensions for child rapists, while at the same time giving their victims next to nothing because the diocese was pleading poverty, Judge Sontchi saw right through that ruse as well. He stated: "You're seeking confirmation of a plan that impairs abused survivors claims and un-impairs abuser priests' claims? You're seeking that. And that's the point."[478]

By July 14, 2011 Judge Sontchi had had enough, and he came down hard on the Bishop and his army of attorneys and other supporters.

THE COURT: All right. Well, to that point, this is most of the time a commercial court and certainly many of the decisions that this Court makes affect real people who are living lives, many of which are in economic uncertainty. And it's sometimes difficult for the person to make their living and [who] live in this courtroom to

-225-

remember that and we throw around hundreds of millions and sometimes billions of dollars in here and it's just simply – becomes a habit. So, I certainly don't hold any personal issue with [the Bishop's lawyer's] comment. It's easy for us who live here to make those kinds of mistakes. But that leads me to my ruling on this issue which is *that this is not a commercial case.* And in my experience as a practitioner and as a judge *it is truly unique.*

This case certainly involves money because our civil system uses money as the way to compensate persons for actions, tort actions, other contract claims, et cetera. The way we deal with dealing – the way we deal with providing some sort of recompense to people who have been injured is money. So, it does – it does involve dollars; there's no question. But it involves a kind of action that go beyond money and it is, perhaps, a flaw in our system that the remedy of money damages for some of these types of abuse is cold comfort and ultimately inadequate. So I keep that in mind or I try to keep that in mind when I make rulings in this case sometimes unsuccessfully and there are certainly issues in front of the Court where the – it's more routine as we would normally see in bankruptcy as opposed to more not in our routine.

And I think this issue of allowing future financial payments, however they are characterized, to the priests who have been acknowledged by the Diocese to be abusers is an issue not just of economics and not just of the technicalities of the Bankruptcy Code. *I think it goes to the very heart of this case.* I'm not making a moral judgment on what kind of charity should be given by anybody. But I have in front of me a civil entity, which is the Catholic Diocese of Wilmington, a corporation that is in bankruptcy and is seeking a discharge of its liabilities and confirmation of a plan that treats different types

-226-

of creditors in different ways. I have in front of me what are called the nondebtor

Catholic entities, the civil entities, who are receiving releases under the plan of

reorganization. And then they're asking this Court for a simple and perfectly appropriate

civil remedy which is application of the Bankruptcy Code as a debtor-in-possession to

receive confirmation of a plan and releases under that plan.

One of the requirements that the debtor has to make and approve to get confirmed

is that the debtor is operating in good faith; that's under 1129(a)(3). And I have an

independent duty as the judge to make the findings under 1129 in order to confirm a plan.

And again, 1129(a)(3) is that the plan is proposed in good faith.

However, this plan impairs, albeit consensually, abuse survivors and it doesn't

impair among others the abuser priests. It goes on to reserve the right as provided for in

the Code to use its post-reorganization property as it sees fit. Under the unique

circumstances of this case, however, I find that doing so, reserving the right to make

payments to the abuser priests while impairing claims of abuse survivors in asking for

that *the debtor is not proposing a plan in good faith* and I cannot make an 1129(a)(3)

finding that allows that.

The language proposed by Mr. Neuberger in his brief, I think with some

tweaking, would solve the issue for the debtor but I'm not here to – to negotiate. My

concern is that a plan that allows the debtor going forward to use property belonging to

the reorganized debtor or the nondebtor Catholic entities to make any financial payment

whatsoever to any of these abuser priests. *I'm not going to confirm a plan unless there is*

some sort of prohibition on that because I don't think the debtor would be operating in

good faith. And that's my ruling on that point.

On the exculpation provision, I'm prepared to rule on that unless –

MR. THOMAS. NEUBERGER: Yes, Your Honor.

THE COURT: – there's anything further.

BISHOP'S LAWYER: Well, Your Honor had asked to identify the docket items at issue but if Your Honor is prepared to rule without identifying them.

THE COURT: I had – I looked at it during our break – four of them which were the ones referenced in your memo.

BISHOP'S LAWYER: Your Honor, I think the only one not referenced in the memo was Docket Item 189. It was a joinder that doesn't itself isn't – itself teed up for any sort of hearing.

THE COURT: All right. Well, I'm prepared to rule on that.

I think that the debtor's request for exculpation for everyone except the Neuberger firm and the Jacobs firm based on their refusal to withdraw certain pleadings is problematic. I'm not sure it reaches a first amendment free speech type of issue but really I think it goes to what I just touched upon which is whether the debtors engaged in good faith and for proposing a plan that allows some professionals and doesn't allow other professionals to receive exculpation based on advocacy.

If we have to withdraw every pleading filed in this case where somebody said something unkind about somebody else, I think we'd take care of the whole docket, all right. This is the type of thing that goes on, albeit perhaps somewhat frustratingly sometimes for the Court given the history of the relationships here.

Frankly, I wasn't particularly disturbed by anything in those pleadings nor did I find them particularly offensive.

So, here's your choice, either exculpate everybody or nobody gets exculpated. It's your decision. I'm not asking you to respond right now but that's – I'll confirm a plan with either. . . .

THE COURT: You either include the Neuberger and Jacobs firm or nobody gets exculpation including the debtor.

BISHOP'S LAWYER: Understood.

THE COURT: It's your call (emphasis supplied).[479]

The last gasp was on September 9, 2011. The insurance carriers had refused to put up their contributions to the overall settlement fund. At a court hearing over this obstruction to the relief which the survivors had earned, Judge Sontchi strongly spoke to this sabotage. [The Court could find them in contempt of court for their actions, if necessary. Of course, that meant they risked imprisonment and fines.] They quickly backed down.

THE COURT: Okay. All right. Okay. All right, I'm ready to rule. . . . And I am *flabbergasted* and disappointed that the insurers would destroy that settlement, blow up this case, on a technicality. . . . I also find that *any delay* of payments to abuse survivors which require the funding by the insurance companies into the trust would inflict significant, perhaps irrevocable, harm on the abuse survivors. And there is a substantial probability that if the settlement date passes and the confirmation order is vacated, that the settlement, that is the result of so many hours of work, would disappear, would be blown up[480] (emphasis supplied).

. . .

While I understand the legal argument of the insurers, I think it's probably one of the clearest examples I've seen in my career of someone asserting form over substance.

-229-

And frankly, it's the kind of thing that lawyers do that make non-lawyers have the opinion that they do of lawyers. I guess, it's the kindest way to put it.[481]

* * *

In February of 2011, two months after he saw the handwriting on the wall when the John Vai trial jury assessed $3,000,001 in damages against his flagship church, St. Elizabeth's, the bishop agreed to pay $77,425,000 into a fund for survivors. This later was coupled with another $24,862,500 which came shortly thereafter from the Oblates, who also recognized the doom awaiting them in state court. These initial funds were distributed to 152 survivors by mid-October 2011. Eventually another $8,000,000 was received from the Capuchin religious order of priests, which was distributed in March 2012. The total fund recovered here was $110,287,500. So with the impartial assistance and fairness of Judge Sontchi, this business court had seen that some modicum of justice was received by survivors, to the chagrin and unhappiness of the bishop, the religious orders and their legal allies.

5

The Trial of John Michael Vai

Following the decision of Judge Sontchi and the federal bankruptcy court, John Vai's long delayed trial began with jury selection and opening statements before President Judge James T. Vaughn, Jr. on October 25, 2010, in the spacious ceremonial courtroom of the Kent County Courthouse located on Dover's historic Green. It then moved for its duration to the cramped confines of courtroom 7 located on the second-floor of that antiquated and overcrowded 1874 courthouse. A courthouse dispensing justice has been located on this site since 1699 near the historic hangman's tree where public executions were held years ago. During the course of John Vai's six-and-a-half week trial, the original sixteen jurors (twelve members and four alternates) were whittled down to seven men and five women who reached a verdict on December 8, 2010.

Looking at the cramped courtroom from the rear of the visitor's section, one could see the judge's bench elevated above the court, but the jurors were visible only in profile. After entering in procession from the jury room off the rear, they sat in two rows against the far right wall. The blinds on a window behind them were pulled against the sun, and the courtroom clock above their heads steadily ticked off the hours.

Directly across from the jurors, on the opposite wall, was an array of audio-visual equipment to be used during the trial.

About three feet in front of and perpendicular to the right side of the jury box sat the cramped attorney tables. A two-foot wide podium had been placed between those tables. The defense sat to the left of the podium; John Vai and one of his lawyers sat on the right, almost in the jury's laps. A lawyer needing to approach a witness or the judge had to turn sideways to squeeze through the narrow space between that table and the jury box in order to enter the well of the court.

Behind the lawyer's table was a row of chairs to seat a few more lawyers and their assistants. A wooden rail separated them from the public area which consisted of four rows of hard wooden church-like pews. There the curious and the supportive endured discomfort as they watched the proceedings. Gates at either end of the rail allowed entry into where the action unfolded.

To the judge's right as he faced the lawyers was the witness stand. To his left was another witness stand from which his staff worked, and spread before him at their tables were the court reporter and courthouse staff from the clerk's office, known in Delaware by the patriarchal ecclesiastical term of *prothonotary*.

October 26

A Southern gentleman with the skill, humility, keen eye and understanding of human nature found in country lawyer Atticus Finch in Harper Lee's 1960 novel *To Kill A Mockingbird*, Thomas C. Crumplar also reminds you of Gregory Peck who portrayed Atticus in the 1962 movie of the same name. A University of Virginia law graduate, dignified in his bow tie and sometimes glasses, Crumplar's appearance can easily disarm and deceive an unprepared witness. But beneath his gentle, polite well mannered exterior beats the heart of a tenacious trial lawyer. Once Tom takes on a client and a case, he never lets go. Famous for his extraordinary work ethic and devotion to his clients, he searches everywhere for new nuggets of evidence with which to build his case and attack the defendant. He is unflappable in the courtroom, his gladiatorial arena. Each move, each question is calculated to a predetermined end. An instrument of truth, always seeking justice for those injured by the powerful, in his final argument he would paint the big picture and assemble the puzzle pieces for the jury.

The day after the jury was selected, on October 26th day two of the trial began with President Judge James T. Vaughn addressing the jury.

THE COURT: All right. Ladies and gentlemen, we're going to begin with the opening statements of counsel. The opening statements are not part of the evidence in the case. The evidence is what you will hear from witnesses and exhibits that are introduced. The opening statements are the attorney's opportunity, at the outset of the case, to give you some information about the case that would be helpful to you as you listen to the evidence. We will begin with the plaintiff.[482]

MR. CRUMPLAR: Thank you, Your Honor.

Ladies and gentlemen of the jury, this case is the story of a young innocent boy, Johnny Vai, shown here in his school picture as he had just turned fourteen. [Here Crumplar pointed to the video screen and a color photograph of young Johnny appeared. He was far different from the wounded older man sitting an arms length from the jury. In the photo, he was boyish and unsullied, with a pinkish complexion, blue eyed, and with close-cropped brown wavy hair. He was dressed in his Sunday best, wool jacket, white button down shirt with a black and maroon paisley tie.] It was the fall of 1966, and Johnny Vai's life was full of joy, hope, and promise. This life, however, was soon to come to a very abrupt and tragic end. The reason why Johnny Vai's life that was so full of joy, hope, and promise, as shown here, would soon take a dramatic and horrible turn for the worse; the reason why his life would never be the same; the reason why he would be forever scarred, confined to live a life of the living dead – is because this also is the story of the conscious indifference of a corporate defendant known as St. Elizabeth's which repeatedly allowed monsters to prey on young innocent boys such as Johnny Vai. Because of the choice this corporate defendant made, young Johnny Vai's life which, in the fall of 1966, was so full of joy, hope, and promise – because of their mistake, their choices, his life had become one full of nightmares, nightmares which continue to this very day.

To better understand this tragedy, we need to begin here, at 1108 South Broom Street, Wilmington, Delaware." [A black and white picture of a modest brick, two-story row home appeared on the screen.] "This was Johnny Vai's home for the first eighteen years of his life. It's where his elderly mother, in her late '80s, still lives. He grew up here with his father, mother, and his three brothers. His parents were both immigrants from Italy who had come to this country on the same boat. Although they didn't know each other previously, they met for the first time on the boat. His mother was an orphan; his father was traveling with his mother. And his grandmother basically took a liking to this young girl who was traveling all by herself, at age fourteen, on the boat. In fact, she wasn't even allowed to get on the boat unless there was a sponsor. And this lady took an interest and said: "I will take you." She was interested in that little boy; but that other little boy wasn't very interested in her.

Sure enough, many years later, they got together, got married, moved to Wilmington, and tried to start the American dream. They both worked very hard. Johnny's father had three jobs. His mother worked part-time as a seamstress. All for a better life for their children. Their neighborhood was full of the same kind of neat row houses full of families who, although from different ethnic backgrounds, shared one thing in common. They all belonged to St. Elizabeth's Roman Catholic Church; a magnificent structure, one of the largest churches in all of Delaware. [A majestic color photograph of the five-story towering limestone and marble church, the largest of over fifty-seven churches in the entire diocese, and which seats thousands, appeared on the screen.] This church was the center of the life for the Vai family. Saturday was confession; Sunday was church. The rest of the week was one church function after another. Johnny's father was a Knight of Columbus. His mother was on the altar committee. Johnny and his three brothers all attended St. Elizabeth's Elementary School. They only walked two blocks to the school, to the church. At the school where he went – from first grade to eighth grade, and then through high school, there was no kindergarten at this time – they were taught by nuns and by priests.

Speaking of priests, I need to pause for a moment to talk about the role of a priest in the life of the Vai family and others in the St. Elizabeth's community in the 1960s. A priest then was a person set apart. He spoke a strange language at the church, Latin. He had awesome and seemingly supernatural powers. He had the ability – and this is what they were taught – to turn ordinary wine and bread into the blood and body of Jesus Christ when he said the mass. It seemed that he held the keys to the kingdom, whether

-235-

you got into heaven or went to hell. He was truly next to God. Therefore, it was a great honor when a priest showed a particular interest in a family and, especially, in one of their sons.

In the Vai home, as was common in those days in a large Catholic family, there was one boy who the mother really put into her heart: Maybe he would be a priest. This young boy was Johnny Vai. He soon became an altar boy. [A color picture of Johnny appeared, his head encircled, with six other altar boys marching in the foreground from left to right in a sacred procession, with two mothers overseeing in the background. Hands folded at the waist pointing up to heaven, Johnny and three others were dressed in black full length robes with a white cassock over top. They looked like miniature Roman Catholic priests. The four young boys before him were dressed more like Roman Catholic bishops or cardinals. They wore red skull caps and red full length robes and white capes. A white sash served each as a belt.]

And there we see him – right there with the circle – being trained, learning his Latin. Life for Johnny Vai – when he was not studying at school, not learning Latin, to be an altar boy – was great. The picture that Johnny Vai, now John Vai, will tell you of that community was: You knew everyone. Even though he was Italian, and they had Irish and Germans, they were all from St. E's. That's how they identified themselves, that was the community. It was a great place, a feeling of safety. You walked to the school. [A picture of the main front doors of the two-story red brick church school appeared on the screen.] You walked to the church. There was a great park right across from the school, Canby Park, huge swimming pool, tennis courts, baseball fields; an ideal place for a kid.

As I say, it wasn't all work. [A black and white picture of a carnival appeared next, – with a Ferris Wheel and other rides just for a quarter.] We can also remember – again, this is a representation of a church carnival in the 1960s. St. E's had a church carnival, a special thing that you would look forward to.

Then one day, in late winter in 1966, a priest in his mid-30s showed up at St. Elizabeth's. Now, it was a little different then because, usually, priests who were transferred in from another parish – they usually taught at the church school. And because school begins in September and ends in June, usually you would have the transfer of priests in June or July so you wouldn't disrupt who was teaching what at school. However, DeLuca, unlike most of the other priests, showed up suddenly one day in late February. [Here the jury caught its first glimpse of the now aged and unrepentant Francis J. DeLuca in a 1960s professional color photo of him in his black suit and Roman collar against an all white background.]

But he seemed to be a regular priest to the Vai family, and he had a special charm. He had an ability to make everybody feel they were very important, that he cared about them. And this priest, Reverend Francis J. DeLuca, soon took a special interest in the Vai family. [Crumplar motioned to a picture of a happy young bride and her groom, the one veiled and dressed in white with her hands holding her bouquet and a rosary, and the other standing proud in his tuxedo, both on either side of a smiling young Francis DeLuca dressed in his long black cassock standing before a church altar.] We see that spring he is marrying Johnny Vai's cousin. That's DeLuca in the middle. And there is young John Vai at that wedding ceremony. [Crumplar pointed next to a picture of Johnny as a junior groomsman, all dressed up standing next to a junior bridesmaid before

-237-

that same church altar.] Father DeLuca had soon begun to play an important part. Even more significant, Father DeLuca was spending a lot of time at the Vai household. His parents felt a special bond to them. If you recall, I said both of Johnny Vai's parents were first generation immigrants from Italy. It turns out Francis DeLuca's parents had come from Italy too. Mrs. Vai felt: Here is this priest, all of a sudden, a sign, he didn't know anybody. He is interested in us; let's invite him over. And she was just beside herself. A priest. And there were, you will hear, over a thousand families at St. Elizabeth's. There were very few priests. For a priest to ever deign to come to your house was like a blessing from God, and especially for a priest to show an interest in one of your young boys. Especially the young boy that you had thought might one day be a priest. What a wonderful chance to mentor young Johnny Vai. What a wonderful chance to teach him the ways of the priesthood.

Little did Mr. and Mrs. Vai know – or any of the other family members or families at St. Elizabeth's – that the spider was beginning to weave his web. He was ready to set his trap. What was soon going to begin is what is known by those who study pedophilia behavior as the grooming process. He had found a boy who wanted to be a priest. More importantly, he found a mother who wanted her boy to be a priest. He had the opportunity, and now he carefully began to set the trap. Part of the grooming process is to start to shower gifts on this young boy. You have to think about this. This is a hard working family, blue collar family. Here is the first picture of Johnny Vai, the same picture I showed you earlier. This suit, this tie, from Father DeLuca; the first jacket he had ever owned in his life. He was very proud when he wore that. The old Mullins store, Clothiers since 1862, – is where DeLuca went and bought him that, the beginning of the grooming process. Now, you have a fine young man; he has a coat and tie. And, in fact, you will hear DeLuca started even teaching him table manners. Here is a picture of the Green Room in the Hotel du Pont, the finest restaurant in the State of Delaware. The Vai family had never set foot in there. DeLuca took young Johnny Vai there. His mother would brag to everyone: My son is going to be a proper gentleman; he is going to be a priest. [A professional photo of young Johnny appeared on the screen, done by Delaware's most exclusive photographer at the time, Willard Stewart, master photographer. Johnny stands smiling, unknowing what dark future faces him, in a different suit this time, wearing a striped Ivy League tie with his button down white shirt, as he looks out at you, one hand is in his left pocket while the other rests gently on the back of a buttoned office leather chair.] Again, this is – still in Wilmington. Although it's no longer a photography studio, taking him up to Stewart Studios to get an expensive portrait which DeLuca then gave to Mrs. Vai at this time. The grooming process had begun.

Now it's the early fall of 1966. Father DeLuca had been a priest at St. Elizabeth's for more than six months. Now, a new pastor, Monsignor Donohoe, had just taken over at St. Elizabeth's. DeLuca decided to make his move to test out the new pastor and the rest of his fellow priests at St. Elizabeth's to see if he could get away with it. Here is how – to see if he could get away with his dark side. He was a serial pedophile, and he was going to strike soon. Now, DeLuca was not only the priest, not only the one that they would see at mass, not only the one that would help Johnny Vai as an altar boy. But he was also assigned by the pastor and the principal of the school – if you recall, I showed St. Elizabeth's had a school. One interesting thing about St. Elizabeth's, and different than most other parishes – in fact, I think there were only two other parishes in all of the

Diocese of Wilmington which had fifty-seven parishes – most of them tried to have, but

not all of them, elementary schools. Because they said if you could afford it, even if you

couldn't at that time, every Catholic family was supposed to send their kids to school.

Most people went at least into – from first grade to eighth grade. After that, the financial

burden was such that many times people would go to public school; and most parishes

didn't have a high school. But St. Elizabeth's – that's why I said it was one of the largest,

most significant churches in all of Delaware. Many of the churches only had a pastor.

They had a pastor, and at least three other assistant pastors. St. Elizabeth's had a high

school. This is also relevant because I mentioned to you that Johnny Vai had three other

brothers. The other brothers – one was older, two were younger – all of them ended up

going to public school. Again, he was the chosen one. It was important that he continue

with Catholic school, especially if he was going to become a priest. So the family

continued to sacrifice. Well, who was his religion teacher in ninth grade? Very

impressionable. Somebody who is going to spend a special amount of time with the

children. Yes, I am afraid you have guessed it, Francis DeLuca was his religion teacher.

Early that fall, in 1966, DeLuca had hatched his plan. He decided he was going to

take a couple of chosen boys on a trip to New York City. [A photo of New York from

the New Jersey side appeared.] In the class, he announced that he wanted Johnny Vai

and two other boys to go. A little unusual because you will hear testimony from the

former bishop of Wilmington that the rule that was always in place is: A priest would

never take a boy by himself, unaccompanied, without a chaperone. Yet, they allowed

him to do it. The first of many times that the policies and rules designed to protect children were ignored time and time again. The result of which was that Johnny Vai and others were abused time and time again. You can imagine that all of the boys' mothers said: Well, if the school says it's all right and, more importantly, if the priest says it's all right – if the pastor, who has to control the comings and goings of the priests, does not oppose it, why are we to oppose it? We will be talking about this. The priests are on duty – it's like the military, it's 24/7. There is no time off. All of your comings and goings are controlled by the pastor. So, sure enough, Johnny Vai, two other boys, headed up to New York City. You have to imagine the special treat this was. This boy had never really been outside of Wilmington, [except] maybe crossing the line into Pennsylvania. He was going back to the very place where his mother and father arrived in the 1930s to start their life in America; how excited the family was.

Of course, Catholic boys that they were, they went to St. Patrick's Cathedral. [A black and white aerial shot of that massive neo-Gothic church emerged with its two tall spires reaching to the heavens.] Again, part of the whole thing. Let's go to one of the seats of Catholicism in America. And DeLuca, part of the grooming process – he did not scrimp in terms of money – had him at one of the fanciest hotels in New York, the Americana hotel. In 1962 this opened up. [This massive Seventh Avenue skyscraper hotel loomed up on the screen surrounded by other tall edifices.] A modern hotel, very dazzling. Shows, other things that you do in New York; it was a great day. DeLuca and the boys, after a busy day, came back to the room. He said: We need to go to sleep. We're going to have another busy day tomorrow; go to sleep. The door was closed, the sign was put in, and everyone went to sleep. [A " DO NOT DISTURB " sign on a door knob was projected.]

While Johnny was dozing off, thinking what a wonderful life it is. Life was so great last year, but now it's so much better. Father DeLuca has an interest in me. Yes, I am certain I want to be a priest. As he began to go to sleep, and the other boys were sleeping, Johnny Vai suddenly felt something on top of him; it had pinned him down. He couldn't get up. It was slowly moving up and down against his body. He was petrified. What is this? What is happening to me? And then he realized what this thing was; it was Francis DeLuca. Johnny was now not only afraid; he was confused beyond belief. This thing that looked and smelled like DeLuca then started moving faster and faster, breathing heavier and heavier. And, then, Johnny felt something wet across his body; and it was over. DeLuca got up and simply said: "Go to sleep." The next morning DeLuca was his same old self, as if nothing had happened; but something had. Johnny returned to his Wilmington home and, at first, life seemed to go back to normal; but it didn't last very long. Father DeLuca soon called his home and said he wanted Johnny to come over to the rectory to help out. His mother was delighted, and encouraged. Now she said, young Johnny move along, you can't keep Father waiting.

[At this point Crumplar walked over to a black and white projection of a rather unattractive two-story cinder block and mortar residence with a large porch and front door, opening up to an inner courtyard behind St. Elizabeth's church. Six windows spread across the front of the dwelling. Then a dark interior hallway appeared where more than a dozen steps with a bannister cast a dark shadow and lead up to a second-floor where bedrooms were located. And there, in a corner, was the closed door of the room which DeLuca had occupied. Ninety degrees to the left of that door was the doorway of the priest bedroom next door to DeLuca.]

-242-

Let's take a moment. This is the rectory at St. Elizabeth's, a term you may not be familiar with. At St. Elizabeth's – and, again, we talked about – being a priest is not like many other jobs; it is a 24/7 job. Like you are in the military, they tell you where to live, when to go to work, when you are off work. In fact, you are never off work; they control your vacation. And all of the priests – the pastor and the other priests all lived in this rectory. This is right next to St. Elizabeth's church, right next to the school. Now, at the rectory – and you will hear the rules that were enforced here in Wilmington and elsewhere, and at St. Elizabeth's, those were the rules that were clear. Unfortunately, at St. Elizabeth's, we'll find out they were not enforced as they dealt with Father DeLuca. You see on the first floor, there was the public area of the rectory where an office was found. People – if they wanted to speak to the priest, they would go there. You *never* went upstairs; that was the *private* area, that was the priest quarters. And in fact, you will hear various church officials say: Why was there such a rule? The rule is there to protect kids.

However, Johnny Vai that day was told by DeLuca: I want you to come up. He comes up the dark stairs, and then enters Father DeLuca's bedroom. And in the room Johnny Vai realized that what happened in New York was not a dream; it was a real nightmare. And it was going to happen again and again. For the next three years it happened again and again. This young fourteen-year-old boy who knew nothing about sex – again, remember the time, especially the culture, it's not talked about at all – was soon going to be the subject of masturbation, oral sex, and anal rape time and time again. The location might change, although it was usually in the rectory in Father DeLuca's room. His room first was room number two. And you will see that he testifies throughout his time he switched from room to room. Sometimes it was on a trip, just like the trip to New York. But other times it was on a trip to Washington, D.C., Rehoboth Beach, and Wildwood, New Jersey. While the location might change, the abuse never did.

DeLuca is a classic pedophile priest. You will hear testimony next week from Dr. David Springer who, in addition to being a board certified psychiatrist, for over eight years served as medical director at St. John Vianney, a treatment facility where priests who have problems with alcoholism or sexual abuse go there. He will testify that classic pedophiles – it's denial; that's how they live with themselves. And if they are caught so that you can see that the proof is irrefutable, then they will just try to minimize the amount of abuse. They will never say it's anal sex. They will hardly ever say it's oral sex. Masturbation maybe. But it's more of a: I was just being friendly and hugging. You will see that when you hear the testimony of Francis DeLuca.

Let me just pause here. I mean, there are two defendants in this case, Francis DeLuca, and his employer St. Elizabeth's. Francis DeLuca is, was and still is a defendant in this case. [Tom looked over to where DeLuca was supposed to sit, but he had fled and refused to attend trial. So no one was there.] We took his – what is called a discovery deposition to try to find out what he would say when we got to put him on the stand. He is supposed to be here today, but he is not here today. He is in New York; and I don't think we'll be able to get him here today. So we may be stuck with simply listening to two discovery depositions. But in those depositions he will admit – and you will hear a little portion of one before I close that, yes, indeed he abused Johnny Vai. But he will try to hem and haw and say: Well, you know, I remember in the rectory one time. It almost

-244-

didn't really seem like anything. Oh, I never took him on trips. Well, then again, remember what Dr. Springer said. But when you confront them with the evidence – and we, fortunately, had this piece of evidence. Not from Johnny Vai, he tried to destroy everything that was associated with DeLuca. We'll get to this later. His mother saved some things.

[Crumplar now projected on the screen several 1960s pictures of young boys at the beach, bare-chested in their swimsuits. On the back of them each of the boys' names were handwritten. Pointing he said,]

This is another boy – remember the name Bobby Quill – who happened to have a book, a book that DeLuca made, which we now know is his trophy book, where DeLuca put pictures of boys. Right here. See in the middle, that's Johnny Vai. Right here. This is DeLuca's handwriting. DeLuca admitted in his deposition it's Wildwood, New Jersey, 1967. We have another. This is a Polaroid. This is, again, DeLuca. Summer – it's blanked out – I believe it was '68, Wildwood, four boys. Johnny Vai is the one – you can see the hand there; but DeLuca has written the name. Again, very consistent with what Johnny Vai says in terms of the abuse.

Johnny Vai was now trapped. He wanted to escape. He wanted to tell somebody. He wanted to make it all stop. But DeLuca was his teacher, his priest; no one would believe him. Again, back at that time period, you were taught to never speak ill of the priest; that would be like blaspheming God. And, more importantly, the other priests did nothing when DeLuca brazenly took him into his room time and time again. So young Vai basically only could survive by turning into a zombie. Every time he had to walk up those stairs in the rectory, he pretended he was dead; it was not real. And he pushed the

-245-

memories of that abuse deeper and deeper into his subconsciousness. All along, his mother thought nothing was amiss. And DeLuca has two faces; one, the abuser in secret, and the other the family friend.

June 1967, this is a birthday card which his mother saved and treasured. It reads "Johnny: This comes today to say hello, and bring a wish as well, that you have a birthday that is just like you, just swell, Father D." "Father D" is how he signs it. 1968, here is another card on his 16th birthday. And again, it just gives you chills. He says – "I am the living bread that has come down from heaven. Your intentions will be remembered by me at mass, and in my prayers, and in my communion on your 16th birthday, sincerely Father D."

June '69 DeLuca is transferred to another parish; but he returns time and time again to St. Elizabeth's. Another thing in his sworn deposition, he denied that he ever came back to St. Elizabeth's. But we happen to have Johnny Vai's high school yearbook that his mother had saved. Right here. [Crumplar opened two pages of the 1970 yearbook on the screen.] Think about this for a second. High school years really sometimes, especially junior and senior year, are one of the most wonderful years in somebody's life. I mean, you are a young person full of promise. You don't have to support yourself yet; I mean, things are great. Think about this when you hear John Vai testify. His high school time is blank. He remembers nothing about it other than the abuse. Now, why? Because everything in his high school is associated with DeLuca, even when DeLuca left his senior year. Junior, senior prom, Johnny Vai's first real date. He has repressed it; tried to put it past him, imagined it doesn't exist. He is there, and who does he see? There he is. There is DeLuca [pointing to him in a picture greeting
-246-

students entering with their dates]. Circle around him, shaking hands. The person next to him is Father Peterman, who lived next door to DeLuca. You will hear Father Peterman testify, and then we have Father Cini. He is there in the second circle shaking hands.

Ring day. You will see this exhibit. But it says right here: "Senior ring day is probably the most long-awaited day in the life of a senior. A participated, concelebrated mass, a most delicious luncheon, and an enjoyable dinner and evening are remembered as senior ring day." And who was the guest speaker at senior ring day? There he is, two pictures of him, Francis DeLuca; Johnny Vai's tormentor. And, finally, graduation. Look at this picture [pointing to a color photo of a grim faced John standing outside the doors of the church with his smiling mother and a smiling DeLuca]. Here is a question: Who is not smiling in this picture? Yes. Remember, just a few years before, this boy was smiling, so full of hope, and promise. There he is now, unsmiling standing next to his tormentor who is smiling like the spider who has gotten his prey, next to John Vai and his mother.

I talked a little bit ago about how Johnny Vai coped with this horrible, horrible tragedy. And he did it in a common way that people who experience horrible tragedy do. Johnny Vai, or now John Vai, has been diagnosed as having posttraumatic stress syndrome; that's something that happens when you are in combat, a horrible event, or you are involved in a crime scene. I mean, all of a sudden, a robber has attacked you, you have been attacked; many times you have a posttraumatic stress. And sometimes, when the stress is so horrible, the only way the mind can survive is to push it down as deep into the unconsciousness as possible. Dr. Springer will be talking about it, that this is a recognized thing. I also have right here the Bible of psychiatry, a medical book we will learn about, the DSM-IV.

Johnny Vai pushed it down. This is like a volcano, but a dormant volcano. [A color photo appeared of a large volcano on some tropical island without any smoke coming out of its top.] That's how John Vai from 1966 until 2007, with one or two brief exceptions, appeared to everybody; quite a peaceful scene, dormant. On the outside, he didn't seem to have any problems. But, on the inside, if you could go into that volcano, the molten lava, the abuse was tearing him inside. But it was capped, and that's how he survived for all of this time.

Johnny Vai went to the University of Delaware. And to further escape, he was no longer "Johnny Vai," it was John Vai. He stopped going to church, started drinking, partying; anything to numb the pain. In 1972 he dropped out of the University of Delaware; drug and alcohol abuse is clear. The nightmares are clear – and there are reports of the psychiatrist for this. Ten years later he continues to have job problems, anger at authority figures. A classic set of conditions of abuse victims. Especially abuse victims – it's not just one time, regularly. In abuse victims – if you are abused by someone you can trust and someone in authority, you have problems with authority figures. Again, who was the priest? He is someone who has respect. He wears black, wears a collar. We have Father Carroll here, do you see that. [Crumplar pointed to the young innocent looking priest that the St. Elizabeth's corporation had chosen to sit at the defense table throughout the trial to try to project a wholesome image to the jury and to counter the awful arrogant and unrepentant face of DeLuca and the other older priests who would appear before the jury in the coming days.] He is someone you are taught to

-248-

respect. He was the ultimate authority. The ultimate authority, but you realize you can't trust him. So it doesn't – it's no surprise that you have a problem with your boss. You have a problem obeying orders. You just think: The last person I trusted with authority, look what he did to me. Some of this is unconscious to John because he's pushed it in. He doesn't know why he snaps at his bosses. He doesn't know why he is having these problems.

Again, that's one of the horrible things – in terms of self-consciously, you push this down to survive, but it messes you up; and you have no way to even deal with it. Then in 1994, John Vai's marriage collapses; and he continues to have many problems. Now, we have the volcano again. [He pointed at a cross-section of a volcano, with the word "abuse" buried far underground and a few spurts of lava shooting out the top.] Here is the volcano, you see, it is simmering; it's had a minor eruption. There was an eruption from time to time.

I mentioned before that John Vai's marriage collapsed in '94. Let's go back to 1985. John Vai has had problems with relationships; you can understand that. One girlfriend after another. He finally finds someone his mother likes; who says it's important that you get married. He is in his mid-thirties. The problem is Cindy has been married before and wasn't a Catholic. In the Catholic religion it was very important to his mother that he get married in the church. So it is important that Cindy have her marriage annulled. Well, you have to go to the priest. And John had not gone to church at all, had kind of washed his hands. His mother kept saying – Well, remember Father DeLuca, he is still around. In fact, he is now a pastor of a church. He is now the Very Reverend Father DeLuca; he has been promoted. He is now a Dean, which is a higher position, you will understand. He has the power. He was so good to us. Go to him.

John Vai had an uneasy feeling. He really didn't know why he didn't want to go see DeLuca. Again, what I told you, in terms of the repression, that self-defense mechanism. He goes; but he has this uneasy feeling. He goes with his bride-to-be to see DeLuca. DeLuca is there, in a careful kind of grin, knowing he has him in his power. He says: Well, you need several thousand dollars to make this work. John couldn't take it; he just abruptly left. His bride-to-be followed him, said: What is the matter? He just looked at her and said: I don't want to talk about it; he abused me. The one memory that was on the surface, the New York trip, came up; and John just pushed it down as fast as possible.

Let me go back. One more time where we had this simmering happen, John thought it was 2004. But if you look at the records, it's really 2006. There was a story in the newspaper by Beth Miller that talked about abuse by a number of priests here in Delaware. John Vai read that and broke out in tears just because of this story of sex abuse by priests. He soon put it back in his unconsciousness, put back that New York abuse at the top. But there was, again, an explosion in 2006.

Now, let me take a moment because we're going to talk about when the volcano finally burst. You will learn of evidence, including from DeLuca, that Johnny Vai wasn't the only boy that DeLuca was abusing at St. Elizabeth's. Johnny Vai thought he was the only one. Again, that's part of the power that DeLuca had on him: I am alone, and nobody will believe me. As it turns out, there were other boys. You will hear from the other boys, at least two of them. Quill is especially important to John Vai. Because Bobby Quill lived right down the street, had an older brother. He was three years younger than John Vai. John Vai could remember actually, when he was smaller, holding his hand and taking Bobby Quill to school. Had a certain sense of remembering him as that little boy he wanted to protect. Unbeknownst to John Vai – at the same time while Francis DeLuca, was taking him up time and time again openly, even in front of the other priests, into the bedroom – he was doing the same thing with other boys, including Bobby Quill.

So in 2007, July 2007, one day John Vai opened up *The News Journal*. [The July 13, 2007 front page of the paper appeared with pictures of DeLuca and Robert Quill. Quill looks strong, angry and determined, taken months before when he stood in front of the Delaware State legislature and testified four times trying to get help for survivors. The caption states that he charged he was abused by DeLuca 300 times.] Front page: – "Clergy Abuse Civil Suit Filed, case first to be brought after change in Delaware law." – There is a picture of now Robert Quill, who is an attorney, an attorney in Atlanta, Georgia. There is a picture of Francis DeLuca. Quill has filed suit, and the guilt overwhelms John Vai. I wasn't alone. And if I could have done something – I should have killed him. I don't know how I would have killed him at fourteen, but I should have killed him. He wouldn't have abused that other little boy.

The volcano erupts. Everything comes out. He remembers bits and pieces that this abuse wasn't just the New York abuse which was the one at the surface, but it was so much more. It was the rectory, which DeLuca will admit. It was horrible, horrible abuse. John's emotions overwhelm him. Just a few days after this article comes out, he sends this message to Catholic officials. He says – this is an e-mail, and you will see this exhibit. I was an altar boy at St. Elizabeth's, too, just like Robert Quill. I cannot hide the

-251-

shame anymore.

Johnny Vai then went to a counselor for the first time. Again, a classic thing – in terms of abuse victims – is you don't want to deal with it. It's too painful. Even though, ultimately, it is necessary. But he goes to the counselor that one time, and he can't deal with it. He realizes the one way he will deal with it is to ensure that justice is done, that this never happens again. He contacts Quill's attorneys because he wants to help out Bobby Quill. He wants to do something about it. He is informed that he has his own rights. And the best thing to do is also to bring our present lawsuit to get justice and to make certain this never happens again; and he files this suit.

How did this happen? Let's think for a moment. A church is supposed to be a sanctuary. In the middle ages, when you were falsely accused of something, you would go into the church and nobody could touch you; that was the safest place possible. The priest – and, in fact, the word "pastor" in Latin means shepherd. DeLuca was an associate pastor. What is a shepherd? Someone who takes care of the sheep, especially the little lambs. His whole life is dedicated to their protection to protect them from the wolves that may destroy him, and that is what we had. The shepherd was really a wolf. And the other shepherds – if they didn't know it, they certainly should have. That is why we are here today.

Remember those stairs that Johnny Vai would go up? When he would go up those stairs – right here, this is an exhibit to DeLuca's deposition. You will have this as evidence; this is April 3rd, 2009. I asked DeLuca to draw a picture of the private upstairs area where no one, other than the priests, was supposed to be according to the rules of all the churches – all the Catholic churches in this area. [He pointed to the stairs leading up

-252-

in this drawing.] That is St. Elizabeth's rectory as the front, room two, three, and big room one. Early on, DeLuca said: I was in room two. Although, later I was in three and one. Now, let's find out who was – you see there are three other rooms. You will see they are close; next to each other. There were – throughout DeLuca's time, throughout his abuse of children, including Johnny Vai – at least two other associate pastors living there right next to him. And the pastor was living in the same rectory in another section.

I asked DeLuca – this is his sworn testimony. [The plain white page from the transcript of Crumplar's earlier questioning of DeLuca appeared on the screen.] Let me read it to you. First of all, I said:

Q. And what was the excuse that you gave his parents for him to spend the night in the rectory?

A. I am not quite sure.

Q. Okay. Did you hide his presence in the rectory? Did you sneak him in and sneak him out?

A. No. I think he just came in and came up to my room. I wouldn't call it sneaking him in.

If you remember one thing I say to you today, remember that. DeLuca paraded his victims openly into the rectory.

Who did he parade him up there in front of? [Three black and white photos framed in a red background were projected on the screen. On the top left was a young bearded hip Tom Cini who for a generation became the most powerful priest besides the bishop in the Diocese. Next to him was a middle-aged Thomas Peterman and below the two of them was the grey haired John M. Donohoe, head of the most powerful church in the Diocese.] The fellow priests. Now, there are a number of priests who served with DeLuca; a number of them are now dead. At the bottom is Monsignor Donohoe who was the pastor; he is now deceased. But the top two priests right there, now Monsignor Cini – he was Associate Pastor Cini – and Pastor Peterman, who also became a very reverend, is still alive. You will hear their testimony in this court. They were living next to DeLuca while he was abusing John Vai and others. And because they did nothing about it, that is why we are here today.

Now, from 1966 to '69, St. Elizabeth's – Johnny Vai was not the only boy to be abused by DeLuca at St. Elizabeth's. From 1966 to 1969, John Doe Two, age eleven to fourteen – he got an even younger one – [was] repeatedly abused by DeLuca in the rectory. You will hear from John Doe Number Two on Monday. We don't have a picture of John Doe Two. Not because there isn't a picture, it's because John Doe Two doesn't want anyone to see his picture that might remember who he is and he has to go anonymously. One thing the Court allows is that, when you are a victim of a sexual assault, you can go anonymous. That's why – sometimes you read in the paper about a young woman who has been raped, they don't mention her name. Especially when you deal with children, there is no mention. It is very difficult. Think of the shame. Think about how hard it is for this man to be here among strangers, the public, and the press, and to state how he was humiliated; the grossest type of abuse time and time again. John Vai is doing this because he thinks it's so important to justice. But I can't fault other people that are still racked by the shame that are willing to come forward and testify. This is going to take real courage for this person to basically come in, who lives as a hermit – for him to come in here. And I can only call his name John Doe Two. He will testify on Monday – just like John Vai – time and time again DeLuca abused him in the most vile way, in the rectory, while there were others around.

There is something more. Johnny Vai was not the first person that we have clear evidence who was abused in the rectory at St. Elizabeth's. Right before John Vai and John Doe Two's abuse began there was another priest, John A. Lind. He happened to be DeLuca's friend. DeLuca's first assignment in the diocese was down in Maryland. And who was he serving with? John Lind. Two years. Then they both got moved up to Delaware. DeLuca was at a church, St. John's. Lind was at the neighboring church. Lind, the trailblazer, was assigned in the summer of 1965 to St. Elizabeth's; and he openly abused boys in the rectory. We will have two of those boys testify. Pat Nagle – this happens to be their football pictures, so it doesn't turn out too clear – and John Loe Number Two.

Let me just – because it may be a little confusing. With Lind victims, we used the term "John Loe." You are going to hear from John Loe Number Six. There are – some Lind victims are willing to go public, some are not. So you will hear from John Loe Number Six. With DeLuca victims we use the terminology "John Doe." You will hear – we'll talk about John Doe Number Two. You will also hear from John Doe Number Eighteen, who is scheduled to come and testify on Monday, about the abuse that DeLuca also performed on him at St. Elizabeth's. The same rectory; the same place where DeLuca came in.

Now to move on, there are two defendants in this case. I don't think you will have any question whatsoever with regard to Francis DeLuca. He minimizes it; but, of course, he admits that he abused John Vai and others. But there is another defendant, it's

-255-

his employer, the corporate defendant St. Elizabeth's. They will get a chance to speak to you in a moment. I expect they will do a couple of things: We didn't know anything about DeLuca they will say.

And we don't have to prove that they absolutely knew. This is a civil case; it's a case of negligence. All we have to prove is they should have known; that they had a heightened duty – and they will admit – to take care of little children. They are not only a church where they invested priests with authority, but they also operated a school. And they had that duty not to turn a blind eye – a duty to be ever vigilant – in terms of the danger to children. That's all we have to prove, that they should have known. They failed to take the proper steps that, if they had done so, would have protected Johnny Vai, Bobby Quill, John Doe Number Two, John Doe Number Eighteen.

That's why it's especially significant that – right before the abuse of Johnny Vai started – there was regular abuse by one of DeLuca's friends who was there in the same rectory. It's not like it's not something to be expected. You will hear the testimony of the current pastor, Father Carroll, who said – who admitted in deposition, yes, it was known in the Catholic community that there was a risk of pedophile priests, at least in the 1950s. You will have other people testifying, including Monsignor Cini, who says it goes back even to the 1880s.

There is a risk – there is a danger that comes with responsibility. To say that they had no responsibility is to say that – it just betrays common sense.

Now, you also will have the pastor's authority over all priests in the parish. Again, think of it like the military. It is a military organization, ultimate; and it's the authority from the top down. The pastor has authority over all priests in its parish. He

-256-

assigns priests. He makes a decision: Does this priest work with the youth or does he work with the elderly? There is a hospice right nearby, a nursing home. DeLuca didn't have to be assigned to work with the altar boys. DeLuca didn't have to be assigned by the principal, who was an associate priest, to teach religion to ninth graders. They approved the vacation and work schedules. They enforced the rules of the rectory as you see it. They did not enforce it and discipline priests.

Now, it's St. Elizabeth's, Inc. You will hear, when we're talking about we're suing the church – and you think about the church as all of the people in the pews. We're not suing the people in the pews. We're suing a corporate defendant. Just like if there was a lawsuit against General Motors or Gore, or something of that kind. Some people say: Oh, it employs all of these people, and they show all these pictures and the good that they do. The church does a lot of good things. St. Elizabeth's does a lot of good things; I am not denying that. But there is responsibility when you are incorporated. And a corporation – you are incorporated so you can sue and be sued. You have responsibility. It is a corporation; the corporation never dies.

You look in terms of: What is the corporation? The corporation doesn't have shareholders. The corporation – members of the church are not members of the corporation. Its legal document shows there are five people that consist of the corporation that we sued. The bishop, who is the president of the corporation, he appoints a chancellor – his right-hand man. In fact, one of the witnesses, Chancellor Rebman, used to be at St. Elizabeth's when DeLuca was there. He later moved on. The bishop appoints the pastor. And the pastor sees that there are two lay trustees. Now, the lay trustees really don't get involved here. They are figureheads, even though you are supposed to have them. We just took the deposition of the pastor. And in over 100 years that this church has been incorporated, they have had one meeting involving the lay trustees. I don't think it was by coincidence. It was just last month. And what did they talk about? The fact that you folks were coming here; the first time they got the lay trustees together. Basically, the corporation is run by the bishop; and he has a pastor for day-to-day operations.

[Crumplar paused and started to move into his final remarks.] The "scales of justice." This is very important because I know – I think, when you go back to the jury room in a few weeks – you will say: I am not certain that Mr. Crumplar – I will introduce myself in a second. I haven't introduced myself yet because I am not the important person; that is the important person [pointing to John Vai sitting next to the jury.] You will say: Mr. Vai's attorneys, they didn't absolutely convince me. I am not certain it is the way it is. There is a lot of good evidence there. It seems more likely that that is the case, but I am not absolutely certain.

This case is not about a crime. For a crime you have to prove beyond a reasonable doubt. We are not seeking to put St. Elizabeth's pastor in jail. We are not seeking to put DeLuca in jail, that's the prosecutor's burden. This is not a criminal case. This is a civil case, just like somebody bumps into another car. Here all we have to do is prove negligence. Negligence is a mistake. You are just a little careless; you just kind of weren't paying attention. There also may be an argument that we'll show gross negligence. What is that? That's just a bigger mistake. I think the evidence will show recklessness, a conscious indifference to the lives of others.

Let me go back to the scales of justice. In order to prevail in the case – for you to have a verdict for John Vai, all that you will have to see is that these scales are just slightly tipped ever so slightly. If you can really study it, you can see that it's just a hair that one scale is tipped a little bit more. It's just 50.0001 percent is on John Vai's side. So if you look at all of the evidence, all of the elements, you can say: The other side had a lot of good points. The other side are ably represented by attorneys. They are going to raise questions; that's what they're paid to do. You might say: I am not convinced. You don't have to be absolutely convinced. At the end of the day, are we just more likely than not [sure]?

I'll talk a minute again about the role of Catholic culture and the power of the priests. In the 1960s you might wonder why Johnny Vai was unable – or any of the other people – to do anything. It was a power that no one would believe them. A vow of celibacy and sexual temptation – this is not an attack on the Catholic Church. It's not challenging any of their doctrine or dogma. The church is certainly right and within their power to say that priests do not marry. Well let's have common sense. Sexual urges are one of the most powerful temptations that people have, very clearly. Look at the *Bible*. There is the story of David and Bathsheba. Good people fall prey to sexual temptation. Priests are not allowed to have any sex. That's what it is; it's a vow of celibacy. It's not just marriage; you can't marry. You cannot have sex, period. Nothing whatsoever. No masturbation. Nothing whatsoever. You are violating that. It's going to be hard. There's going to be temptation. There are going to be priests that are going to err; that is a fact. It is a fact. Where are they going to err? Where is the opportunity? Really, a bank robber was once asked: Why did you rob the bank? That's where the money is. Priests in 1966 – there weren't altar girls, there were altar boys. And what better opportunity as

a

young impressionable boy; that's who DeLuca preyed on. You will have to decide that: With that risk, did the church take proper steps to protect against that?

Then we have percentage of liability. I put DeLuca up there first because I don't think there is any question. You will find he has responsibility. We have St. Elizabeth's here, too.

The judge will instruct you: There can be more than one cause of an injury. You can have an auto accident that is due to the manufacturer didn't make the car right; plus, the other driver did not brake. They can both independently combine to cause the injury or they can work together, as is the situation here. DeLuca was the final agent. But for the negligence of St. Elizabeth's – the gross negligence of St. Elizabeth's – the conscious indifference of St. Elizabeth's, DeLuca would have never had the ability to abuse Johnny Vai, John Doe Two, John Doe Eighteen, Bobby Quill. I believe the evidence will show that there is liability. It may be less liability than DeLuca, but there is still liability.

Now I would like to get to damages. One thing that there will be no evidence for in this case for is: What is the proper level of damages? Under Delaware law, I am not allowed to tell you how much 100 rapes are worth. Under Delaware law, I am not allowed to tell you what is a life destroyed worth. Under Delaware law, I am not allowed to tell you what is worth the fact that you can't really love someone. Under Delaware law, I am not allowed to tell you what is the fact that you are alienated from your mother worth. Your mother whom you love – but, to go visit her, you have to drive around the block and detour so you don't go past St. Elizabeth's church. I am not allowed, under Delaware law, to do those things.

You are the experts here. You will have to look at all those elements of damage; and you are going to have to find damage certainly against DeLuca. And what is proper damage to compensate young Johnny Vai and now older John Vai?

We will have some experts that will help you in this process. First is Diane Langberg. She's twenty-five years a licensed psychologist, nationally known author and speaker, exclusive work with survivors of sexual abuse. And consistent with just saying: It's not only a Catholic church problem; she is a Protestant. She first got involved because there was a Protestant youth worker doing it; and she saw how important it was. She will talk about classic problems with people who are victims of sexual abuse, especially at the age of John Vai – especially when it's a trusted figure, such as a member of a church.

Loss of childhood, think about that. Most people's most precious memories is how wonderful it was as a child. When John Vai thinks about his childhood, it's DeLuca. Loss of intimacy. Sex really is one of God's greatest gifts; it's a chance for two people to show affection and love. John Vai's first introduction to sex was one person abusing him, somebody on top of him. It's very difficult for him to have that relationship without thinking in terms of what is seared in his consciousness. Loss of trust. He and his family trusted Father DeLuca implicitly. How can he trust anybody else?

Loss of faith. His problem is believing in God. He can't go to a church. Think about that. Think about that responsibility. Loss of spirit, and loss of joy. One thing about John Vai which you will see, and you will hear from the witness stand, he is a stoic. Let me just tell you what stoic is: It's someone who doesn't show emotions. Many times it's men who do that. You talk about: men don't cry. It's the John Wayne

-261-

syndrome; you don't show your emotion. And that is John Vai in spades. That fits, in terms of the repression. But while he is not showing emotion on the outside, on the inside he is being torn up. The only way he really lives is he is basically living dead.

We'll have Dr. David Springer testify. He has extensively examined John Vai, looked at medical records; twenty-five years board certified psychiatrist. Again, medical director of the St. John Vianney Center treating pedophile priests. Clinical experience: Professor, Drexel University; vast experience treating sexual abuse patients. A few of the key items that he will testify to: Mr. Vai suffered greatly from being sexually abused by Father DeLuca, and continues to suffer. Vai has been racked with memories, flashbacks, nightmares and guilt. He uses alcohol to avoid truly confronting and addressing the emotional pain he is in. He numbs the pain with a lot of stiff drinks, has become a functional alcoholic. Mr. Vai continues to have symptoms of posttraumatic stress disorders such as nightmares, avoidance, anger, and irritability. The lava is still burning inside, and it comes out from time to time. You have to look at your damages of both the damages to John Vai in 1965, 1966 – 1966, '67, '68 and '69, when the abuse happened, and, then, for the rest of his life to the present, and for the life to come. Until he dies, there will always be that churning lava inside.

Remember, how much is one rape worth? I can't imagine an amount. How many rapes have we had? In terms of defendants here, we've talked about St. Elizabeth's church. Again, it also was St. Elizabeth's school. Think in terms of the duty and the responsibility. And how did this abuse really start the first time? It was a trip. The teacher took him out of school. They did not enforce the rules of chaperoning. I think there will be agreement with both sides that John Vai was abused. There will be disagreement in terms of the amount and type. Vai will testify reluctantly – it's very difficult, and very hard – how often it was and how vile it was. DeLuca you will see – and I don't think I will have the opportunity, although I would dearly love to get him on the witness stand so John Vai could look him in the eye, you can look him in the eye – he will deny it.

St. Elizabeth's, in their pleadings, have not agreed with John Vai. They have taken the side, really, of DeLuca, that they don't know whether there was any other abuse. You are going to have to decide: Is DeLuca lying or is Vai lying, in terms of the amount of abuse? But remember in terms of the amount of lies that DeLuca has told. Let me just read one thing that DeLuca has said in his deposition. And you will hear him state this on the video tomorrow:

Q. And when you were at St. Elizabeth's, Pastor Donohoe didn't have any rules that prevented you from bringing young boys into the rectory?

A. Not that I think was ever discussed.

Q. It's your testimony that you simply do not recall who the first child you abused; is that correct?

A. Yes.

Q. You can't tell us whether the first child you abused was when you were working at a boy's camp in Upstate New York training to be a minister, whether you were a new priest at St. Francis de Sales, or in your second assignment at St. John the Beloved? You simply can't tell us who was the first boy; is that true?

A. Correct.

So many boys, so little time. Back to the defense case again. They will come up,

-263-

as is their right, with their witnesses to counter. I would ask you to carefully listen to them and use your common sense. They have their doctor. He examined John Vai. Forty-one years a practicing psychiatrist; but the majority of his practice is coming to testify in court not treating patients. And I find this to be most significant: In forty-one years, he can only identify one – one instance of ever treating a victim of childhood sex abuse. In fact, when he examined John Vai, he didn't even want to talk to him about his abuse. He wanted to move on to other things. Use your common sense, in terms of whether to believe him.

With regard to the question of liability, you also will hear from Father Thomas Doyle, an ordained priest from 1970 – still a priest. He served as a parish priest and a U.S. Air Force chaplain here in Dover, Delaware. He can explain to you the structure of the church, and how it's very similar to the military. The bishop may assign somebody, just like the general in the Pentagon says to the base commander here in Dover: You are taking this man. But once he is there the base commander, the pastor, is responsible. Of course he's going to look into the background of this person. Of course he's going to find out what did this person do at his last assignment. Of course he's going to decide the right fit. You have to look at that, in terms of seeing whether there is negligence. He was appointed by the Vatican to investigate sexual abuse in the U.S. Catholic Church. And he has authored books and articles on the clergy and sexual abuse.

To conclude, why are we here today? They made a number of choices, St. Elizabeth's. They chose to assign DeLuca to teach religion. They chose not to enforce the rules about no boys into the rectory. They chose to allow DeLuca to take boys on trips.

Ladies and gentlemen of the jury, there is evil in the world. Governments are created. And you, as members of the jury, are part of the government of the State of Delaware to restrain, [to] punish evil, to compensate people who are the victims of mistakes. Churches are held to the same responsibility; they must abide by the rules. In this case, the evidence will show that the corporate officials of this church turned a blind eye. They failed to listen; they failed to speak. And so it is the case of: see no evil, hear no evil, speak no evil and evil itself. [As these words were spoken, images of priests Cini, Peterman, Donohoe and DeLuca rolled across the screen.]

Let's hear Father DeLuca, as I close. [A short video excerpt of the unrepentant and absent DeLuca was played for the jury, and more excerpts followed on day two of the trial. Then Crumplar concluded.] That is the voice of evil. The voice of evil that was allowed to prey on John Vai, and many other boys. Throughout the trial, I want you not just to look at this man who has been destroyed; look at this boy too [he pointed to the original picture of young Johnny Vai with which he had begun], because they are both plaintiffs. This boy will not be sitting here, but I have this picture so you do not forget this boy. Thank you very much.

THE COURT: Fine. We'll take a brief recess.

* * *

The opening statement of the lawyers for the church was significant because John Vai took it in part as a personal attack on his elderly mother and adult daughter, enraging him and locking in his determination for the ultimate face-down later in the case when he would take the stand and be cross examined with all the church could throw against him. The attack on him personally – that he was a liar, had concocted an elaborate story in tandem with his unscrupulous

-265-

lawyers – which was made during the church's opening statement, made him so physically sick that he was ill and absent from the next full day of testimony.

October 27

At ninety-five years of age, William E. Jennings was the oldest living priest in the Diocese of Wilmington. He was the very first witness the jury saw, on the third day of the trial. Jennings was not present in the courtroom. Instead the jury viewed his affable and honest video testimony which was taken by me as John Vai's attorney at the nursing home where Jennings lived.[483] By using Jennings' responses to my questions, I firmly planted in the jurors' minds the cardinal rule of the diocese: that children were never to be taken to the bedroom of any priest, a theme that they would hear twice this day and also throughout the trial. Jennings additionally explained that it was the pastor to whom DeLuca reported who was responsible for guiding and overseeing his development as a priest.

Of the many church officials I had questioned in many cases, Jennings was the first ever to compliment me.

JENNINGS: How are you Tom? Yeah. I never met you officially, but I've heard a lot about you. A long time ago. Yeah. A lot of good things said about you, by the way.

MR. THOMAS NEUBERGER: Thank you. That's very nice of you.

Now you were ordained on May 14th, 1940?

Right.

And then sometime in 1970 you retired?

Right.

So is it fair to say from about 1940, when you were ordained, to 1970 that you

-266-

were a parish priest in the Diocese of Wilmington?

Right.

And even after you retired, is it fair to say that you'd fill in during the '70s and even the '80s?

Oh, yes.

Okay. When did you basically stop filling in because maybe you had gotten too frail or things?

Well, really, I've never stopped filling in. If they call on me, I try to do what they ask me to do.

I want to talk about from, let's say, '46 to '70 when you, quote, officially retired. Is it true that priests weren't supposed to have children visit with them in their bedroom in the rectory during that period of time?

Yes. I've never heard of the prohibition, but I think it would only be wise to obey that law.

Okay. In that time period, from '46 to let's just say '70, a priest wasn't supposed to take a child regularly to their bedroom, were they?

Right.

Thank you. So just going back to '54, let's talk about eight-to-ten-year-old children. Okay? Was it wrong in '54 to take an eight or ten – eight- or ten-year-old young boy to a priest's bedroom on a regular basis?

That's true.

Okay. Well, while you were an assistant pastor, let's say at St. Ann's or at St. Paul's, if you saw a priest regularly taking a young boy to his bedroom who wasn't a nephew or a relative, is that something you would have looked into?

Oh, surely.

In the 1950s, if a priest was taking a young boy up to his room on a regular basis, would you agree it would be a very bad mistake to let that go on?

I think so.

[Changing gears, I asked,] Now, since you were a pastor for quite a few years I wanted to ask you some things about the kinds of things that an assistant pastor does – and what a pastor did back then at that period of time. Okay? Did the pastor put you in charge of being – the priest in charge of the altar boys?

That's right.

Okay. Was the pastor your boss while you were there?

Oh, yes.

So is it fair to say your pastor helped train you as a priest?

That's right.

And was your pastor supposed to guide you in being a priest?

Yes.

Was the pastor, in the absence of the bishop, the person who was supposed to be counseling you and guiding you?

That's right.

However, as the jury would come to learn, none of this counseling and guiding was provided for Francis DeLuca at St. Elizabeth's.

* * *

As had been allowed earlier in bankruptcy court, so now the jury heard by video from deceased Bishop Michael A. Saltarelli, who previously admitted during questioning by me the grievous harms suffered by survivors like John Vai.[484] Bishop Saltarelli had admitted that the multiple injuries caused by the sexual abuse of minors are absolutely devastating and long-lasting for all. In his words, they are the "walking wounded" and they suffer terrible enormous pain, anger and confusion. He stated that no words can ever describe the pain and suffering inflicted on a child-abused by a priest and he agreed that these effects can reverberate through a child's life and reach extensively into his or her adulthood. Saltarelli explained that the many consequences of childhood sexual abuse include: alcohol abuse, drug use, suicide, confusion over sexual identity, divorce, inability to maintain a stable marital relationship or relationships with others, guilt, anger, grief, feelings of worthlessness, loss of faith and loss of trust in God. Finally, as would be explained by expert witness Thomas Doyle a few days later, because of the unique role of the priest in Roman Catholic culture, since Catholics are taught that he is a direct intermediary between God and a child, bishop Saltarelli admitted that it would have been very difficult back then for any abused child ever to have attempted to report wrongful conduct of a priest to anyone at all.

* * *

That same day the jury also heard by video from another former bishop of the diocese, Robert E. Mulvee, who agreed that a child should not spend the night in the bedroom of a priest.

MR. THOMAS CRUMPLAR: Now, at any of the rectories that you ever lived at, were there any rules prohibiting a priest from having a young boy spend the night with him?

MULVEE: Yes.

Q. Okay.

A. Well, in other words, no one stayed the night in the cathedral rectory –

Q. Okay.

A. – except another priest if there was a room vacant and the rector approved.

Q. But in every place that you've ever lived, that's always been the clear policy?

A. Yes. I would say that I would presume that was the policy.

Q. If you had learned that pastors were allowing – excuse me – pastors were allowing assistant priests to have young boys spend the night at the rectory, you would say you have a problem with that; correct?

A. Yeah. I think there had been a policy to that.

Q. All right. And that was a policy in 1960? 1970? 1980? The time didn't matter in terms of the policy, did it?

A. No.[485]

November 1

On day four of the trial, jurors first saw the human face of survivors when John Doe Eighteen took the stand, followed by three other victims. John Doe Eighteen was the first witness called by John Vai's attorney Raeann Warner, the youngest member of his trial team who was known for her ability to earn the trust of survivors, for her unsurpassed work ethic and for her persistence in seeking justice for them.

Earlier the church, through its attorney, had argued during its opening statement that the church and its pastor and other officials just were duped by DeLuca, as were all the other families at St. Elizabeth's. The church claimed that its pastor and all its other priests were totally in the dark about DeLuca's alleged behavior and his alleged crimes.

The jury was mesmerized by this sincere fifty-nine year old witness who had nothing to gain by coming forward to testify. He had never filed a lawsuit against the church and he had kept his shame hidden his entire life. But he had decided to step forward to counter directly what he understood were the falsehoods being told in the media about DeLuca's criminal behavior.

Despite a lengthy unsuccessful attempt in the middle of his testimony by the church's lawyers to keep this vital information from the jury, John Doe Eighteen explained that, despite the church's protestations of innocence and claimed lack of prior notice of DeLuca's crimes, DeLuca frequently would ride around in his car loaded with young boys, one of them always sitting on his lap for sexual gratification. On one occasion as they returned to the church after a joy ride, pastor John M. Donohoe and another priest came out of the rectory, with Donohoe screaming at DeLuca that he was not to still be doing this, that he had said he would stop this behavior. Soon thereafter, Thomas Cini, a rising star of a priest at the time, confronted John Doe Eighteen and accused him of sexually tempting DeLuca and claimed that all the fault lay *not* with DeLuca but with this seductive young boy. [This is similar to one bishop's excuses for the conduct of priest Walter D. Power which surfaced in a document in bankruptcy court.]

MS. RAEANN WARNER: Your Honor, plaintiff will call John Doe to the stand.[486]

Good morning, sir.

THE WITNESS: Good morning.

Would you tell us your [age]?

I am fifty-nine.

Mr. Doe, will you tell us why you are not revealing your name today?

-271-

Afraid of retaliation.

Sir, can you tell me when you first contacted me?

The summer of 2008.

Why did you do so?

I saw an article in the newspaper that said that there was a trophy book of pictures that DeLuca had. I knew I was in that book. And I didn't – I have spent my whole life – thirty, forty years – trying to forget this and trying to hide it from everybody. And I was afraid it was going to come out, who I was; and I didn't want that to happen. Called you just to ask – and I explained what pictures I would be in, and to see if those pictures were in that book and whether my name was in that book.

Why were you concerned that you would be in the book?

I knew I would be in the book. I knew what pictures I was in. And I knew – I knew that I was – I had been with Father DeLuca.

Sir, when was the first time that you told anyone about the abuse by DeLuca?

When I was talking to you on the phone in the summer of 2008.

Who is your attorney, sir?

I have no attorney.

Have you filed suit?

No.

When did you first meet with or speak with Thomas Neuberger?

Today I saw him in the elevator coming up to this floor for the first time – first time I talked to him, I was introduced to him in the elevator.

Sir, can you tell us why you are testifying here today?

When I talked to you the first time – before you would tell me anything about what was in the book, you asked me why I wanted to know; and I explained my story. I kept following it in the newspaper. I know, before the time line was up, you asked me if I wanted to file suit or be involved with it. I told you, again, no, that there was no reason. I wanted to forget this. I didn't want to remember it. I tried to forget it. Then, about – I don't know – two weeks, three weeks, you called me, asked me my story again. I told you my story again. And you told me that my story isn't the same as St. Elizabeth's story. Father Cini said something different. I said I'm sticking by my story; I know what happened. I know what I said and who said – I have nightmares about this all the time. I said I would tell you my story.

Sir, let's get a little background. Tell us where you grew up.

I grew up in Delaware. I went to St. Elizabeth's High School, from 1965 until I graduated in 1969.

How did you know Francis DeLuca?

He was a priest assigned to the parish. He was also my religion teacher. I think that's where I met him and knew him. I wasn't a regular parishioner at the church.

Understood. What kinds of things would you do with DeLuca?

It started off – he would just take a bunch of boys to different school events, sporting events, basketball games. We would ride with him, rather than on the chartered buses.

So the sporting events that you attended, where would they be held; were they at St. Elizabeth's, or were they somewhere else?

No. They would always be away games. Some of St. Elizabeth's home games were played at Baynard Stadium, but most of the other games, away games, different

high schools, Tower Hill, Friends, Sanford. In the beginning it was a normal, whatever,

Chevrolet, four door. Then he got a Camaro, blue Camaro RS. I really liked the car. I

liked to ride in the car. As it went on further, after I got my license, I would drive the

car; and I would be the driver all the time with DeLuca in the car with me.

Who else would typically ride in the car as well?

It was other boys from the school.

Who did you typically sit with at those games?

I think we split up. I don't believe that everybody stayed together. I don't

remember. I don't remember.

Okay. With whom would you leave those games?

Same, Father DeLuca.

Who else from St. Elizabeth's, in terms of faculty, staff, would typically be there

at the away games?

A lot of the nuns would be there. Father Tom Peterman was always there, the

principal. Father Duncan went a lot, freshman, sophomore year. He left sometime, I don't

remember when. The priests were there; the teachers were there. There was a couple of

lay teachers.

Did DeLuca do sick calls or visits to the sick?

He had a pager; and, apparently, he was on call. He shared call times with the

other priests at the parish. There was a hospital that he was assigned to; it was down

Maryland Avenue someplace. His pager would go off, and he would – if somebody was

dying or they asked to see a priest – and I guess if there were no chaplain – it was always off hours, it was always night, weekends – the pager would go off; he would go to the hospital. There is a sacrament of extreme unction that he would perform, last rites. Sometimes he would bring communion with him.

How are you familiar with his routine?

There were times when I was with him that the pager went off. And as long as I was still dressed – like from school – we wore a shirt, tie, sports coat all the time. In the beginning he wouldn't take with me him; but after a while he took me with him.

How did your relationship with DeLuca begin?

I don't know. He was my religion teacher. At some point – fifteen years old, fourteen years old – I had wanted to be a priest. I had been groomed to be a priest. I have relatives that were priests. My grandmother, my mother – I was groomed to be a priest.

What did a priest mean to you at that time?

A priest was a – someone to be respected, the highest respect, authority figure.

Now, when you would be riding with DeLuca in the car or driving with him, what was the typical seating arrangement?

In retrospect, I look and see that his goal was to put as many people in the automobile as he could. He always had somebody sitting on his lap. He would always put one extra person in the car. When it was the Camaro, he sat in the back a lot. And my junior year – this was a different time; my junior year I would drive. And as long as he was sitting in the back, I could drive longer; we would ride around longer.

How many times do you think that you drove in DeLuca's car with him to go to games or for other reasons?

-275-

A lot. Forty, fifty maybe. I was trying to figure it out when you asked a week ago for the first time. A couple of times a week over, maybe, three years; maybe more than what I just said. Some weeks not at all.

Now, what type of beverages, if any, would DeLuca buy for you and the other boys?

I am not sure what he bought for the other boys. He bought me cigarettes and beer.

When would he do this?

Usually we had the beer. We never stopped to buy it. It was always dark. So he was always coming back, returning, from wherever we were. It was always dark.

I know this is difficult, but can you tell us what type of sexual things DeLuca did to you?

It always started with just – because we were close together, he would touch you until you became aroused. I know he was aroused. And it started – I didn't do anything to him for a long time. And I don't know why I kept going back, but I did.

When you say he would touch you, where would he touch you?

I would have an erection.

Where would this take place?

Always in the car, except one time.

Where was that?

We went to Rehoboth Beach one time; and it was somebody's house that he had the keys to. We went to the beach. It was a private house. Somebody's private house, I don't know whose it was. I know it was – when you go into the main drag, if you go on

-276-

the main street, there is a traffic circle at the end. About one block back you would make a right-hand turn, and it was on the right-hand side. There were a lot of trees around. I don't remember whose house it was.

After some time of spending time with DeLuca, would he do other types of sexual things to you?

Yes. Never went past oral sex, but he never – we never had anal sexual intercourse. Oral sex.

Can you tell us what time frame this sexual abuse took place in?

I think it started at the end of my sophomore year or sometime during the sophomore year. I don't think it was the freshman year. I knew the only way I could get out of this was to not be around, so I got a job where I had to be at work as soon as school was over. I was always working. That's how I tried to break it off.

Who was Monsignor [John M.] Donohoe?

He was the pastor of the parish.

What happened during this time with Monsignor Donohoe and DeLuca that you observed?

I think it was in my senior year. It was during the day. It was bright out, so it was during the day. There was [sic] other people in the car with myself; I was driving. I turned off of Maryland Avenue onto Cedar Street, and was heading up the hill on Cedar Street. I used to park my personal car, my family car, in a small parking lot on the side of the school building. I stopped the car, DeLuca's car, on Cedar Street. I think – I don't know what the name of the side street is; I can't remember.

The pastor came out of the basement door of the church. I believe it's – Grant

Hall it was called; it's a kitchen/cafeteria. And he started walking toward DeLuca's car. Another priest came from the right-hand side, I believe it was from the rectory, and the pastor was yelling at –

DEFENSE LAWYER: Your Honor, if this is going to get into hearsay testimony of a deceased person, I think we have a problem here. [A side bar discussion was held outside of the hearing of the jury.]

DEFENSE LAWYER: Your Honor, out of caution, it sounded like he was going to talk about what he heard Monsignor Donohoe or some other priest say; and I think that would be impermissible hearsay.

MR. STEPHEN NEUBERGER: Your Honor, by definition, hearsay is an out-of-court statement offered for the truth of the matter asserted. This evidence is being offered – the testimony that this witness is about to give is being offered for the non-hearsay purpose of demonstrating notice; notice that Father DeLuca was not supposed to be with children, notice that Father DeLuca –

MS. WARNER: Was violating the standard.

MR. NEUBERGER: – was violating the rules and the standards, and things of that nature. I believe the witness is going to say – going to testify something along the lines that the pastor began yelling at him, telling him: You are not –

MS. WARNER: I told you not to be in the car with boys.

MR. NEUBERGER: – I told you not to be in the car with boys. And we're offering this, Your Honor, to demonstrate that DeLuca was getting into trouble for being –

THE COURT: Since he was the pastor, why wouldn't it just be an admission.

-278-

MR. NEUBERGER: It would be an admission. I was getting to my basis. I think it was an admission.

DEFENSE COUNSEL: Your Honor, there isn't any other evidence other than this witness' statement that that occurred. This is a deceased individual. There is no record of this having occurred. And this is being offered for, both, the truth of the matter — suggesting that, in fact, Monsignor Donohoe was indicating that he was abusing boys. And it also goes to the crux of the case, whether or not St. Elizabeth's had notice. To allow it to come in through hearsay testimony of a deceased person, where there is no other evidence to support it other than this individual's testimony, I think that's highly problematic and prejudicial to St. Elizabeth's.

MR. NEUBERGER: Your Honor, there is no corroboration requirement under the Delaware Rules of Evidence. Testimony given by a witness from the witness stand is a valid form of evidence. Defense counsel has made the same argument to the Delaware Supreme Court, and has yet to cite a case in that regard. This is, by definition, not hearsay. More fundamentally, Your Honor, any statements which are being offered for the truth of the matter asserted are admissions. This is the pastor of the St. Elizabeth's parish corporation, an employee of the parish.

THE COURT: Okay. The objection is overruled. [The side bar discussion concluded.]

THE COURT (to the jury): The objection is overruled. Proceed.

MS. WARNER: Mr. Doe, do you remember where you left off? You were telling us what happened.

The monsignor came out of the Grant Hall door and started walking toward the

-279-

car. We were stopped because I was going to get out and go to my car. The pastor was yelling at DeLuca as he came across the parking lot – as he came across the grass toward the car. Another priest was coming up out of the rectory. And they all met, DeLuca, the pastor, and another priest.

About thirty feet from the car the pastor was yelling at DeLuca and waving his arms up and down about: I told you – you told me – DeLuca told him he wouldn't do this anymore. What are they doing in the car? What are you doing now? And he kept yelling that, screaming. I had never heard the pastor – other than a sermon, I had never heard him raise his voice. He was screaming, and I was scared. I got out of the car. And I ran to my car, and I left. I don't know where everybody else went, I can't remember. I know I got to my car, and I left. When I pulled out of the parking lot – and it's a little parking lot; it only fit, six, eight, ten cars. And I only knew one way in and out of town. I made a right-hand turn to go down Maryland Avenue – down Cedar Street, down the hill. They were still standing thirty feet from his car; and the pastor was still yelling at him, at DeLuca. And I drove away.

When the pastor was flailing his arms up and down, who was he pointing at?

Me. He was yelling at DeLuca, and pointing to me.

Was anyone besides you and DeLuca in the car at that point?

Yes. I think there was. I don't remember who. During this time, I don't remember anybody else in the car except in – earlier than that, in the Camaro, I remember he used to bring – DeLuca used to bring somebody younger. He would sit in the middle. It wasn't – a Camaro was only a five-passenger car. He would sit in the middle. And he brought a younger person, younger, that would always sit on his lap. I always thought it was strange because they weren't in the high school I don't believe. I believe they were in grade school. He brought them. I got to drive; I didn't care.

Who was Father Cini?

Father Cini was a priest assigned to the school – assigned to the parish, I guess. He was also a teacher. He was my religious [sic] teacher.

What happened with Father Cini during this time when you were being abused by DeLuca?

I think Father Cini showed up – was assigned to the parish in my senior year, I think. So that must mean he was my religion teacher in the senior year. I think the incident with the monsignor happened on a weekend. The reason I think that is because it was bright; the sun was out. And I can't imagine why – I knew I worked during the week. There would be no sporting event that I could be going to. And I don't know why I was with DeLuca then, but I was. I was afraid that I was in a lot of trouble. I knew that I wasn't supposed to be in the car I don't believe. I think there was either an announcement – I think that I knew I wasn't supposed to be in the car because I knew I was in a lot of trouble for something. I can't remember why I thought I was in trouble; but I knew I was. I don't know if it was the pastor pointing at me, but I knew I was in trouble. And I thought I was getting kicked out of school.

After that, Father Cini and I had a conversation. And it was in this small hallway coming out of a classroom. Father Cini stopped me coming out of the classroom, asked me if there was anything I had to talk about; and if there was anything that I had to talk about, I should talk to him about it. This time I'm thinking I'm in trouble, getting kicked out of school; this is what I thought. Father told me – Father Cini told me that Father

DeLuca was in trouble. That, by me riding with him or being with him, I was tempting him, DeLuca; and that I was part of the problem that DeLuca had. That I shouldn't have – I should have known better than to be putting myself in that position to be with DeLuca. He told me, again, that if I ever had to speak to anybody that I should speak to him; that if I wanted to go to confession that I could go to him. I haven't been to confession since then.

Was there any mention of feelings or inappropriate feelings?

Yes. He – the reason for my confession would be that my feelings were inappropriate, that I have to control my feelings. I had to control my emotions, not feelings. He didn't use the word "feelings," he used emotions.

Is there anything else that you can recall from the conversation?

I knew what he was talking about without him saying anymore. That he knew that I was with DeLuca, and I shouldn't have been. That I was partially responsible for continuing to go in the car, and I shouldn't have put myself there. And I had been told not to. I wasn't directly told not to. Everyone – I think everyone was told they had to ride the bus, the charter bus, not to be in private cars, [and he concluded his testimony].

When this testimony by a highly believable witness ended, it appeared that the church's case had been demolished. The story of DeLuca's crimes had been told by a disinterested witness and the church's claim that it had no knowledge whatsoever of DeLuca's misdeeds had been rebutted. But nothing is certain in a trial and so other credible victims of DeLuca followed. To show that children had been raped in those upstairs bedrooms in the rectory for years, two retired police-officers, both victims of DeLuca's predecessor, John A. Lind, also took the stand.

* * *

The first of the two officers was Phillip A. Saggione. He explained that, as a retired

master sergeant of the Wilmington Police Department taking the witness stand, he still was

living his oath to protect and serve the public. From Saggione, the jury learned that DeLuca was

the second child-abusing priest serving at St. Elizabeth's in the 1960s. John A. Lind, a priest at

St. Elizabeth's immediately before DeLuca arrived, also had been a child-abuser. The practice

of this church in allowing priests to take children up to their bedroom was no mere mistake made

only during DeLuca's tenure; it was the accepted practice, despite whatever rules to the contrary

the diocese claimed were in force.

> MS. RAEANN WARNER: Can you tell us your [age]?
>
> THE WITNESS: I am sixty.[487]
>
> Where did you grow up?
>
> City of Wilmington.
>
> At one time were you referred to as "John Loe Number Six?"
>
> Yes. I did this for several reasons. Basically, when it got to this stage of this
>
> procedure and this process, I just couldn't handle the stress anymore, keeping it
>
> confidential. Mainly, I did it for a couple of reasons – kept confidential for several
>
> reasons. One, my father is up in his age, he is in his 80s. He is a member of St.
>
> Elizabeth's parish, a very close member, and has a lot of friends in that parish. I didn't
>
> want to put him through the stress of this. I also have a brother and a couple other
>
> relatives who are employees of the Diocese of Wilmington, very close to the bishop,
>
> work directly for him. And I was very concerned about who knows what could happen to
>
> them for retaliation, or just – maybe not intentional or unintentional. At that point I kept
>
> it as John Loe, when we started this process up to this week and got to this stage. I spent

my entire life as a police officer to protect, serve, and that's what I'm doing. Just, you know, I'm here to make sure this doesn't happen again.

Can you tell us a little about your employment background?

I graduated in 1969 from St. Elizabeth's High School. And I first went into the union as a carpenter, a carpenter apprentice. So, from '69 to '72, I was a union apprentice. I was not a college-bound individual at that time, so I applied for the Wilmington Police Department in 1972; and I was accepted. And I was a police officer for Wilmington from 1972 through 1992. And, then, in 1992 I retired. I took employment with the State of Delaware. And for ten years I worked for the State of Delaware; three years with professional regulations, and, then, seven years with the State insurance fraud bureau. And, then, in 2002 I retired, took a pension with the State, and went [into] private industry. And I am presently an insurance fraud investigator for a private carrier.

With the Wilmington police, what was the last rank?

Master Sergeant.

During your employment there, how often did you have to testify in court proceedings and such?

I couldn't count the number of times.

Did you always tell the truth?

Absolutely.

What parish did you attend?

St. Elizabeth's with my whole family. I have two brothers and two other sisters. There were five siblings, my mom and dad. Very religious, very Catholic family. I went to the church elementary school. When I got out of eighth grade, I became a seminarian. I was a seminarian at St. Elizabeth's parish. My first year was in a seminary with Mother Savior Seminary in Blackwood, New Jersey; that was '65 through '66. I left after the first year of the seminary. And I went to public high school for the first quarter of that '66 to '67 time frame. And that got to be too much for my parents, picking me up. I played football and sports; they had to pick me up late, get me to school early. St. Elizabeth's was a block and a half from my house. So after the first quarter semester, I ended up going back to St. Elizabeth's; and I graduated from St. Elizabeth's high school.

What year did you graduate from the eighth grade at St. Elizabeth's?

1965. It was a long time ago. The best that I can remember – I am not 100 percent sure who the pastor was in 1965; it may have been Monsignor Grant or Monsignor Donohoe. I don't remember who the pastor was. Father Lind, John Lind, was a priest at that time. I was an altar boy. I think we started altar boys back then in sixth grade, if I remember correctly. I was in the choir, played sports, a member of the CYO; everything that a normal Catholic grade school boy did.

When you met Father Lind, what kind of things stood out about him to you?

Fifteen years old, Father Lind was always a priest, you know, which we looked up to. Back in those days our religion told us that priests were God on earth; and you lived up to what they wanted and listened to them, and abided by what they said. But he was kind of cool. He had a white 'Vette and a cowboy hat and boots, fairly young. So that was kind of cool, for us to hang around someone with a 'Vette.

Now, where was St. Elizabeth's parish in relation to your family home growing up?

About two blocks away.

When was the first time that you recall being in Father Lind's bedroom?

Specifically, I can't say when the first day was. But there was one day that I will never forget that kind of is my benchmark, I will call it, as to when the activities and the abuse by Father Lind took place with me. That was June – to be exact, it was June 12, 1965. I remember that day specifically because, after we were finished with Father Lind's activity with us, he took us out to eat. That was sort of a reward, he'd take us on a ride around in his 'Vette. St. Elizabeth's had a pretty good length driveway. He would let us get in the car, drive it up to the driveway, to the end. You would get out, and switch. He would take us to eat. He would always take us to what was called then the Chuck Wagon; it was a hamburger restaurant on Kirkwood Highway. And we would go there, and we would sit in the parking lot. That particular day there was myself – he was driving. Pat Nagle was a passenger. And Father Lind's 'Vette was one of those, like, coupe 'Vettes so you could sit behind the seat, put someone back there if you wanted to sit back there. I was sitting behind the seat, the driver was here (pointing). And Pat was the passenger on that particular occasion.

I remember listening to the radio. And on the radio came a shocking news report that a friend of ours – he was a year or two older than us – but a friend of ours had just been killed in a motorcycle accident earlier that day. And his name came across the radio, and right away we took notice to that. I made a comment to Father Lind. I said: Father that boy lives – Father Lind was fairly new. I said, Father, that boy lives across the street from the church. Do you maybe want to go, go back? We went to school with his sisters, and things like that. So I will never forget that day. I mean, that was clearly one of the days of the abuse. Whether it was the first day, second day – but that's my benchmark; and, then, a few times after that. But I left and went to the seminary around – I guess it would have been sometime in August of 1965. So I left, after that, and went to seminary.

Okay. What happened earlier that day with Father Lind that you mentioned?

Well, what Father Lind would do to us – we would go to the rectory to see him. For the life of me, I can't tell you why or what drew us there or why I would go there. But we would go to the rectory – or I would go to the rectory – and knock on the back door and ask for Father Lind. Usually, you know, on some occasions the housekeepers – I don't know her name or anything, I just remember an elderly lady, housekeeper, middle age, elderly ladies – would allow us in. And we would sit at the kitchen table. In the back of the rectory is the kitchen. We would have cookies. They would give us some soda or snacks or something, and wait for Father Lind to come down from wherever he was at. On that particular occasion there was two, possibly three, of us. I can't say for sure whether there was a third John Doe there that day. I envision a third one that day. But I know, when we went to Chuck Wagon, there was only two of us on that particular occasion.

He would take us upstairs to the second-floor of the rectory to his bedroom, which was in the – what I would call the front of the rectory; it faces out to the convent. St. Elizabeth's has a convent which was a separate building. You walk in – the best I remember, forty-five years ago – but you walk in, his bed was to the right of the doorway. There was a night stand on both sides, a box of tissues on the night stand. If I remember correctly, the bathroom was like the far left-hand corner. And then there were windows similar to like what you see in here, rounded corner windows of the room.

He had me get on the bed. And he said – he went in the bathroom and brought out Playboys and Penthouses. I was on the bed with the Playboys; and Pat was in a chair. I am laying in the bed, this way. Pat was towards that direction, by a window, sitting in the chair with him. And I believe the third person – if there was a third, I can't be 100 percent sure – Pat is over there. We would be looking at the Playboys. And then, he got on the bed with us – or with me. He would undo my pants and put his hand down my pants. He would start playing with us, and masturbate with us until we had an ejaculation. And, then, got some tissues, clean us; and the next boy would get on the bed.

Do you remember how long the whole sequence of events took place in Father Lind's room in the rectory?

I would say we were up there for a while. There was a couple of us that this act was taking place. It probably could seem like an eternity back then; but, no, it's too long ago.

How often did this occur, that Lind would bring you up to his rectory bedroom and abuse you in that fashion?

As I – I believe I told the investigator it could have been anywhere from a couple of times to maybe a half a dozen because, again, I left and went to the seminary. But it was more than once, and it was more than twice in that June, early July, maybe month and a half time frame. Because I didn't know when Lind came to – I don't recall when Lind came to St. Elizabeth's. And I never knew when he left because I left and went to the seminary and wouldn't come back. I went back and forth for holidays, and things like that.

Right. Each time who would let you in to see Father Lind?

It would vary. A housekeeper, maybe. Sometimes him. You know, I can't picture exactly who on any particular occasion.

Did you have to come up with an excuse for being there, or what was your reason?

I don't remember. I have been beating myself to death trying to figure out why – especially after the first time – we would go back. The only thing I could think of was we get to ride in the 'Vette.

Was the nature of the abuse similar to what you described each time?

Yes.

No further questions, Your Honor.

THE COURT: All right.

CROSS-EXAMINATION BY CHURCH LAWYER: Just one question for you, sir. Did you ever tell anyone, before filing your lawsuit, about your allegations of abuse against Father Lind?

THE WITNESS: Exactly, specifically, never told no one [sic]. I was going to take it to my grave. When we got married, I told my wife: Yeah, we used to go up in his bedroom. But I never told her anything about the touching, the masturbate, anything, no.

The first time I told anyone was when the investigator was standing in my driveway and I was standing at the door. He came to the door, knocked on the door. And I thought he was there for another reason. Because I am an investigator, I thought it might have been something related to something that I was doing. I knew who he was from my years in law enforcement. I knew he worked for another police department. I

-289-

said "hi" to him. I said: "Are you here for something specific?" And he said the word "Pat Nagle." Before he could say another single word, it came out. I said "Father Lind," and he looked at me. And I said: "Well, what he told you is true." That's the very first time I ever spoke those words in forty-five years.

THE COURT: All right. Sir, you may step down.

* * *

And then John Doe Number Two was called to the stand. He had lived for years with a fear of the courtroom and public exposure of his shame and that of his family. But somehow he found the courage and fortitude to stand up to his tormenters and their enablers, and he became another man on the stand, sincere and forthright as he bared his soul to the jury. His testimony was devastating to the cover-up by St. Elizabeth's of its complicity in DeLuca's crimes and its false claim that no one could ever have known that DeLuca was constantly taking children up that long dark stairway to the hell that was his second-floor bedroom. As a fifth-and sixth-grader John Doe Two was abused by DeLuca on nights when John Vai was not available. He also added still more corroborating evidence to the fact that the pastor and all the priests in the rectory knew full well what DeLuca was doing to children but they still sat on their hands and did nothing about it.

MS. RAEANN WARNER: Your Honor, John Vai calls John Doe Number Two.[488]

Good morning, sir. Now, how difficult is it for you to be here today to testify?

THE WITNESS: It's extremely stressful for me. I don't like speaking publicly about something that happened that was so traumatic and horrible for me. It's hard for me.

Okay. Have you ever testified in any capacity before?

Well, I had a deposition. I testified in the deposition. That was in my own case. That experience was also very stressful. I don't like confrontation. I was anxious. Before my deposition, that entire previous evening, I couldn't sleep. So I actually had the deposition without any sleep, but I got through it.

Okay. Now, can you tell us why you are using the anonymous pseudonym of John Doe Number Two instead of your own name?

I am using John Doe because I feel the negative perception and judgment from my peers, my family, my friends, my neighbors, and anybody that would know me – how they would judge me after knowing this happened to me.

Okay. Now, can you give us your [age]?

Yes. I am fifty-five years old. I live and grew up in Wilmington, Delaware. We were Catholics and attended St. Elizabeth's parish. All of my family. I have three siblings, and my parents. I went to elementary and high school at St. Elizabeth's and graduated in 1973.

Okay. Now, what school or church activities were you involved in?

Well, I remember being a part of glee club. I was in Cub Scouts, Boy Scouts; and I attended mass regularly. My home was directly across the street from the school.

When did you first meet Francis DeLuca?

I first met him when I was studying to be an altar boy in fifth grade with Sister Gerard.

What did a priest mean to you at that time?

A priest was, to me, at that time, an extension of my parents. They were

-291-

somebody that I could trust; that I could count on, that could teach me, mentor me. And they were the closest thing to God on earth is how I felt at the time. They were my direct link to God is how I felt at the time.

When was the first time that you recall being in DeLuca's bedroom in the rectory?

It was when I was asked to help him bring some articles over to the rectory. He had asked for my assistance. I asked him – he asked me to bring these items over, and that's how I wound up in the rectory.

Where was DeLuca's bedroom in the rectory?

It was on the second-floor. There was a staircase. I entered through the main entrance, I think there was like a screen porch. The main door was beyond the screen porch, the vestibule. To the right of the vestibule is a big staircase; and that's how I got up to the second-floor.

What happened in DeLuca's bedroom that first time to the best of your recollection?

What happened the first time, as I recall, is that he was asking me about my school activities. I remember definitely he was asking about some mischief that I was getting into. Do I get into mischief? He used that word constantly. I wasn't understanding what he meant. I thought maybe he knew something, I was in trouble or something. And he asked me about sports, gym class, and if I felt comfortable being around other boys.

After that he started – he sat next to me. He started massaging my leg, my thighs, eventually massaging my groin area, and started to undo my pants and lower my pants.

What particulars do you remember about this first incident of abuse?

What I remember about the first incident is: after he lowered my pants, he put his mouth on my genitals, and he orally raped me. He had oral sex with me and, at the same time, he lowered his pants and was playing with himself. That's what I remember about that first time.

Where was the next place that you went? Did you go home?

I think home, yeah. What had happened when I got home was: I went to the bathroom, and I realized – and I was horrified to discover that I was somewhat deformed. I didn't look right. I didn't look like I did before; and I couldn't understand what it was. I became very nervous, agitated. And I thought that I have to summon my parents and to let them see what was my situation; my "situation" being that I was very, very swollen. I was swollen, and it looked like I got hurt – I got hurt physically.

Why did you not tell your parents at that point what had happened?

I did not tell my parents because I definitely thought that if they knew I would be in huge trouble. I couldn't speak ill about a priest. I was very young. And I thought that maybe I could just get through it by myself.

How often did this type of abuse occur?

The abuse occurred one, two times a week normally. Sometimes it didn't occur during a few weeks. It was intermittent.

What was the duration or number of years that this went on?

I continually had relations with DeLuca for fifth, sixth, seventh, going into the eighth grade. I remember seeing him as he came back to do some work at the parish. And, occasionally, we would get together when he returned to do special functions at St. Elizabeth's.

Okay. And where would this abuse take place?

Mostly it occurred at the rectory. It was usually after school.

Who would let you into the rectory?

Whoever was there at the time, priests. There was a housekeeper there at the time, and whoever was there. Normally, what I remember was that I used to actually go over to the rectory with DeLuca; so, actually, it would be him letting me in. But occasionally, like I said, either a priest or a housekeeper would let me in.

I know it's difficult, but can you describe the typical type of abuse that DeLuca perpetrated on you?

Mostly it was an oral – oral rape. He had many, many attempts with me to have intercourse with me. I don't ever remember him accomplishing that or being successful. He became insistent many times. And what would happen a lot is: He would get on top of me and simulate sex, a lot of times putting his penis between my legs.

What was bad about that was that he would hold me down until he was finished. And that was horrific for me because it was very – because, when I would try to get up, he would just keep me down until he was finished. A couple of times it would sort of get on the violent side. I would sort of push him off of me; what are you doing? You know, I was uncooperative. Like I said, he was never successful in entering me.

Now, other than the rectory, did this abuse take place anywhere else?

Yes. It happened frequently also in the school. It was on the lower level. I guess you could call it a terrace/basement level; there was an office down there. It was an office that encompassed two small offices, and the office in the back had a lock on it. So we would go into the office, to the back office, and he would lock the door there.

-294-

What would people at St. Elizabeth's, your friends, teachers, tease you about with regard to DeLuca?

I was known around the area and in my neighborhood as his buddy, and people would refer to him as my buddy. It got me upset. It made me think that maybe they knew what was going on. It made me feel trapped and very fearful, intimidated.

Who was Sister Mary?

Sister Mary was a teacher at St. Elizabeth's.

What would she tease you about with regard to DeLuca?

She used to tease me, I think, more than ever, about: Your buddy, your buddy. I remember feeling a huge sense of paranoia that she knew what was going on. And I was always afraid that she was going to call me on it or to reveal it. I didn't like anybody calling him my buddy. It made me feel that – at that time, I remember thinking that people knew, but that was their way of expressing it; that that's your buddy. Your "buddy" meant that that's your lover, so.

Now who was Sister Mary [referring to a different person]?

Another teacher at St. Elizabeth's. She got me in the hall one day and approached me, grabbed my shoulders, and looked right into me with her piercing eyes and said: I want you to understand I know what is happening to you. The same thing happened to me. Don't you understand what I'm telling you? The same thing happened to me. And I looked at her, I was horrified. I didn't know – I thought for certain that she knew what was going on, and this was the end of it. She knew what was going on. I told her at the time that I didn't know what she was talking about. I was extremely nervous. And she asked me to please see her – it was very important – at the library after school. I agreed that I would go.

Did you go?

No, I did not. No, I did not. I was so scared. I actually – she got before lunch [sic]. I went home for lunch, which was right across the street. And I thought that there is no way in the world that I could go to see her because I was just trying to escape the confrontation that I knew she had waiting for me that, basically, she knew what was going on. So I did not go to see her, and that's something I have regretted all my life. I should have – I should have went [sic] to go see her.

To the best of your recollection, who would have witnessed your interactions with DeLuca at the rectory, just the fact that you were there to see him.

Well, people saw me a lot around the rectory, like I said, if a priest let me in. I can remember many instances the housekeeper being there. She let me in, she was there. A lot of times she was in the kitchen with us; so she was aware that I was at the rectory.

Okay. Can you please tell me, to the best of your recollection, the number of times you were abused by DeLuca in the rectory?

Well over 100 times.

How do you come to that number?

Well, I know it happened consistently for three years. There are fifty-two weeks in a year. One to two times a week. That's a very conservative number, a hundred; it's probably a lot more than that. Also, if you include what happened with us at the school.

CROSS-EXAMINATION BY CHURCH LAWYER

Just one question for you. Sir, when is the first time that you told anyone of your allegations of abuse against DeLuca?

-296-

I tried to keep it hidden the best I could. I felt that if I showed myself as a victim of this abuse that it made me seem not adequate as a male. I believe that I told some medical practitioners early on about my abuse. That was maybe when I was seventeen, eighteen, nineteen.

THE COURT: All right. You may step down, sir.

* * *

Patrick Nagle, a disabled retired Wilmington Police officer was the last witness for the day. Like Phil Saggione, Nagle was another victim of John Lind. Severe kidney failure prevented Patrick from testifying in person, so the jury reviewed the video of his sworn testimony which I took from him and which was recorded one week earlier.

MS. RAEANN WARNER: Your Honor, at this time, plaintiff John Vai is going to call Patrick Nagle. Mr. Nagle is unavailable due to his medical condition so he testified by a deposition on October 28, just last week. St. Elizabeth's counsel was present. We're going to play the videotape deposition. [The video recording began.]

MR. THOMAS NEUBERGER: Why don't you, for the record, state your full name for the jury.

THE WITNESS: Patrick Emmett Nagle.[489]

What is the health problem that you have?

Well, I have diabetes and I have kidney failure, and I have to take – I have dialysis three days a week, which are Mondays, Wednesdays and Fridays.

Now, how old are you, sir?

Sixty.

And where did you grow up?

Canby Park in Wilmington.

What about your family?

My father was Gerald J. Nagle, Sr., and my mother was Elizabeth Nagle. I have five siblings.

Now, do I know one of your brothers?

Yes. You went to school with him at Sallies and played on the basketball team with him.

Do you have a court case against St. Elizabeth's Church, Incorporated, because you charge that you were sexually abused by one of its priests, a Father John A. Lind, who was there some time in 1965?

Yes.

Now, despite all that, you just took an oath to tell the truth today. Do you remember that?

Yes.

And will you uphold that oath today to tell the truth?

Yes.

And will you not – are you not going to tell the truth today because I was a friend of your brother's?

No, there's no reason for that.

Okay. Will you not tell the truth today because myself or my son and partner, Mr. Neuberger, or Jacobs & Crumplar are your lawyers?

No.

Now, before we go on, why don't we just tell the jury if you had like a primary career in your life so they know something about you.

Well, I was a police officer in the City of Wilmington from 1971 to 1986. Okay. Fifteen years as a patrolman.

When you testified in court as a policeman, did you always tell the truth?

Yes.

It looks twenty, like you were on the force for fifteen years. Why did it end after fifteen years?

Well, I went on disability because I was punched in the face by a six-foot-six, 350-pound mental patient. And when he did hit me, my back hit the car door and my neck went over the door, and I have a herniated disc in my neck and my back. These injuries prevented me from continuing my career as a police officer and I retired with a disability.

So let's just say in 1965, we're focusing on '65, were you Catholic back in '65?

Yes.

Now what parish did you attend?

St. Elizabeth's. We lived near the church. So we would walk to school every day.

And did you graduate from an eighth grade in an elementary school?

Yes, in 1965 at St. Elizabeth's.

Okay. So would it have been some time in like in June of '65 when you had the graduation ceremonies, that kind of stuff?

Yeah. Usually it's like the first week in June.

Okay. Now, the church building, is the St. Elizabeth's church building a little one-room church building like you see out in the country somewhere with a picket fence around it?

No. It's probably one of the biggest ones in the city – or in the state. They usually have somebody of high status that dies, they usually have the burial there because there's so much room.

Was there a building where the priests would live?

Yes, the rectory.

Could I ask you how many times you might have been in the rectory, if you remember?

I would say probably maybe five times, around that time. Not many more.

Thank you. Okay. I want to focus in on priest John A. Lind. Church records in this court case will show that John A. Lind worked for the St. Elizabeth's Church, Incorporated, in 1965. Does that time sound about right to you?

Yes. Spring of '65 I think is when he came.

Now, when you met Lind, was there anything that stood out about him when you interacted, you or other boys interacted with him?

Well, the thing that attracted us is – the boys to him – was because he had a Corvette, and to have a priest with a Corvette, you know, was something different, you know, than what you've seen. So it attracts everybody's attention to him. When he wasn't dressed, you know, in the regular black jacket and pants and stuff, he would wear jeans and cowboy boots, you know, and never really dressed as a priest when he wasn't, I guess, working, you know, in a sense.

What kind of a position did a priest hold in your eyes back there in the middle 60s in your religion?

Well, a priest couldn't do anything wrong, you know, from what your parents taught you and how you have respect for them. You know, it's no different than with the nuns. They tell you what to do, and you do it, you know. And the priests, you always felt that at that time, he was the right hand of God and, what he told you was what was supposed to be the truth.

Did you interact in any way with Lind in the spring of '65?

Yes. Well, we got to know him. There was three of us, including Phil Saggione. Yeah. I mean he would park over by the school with his car and we would talk to him, you know, at lunchtime or at the end of school. Then we started going for rides with him, you know. One would sit in the front seat, the other two would get in the back, because it was a hatchback Corvette. We would, every day, see him or talk to him and start getting to know him. And then he would – well, he invited us over to the rectory. He would ride around, and say, well, why don't we go back to the rectory for a while. The rectory parking lot, is in the back of the building. And then there was [sic] two entrances, one to the kitchen and one to the rectory in the back.

What happens next?

We go up to his room up on the second-floor. All three of us.

Did you enter a door?

Yeah. There's, like I say, there is a door for the kitchen to the left, and then there's a door to the right that goes into the rectory part. We went in the right door where you're right in the main area, the dining area, the parlor. I think they had a couple of small offices or an office in there, you know, and then the stairs that went up to the second-floor.

Okay. I forgot to ask you, what time of day was this happening?

This was late afternoon.

And did the four of you go to the second-floor?

Yes, apparently to his bedroom on the second-floor.

So then what happens in the bedroom?

Well, once we're in the bedroom, he pulls out these magazines of nude men and women and gives them to us, you know, the three of us. And we're – you know, never seen anything like that, you know, we're all looking at them, you know. Then he started wrestling with whoever was sitting on the bed at the time. And then it ended up all four of us wrestling on the bed. And while we're wrestling, he's grabbing our private areas. More of like accidental, but it continued. And he would pin somebody down, and he would put his hands down their pants. You know, all three of us – it happened to all of us, and we were, I think, all scared and didn't know what to say, we didn't know what to say at the time. I mean we were loud, you know, when we were wrestling, so if there was anybody else in the house, they had to hear three kids up there wrestling. After about an hour, then he took us all home and that was that for that day.

Ok, this is just math. Do you remember how old you would have been in – let's see, you're saying this is the spring of '65.

I was fourteen. I would have to say the other two were the same age.

So you're saying this wrestling started – well, first of all, there were the magazines that you were shown. Was it more than one magazine?

Oh, yeah, yeah. There was – each one of us had maybe two to look at, you know, at the time.

Do you recall if it got you sexually aroused looking at those magazines?

Yes, it did.

You said you were loud. Does sound carry in that rectory?

It's an old building. I would assume, you know, that they could hear you on the first floor.

Did Lind ever take you, after that day, to another place?

Yes. That was his parents' house out in Woodcrest.

So what would happen at that location?

He would have oral sex, he would perform oral sex on me.

Would he masturbate you?

He would play with me, yeah, you know, he didn't – but he had oral sex. And one time we had anal sex. I had anal sex with him. Then after that he said, "What's good for one is good for the other," and he had anal sex with me.

Okay. Would there be any showing you these kinds of magazines again?

Oh, yeah, they would be there. He'd have a pile of them.

Do these things come back to you easily?

No.

Why's that?

No. There's things that are buried that I, you know, don't bring up or don't want to bring up. I have no idea. But, you know, it's like after I got married, I was in Gaylord's on Centreville Road, and he was a security guard there. And I saw him and he followed me around in the store. And I finally grabbed my wife and said, "Let's get out of here." Never told my wife why, and she knew something was wrong, but she didn't know what. Not until I filed the suit that I finally sat down and told her why we left the store.

And it just brought back a lot, a lot of memories, you know, of what happened, and I just couldn't handle it at that time with her.

So is it hard or easy to remember these things?

I think it's hard, because I buried it so much that I just got on with my life and didn't let things bother me.

So just to wrap it up, you said he would take you to his parents' house and these kinds of things happened. About how – over what time period did that continue?

Until around '66. I mean he would, he would come over the house for dinner, you know, and my parents, you know, the Catholics that they were, you have a priest in your house for dinner, you're like the neighborhood saint. And then he would say, "Well, can I take your son?" And you know, and we'd go for a ride and go right to his mother's house.

* * *

The afternoon of day four of the trial concluded with priest Clement Lemon, a hostile diocese witness who had been a priest since 1964, was now a monsignor, the current vicar of priests (their personnel director), and who also was one of the three chief staffers to several bishops, "in fact, a high ranking church official in the bishop's inner circle."[490] Reluctantly, under Thomas Crumplar's controlled questioning, he had to supply several pieces of the puzzle which the jury was piecing together.

He first explained that St. Elizabeth's in the mid-1960s was one of the largest and most influential churches in the diocese,[491] with the largest high school and a church staffed by pastor John M. Donohoe, and priests Francis DeLuca, Thomas Cini and Thomas Peterman.[492] In 1966 the bishop had moved Donohoe there to become the pastor and Peterman to be his assistant. Deluca also arrived in 1966 to replace Lind.[493]

Next, against his will, Lemon admitted the facts needed to establish that there was only a tiny and intimate community of priests in the diocese at the time. With only 108 diocese priests in total, over eighty-five worked in the small geographic area where St. Elizabeth's was located. So most diocese priests were familiar with each other in that close community and interacted in many ways (such as being aware of each other's problems).[494]

As far as the rectory at St. Elizabeth's was concerned, the site where boys spent so much time in the bedrooms of Lind and DeLuca, Lemon explained that this was the very church where Lemon himself grew up, and he testified that residence was very old, drafty, and without the best of insulation. (So sound would carry from one priest's bedroom to another's.)[495]

Even more important, for every crime there has to be a motive, and Lemon was forced to admit what had been the overriding historical motive for pastors and bishops to keep child molesters on staff in the diocese: the need to staff their business operations during a priest shortage took precedence over the protection of innocent children. (Abundant church business records in that regard were identified in chapter one regarding predator Edward Carley.)

MR. THOMAS CRUMPLAR: I think you testified that there is a priest shortage today in the Catholic church; and there has been a priest shortage since you have been a priest in the Catholic Church, correct?

THE WITNESS: Correct.

That priest shortage even goes back before you, back in the 1940s at least?

Right.[496]

Lemon also provided vital information needed to prove the gross negligence of the pastor of St. Elizabeth's, John M. Donohoe, and his assistant pastor, Thomas Peterman. Basically, that when DeLuca was suddenly sent to St. Elizabeth's in mid-year out of the normal rotation cycle, ostensibly after a public sick leave, all the pastor had to do was to check up on him to ascertain that DeLuca was not a danger to children.

MR. THOMAS CRUMPLAR: The pastor would be the one who would set up the rules of the rectory, correct?

WITNESS: Correct.

Now, if a pastor didn't really know an assistant pastor that had been given to him because he didn't go to school with him, hadn't served with him, he didn't know about him – he could talk with his friend, that assistant pastor's boss at the prior church, and find out something about him, correct?

He could.

Right. And so there would be just a kind of informal to small community of only 108 priests that – if you didn't know something about another priest, you could find out by asking about him, correct?

You could.

And in fact, you would agree that: If you had a new priest with you and you knew nothing about his background, strengths or weaknesses, his past track record, you could ask his former boss, his former pastor, correct?

I could.[497]

Then, after further questioning, Lemon conceded that once it was observed that DeLuca repeatedly was taking children up to his bedroom and on trips with him, he easily could have been reported for his wrongful activities.

MR. THOMAS CRUMPLAR: You also told us that – back in 1966, '69 – there was no formal policy within the Diocese of Wilmington on reporting child-abuse. But it was common sense that: If you were in the rectory and something just wasn't making sense that you would call in to question that, correct?

THE WITNESS: Right.

That if there was something that raised a red-flag that caused a concern you, as a priest, would have an obligation to bring it to the pastor's attention, correct?

Sure.

And, certainly, you would agree that a fundamental duty of all priests is the protection of children, correct?

Agreed.[498]

Crumplar then concluded questioning Lemon with a powerful indictment of the pastor and assistant pastor, both of whom constantly ignored DeLuca's conduct which was repeated day after day, before their eyes, as children were brought up the long dark stairway to his second-floor bedroom.

MR. THOMAS CRUMPLAR: You will agree with me that – as part of your role, and every other priest in the Diocese of Wilmington, that: If you see a situation where the acts of another priest may put somebody in danger, it's incumbent upon you or any

-307-

other priest in the Diocese of Wilmington to take steps to protect the children?

THE WITNESS: Correct.

And that, certainly, is something that was the rule that all of the priests would have had to follow at St. Elizabeth's in the period 1965 to 1970, correct?

It would be a lifelong rule.

And priests have the opportunity to really watch their fellow priests, correct?

Can you clarify?

Okay. Well, you know, you have a – in a public school setting, teachers come together; but then, at the end of the day, they separate. You know, one teacher, say, at Dover High School may live in Elkton, another one lives in Milford, another one lives in Dover; and they don't see each other, correct?

Correct.

Whereas the priests who are there, let's say, teaching at St. Elizabeth's, they all come back and live together at the rectory, correct?

Yes. But you have to understand there is a day off and a time when they go visit their friends and there is no connection.

I understand that. But you have a seven-day week; they get one day off, correct?

Or an overnight.

Or an overnight. And many times priests are going to – they should be concerned about their brother priest. They might want to know where this brother priest is going on vacation, correct?

They might.

And if, let's just say, a brother priest found out that his fellow priest – when he went on vacation, he wouldn't travel with other priests; he wouldn't go to see his mom and dad. When he went on vacation, he would take three or four boys with him to spend a week consistently at the beach. Would that raise any questions in your mind?

In my mind?

Yes.

Yes.

MR. CRUMPLAR: Okay. No further questions. Thank you.[499]

November 3

On day five of the trial Thomas Crumplar changed the focus in order to help the jury to understand what the church culture looked like to a young altar boy in the mid-1960s in order to explain how he could fall prey to a priest who wanted to use him as his sex toy; to help the jury to understand how the Roman Catholic Church operated at that time; and to show the jury evidence that the pastor at St. Elizabeth's – where John Lind recently suddenly had been removed – knew DeLuca was dangerous for kids. He chose for this task Thomas Doyle, a priest expert witness who the Vatican ambassador in Washington D.C. previously had selected to study the American child-abuse crisis within that church.

The witness began by introducing himself –

I am Thomas Patrick Doyle, a Dominican priest in good standing, and I live in Vienna, Virginia.[500] I have been a Roman Catholic priest since 1970, forty plus years.

Before I get into my background, I first want to explain for the jury the different types of priests who operate in the Roman Catholic Church and how it is organized. The Catholic Church is divided generally into geographical sections called dioceses. Each one is headed by a bishop, a man who is a priest. A priest who is officially attached to a diocese in one of those sections is called a diocesan priest. He is ordained; he becomes a priest in that diocese. And he serves there for the duration of his life, unless he's officially detached and attached somewhere else. The other basic division or distinction would be priests who belong to what are called religious orders or congregations. A religious order or congregation is a group or an organization of men who live a common life. And, usually, they belong to an order that has a specific mission or occupation, in civilian terms. In other words, some may teach; some may work in parishes; some may do hospital work. For example, the Benedictines are monks, they're fairly well-known; that is a religious order. The men who belong to that – the priests who belong to that order, they are transferred around to different places in the country or the world where that particular order has its work or its missions.

Now I am a member of a religious order known as the Dominicans. It's an international religious order founded in the 13th Century which has membership in many countries of the world. I believe there are about 10,000 members. Initially, its primary work was teaching, intellectual work, research, preaching. Right now it does a variety of things. There are superior officers, to use a military analogy, in the Dominican Order. They are all elected. The head of the worldwide order is called a master of the order. And, then, each geographic division is called a province, as opposed to a diocese. And each province is headed by what is called a provincial superior.

Now, as far as my background goes, I joined the Dominican Order in 1964, was ordained as a priest in 1970. My first assignment was in a significantly large suburban parish in the Chicago area. I was a parish priest full time for three years and part-time for about another six. Full time parish priest, '71 to '74. Then '74 to '81 part time. It was a large suburban parish in a suburb of Chicago, Illinois. I believe they had about 3,000 families; church held about 1,000 people. I was one of five priests. There were about fifteen of us living in the – what was called the priory – the equivalent of a rectory, where diocesan priests live. Some were retired, some had jobs elsewhere. And I believe six of us, at one point, were working only in the parish.

I was in the Air Force from 1986 to 2004. When I finished my Air Force career, I finished with the rank of Major. As a matter of fact, my first assignment was at Dover Air Force Base here in Delaware near this courthouse. I have very warm memories of being around here many years ago. I served as a chaplain in the Air Force from 1986 to 2003. I served in a number of countries, a number of states in the United States – a number of bases in the States. I served in Germany, Italy; Thule, Greenland. I was in three conflicts, Desert Storm, Operation Iraqi Freedom in 2003. I was stationed – deployed to Kuwait and, also, to the Balkans when that was a conflict situation back in '98, '99. I have gotten, I think, sixteen decorations for service in combat and, also, outside of combat. I am honorably discharged.

For my education, I got my bachelor's degree in 1966. I've also received five master's degrees. One is in philosophy, another in theology, political science, administration, canon law, and Soviet studies. I also have a Church legal degree. The Catholic church has its own, for lack of a better term, legal system; it's called canon law. And I happen to have a doctorate in canon law, which is a research degree. Canon law actually is the oldest continuously functioning legal system in the world. It goes back to the early Middle Ages when it was set up as a separate legal system. I have a degree in that.

Canon law is not doctrinal information; it's not a question of faith. It's, for lack of a better term, a legal system, but it's the internal regulations, structural norms of the institution of the Roman Catholic Church. The Catholic Church is a way of life. It's a spiritual entity called by the Vatican Council the People of God; but it's, also, a political organization with officeholders, with different levels of organization that have rules for property ownership, for disposal of property, and so on and so forth. Canon law is an ancient – it's a legal system very similar to the continental legal system in that it's set up in terms of a code. It also has the rules or the norms for different positions in the church, different officeholders, requisition requirements for holding an office, how that office is attained, whether it's by appointment or by election, what some of the requirements are, the responsibilities, the duties of the officer.

So if someone wanted to kind of understand the relationship between a bishop and a pastor or the relationship between the pastor and his assistants at the church, canon law would probably be the best place to find a description of what the rules and regulations are, what the norms are. Also what the terminology means, the church has its own unique terminology in many ways. The Code of Canon Law is a good place to find what these words mean.

I also have been, I guess, a visiting lecturer at Catholic University of America in Washington, at the Catholic Theological Union in Chicago, Mundelein Seminary in Chicago. I have given lectures at several law schools in the United States – but not as a faculty member, just a guest lecturer. I even have given lectures in Australia, New Zealand, Canada, Ireland, and Great Britain.

Moreover, I have written some articles on pastoral psychology. *Pastoral Psychology* is a journal that's published by one of the universities in California; I believe it's Santa Clara University. It's a professional journal that publishes primarily articles related to psychological issues related to religion, ministry, religious issues. It is peer reviewed. I have published [articles] dealing with the psychological effect and the relationship, psychological relationship, between a Catholic child and a priest. I published four articles – three articles on the direct relationship of not only the priest, but the institutional church on the emotional reaction of victims and their families to sexual abuse. And I co-authored an article with a psychiatrist named Dr. Marianne Benkert on the impact of what we call a complex PTSD, posttraumatic stress disorder, the impact of religious training and nurture on the victims of sexual abuse, how this affects them, how it affects their decision making, how it affects their ability to disclose what has happened to them, and to pursue the issue, et cetera.

I have been a judge in the church. I was a judge in an ecclesiastical church court in the Archdiocese of Chicago for a period of time when I worked there full time. The Catholic Church has its own legal system and its own court system which is, in some ways, very similar to the continental system in Europe. And in '75 I was appointed a judge in that court system in Chicago. I first was what is called an advocate, which would be the equivalent of an attorney, representing people who were seeking annulments, ecclesiastical annulments, which is a separation of a couple in a marriage situation. I think I was an advocate for a couple of years. Then I went away for studies, and I came back. When I returned, I was made a judge. And I stayed there until 1981.

While I am presently sixty-six years old, I am not retired. I do a lot of writing. I
-313-

write articles. I do research. I do a lot of work with victims of sexual abuse, with their families; one on one work; counseling, supportive work. I do consultative work with attorneys, with psychologists who deal with the issue of sexual abuse. I also do a lot of – I am a licensed addictions therapist. I try to do some research in that area, plus some family counseling, family work; and I do a lot of hospice, volunteer work. Presently I am doing work with – the past two, three years with an organization that specializes with working with children with terminal illnesses. I work with the families and, also, try to provide counseling and support of the care givers. It's extremely traumatic to be with dying children, as you can imagine.

As an additional area of my expertise, in 1981 I was asked to go and work at the Vatican Embassy in Washington, D.C., which I did. I was there from '81 to '86. While the Vatican is not a country, it's unlike any other religious denomination. It's recognized by the community of nations as a separate state, so they do have a diplomatic corps. The man there, the so-called ambassador, was the representative of the Pope to the Catholic Church in the United States. And a couple of years after I was there, the United States entered into diplomatic relations with the Holy See, which is the legal term for the Vatican as a political entity.

During my service at the Vatican Embassy in Washington, D.C. my primary job there was to monitor or manage the program whereby men were selected to become bishops, whereby they were appointed to be a bishop of a diocese or whereby they retired or a diocese was created. I also was the staff canon lawyer. And I handled many issues that came along that involved ecclesiastical maters.

In 1984 my boss, the head of the Vatican Embassy, gave me a special assignment dealing with sexual abuse of clergy. In the summer of 1984, I was asked to handle the correspondence that came to us with regard to a particular situation in Louisiana whereby a priest had sexually abused a number of children. And six families complained about it consistently and entered into a confidential agreement with the Catholic diocese down there. Shortly after the initial communication between that diocese and the papal nuncio, the papal ambassador, one of the families pulled out of the agreement and sued the diocese. That, basically, started the process whereby a lot of publicity became attached to these revelations of sexual abuse by the clergy. I was asked to prepare a series of reports on what was going on down there for my superiors, the papal ambassador. But, at the same time, two of my colleagues and I – one was a priest psychiatrist and the other an attorney who was involved – on our own decided to write a memo or a manual to assist the church, to assist bishops, in dealing in a practical way with these problems as they were coming up. This at the time – the publicity attached to it and the public revelation was seemingly new.

The paper was divided into question-answer format into several sections, mainly questions about the civil law, dimension of sexual abuse by clergy of children, psychological or medical questions, canon law and pastoral questions, and insurance questions. We set it up on the advice of several bishops, question and answer format, and it ended up being about ninety-five pages long. Attached to it there were several professional articles that the priest psychiatrist selected explaining what pedophilia was, which is the disorder whereby men are sexually attracted to children. These are professional articles from psychological psychiatric journals Because of my position at the embassy, I also spent a great deal of time discussing this issue informally with a lot of other bishops, several archbishops, and a couple of cardinals looking for guidance. At the time it was a very intense issue, back in '85, '84. to help the bishops to understand what this was and what the best way to deal with it was.

And now, with my background and expertise and experience out of the way, it is time to get to the point of this trial, Francis DeLuca and how St. Elizabeth's church handled him. I have researched this back to the Fourth Century, and I have reviewed thousands of ecclesiastical files, hundreds of thousands of pages of church documents. And I have reviewed documents dealing with the issue of sexual abuse within the clergy within the Diocese of Wilmington from the '50s up through the '70s. I also have reviewed documents to obtain a familiarity with a priest known as Francis DeLuca and reviewed documents and materials to get a familiarity with a parish in the Diocese of Wilmington, St. Elizabeth's. Moreover, I am familiar with the particulars of Mr. Vai's case. I understand that he grew up in a strong Catholic home, his mother wanted him to be a

priest, and he was an altar boy.

So given the research I have done and what I know of the facts of this case, I can explain a little bit in terms of the unique relationship between a young boy who wants to be a priest and the power or control that the priest would have over him.

In the 1960s, the period involved here, children were taught – adults were taught as well – that priests were significantly different from lay people after they were ordained. They were taught that priests take the place of Jesus Christ, especially when the priest is celebrating mass and he says the words: I turn the body – the bread and wine into the body and blood of Christ. They were taught that the priest is the intermediary between the Almighty and the lay person, the child and the adult. Catholics were taught then, and still are taught, that the ultimate goal of being a Catholic is salvation; in other words, living in heaven after you have crossed to the other side. And that essential to that is participation in what we call the sacraments, the seven sacred rituals that correspond to key moments in life such as birth, adulthood, death, et cetera. Participation in these rituals is essential. And that the priests and the bishops are the – they are the guardians of these sacraments, of these rituals. You must deal with the priests. You must go through them to receive these sacraments because they are the administrators in most cases, except for marriage when the couples are – but that's another issue.

So the child and the adult were taught – officially taught to view the priests as an Alter Christus, another Christ; to view the priest as someone who lived in an exalted, almost in a mysterious world.

Culturally this was reinforced by the fact that, in the religious services that take place, the priest is on an altar removed from the people wearing very special clothing called vestments. They live in a rectory which is, in many ways, an isolated place, a place of mystery. These are the cultural reactions to the role of a priest in the lives of Catholic children and Catholic adults at the time.

It was a role – an exalted position; one that demanded great deference and respect. You were taught never to question or harm or insult a priest, that that would incur the divine wrath, either in this world and/or the next.

The fact is that you are taught that you need – you have to have the priests and the bishops for the ultimate goal which is salvation, which is your safety in the eyes of the Almighty. You need them to forgive your sins because, if you commit a grievous sin, that is going to amount to a life sentence in hell. The way for absolution from that sin is a confession to the priest, and absolution. He is the only one that can do it. You can't do it in the mirror to yourself.

If you are refused absolution, if you get a priest angry at you or something like that, it can instill incredible fear into an adult or a child that: He is not only angry with me, God can be angry with me.

Now in this process, John Vai was an altar boy in the 1960s. I myself was an altar boy in the '50s in upstate New York. And we were taught that, first, the mass was this great mysterious ritual surrounded with a great deal of mystery and awe; and that it was a tremendous honor for little boys like myself, in the sixth-grade, to be that close to the priest. At that time the rules in the Catholic Church were such that lay people did not get into the area where the sacrifice – where the mass took place, what is called the sanctuary. Lay people could not even touch the sacred vessels, the chalices, and the other vessels that were used. You couldn't even touch those. So the altar boy had a tremendous role, a tremendous honor and awe to be that close to the priest. You were taught, and it was portrayed in such a way that there is this immense power surrounding priests, kind of a mysterious power, and you were close to it. I still recall vividly the feelings of awe and fear when we were beginning to be taught to be altar servers, and when we were allowed to actually serve at the services which, at the time, were very complex. They were conducted in Latin with a lot of Latin music. And so it was a very other-worldly experience.

During the 1950s and throughout much of the '60s, when the priest was up there conducting the service, the services were never allowed to be used – to be conducted in the vernacular languages, like English, until, I think, 1966 right after the Second Vatican Council which went on from '62 to '65. Prior to that, everything was in Latin except the sermon; and any request for increased donations was in English. The altar boys had to learn a certain amount of Latin, what we called responses to the prayers the priests said. We may not have known exactly what we were saying, but we had to learn to pronounce those words.

Now in this time period, let's just say that you have a young boy who has grown up in the faith, born in 1952, like John Vai, altar boy, thinking about being a priest, and a priest does something wrong to him in '66, '67. Let me ask, in terms of what he's taught, would there be any disincentives, in terms of the teachings, to make a complaint about what this priest had done wrong?

Of course there were. There would not only be a disincentive, you would be incredibly fearful. First off, the shock that the priest – I remember the first time a priest got angry; and I was stunned, I didn't think that ever happened. But if a priest did something of the nature of what we're speaking, that would entail shock, disbelief. I have spoken with more victims that I can count. Many of them said they were just absolutely stunned when this happened. They could not even think of words to use to describe it, and were in tremendous fear of ever saying anything because we were taught to say anything ill about a priest would result in God's anger.

The impact of this testimony by Thomas Doyle on the non-Catholic members of the jury was fundamental to their understanding why children in the 1950s and 1960s were helpless before their priest predators. Doyle had placed them in the shoes of a young boy living in the church in the 1960s. They now understood how confused and helpless a boy would be when he

-319-

became the victim of someone who he was taught was not much less than God to him and who held the keys to heaven or hell for his eternal existence. They now also understood that, within the mysteries and rituals of the Roman Catholic religion, it was impossible for any of its followers to even comprehend or believe that a priest would be capable of sexual abuse.

The theme of the unique role of a priest in Catholic culture was heard throughout this trial from many witnesses. In the video testimony which the jury had seen on day three of the trial, former Bishop Michael A. Saltarelli also had explained the unique role of the priest in Roman Catholic culture. Because every Roman Catholic is taught that the priest is a direct intermediary between God and a child, Saltarelli admitted that it would have been very difficult back then for any abused child ever to have attempted to report wrongful conduct of a priest to anyone at all.

Under questioning by Crumplar, the focus of Doyle's testimony then turned to what the pastor of St. Elizabeth's had the reasonable opportunity to learn from his bishop when DeLuca was suddenly transferred to that church after a sick leave and John Lind was uprooted from his assignment there. Doyle explained that the bishop "certainly could have told the pastor if DeLuca had been away for medical treatment for whatever. And there was nothing which would prohibit the bishop from telling him that father so and so is coming back from alcohol rehab or he has been in a mental institution for a breakdown of some sort. The bishop would have to tell that as a moral obligation to the incoming pastor."[501]

Doyle then also commented upon the fact that DeLuca replaced John Lind who after just two-and-a-half months at the local church, where he abused several boys, was sent to Seton Psychiatric Institute in Baltimore Maryland. The jury learned, as had the jury in Jimmy Sheehan's trial, that Seton Psychiatric Institute was a well known mental health institute founded

-320-

and sponsored by the Roman Catholic Church in 1844. It closed its doors in 1972. It was a fully accredited mental health facility where Catholic clergy, among others, were sent early on in the twentieth century for treatment for psychosexual abuse disorders.

Doyle moved toward concluding by stating that St. Elizabeth's church and its pastor back then were well aware of the danger of their priests sexually abusing children because church law, canon law, dealt with the danger of priests abusing children. He testified that "the church's internal system has a section called penal law or criminal law. In it, they have a number of specific acts or actions that are considered to be criminal according to the Catholic church's rules. One of these is sexual abuse of a minor by a cleric, that's a priest, a deacon or a bishop; that is considered a crime. And the law itself says that these men guilty of this crime can receive a number of punishments up to and including dismissal from the clerical state, commonly known as defrocking, being kicked out of the priesthood. This was codified in 1917 as a crime, but it had existed in various form even earlier in the church."[502]

And then Doyle ended his testimony with one last thought for the jury. As had Father Jennings earlier on day three of the trial, he explained that the private living quarters of priests in a church rectory were off limits to children. He indicated that there always have been either unwritten or actual written rules that restricted access to the private quarters, the bedrooms, the living quarters of the priests just to the priests. And only on rare specified occasions were lay persons allowed in those areas. He underlined this by sharing a personal experience.

THE WITNESS: I can remember one incident. This was in Canada where we were living. I was – there was a priest of the parish that was active with a bunch of us who played hockey. He invited a couple of us up to his bedroom. I don't even remember what the discussion was about, something about a hockey game somewhere. There was a knock on the door, and it was the pastor. He called the priest out, and a few minutes later the priest came back in. He said, unfortunately, we're going to have to continue this downstairs because I am not allowed to have young people in my quarters, in my bedroom.

MR. THOMAS CRUMPLAR: That was an example of the pastor enforcing the rules?

That's right.[503]

At this point in the trial, it was abundantly clear to the jury that the pastor of St. Elizabeth's never enforced this rule in his rectory and that children often went up that dark rectory staircase to John Lind's and Francis DeLuca's bedrooms.

* * *

Three and a half years after Carol A. Tavani, M.D. first had explained to a federal court jury and to the general public, at Kenneth Whitwell's trial, the ramifications of childhood sexual abuse on the life of an individual, in the afternoon of day five of this trial David Springer, M.D. next was sworn to testify before another citizen jury to inform them of the same problem in all of its aspects. The first of three medical experts to testify for John Vai at trial, aside from his professional credentials, his experience within the Roman Catholic Church medical system added to his expertise.

He identified himself as –

David Springer, M.D. a board certified psychiatrist who has been in practice since 1989.[504] My experience has included private medical care, medical care for governmental agencies, such as the prison system, the veteran's administration or institutions for the care of the mentally ill, along with supervision of physicians in

-322-

training during their medical residency in psychiatry.

Since both medical doctors, known as psychiatrists, are going to testify in this case, along with psychologists, let me explain the difference between them. A psychiatrist is a specialist in the field of medicine, so it's – a person gets a medical degree – receives a medical degree, and then they go on to specialize in psychiatry, but it's a subset of medicine. For psychology it's a graduate degree, so some go through four years of college, then they go on to a five year – depending on the length of their program, but a five-year graduate degree and a Ph.D.; they actually do the Ph.D. paper. There are some similarities in the training, but psychiatrists are physicians, so that they get the training, the whole gamut of all kinds of medical disorders, as well as have the ability to prescribe medications.

The fact that I have medical training assists me in dealing with someone such as John Vai when I do his psychiatric evaluation. Given our medical training, psychiatrists tend to look at the entire history of a person in a very holistic way, including their medical background, what medical conditions might impinge on their psychiatric symptoms, what psychiatric symptoms might affect them medically, et cetera; so it allows for – in my opinion, I might be a bit prejudiced, but a more thorough kind of diagnosing. For example, there are numerous medical conditions that have psychiatric side effects; Parkinson's disorder, for example, which has psychiatric symptoms.

A significant percentage of the patients I see, such as combat veterans, have posttraumatic stress disorder. Posttraumatic stress disorder is subsumed under anxiety disorders. And it involves a reaction that somebody has to an event that's out of the ordinary human kind of events; in other words, an extraordinary event that would be very

-323-

traumatic. So, like combat, like sexual abuse – could be a severe car accident, so it could be a serious illness even. And what happens is people's abilities to cope with that get overwhelmed; and when it gets overwhelmed, it's kind of like two sets of different kinds of symptoms they get. One is that their nervous system just can't handle it, so they get irritable, angry; they can't sleep well; they get flashbacks to the incident. They might have nightmares, panic attacks, et cetera. And then, on the other hand, as a kind of a protective measure, the body tries to kind of not deal with it at all, so they might shut down, they might feel numb. Often, substance abuse is involved or alcohol to kind of keep those thoughts away. There's avoidance. So, if they were in a car accident, they might not want to be in a car or near the place where something happened that was traumatic. They might not feel like they have much of a sense of future because they just feel like their world is coming to an end.

So those are two kind of general areas. One is kind of reactivity because their system is overwhelmed. The other is avoidance. On avoidance that would be a situation where if somebody was in combat, had a horrible experience, he would want to avoid anything that reminded him of that experience. For instance, they will not meet with any of their fellow, you know, combat buddies if they have reunions and things like that. They just will not go. There are some that refuse to go down to the Vietnam Memorial down in Washington DC. It just – even the idea of it, or even just seeing news reports about Iraq or Afghanistan on the news, they just can't even tolerate anything like that.

Let me explain about my medical experience with the Archdiocese of Philadelphia in nearby Pennsylvania. I was the medical director for, eight years, May 1, 1999 to December, 2007, at St. John Vianney Center. St. John Vianney Center is a small psychiatric hospital. It's in Downingtown, Pennsylvania, outside of a Philadelphia. And it's owned by the Archdiocese of Philadelphia. It's actually accredited as a full psychiatric hospital, but the patients are all religious Catholics, so it's priests, nuns, religious brothers or monks. And it – you would see the gamut of different kinds of people there from depression to bipolar disorder, even dementia, people having adjustment problems. And during the time that I was there, we also had a number of people who came in because they were – had – were pedophile priests, so we ended up treating or attempting to treat some of these folks. As medical director, I was actively involved in the development program and the overall treatment there, as well as I had my own case load. And so in that treatment of pedophile priests that had been sent there I gathered some appreciation and understanding in terms of the problem of pedophilia within the Catholic culture.

In my professional career I also have treated dozens of victims of childhood sexual abuse. I can't put an exact number to it, but many. Unfortunately, at St. John Vianney, a very high percentage of the nuns even had a history of being sexually abused.

Let me now explain some of the tools a psychiatrist uses in making a diagnosis and prognosis. [Although this information was noted in great detail by Dr. Springer for the jury, the decision was made not to repeat it here because of Dr. Carol A. Tavani's testimony in chapter two which covered the same information.] Like most specialties in medicine, but especially in psychiatry, the history is the key. So taking a history from a person, getting a time line of events, using any corroborating evidence or information like medical records or other people that might be involved and knowing the person, putting that together in totality is the way that psychiatrists come up with the diagnosis.

And there are various parts to that. So there's, obviously, the current issue, the thing that's going on currently, and all the surrounding events around that. There's the past psychiatric history, so just kind of going through does the person have – excuse me – does the person have an anxiety disorder, depression disorder, bipolar disorder, psychotic? Do they have a whole range or gamut of other psychiatric disorders that might be present? Medical problems, what medications they're on, their social history, you know, marital history, children, alcohol and drug history, any family history of other psychiatric disorders, et cetera. And then a total mental status exam, which is kind of like the psychiatrist's physical exam.

So let's turn now to my mental status exam of Mr. Vai and my written report on him. I saw him for about five and a half hours or so, something like that. On October 2nd of last month, I wrote that "Mr. Vai's appearance was well-kempt. His manner was pleasant and cooperative. His speech was clear and goal-directed. Mr. Vai had no movement disorders observed. His mood was sad, 'sad – have to go through this again.' His affect was appropriate to his mood and full range; at times, he became angry and sarcastic."

Let me put mood and affect together. The mood is, you know, sad, happy, angry, whatever you're feeling at the time. Affect is how you're expressing it. So a person can say they are any one of those things, but their degree of expressivity can be along a continuum, so they could be very constricted, they could be screaming and yelling, so it could be appropriate to the mood. They could say they're happy and they look sad, so that's what the affect is.

"Mr. Vai exhibited no auditory or visual hallucinations or suicidal or violent ideation. He had no obsessions, compulsions, racing thoughts, paranoia, delusions, special powers, hyper-religiosity or grandiosity." He is totally normal in that there is no indication, either in anything that I found in my mental status exam, history, or review of medical records, that Mr. Vai had ever exhibited any delusional, paranoia, schizophrenic behavior. That means that he's not given me any history that's based on something that is delusional, meaning a false, fixed belief, or he's not having hallucinations and making things up in that regard. So it would, obviously, increase a person's reliability when they're not psychotic. [And so the jury had heard here an expert medical reply to any contention or implication that John Vai was either a liar put up to his case by unethical lawyers or simply crazy.]

"His thought process was normal. Mr. Vai's sensorium was alert and oriented to person, place and time." While his functional memory was ok, to jump ahead in my report I did conclude that he did have memory problems, with specific memories, specifically tied into the abuse by Father DeLuca. Well, in Mr. Vai's history, he was abused by Father DeLuca for a couple-year period between, I guess, 8th or 10th grade, somewhere in that neighborhood. He kind of had very vague memories thereafter for a couple of years or during – actually during that period after the initial abuse. And he – as he says, he kind of shut down those memories for a long time.

The next significant period in which he remembers the abuse is when he's thirty-five years old. At that time, he was getting married, and his bride-to-be had been previously married, but not in the Catholic church, and he wanted to get an opinion about whether or not they can get an annulment and he could be married in the church. And John goes to his mother, and she suggests, "Why don't you go to Father DeLuca and see what he has to say about this?" Obviously, she had no idea about the abuse. Mr. Vai had never told her about the abuse, and Mr. Vai clearly had not remembered actively about the abuse at that time. So, he goes with his fianceé and meets with Father DeLuca, and he has an intense visceral response. He feels very uncomfortable. He had to get out of there. He wasn't quite sure what it was. And after a relatively brief time, he leaves the meeting. And, subsequently, he told his fiancé that he had been abused by Father DeLuca. So this was an example of what is called a repressed memory. The trauma of being abused was so great, so significant, that in order to psychologically protect himself, Mr. Vai literally did not remember the abuse 'til such time as he had then confronted Father DeLuca; and part of it was, and very common with these kind of situations. Father DeLuca had a certain kind of smell, some aftershave or some kind of smell that he had that was very distinctive, and that brought back the memory.

And that's very common in people who have this kind of trauma; and what's, you know, called "traumatic amnesia" is another kind of medical term, for it is part and parcel of people very commonly who have posttraumatic stress disorder.

This is a means for the body or the mind to protect itself. It's so painful to see something or to remember something that happened that was so horrible and so traumatic that, literally, the brain shuts down, and the memory can go away. I mean, I can give you an example of a more benign kind of situation which had nothing to do with PTSD, nothing to do with trauma, but shows you just as an example to explain this phenomenon.

I had a patient who I was seeing in my private office for a matter of literally three years. In my office, I have my chair and a couch that's next to me and a couch that's kind of on the other side of the office; and for three years, this gentleman sat in the couch on the other side of the office; and he was dealing with issues of trust; and many issues were in intimacy and trust. And after literally three years, he looked at me and he said, "When did you bring that couch in that's right next to you?" And he didn't even – he had not seen it. Those are just the process of the brain, because he didn't want to sit there. That would have been too uncomfortable for him to sit next to me or to sit relatively close to me. And so what happened is, literally – and he's not a psychotic person. He's just an anxious guy. And – but he literally thought that I had just brought that couch in, and that couch was never there. He had walked into my office weekly for three years. Now, that's just a phenomenon of the brain, how it works to protect itself. That was not a traumatic situation. I mean, he didn't have anything like any sexual trauma, but he had issues around intimacy and trust in his life. Mr. Vai's situation is, you know, through the roof. And so you could see where the mind can work to protect the person and where they literally can not remember what happened.

At certain times with repressed memory, the memory can come back, as it did in the example I gave with – when Mr. Vai was getting married. Now there also is a difference between suppressed memory and repressed memory. Sometimes it's a matter of degree, but a repressed memory would be something that really is out of a person's conscious awareness. A suppressed memory is more of a memory that you can bring into your awareness. It's almost like I don't want to think about it, but if you, you know, try to think about it, it will come back; so it's just a matter of degree. And there is no reason why someone can't have both repressed memories and suppressed memories at the same time. Let's say, there's a series of traumatic events, and someone has repressed a number of them, so they're in the unconsciousness, but one of the events is suppressed, it's at the surface, but he tries to avoid it.

Concerning repressed memory, I recently was treating a veteran who was in combat in the Vietnam War, and literally forty years after he fought there, was diagnosed for the first time with posttraumatic stress disorder. And he had no idea that he had it. He just thought he had bad dreams, I got a drinking problem, my relationships are bad. I don't know what's going on. And then he began to realize that those bad dreams were part and parcel of his trauma that he experienced in Vietnam.

Now there also are significant differences between the combat veteran and a teenager or a young boy and being an adult. As an adult, presumably, we have more defenses. We have life experience. We know how to protect ourselves psychologically more so than a child who's naive and innocent and had really no idea why this thing is happening to him. In the particular case of priest abuse, the priest is also an exalted person in the community. He's a person who has, you know, been elevated to a position where they are kind of an intermediary to God, and so there's almost no question this person is going to be caring for you and look after you. So when that happens – and then to an innocent child who doesn't have defenses, doesn't have the ability to protect themselves, it's much more traumatic, much more damaging than the example of someone who's been, you know, traumatized in a war situation, which is also very traumatic. But because of the child, they can't protect themselves.

And what often happens is that they blame themselves. That's almost the universal situation in victims of pedophile priests, is that they blame themselves. They think that they were at fault. And why do they do that? They think it's – we think it's not logical, but from a child's point of view, either the priest is a sick, sick person, or something's wrong with them; but they couldn't consciously come to the conclusion that this priest is sick. They're – their parents love them, the community loves them. They're up on, you know, the altar. There is – not a person that can – you consider to be doing these horrific things so, it's got to be – got to be the victim. That's who the person blames. And that blame, that self-blame is what oftentimes is a driver for a lot of the other problems a person has in life, you know, poor self-confidence, a sense of unease, depression, anxiety, which I think all fit for Mr. Vai. Even though we didn't even have "the memories" active because he repressed them, it's that self-blame that I think has caused him to suffer silently or quietly for all these years.

With a priest is like – almost like a parental figure for a young boy, especially in the time period we're talking about, which was in the '60s where priests were much more respected at that time; even all authority figures probably were more respected at that time; and, so, the idea that this was a trusted person changes from just an anonymous, you know, stranger who might commit a horrible act of abuse, because it's now just not the trauma of being abused, it's the trauma of being abused by a trusted person. So the idea is how can you really trust somebody again? If the person – this person who's supposed to be beyond reproach can do that to you, how can you really trust somebody? And, in Mr. Vai's case, he's had trouble in relationships. He's isolated himself. His first marriage failed. I think, over the years, he's managed to get to a certain point of trust with his current relationship; but even there, it took them years before he was even able to tell her that he was abused. So – and even there, they haven't really talked about it too much, because it's so hard for him to open up to people.

It also affected his relationship with other authority figures, such as his

-331-

employers. Mr. Vai, although he's had a good career overall, it probably could have been significantly better in that he either was fired, or he quit a number of different positions after getting into conflicts with people. And, as he put it kind of bluntly, it was kind of like: If you do something to me, I'm going to do it back to you. It was kind of almost like: I'm not going to let anybody take advantage of me, which I think comes out of this idea of, you know, I'm not going let somebody again take – you know, abuse me. And I think that's affected his ability to relate to people in authority.

I think it is so difficult for Mr. Vai to think about these matters, let alone talk about these matters, that he visibly becomes shaken when – when the topics are discussed. Oftentimes a child doesn't even know what happened to them. They're not even sure what's going on, but if they – they certainly sense something is wrong going on, but they often don't come forward. They don't really think somebody's going to believe them. And in Mr. Vai's case, he actually thought that if it came out, he would become suicidal, so there was another aspect of this just out of sheer embarrassment. I mean, if you think about the idea that it's going to become public knowledge, even public means not only your family, but it might go to the Diocese or to St. Elizabeth's, etc., that these acts happened. I mean, think about how humiliating that is. I mean, it's extraordinarily humiliating.

Today, in terms of my evaluation, Mr. Vai also has some concern that people will not believe him, call him a liar [as the defense was doing in its case]. Well, I think this is a conflict for Mr. Vai, because on one level he wants to tell people these are the instances of the abuse, exactly where they happened, and what exactly happened on this particular date in this particular place, but he is not capable of doing that. He has snippets of memories about various kinds of abuse, one incident being much more detailed. That's the first major incident of abuse, but he can't get to those kinds of things. So he might think that because he can't be explicit about these kinds of things that he's not going to be believed. On the other hand, he's barely able to say the little that he is able to say. So I think it's very, very hard for him. I think he wants to say it, but on some level his body is saying, no, we're not going there, and maybe we'll never go there.

Now Mr. Vai also was examined by Dr. Carol Tavani who recorded that he has one detailed memory of a single abuse, but the other instances of the abuse are snippets, foggy. That is absolutely consistent with the injuries he has. And oftentimes, these snippets of abuse do become more detailed over time as some of these memories become a little bit more recovered. It doesn't mean the person's making up more stuff. It just means that, you know, as the person gets a little more comfortable with accepting some of these memories, some of these memories do come back. And also, there is a fact from the – you know, as there is litigation going on and evaluations, you know, those are other aspects that a person has to answer questions and has to talk about these things when they ordinarily might want to put it away and not want to talk about it.

The doctor then explained that John Vai's alcoholism since his teenage years (like that of Jimmy Sheehan earlier in chapter three) –

was caused by the abuse he suffered at the hands of DeLuca. First of all, DeLuca introduced Mr. Vai to alcohol at a young age, and so that certainly, you know, contributed to his later drinking problems; but as far as the drinking problems that have existed throughout Mr. Vai's life, I believe that Mr. Vai's essentially self-medicated, that he's using his alcohol to numb himself because he does not want these thoughts to come into his head. And he typically will drink it in the evening when things are

quieter, thoughts are more easily – you know, enter one's mind when things are quiet, at

nighttime, and he needs to drink a substantial amount of alcohol in order to quiet his

mind down.

Dr. Springer concluded by testifying that, to a reasonable degree of medical probability,

"the symptoms that I have described today are a direct result of him being abused by Francis

DeLuca." Dr. Springer also stated that John Vai's "prognosis is somewhat guarded in that he's

quite ambivalent about getting psychiatric treatment at this time. As he is fearful of the painful

memories that might come up in the process. He also is – continues to drink to excess; and, you

know, that's another issue that needs to be tackled. And my opinion is that needs to be tackled,

probably first, before other treatment can proceed. Given the degree also of Mr. Vai's

defensiveness and kind of stoic attitude, it may be hard for him to let his defenses down in order

to deal with some of these issues."[505]

November 8

Trial day six began with attorney Raeann Warner directly challenging the defense claim

that John Vai was a liar by calling Dianne Langberg, Ph.D. to the stand on behalf of John. Dr.

Langberg was chosen as an expert witness because she is a psychologist whose work focuses on

the treatment of survivors of childhood sexual abuse and the world-wide sex-traffic trade of

children. Dr. Langberg explained to the jury that sexual abuse is an interpersonal trauma caused

by a trusted figure, and is usually repeated. Consequently, it does tremendous permanent

damage to children and teenagers' relational and emotional well being. In this way it is

completely unlike the trauma of a terrible car accident or similar events. Dr. Langberg movingly compared John Vai's amnesia as a child's normal reaction similar to the way many reacted who survived the destruction of the Twin Towers at Ground Zero in New York City on 9-11.

MS. RAEANN WARNER:

Q. Good morning, Dr. Langberg.

A. Good morning.[506]

Dr. Langberg, what is your profession?

I am a licensed psychologist in the State of Pennsylvania.

Can you explain a little bit about the type of practice that you have?

I have a large group practice in Jenkintown with psychologists, social workers, and licensed counselors; and we cover just about everything between us.

What type of work do you do there?

Most of my work over the last decades has been working with victims of various kinds of trauma, which would include child sexual abuse, domestic abuse, combat vets, and trafficking victims. And I also have spent a good number of years working with clergy.

Is that clergy victims of sexual abuse?

Victims and offenders, both.

And when did you receive your license to practice?

1977.

Can you tell us just a little bit about your educational background, how you got to the point of being a Ph.D.?

I have a bachelors in psychology, a masters in psychology, and a Ph.D. in counseling psychology from Temple University, which was followed by a two year clinical internship, and an exam.

Can you tell us how you got involved in the type of work that you do, specifically treating those who have been sexually abused as children?

I started working right after I acquired my masters degree and began hearing from counselees about being sexually abused as children, though they didn't call it that back in the earlier '70s. They would just say things like: My father did weird things to me. I was not taught anything about that in graduate school, nor was there much of a literature at the time. I went to a supervisor who told me not to believe their stories. In hearing about it over time from several people, I chose to believe my counselees rather than the supervisor; and that began a lifelong journey.

And for how long have you been specifically treating victims of sexual abuse and also clergy sexual offenders?

Victims of sexual abuse, I'm moving into my 38th year. Clergy sexual offenders, probably twenty, twenty-two years.

And besides your daily practice of treating patients, what other professional activities are you involved in?

I am an author. I lecture. I do training in workshops and, also, in graduate schools, speak at conferences.

On what topics have you spoken nationally and internationally?

Most of the time I'm speaking about trauma and how to treat it, training other therapists, sometimes training church communities how to walk alongside those who have suffered sexual abuse. I have done teaching and training on sex offenders and some things about treatment there. And I have done international work working with other kinds of trauma, such as in places like Rwanda where there has been a genocide, and there are victims of trauma there.

When you say you work with church communities, what denominations or religions does that include?

It has been Protestant churches, across denominations.

What organizations are you a consultant with in regard to trauma, abuse, trafficking, those types of issues?

I have consulted with World Vision, which is a global-like humanitarian organization, and done some working training their care-givers in some of these issues. I have consulted with International Justice Mission, which is largely a group of attorneys. And they do investigations and training and, also, rescue globally for minor victims of sex-trafficking.

Can you tell us what is The Place of Refuge?

The Place of Refuge is a nonprofit inner city trauma and training center that I founded in about 2004. It's in the north Philadelphia Badlands.

And what type of services does it provide?

Counseling and training specifically related to trauma dealing with the violence and things like that in the inner city.

What is your teaching experience, if any?

I have done teaching for graduate level courses around the country to train therapists who are either in graduate programs and will be therapists, or therapists who are already working in the field, how to treat victims of sexual abuse. I have also taught classes on clergy sexual abuse and taught in several seminaries for divinity students and what they need to be aware of in that area before they graduate.

How long have you been teaching in the seminaries?

Twenty years.

What is the goal or purpose of the classes or seminars that you would give to those students?

Well, I teach – for example, in one of the seminaries annually I teach a four-hour workshop for the graduating masters of divinity students who are the ones who will finish and then go into pastorates. So we focus a great deal on what it means to be a shepherd. I talk to them about how people in positions of power can abuse power and what that would look like, and how their role is to protect the sheep and not feed off the sheep; how easy it is for people in power to feed off of sheep financially, feed their egos, feed their lust; and that their job is to protect and nurture those who are weak and small and vulnerable, not to use them.

Can you tell me briefly about your book: *On the Threshold of Hope, Opening the Door to Healing for Survivors of Sexual Abuse*, which was published in 1999? What is it about?

That is a book that is written for adults who were sexually abused as children. I tried to write a book that they would be able to read. The chapters are very short, but it helps them understand their symptoms. It helps them put words to their stories and understand why, as adults, it is still so profoundly impacting them, even though it occurred many years ago. And as the title suggests, it hopefully offers hope to them for healing that can come.

Also, you wrote a book entitled: *Counseling Survivors of Sexual Abuse*, which was published in 2003. Can you tell me briefly what this book is about?

It's a treatment book for counselors and psychologists who work in this field. Because I came to the field at the very beginning and there was not much knowledge about it, I wanted to present a model for how to do the treatment that was therapeutically sound, was ethically sound, and was based in the research and writings that had been coming about over the '90s.

And what is unique about treatment for survivors of sexual abuse, as opposed to treating survivors of other types of traumatic experiences?

Sexual abuse is an interpersonal trauma. The vast majority of children who are abused are abused by a trusted figure. And so it's interpersonal trauma by a trusted figure, it is premeditated, and it is usually repeated. And so unlike, say, a trauma of a terrible car
accident or something like that, it does tremendous damage to self, the identity of the self, in the child and the teenager, and it does tremendous damage to relational and emotional pieces because it's interpersonal in nature.

In your treatment of survivors of various types of trauma, do you use testing materials such as MMPI or TSI, Trauma Symptom Inventory, in your practice?

I do not. I used to use things like that many years ago. But at this point I use my clinical judgment and intuition, and the kinds of questions I have learned to ask and things like that. So, no, I don't do testing anymore.

What about articles? How many articles on the subject of sexual abuse and treating patients who have been sexually abused have you authored?

I don't know. A lot.

Now, have you ever previously served as an expert in childhood sexual abuse cases?

Yes. This is my first time in court; but I have written reports and read depositions, and things like that.

Can you estimate how many of those you have done?

Well, if you count the eight DeLuca cases as eight, probably twelve or so.

And for what firm have you provided these services?

Jacobs & Crumplar and also the Neuberger firm.

And what type of advertising do you do for consultation, expert work?

I don't do advertising at all.

Then how did the Jacobs & Crumplar and Neuberger firms come to you, get in touch with you?

I believe the story is that Mr. Crumplar's daughter heard me speak in St. Louis, Missouri on these issues and told her father about me. And he came up to the office to interview me about my work, and here we sit.

Now, what were you asked to do in this case by the plaintiff John Vai's law firms?

Well, I was asked to read documents. I was asked to write a report on the general effects of child sexual abuse based on my experience and on the research. And, then, I was asked to make some specific applications to John's case.

Well, aren't the effects of childhood sexual abuse basically the same across the board for all those who experience it?

There are general categories that pretty much impact almost all victims. But there are also specific applications because it happens a different number of times for people, it happens at different ages. Children have different personalities and strengths and coping mechanisms. They live in different families and communities, so there are many other factors that can heighten some of the issues and lessen others depending on what happens.

How much are you charging for your testimony?

A thousand dollars.

What do you base that on, if anything?

The amount of work I have lost.

[The focus then shifted to John Vai's injuries.] What information were you provided with in order to formulate your opinions in this matter?

John's deposition and the medical records.

Did you interview John?

I spoke with John on the phone for about thirty minutes.

What else, generally, do you use in formulating your opinion, and – to formulate your opinion in this case in particular?

Thirty-seven years of reading every book I could get my hands on – and professional articles, and sitting in workshops that other professionals have run, and listening to and working with treating hundreds of victims over the years.

When I ask you for your opinions as to the general effects of childhood sexual abuse which are applicable in John's case, will you give your opinions to a reasonable degree of psychological certainty?

Absolutely.

What does that mean to you?

It means that what I say can be supported both by clinical experience, clinical writings, and the research.

Okay. And what was your methodology or process in formulating your opinions in this case?

Well, it was reading through all of the things and looking for the patterns and things that reflect what is common knowledge about victims of sexual abuse, looking for differences that might be unique to the case. Trying to understand, particularly, John's coping mechanisms and how he dealt with the abuse, both as a child and as an adult.

[John's amnesia came to the fore.] In your review of John's specific records and materials in this case, have you seen that he has had repressed memories for some period of time of the abuse?

Yes. It is not uncommon for those who have been sexually abused as children to experience significant amnesia in response to it. And, yes, he would qualify as one of those.

Why is that a common experience?

Well, you have to think about the abuse as happening to a child. So you have someone who is physically smaller, who doesn't know as much as adults, and who is having something horrific happen to them by somebody they thought was good and trustworthy. And they usually either can't get away because the other person is stronger, or they freeze and can't get away. So they just passively stay there because they are so overwhelmed they can't think straight. So what happens is the only thing that can get away is the mind. The body can't get away, and so the mind goes away. The mind goes away by saying: This can't be happening to me; this can't be true; this has got to be a dream; I am sure this isn't so. And if you say that to yourself long enough, you actually believe it. Not too long ago – this is just an example of that. I was interviewing somebody who was – a woman. When she was twelve years old, she went for a sleep over to a neighbor's house. That night, the father of her friend raped her. And after he washed her off in the shower and took her back to bed, she remembers laying [sic] in bed at twelve years of age saying: Okay. If this really happened, I am not going to be able to get up tomorrow. I am not going to be able to function. But if this was just a bad dream, then I can go down tomorrow and eat breakfast with my friend. And so it was a bad dream. She spent years not remembering the event. And many years later something happened that triggered the memory, and it came back. It's been corroborated by the girlfriend that she spent the night with, so it is a true memory.

One of the articles you wrote is entitled: Coping with Traumatic Memory, and that was published in the *American Family Journal* in 2002. Can you explain to me how traumatic memory is different than other types of memory?

Yes. That article was actually originally a presentation that I gave thirty days after Ground Zero in New York City for counselors who were working with victims of Ground Zero. And they were, of course, going to be dealing with traumatic memory. So I was wanting them to understand the differences. When we think of normal memory, which the literature calls either common or narrative memory, that would be the kind of memory that you would use when you sit down at the dinner table and tell your friends or family: This is what I did today. I got up, I went here, I did this, whatever. It's a memory that tells a story. Trauma memory usually does not tell a story unless you work

-343-

really, really hard at it for a long time. In treatment, what it is is stored in fragments. It's because the whole of the memory, the physical sensations, the emotions, the confusion, the fear – all of those things so overwhelm the victim that they cannot, as it were, put all of that in one file in their head. So it gets divvied up in fragments. So, for example, one of the women who survived the Twin Towers falling down that I was meeting with kept talking about: I saw the color of their ties; I saw the color of their ties. What that meant was she remembered the colors of the ties of the people who jumped from the windows. She could not tell me what happened before and she could not tell me what happened after. So that's traumatic memory, it's fragments. It's often sensory. You can remember a feeling or a smell or a touch or an emotion, but you can't tell the story.

How common is it for a survivor of sexual abuse, such as John Vai has done, to misplace exact years or ages of abuse especially in the beginning?

Well, it's very common. Oftentimes people will misplace the age; and, again, it's just because the details of things. You know, they can tell you they were abused; they can

sometimes tell you where it was. They can tell you some of what happened. But because the narrative piece gets shattered in the telling. They can't say, you know, this was during

this year of my life when these things were happening; and, then, I was sexually abused. It doesn't work like that.

Does the psychology or literature discuss the accuracy rate of those who have memories of being sexually abused as compared to other memories?

Yes. Actually, there have been quite a few studies about that since, of course, people raise questions about memories that come out in fragments rather than narrative. There was a study in the mid-'90s which was quite fascinating in that the researchers went back and got hospital records of those who had been sexually abused as children and brought to the emergency room; so this was documented abuse. Seventeen years later they did follow-up with these now adults who had been children at the time. And they found two things. One was that thirty-eight percent of the women and fifty-five percent of the men did not remember that they had been sexually abused. The second thing they found was: When they went back and looked at the story that was in the emergency room documents and compared it with the recall for those who did remember, the accuracy rates were the same. So the telling of the story originally, when the child was brought in by the parents, and the telling of the story upon recall was identical.

In your experience and knowledge, how common is it for victims of sexual abuse to be unaware of all of the instances of that abuse when they begin treatment -- in the case of John Vai?

That's the vast majority of them. And, in fact, many of them even finish treatment knowing there are things they have not remembered. One of the things I always tell my patients is that in trusting the process – their minds will bring to them what they need to remember in order to heal. They don't have to remember every detail in order to heal.

Doctor, what is the significance and the effects of childhood sexual abuse when it occurs to an adolescent, a young boy in his early teens, for example, such as John Vai, as opposed to a child or someone who is older? And just, you know, for effect, I will remind you that this is how John looked when he was abused. [The photo of young Johnny Vai shown earlier appeared on the screen.] He was abused between the ages of

-345-

fourteen and sixteen.

How abuse impacts a child depends, in part, on the developmental stage. So, I mean, obviously there is a difference between a three year old who is being abused and a fourteen-year-old who is being abused. Early teens are profoundly impacted for several reasons. And I am sure you all remember being an early teenager and thinking it was an awful period; and probably most of us would not want to repeat it. Part of what you are trying to figure out are your relationships, your value in your culture, do you belong to the right group or not kind of stuff, your sexuality, your identity as male or female and what does that mean; and you're trying to develop some sense of self-confidence. You know, that's when everybody wants to be cool. So all of those things in an early teen are impacted. For example, when it's a male, part of what you are becoming aware of is identity as a male. Not just in terms of your sexuality but, also, gender roles in society and the culture that you live in. So if your culture says: Males are never victims, males are never weak, males are never powerless, all of those things are shattered for you when you are sexually abused. And you feel a great deal of shame because you don't feel like you meet that qualification for male identity. You feel little and weak and powerless, and not a strong and brave and handle anything kind of person.

What is the difference in the effects or repercussions of abuse when the abuser is a trusted person such as, in this case, John's priest, versus a stranger, someone who isn't as well-known?

Well, I would like to say first of all that, again, the vast majority of abusers are people known and trusted to the child. We typically raise our children and tell them to be afraid of strangers; that's quite backwards, in terms of statistics. So you have somebody who is held in high esteem, you have somebody who represents good, you have somebody who is supposed to protect you and nurture you and teach you; and that person that you trust acts in a way so contrary to that trust that it brings into question trust in anyone. Because if this person can do this, then I can't really trust anybody. So there is much more power to do damage when it's a trusted figure.

In your experience, how difficult is it for survivors of abuse, including John Vai, to come forward?

Well, first of all, according to the Centers for Disease Control, this is one of the most under-reported crimes in the United States. One of the greatest fears that most victims have is of disclosure. This is true particularly of – this is true of adults who have been raped; so it's even more true of children and teenagers because they do not think they will be given credibility. And, in fact, they are often not. I can't tell you how many victims I have worked with who have gone to a parent and said: Mom or Dad, you know, uncle is doing some weird stuff to me. And the response is: Oh, honey, you know how he's weird – and it's blown off. They don't have the vocabulary to say what has happened because they don't have real knowledge of body parts and sexuality and what people are doing to them. So they use language that is more vague, and they are not credited. If they literally say it, the frequent response has been to attack the child for saying terrible things about a good person; so they don't come forward. That's why, if you look at the research, most of the people who come into treatment for childhood sexual
abuse come in their 30s, 40s and 50s.

Dr. Langberg, what psychological functions aid in a child's ability to cope with being sexually abused as is applicable in John's case?

Well, repressing is certainly a main one, amnesia. Using disassociation, which is just a way of removing the mind. People look out windows, look at ceilings, look at wallpaper, all kinds of things, to tell their mind this isn't really what is happening to them.

Children are much more capable of doing that than adults, so they access that as a coping mechanism. Functioning and achieving is a coping mechanism; you know, I will be okay. I will get up and go back to school. I will go back to my job. I will go home and have breakfast, or whatever. So a lot of times you will find those who have achieved and things like that, but it's driven by the trauma; it's not something that is free. So they will do that. You know, sometimes then, on the other hand, you will get kids who do acting out kind of things. You will see a lot of substance abuse. You will see a lot of anger outbursts. You will see sometimes criminal acts, things like that.

Now, what are the types or categories of aftereffects common to child sexual abuse victims that are applicable in John Vai's case?

Well, there are categories of aftereffects, one is physical. That would include things that happen to the body, which would include nightmares; it would include insomnia; it would include substance abuse. Then you have emotional aftereffects, which include a lot of fear and – emotional/relational I would say; fear, a lot of rage, difficulty with intimacy emotionally, difficulty with authority figures. And then you also have the spiritual effects – this is true for all victims. It attacks faith in the child. But when the abuser is someone of faith, of course, that makes it even more so, if you have someone who represents God acting not like God; and so it's very destructive to the child's faith as a result.

And what are the common physical aftereffects of childhood sexual abuse that you have seen present in John Vai?

History of substance abuse, nightmares, flashbacks.

Can you tell me why substance abuse is a common aftereffect?

Well, in trade – in the counseling trade, we call it self-medicating. Rather than saying: I can't function, I can't sleep, I can't do this, I can't do that, and going to a doctor for medication – particularly adolescents and early adults and, then, into adulthood because of addictions use drugs or alcohol to medicate themselves. They're just numbing pain that they really don't understand.

Now, with respect to the emotional aftereffects of childhood sexual abuse, can you tell me which are consistent with John Vai's response to the sexual abuse that he suffered?

Anger, difficulty with authority, difficulty with emotional intimacy, a lot of isolation, a sense of disconnection to people.

What about spiritual aftereffects, which have you seen that are present in John Vai's case?

Well, he lost his faith so – it's just gone.

Now, can you tell us what factors specific to the abuse suffered by John Vai affected the severity of aftereffects in his case?

There has been a lot of research that talks about what makes sexual abuse worse through the years as opposed to getting better. Let me just say the kind of abuse that gets better, outside of treatment later, is: if the child or teenager can go to a trusted figure, tell what happened, the trusted figure believes them, the trusted figure takes action against the perpetrator and protects the child, and there is only one instance of abuse. So, in all of those factors, then you don't have the same kind of factors you do otherwise. When it's a trusted figure, when it is not disclosed or is disclosed and receives no help, when you don't know that anybody else is being abused and you think you are the only one, that really messes with your head in terms of: What is it about me that is making this happen, so you have to go through life isolated, or with it. So all of those things exacerbate the consequences.

What is it about the responses that some child victims, such as John Vai, had to the abuse as it is happening, that can affect them more severely as adults?

Well, one of those is freezing, which many children and teenagers do. So you are, in essence, passive. You let somebody abuse you is how the child thinks about it. The freezing is – you know, I'm sure you all know that when something bad happens we all have this flight or fight symptom. So something dangerous is happening, you either want to run away or you want to put your dukes up and slug it out. Oftentimes with sexual abuse you either can't fight because the person is bigger, and you can't flee because you don't know where to go. For example, in John's case, he was in New York City; where was he going to go? He was a kid. So you freeze, and that's when the mind leaves instead. But then you later interpret the freezing, which is a normal response, as passivity in allowing it. So then you carry tremendous shame and guilt that you did that, even though it's based on a misunderstanding of the dynamics, that conclusion.

Have you seen that shame and guilt evident with respect to John Vai?

-350-

Yes.

* * *

To finish refuting the church's claim that John Vai was simply a liar acting at the behest of sinister lawyers who were persecuting an innocent church, a third medical professional took the stand that day via video testimony since she was out of town on medical society business. As she did for Commander Kenneth Whitwell, Carol A. Tavani, M.D. confirmed for the John Vai jury the medical explanation for his injuries.[507] Her previously recounted exceptional qualifications and probing interview technique need not be repeated here (see chapter two), although the Vai jury was fully informed in this regard.

Because the church sought to prove John Vai a liar since his memory of dates many decades earlier was not exact, as Raeann Warner had done with Dr. Langberg, Thomas Crumplar explored the effect of trauma on memory and as a consequence the fact that often dates are confused with abuse survivors.

Q. His memory, how did his memory seem to be?

A. Well, in the ordinary day-to-day executive functions, his memory is intact. However, there are periods for which his memory is not intact.

Explain what you mean: ordinary day-to-day functions, his memory is fine.

Except for periods in question, which got blocked out.

By "periods in question," are you talking about the abuse?

Yes. Except for that his long-term memory appears intact. His short-term memory appears intact. He can tell you what he had for breakfast that day, etc. If I ask him to remember three complex objects, he can remember them in five minutes. I mean, he does not have a primary cognitive deficit.

Doctor, can you compare the sequence of events that Mr. Vai gave to you versus what he gave to other doctors after you and what he gave in his deposition?

When I talked to him, it wasn't really the events that were often inconsistent, it was just the time-line. The time-line was off. And he was kind of struggling with the time-line. I know that when he spoke with others, he got the time-line closer. And when he came back the second time, the time-line was better. For example, I think he – for example, I think he confused, like, a high school graduation picture, he thought it was a grade school picture, I think.

Doctor, does the fact that you have someone who is a victim of childhood sex abuse – the fact that that person initially had problems figuring out what year that happened, is that unusual?

No. That's not unusual because – especially with children, the mind tends to block these things out. When a child is being abused, they don't have the complicated defense mechanisms that we do. This is the best way I can explain it. So what they do is, they take themselves out of the situation, that the mind just sort of goes somewhere else. And that's how they can bear it. So things like time-line are often off, like that.

Doctor, does the fact that you found out that he was off by three years as to when the abuse happened but all the other things fit, did that call into question your initial evaluation and diagnosis of him?

No, no. A good example of that – it's a little bit different, but I think the same principle applies. If you are in a car accident and you get hit on the head and lose consciousness, and so you have amnesia for the event. Sometimes it's not just for the exact event, but there is a window where you don't remember what happened for a time before it and a time after that. We call that retrograde and anterograde amnesia. And I think there is sort of a similar mechanism there. So maybe that's an understandable analogy.[508]

Dr. Tavani also noted some of John Vai's lifelong symptoms demonstrating the consequences of DeLuca's sexual abuse.

A. He has horrible nightmares.

Q. And how long has he had these horrible nightmares?

He told me he has had them since the abuse.

And has that been consistent? I believe you talked to his ex-wife and his current girlfriend.

Oh, yes. Cindy, his ex-wife, told me that throughout their marriage, and they were married pretty young, that he would have these horrible nightmares where, I mean, he would wake up and look like he was going to hit somebody. And that he had them as long as he knew her. And I think he met her in college, if I'm not mistaken.

And how about his current girlfriend?

The same thing. And she also said that he is very sensitive to like somebody touching him. And if she would go to touch him to try to abrupt these [sic], that he was, he would react badly to that.

How does the fact that someone is sensitive to touch, is that consistent with the history of sexual abuse as a child?

It is. It often is.

Explain that.

Well, there is a feeling, there is a pervasive feeling that people are left with that the world is an unsafe place. And there are problems with trusting people. So because the abuse involved tactile phenomenon and touch, one is often very sensitive to being touched, especially startled. They – in fact, it's one of the diagnostic criteria of Post Traumatic Stress Disorder that they have an easy startle response, an exaggerated response as to things like this.[509]

Finally, Dr. Tavani also addressed the church claim that John had only been abused by DeLuca on just one occasion, if at all.

Q. Okay. Ma'am, just a few last questions. Based upon your evaluation of him, was he able to quantify the amount of abuse? Did he ever tell you the total number of times?

A. He didn't tell me a number of times. He – there was one incident that was pretty clear in his recall. There were a lot of details that he recalled. And then what he told me was that he had, as I said, snippets, he called them. Bits and pieces and fragments. They were more – they weren't so much visual or auditory recollections that he saw and heard, most of what he told me he remembered were more what we would call somatic or affective. For example – well, here is one thing that comes to mind, when he saw these pictures – his mother had kept this wonderful anthology apparently of pictures of their whole lives. And he was going through these pictures. And there were recollections that came back then that Father had taken him to get a portrait done after he had taken him to – was it Mullin's haberdashery that used to be in Wilmington? And he outfitted him, soup to nuts, neckties and everything else, and all he had had was hand-me-downs, so this was a really big deal. And he remembered that. And he actually went back to where that portrait studio used to be. But anyway, he felt emotionally, he got this intense feeling. It was extremely uncomfortable. So it was the feeling that came back. It was like this yucko feeling.

So what you are saying, in terms of the one incident – that was the incident in New York; is that correct?

Yes.

Okay. That he has the kind of full recall, auditory, hearing, seeing, smelling, but these other incidents he doesn't have all that clear, he has much more of the somatic feeling; is that correct?

It's more – physical, that's what we mean by somatic. And affective, meaning it's the feeling that comes back. It's like when you hear a song that you heard maybe with your first girlfriend or something like that or boyfriend and that whole feeling comes back. It's the recapitulation of the feeling. There are some things that – as I said, it's fragmented. This is generally what happens. Like he gets this terrible feeling at the back door of the rectory, but not the front door of the rectory. So there – he can kind of tell from that. And he doesn't know why, because the data is not there yet. The actual recollection of events is not there yet. What typically happens is it does continue to come back, but it comes back in a very, like a jigsaw puzzle like way, with little pieces, and gradually, you know, more and more pieces come together. And then once in a while there are pieces that will fit together. That's the best I can describe it.

And when you saw him in September 2009, over a year and a half after you saw him the first time, had more of these bits and pieces come back?

Yes.[510]

* * *

The time had now come to call to the stand the remaining priest-witnesses from the church hierarchy, to assemble and confront them with the evidence against them and to force from their lips through careful questioning the remaining pieces of the puzzle concerning the guilt of St. Elizabeth's. After that John Vai and his daughter would be called. At this point, after six trial days of sitting attentively before the jury, and by prearrangement with lead counsel Thomas Crumplar, attorney Stephen Neuberger took the lead in questioning witnesses.

He first called to the stand priest Joseph F. Rebman, former chancellor or administrative assistant to the bishop, and presently one of two vicar generals for the bishop, one level right below the bishop.[511]

Rebman was compelled to confirm the earlier testimony by priest Clement Lemon that, upon the sudden transfer of DeLuca to St. Elizabeth's, all its pastor would have had to do to check up on the possibility that DeLuca could be a danger to children was simply to pick up the telephone.

> MR. STEPHEN NEUBERGER: If a parish pastor has a question about a new priest who is being assigned to him and hasn't worked with that priest in the past in a prior assignment he can, for example, look at the local Catholic directory to find out where the priest's last assignment was. And, if he had any questions, he could call up the previous parish pastor, couldn't he?
>
> WITNESS: If he wanted to. Yes.
>
> If he wanted to. If he had a question?
>
> Yes.[512]

Next, through precise questioning, Rebman was made to corroborate the testimony of several witnesses, such as former Bishop Mulvee, that children never were to be taken to an

-356-

upstairs bedroom in a rectory, such as at St. Elizabeth's where Rebman himself lived "for about three months" in the summer of 1966.[513]

Q. You would agree that, as a matter of common sense, going back to your earliest days in the diocese, that a priest was not to have any person at all, be it a child or an adult, into the second-floor of the rectory where the priests lived?

A. That's correct. . . .

But you understand that what the norms and expectations of conduct were throughout the diocese at that time, right?

That is right.

One of those was that you couldn't generally take people up to your rectory bedroom?

That's right. Yes.

I think you also previously testified that it would be common sense that you would not take a child up there, right?

Yes.

And you would agree that: If you had seen a child up there, that would be something that you would have to inquire about, you would want to inquire about; correct?

Yes. I think I would have done that, yes.

That would have been a reportable offense to the pastor? You would let someone know?

Yes. I would say that.

That's just common sense.

Yes.[514]

Last, he had to corroborate the expert testimony of Thomas Doyle, and even deceased Bishop Michael Saltarelli, on the elevated role of a priest in Roman Catholic culture during the 1960s and the feeling of helplessness, even paralysis into which survivors were thrown upon their victimization.

Q. Now, just to focus a little bit on the role of a priest in Catholic culture, is it fair to say that in the Diocese of Wilmington in the 1950s, the 1960s, and the 1970s that the parish priest played a central role in administering what is called the sacraments to parishioners in the parishes?

A. Yes. . . .

Is it fair to say that children were taught that the priests in their parish represented Jesus Christ in a very special way?

Yes.

You would agree that children were taught that the priests possess the authority to act in the place of Jesus, correct?

Yes.

You would also agree that, in the 1960s, parish priests were known as the enforcers of the church's moral code? You would agree with that, wouldn't you?

Yes.

You would agree that it is the first principle of canon law that the faithful owed reverence to their priest and that if you injured a priest you committed a sacrilege?

Yes. . . .

So clergy were entitled to reverence in the 1960s?

-358-

That's right. Yes.

This was taught to Catholic school children in the 1960s?

Yes.

This was taught in the parishes within the Diocese of Wilmington in the 1960s?

Yes.

It's your understanding that this was taught at St. Elizabeth's parish in the 1960s?

Yes.[515]

* * *

Only two key players from the DeLuca era in which John Vai was trapped remained,

priests Thomas Peterman and Thomas Cini. So next Stephen Neuberger called to the stand

Thomas J. Peterman, who was already an experienced priest[516] when DeLuca arrived suddenly in

1966 at St. Elizabeth's. Peterman was the assistant pastor of that church, the veteran principal of

its high school where DeLuca taught and which John Vai attended, and previously the principal

of another diocese high school in Dover.[517] At the time of trial he had been a priest for fifty-

three years and he also had acted as the historian for the diocese.[518]

Peterman first testified that the now deceased pastor, John M. Donohoe, in whose rectory

DeLuca constantly took children up those long dark stairs to the upstairs bedrooms, "was a

hands-on pastor" who "tried to pay attention to detail" and who "tried to leave no stone

unturned."[519]

Concerning the ultimate failure of Peterman and St. Elizabeth's church-run high school

to protect John Vai from DeLuca, he admitted that generally he as the school principal had a

"duty to protect those children [in the school] from things that could hurt them."[520]

MR. STEPHEN NEUBERGER: . . . you would agree that you also had a duty to protect students from people that could hurt them, correct?

PETERMAN: Yes.

For example, under your watch, St. Elizabeth's just didn't let any member of the public walk into the school and have access to the students, right?

That's right.

The safety of the kids in your school, that was probably the most important duty you had as a principal?

Yes.[521] . . .

You didn't want them exposed to some kind of a zone of danger of any kind, did you?

No.

And you didn't want them being exposed to a person who really had no business being in a classroom, correct?

That's right.[522] . . .

And if you have a teacher or a potential teacher who you eventually learn has a history of sexually abusing children, you might not want that person to be a teacher in your school at all?

That's right.

Is that just common sense?

Yes.[523] . . .

Then you're aware that sometimes people can be hospitalized in the 1960s for sexually abusing children, right?

Yes.

And that's something you would definitely want to know as a principal, right?

Yes.

And having served with Monsignor [John M.] Donohoe for as many years as you did, those eight years, you would agree that that's something that monsignor Donohoe would have wanted to know as well?

Yes.

And the point being, of all this, if you knew that one of your teachers had been sent to a hospital of some kind, you would want to know about that, not only so that you can try to take care of them, but also to make sure that your students and your school were not in danger, right?

That's right.[524] . . .

Now, if you were looking at the local Diocese of Wilmington directory, and you saw that a priest who had been transferred into your school as a teacher had been hospitalized, that was his last assignment, would that have raised a red-flag in your mind?

Yes.

And would that be the kind of red-flag that you would feel compelled to look into?

Yes.

That would be the kind of red-flag that you would want to investigate and get to the bottom of to make sure that your students, your 400-and-some students in your school were protected, correct?

Yes.[525]

Stephen then changed direction and asked this witness, who had served as the historian of the diocese and who had written several books about it from its 1868 founding in the aftermath of the Civil War to the present,[526] to address its historic shortage of priests which led to the business decision to make the staffing of diocesan churches more important than protecting children from priests who were child-abusers. Here Peterman admitted that since he first had become a priest in 1957 "there's been a priest shortage in the Diocese of Wilmington . . . and it has gotten worse rather than getting better."[527]

November 9

Peterman's testimony carried over to the morning of the sixth trial day. Now it became more contentious and confrontational, resulting in his being impeached repeatedly by his previous sworn testimony which differed from what he started telling the jury this day.

Q. So from 1965 until 1970, which includes your time at St. Elizabeth's, you would agree that you knew it was the policy within the Diocese of Wilmington that when a priest had sexually abused children he would be transferred from his [present] to another parish? You were aware of that, weren't you, Father?

A. I was not aware of it as a policy. It happened.

[Confronting the sudden lack of cooperation by the witness, Stephen immediately asked,] Now, Father, do you recall coming to Mr. Crumplar's office on September 10 of 2010 to give a deposition?

Yes.

Now, Father, at the very beginning of that deposition, do you recall giving an oath to tell the *truth*, the *whole truth*, and nothing but the *truth*? [Stephen added the emphasis for the jury.]

Correct.

Do you recall being asked that it was very important that we didn't want you to guess?

Correct.

Okay. Could you turn to page 118 of that deposition, please, Father?

118.[528] . . .

Q. Father, just to direct your attention to that question again, you would agree that that line says that: From 1965 to 1985 it was the policy of the diocese that when a priest had abused other children he would be transferred from that parish to another parish? And then you were asked the question: Are you aware of that as being the policy?

A. No.

Q. And your answer that day was "yes," was it not? [Stephen stressed the word "yes."]

A. It was that day, I guess.

So, specifically, line 16 of your testimony says "yes," correct, Father?

Correct.

And that answer of "yes" is different than the answer "no" that you just gave me, correct?

Well, it wasn't all that clear to me.

"Yes" and "no" is not that clear, Father? [He raised his eyebrows in disbelief.]

Well, I wasn't involved in the policy. The bishop was the one who would decide that. [The witness was struggling.]

Sure. And in these lines you said you were aware of that being the policy; not

that you set the policy, not that you didn't know the policy. You said – you were aware

of that being the policy? And your answer was "yes" was it not? [Now Stephen was

almost shouting out the word "yes."]

Yes.[529]

The possibility was established here for the first time that Peterman, a key witness in this

trial, may have directly contradicted his sworn testimony to the jury that day by swearing to the

opposite on an earlier occasion. Stephen left it to the jury to assess later how this would affect

the weight it might give to other statements this witness would make in the case which might

favor exonerating the church, or which Thomas Cini, the next witness to follow, would make

after he also was impeached time and time again by his prior sworn testimony. In this regard,

Judge Vaughn at the end of the trial, in his instructions to the jury, explained the governing law

to the jury and their power in this area. The Judge stated:

> If you find that a witness made an earlier sworn statement that conflicts with the
>
> witness's trial testimony, you may consider that contradiction in deciding how much of
>
> the trial testimony, if any, to believe.
>
> You may consider whether the witness purposely made a false statement or
>
> whether it was an innocent mistake, whether the inconsistency concerns an important fact
>
> or a small detail, whether the witness had an explanation for the inconsistency and
>
> whether that explanation made sense to you.
>
> Your duty is to decide, based on all the evidence and your own good judgment,
>
> whether the earlier statement was inconsistent and, if so, how much weight to give to the
>
> inconsistent statement in deciding whether to believe the earlier statement or the

witness's trial testimony.

A witness may be discredited by evidence contradicting what that witness has said or by evidence that at some other time the witness has said or done something or has failed to say or do something that is inconsistent with the witness's present testimony. It is up to you to determine whether a witness has been discredited and, if so, to give the testimony of that witness whatever weight that you think it deserves.[530]

Stephen, immediately tried to get Peterman to admit that he knew DeLuca was abusing children at the time he lived with him in the rectory, with the hope that the jury now would recognize that the denials by the witness would indicate that he was trying to shade his testimony to protect the church. Here Peterman again contradicted his sworn testimony that very day, both when the jury had been asked to leave the courtroom and when it had returned and again began listening to the evidence. Stephen began –

Q. And just specific to Father DeLuca, you never witnessed him sexually abusing a child; correct?

A. Correct.

But you had some suspicions about him, didn't you?

I think it was natural that I would have maybe a question. But I didn't have any serious suspicions enough to speak to anyone about it

So you think it was natural that you would have a question, but your question was not serious enough such that you would speak to anyone about it?

That's right.

Right. You would agree that you usually saw Father DeLuca in the company of quite a few of the same fellows at basketball games, correct?

Yes. That is correct.

And ultimately, putting aside the time, when you finally did learn that Father DeLuca had sexually abused children, you were not surprised by that, were you?

Yes and no. I can't say.

Q. So yes and no. So let's focus on the "no."[531]

[The church attorney here sought to prevent this inquiry into what Peterman knew about DeLuca at the time in the 1960s. The jury was sent out of the courtroom and Peterman gave the following sworn testimony, known as *voir dire*, just to the judge.]

MR. STEPHEN NEUBERGER: Were you surprised – would you have been surprised to learn, based upon what you knew pre-1970, that Father DeLuca had sexually abused boys?

WITNESS: No. . . .

THE COURT: Well, it's a proper question. [And the defense objection failed.]

CHURCH LAWYER: It's a proper question.

THE COURT: Bring in the jury.

THE BAILIFF: Yes, Your Honor.

(The jury returned to the courtroom.)

THE COURT: All right. Proceed.[532]

MR. S. NEUBERGER: Father based on what you knew about Father DeLuca pre-1970, drawing upon that base of knowledge, would you have been surprised to know that Father DeLuca had sexually abused boys?

A. Yes. [Peterman here contradicted his sworn testimony to the Court just seconds before! Neuberger looked to the Court with amazement, and the judge

-366-

directed:][533]

THE COURT: You can cross-examine him about the voir dire.

MR. NEUBERGER: Now, Father Peterman, when the jury walked out, I asked you a series of questions, did I not?

A. Yes.

One of those questions was: Based upon what you knew about Father DeLuca pre-1970, would you have been surprised to know that Father DeLuca had sexually abused boys? Do you recall me asking you that question approximately two minutes ago?

Yes.

And your answer was "no," was it not? [Stephen stressed the word "No."]

Yes.

Okay. And when the jury just came back in you changed your answer, did you not, Father, and gave the answer of "yes" to that exact same question; did you not, Father?

I don't think so. I am not clear of how – what surprise, to what extent?

But you do agree that you gave the answer: "No," you would not have been surprised, before the jury came back in, correct?

Yes.

So we're in agreement on that.

All right. [And so twice in succession the jury learned that this witness had changed previous sworn testimony in a way that favored the church.][534] . . .

[Concluding, Stephen asked about the negligence of the church and its officials.]

-367-

Did you ever feel that DeLuca may have been a little too chummy with some of the boys that he was hanging out with?

Yes.

Did that raise a concern to you?

Yes.[535]

Stephen then switched to ask Peterman about priest John Lind who had sexually abused at least two students before DeLuca arrived to replace him and with whom Peterman had worked at a different church. The witness first denied knowing that in 1965 Lind had been removed by the bishop for sexually abusing boys. And for the third time he was impeached by Stephen because he previously admitted under oath that he knew in 1965 that Lind actually "had been removed for reasons of pedophilia."[536] Peterman's credibility before the jury now was in tatters, as was the effort by St. Elizabeth's to deny responsibility for DeLuca's misconduct. After all, Peterman was its assistant pastor when DeLuca worked there and he also had been the principal of its high school whose admitted duty was to protect the children entrusted to his care by their parents.

Stephen ended with this question which illustrates the "I don't care attitude" found in the Roman Catholic Church of the time towards the protection of children. "Did you ever tell Monsignor [John M.] Donohoe about the suspicions you had about Father DeLuca?" To which Peterman simply replied – "No."[537]

* * *

When he lived in the second-floor bedroom right next to DeLuca in St. Elizabeth's rectory where sound carried easily, priest Thomas Cini was a young, rising star in the diocese. He went on to serve as the right-hand man to four bishops over a period of thirty-three years.

-368-

Bishops in this diocese came and went, but Cini remained. For each and every survivor who was sexually abused by a priest of the Diocese of Wilmington, Thomas Cini is the object of their anger and frustration, the embodiment of the cover-up by their church together with its lack of compassion for them and also the manager of its effort to injure them still further by its hard-nosed delaying tactics regarding their claims for justice. So the courtroom was full of survivors that sixth day when Stephen called Cini to the witness stand, forty-two years now a priest, to face Cini's public accountability for the torment they had endured throughout their ruined lives. The survivors hoped that Stephen Neuberger would be their avenging angel who would humiliate Cini into admitting the very bad mistakes of the diocese in its failure to protect them from known sex abusers and also covering-up its misdeeds.

[Stephen first addressed Cini's background and stature within the diocese.]

MR. NEUBERGER: Q. Your first parish assignment was as an associate pastor at St. Elizabeth's parish in 1968, correct?

WITNESS: A. That is correct.

And in the course of your career since then, you have climbed to the second highest rank in the Diocese of Wilmington, correct?

I am a vicar general, yes.

That's one step below the bishop, correct?

Yes.

And you would agree that you share in the bishop's authority throughout the diocese?

For administrative matters, I do, yes.

You are the vicar general of administration, correct?

-369-

That's correct.

You are like the chief of staff to the bishop, correct?

I am.[538] . . .

So, Father, would it be fair to say that you manage the day-to-day administrative affairs within the diocese?

Yes, sir.

And although your job title has changed several times, you have had the same basic position and job duties since about 1977?

I was not a vicar general until 1996. However, I was an Episcopal vicar, which is a different type of vicar; but I was in charge of administration for the bishop's staff, yes.

You had the same basic position and types of job duties even though the title is changed?

Some of them, yes, sir.

You have been in that position for about thirty-three years, correct?

A. Yes. . . .

So you went from being a freshly ordained priest in 1968 to joining the bishop's inner circle in 1977?

I was appointed to the bishop's staff in 1977, yes, sir.

And then you served within the inner circle of four bishops, correct?

I have, yes.[539]

First you were a parish priest at St. Elizabeth's, right, Father?

Yes, sir.

And you also taught at St. Elizabeth's High School, correct?

I did, yes, sir. [Here he corroborated John Doe Eighteen's testimony that Cini was a teacher there.][540] . . .

Then eventually – you served under Father Peterman at St. Elizabeth's in the school, right?

He was principal of the high school, yes, sir.

Right. So he would have been your boss in the high school, correct?

Yes.

Sometime around 1970 Father Peterman moved on to a new assignment, correct?

He did. Yes, sir.

And you became principal of the high school at St. Elizabeth's?

Yes, sir.[541]

[Considering what had just happened to Peterman when he sought to deviate from the sworn testimony which he had given previously, Cini tried mightily to stick to every answer he had given earlier under oath before trial in this and other cases against the diocese.] After establishing that St. Elizabeth's was its own Delaware corporation separate and distinct from the corporation which was the diocese, and that St. Elizabeth's owned its own assets from which financial compensation could be paid to John Vai,[542] Stephen also had Cini confirm the prior day's extensive testimony by Peterman that in the operation of its schools the church recognized the important obligation to protect the children entrusted to a school by their parents.[543] Stephen then turned to the topic of the history of sexual abuse of children within the church and the need to keep children out of the bedrooms of priests.

Q. You would agree that there are specific provisions of canon law that are designed to prevent sexual abuse by priests operating within the Diocese of Wilmington?

A. There are in canon law, yes.

And you would agree that child-abuse is a crime under canon law, correct?

It is.

The same way it is under civil law, correct?

Correct, sir.

These canon law criminal provisions have been in existence since the 1917 Code of Canon Law, correct?

I believe so, yes, sir. . . .

Now, Father, you would agree that the Roman Catholic Church has recognized, since at least the 1800s, that it has an obligation to protect children from sexual abuse, correct?

Yes, sir.

And these rules exist because the church authorities have recognized the possibility of priests sexually abusing children in their parishes?

Yes, sir.

And these rules were designed to try to prevent that, right?

Yes, sir.

Would it be fair to say that there is no dispute between you and I that: In the 1950s forward, the Diocese of Wilmington knew that there was a danger that some of its priests could sexually molest children?

A danger, yes, sir.[544]

[Despite his efforts to appear credible, Cini then began to stray from his prior sworn testimony.]

Q. Now, Father, you would agree that if a priest in the '50s, '60s or '70s was spending an inordinate amount of time with a particular child – a child who was not a blood relative – you would agree that that could be a warning sign, correct?

A. It *could* be [and Cini emphasized the word "could"].

Q. You would agree that that *would* be a warning sign, wouldn't you? [Stephen sought to have him admit that it also "would" be a warning sign.]

A. It *could* be, sir. [Cini stuck to his claim and so his impeachment began.]

MR. NEUBERGER: Okay. Your Honor, may I approach the witness?

THE COURT: Yes.

[Stephen had before him on the top of the attorney's podium a tall stack of the various sworn pre-trial depositions which Cini had given over the years. He pulled one of them from the pile and walked up to Cini and placed it in front of him.]

Q. Now, Father, I have just put in front of you some sworn testimony you gave on March 4 of 2009. Do you generally recall giving this testimony?

And it was in what context? Was it a deposition?

Yes. It was a deposition.

Thank you. Yes.

Could you please turn to page 139 and 140 of this deposition, Father?

I have it. Thank you.

I want to direct your attention down to line 19 on page 139. Then I'm going to read through line 5 on page 140.

QUESTION: If a priest in the '70s, '80s or '90s was spending time alone with a child – an inordinate amount of time with a child that was not a blood relative, *would* that

-373-

be a warning sign?

One of your attorneys says: Objection as to form.

Then you responded: You are saying in the '70s and '80s?

QUESTION: Yes.

ANSWER: I *would* think so [and Stephen stressed the word "would"].

Q. Correct?

A. Yes, sir.

You used the word "would" there as opposed to "could," didn't you?

A. I did [reluctantly].

Does that same logic apply to the '60s?

Yes, sir.[545]

Q. Thank you, Father.

Stephen then returned to the repeated theme, from priest Jennings, through Bishop

Mulvee and others, that children were never to be taken to the bedroom of any priest. He

emphasized for the jury, which soon would have to decide whether St. Elizabeth's had been

negligent in allowing children into DeLuca's bedroom, the "very bad" nature of this mistake, to

use Cini's own words.]

Q. Now, Father, you would also agree that from 1954 until about 1968 it was one

of the rules or expectations of conduct within the Diocese of Wilmington that those rules

and expectations prevented a child from visiting a priest in his bedroom, correct?

A. Yes, sir.

Is it fair to say that: Going all the way back to the mid-'50s through about 1969,

that applying the standards of the day a priest should not have been allowed to take a child up to his rectory bedroom?

I would think so. Yes, sir. . . .

And you would agree that it would be *a very bad mistake* to let an associate pastor take a child up to his bedroom, who was not a blood relative, one time?

He shouldn't do it, no, sir.

Would you agree that it would be *a very bad mistake* if he did that two times?

Yes, sir. [Cini had been forced to admit the extraordinary nature of such a mistake.]

Three times?

I would agree.

All the way up to ten times or more?

I would.

Okay. Is it fair to say that if a priest in the 1950s and 1960s was taking a child up to his rectory bedroom at St. Elizabeth's repeatedly and that the associate pastor or one of the associate pastors or the pastor were aware of that and did nothing to stop that from happening, you would agree with me that it would be *a big mistake* not to intervene? [Stephen carefully emphasized these words for the jury.]

You said "repeatedly," and I would agree with you. [Again these words had been spoken by Cini to the satisfaction of the survivors sitting in the audience.]

Okay. Is it fair to say that a priest bringing a child up to his rectory bedroom is disturbing, red-flag behavior?

I would think so.

That included your time at St. Elizabeth's in the 1960s and the early 1970s, correct?

Yes.[546]

Now, Father, you would agree that a priest who spends significant portions of his free time with individual children should have been reported, correct? [Cini next tried to deviate again.]

I would have to know the reasons for spending the time.

Okay. Father, could you turn to page 138 of that March 4, 2009 deposition, which I think you already have in front of you?

Yes.

Have you found that page, Father?

138, yes.

Let's pick up around line 11. You are being asked a question that: If a pastor or another employee learned that a particular priest was spending significant portions of his free time with individual children, would that be something you would expect that they would have alerted the chancery office to? Father, you understand that the chancery office is the headquarters of the Diocese of Wilmington, right?

Yes. Yes.

And your answer there was "yes," correct?

Yes.

And then the question was asked: And the reason for that is there was a risk of inappropriate behavior? And your answer there was also: "Yes." That is among the reasons.

Among my reasons, yes.

You would agree with that?

Yes.

Okay. Father, you can put that down.[547] [Cini had admitted that spending significant portions of time with individual children should have been reported.]

[At this point the court took a lunch break. Immediately afterward Cini sought to defend pastor John M. Donohoe's lax oversight of DeLuca by fleeing again for the third time from his prior sworn testimony.]

Father Cini, you would agree that in 1960 to 1969 you and Father DeLuca would be evaluated by parish pastor monsignor Donohoe, to see how you were performing your roles as assistant pastors, correct?

He never made a formal evaluation of me that is related to me, an evaluation, but I suspect he was evaluating, in his own mind, how we were doing.

[Stephen now pulled another deposition transcript from the large pile before him.]

MR. NEUBERGER: Your Honor, may I approach?

THE COURT: Yes.

MR. NEUBERGER: Father, I'm putting in front of you your deposition dated March 13th of 2009.

Okay.

Do you recall giving testimony on that date in this case?

It says so; yes, sir.

Could you take a look at Page 107, please, Father, and tell me once you've found that.

I have the page.

Okay. I want to direct your attention to Line 5. Does it say, "Question: Would you be – would you and Francis DeLuca be evaluated by Father Donohoe to see how you were performing your roles?

[Raising his voice Stephen said] "Answer: Yes, very definitely"?

Correct.

That was the answer you gave on that day, Father? [This again contradicted his initial testimony to the jury]

I did.

Okay. You can put that down, Father.[548]

[Because the church constantly tried to blame parents for the abuse their sons endured, Stephen defused any thought in the mind of any juror that perhaps fault lay with the parents of John Vai who naively trusted him to parish priests of their church.]

And, Father, you would agree that it was reasonable for parents, in the 1950s, and the 1960s, and in the 1970s, to expect that the parish priests who their children interacted with in the parish were safe?

Yes.

Okay. And you would agree that it was reasonable for those same parents to expect that the parish priests would not sexually abuse or molest their children?

Yes, sir.

And you would agree that it was reasonable, in that same time frame, for the parish parents to expect that the priests who their children would interact with would be celibate?

Yes.[549]

[Stephen next turned to Cini's association with DeLuca and had him identify a picture from the 1969 St. Elizabeth's High School yearbook that showed DeLuca, Cini and Peterman together. Stephen also asked him to identify by name all the priests who lived in the rectory with DeLuca in 1968. The list included: John M. Donohoe, Thomas Peterman, Howard Clark, and Francis Duncan before Cini replaced him. Cini also was forced to admit that in 1966 DeLuca was carried in the official diocese directory as "on sick leave," a red-flag about which Peterman had previously been questioned.[550] And then for some, perhaps with the most damaging evidence of the day, Cini was questioned about DeLuca's bedroom where so many boys found themselves trapped.]

Q. And specific to Father DeLuca, you would agree that your room was right next door to his on the second-floor of the rectory, right?

A. We were adjacent.

You were adjacent?

Yes. . . .

And you would agree that you worked for father – with Father DeLuca for about a year at St. Elizabeth's, right?

Yes.

Okay. And both of you were both assistant pastors there?

We were.[551]

[Although Cini next tried to portray himself as a figure caring for victims of sexual abuse, he found himself in his fourth sworn contradiction with his prior testimony under oath.]

Q. And would you agree that you've previously testified that, as a teacher at St. Elizabeth's in 1968, it would *not* be important to you to know whether Father DeLuca had

-379-

previously sexually abused children before coming to St. Elizabeth's? [Stephen raised his voice to draw to the attention of the jury to this lack of concern for the safety of children.]

A. Could you ask the question again, please?

Sure. Would you agree that you have previously testified that as a teacher at St. Elizabeth's in 1968, it would *not* be important to you to know whether Father DeLuca had previously sexually abused children before coming to St. Elizabeth's?

If that's my testimony then, I don't agree. If I heard you correctly, I believe I hear you saying that it would not be a concern to me that he had abused people.

Correct, Father.

If I had known that, it would have been a concern, yes.

If you had known that, it would have been a concern?

It would have been.

[Stephen then pulled still another sworn deposition transcript from the large pile on the top of the podium.] MR. NEUBERGER: Your Honor, may I approach the witness, please?

THE COURT: Yes.

Q. Now, Father, does this appear to be a deposition you gave in this case on November 18th in 2008?

That's what it says here, yes.

Could you turn to Page 160, please, Father?

I have it.

I want to direct your attention to – just read quietly to yourself the questions

-380-

beginning at the bottom of Page 159 and through the first seven lines of Page 160. Just read that quietly to yourself, and tell me once you've finished.

It's a long question, and the last question is, "Did you know that?" And the answer is, "No."

Q. Okay. And then the question after that says, "Did you think that would have been something that would have been important to know?" And that something is whether Father DeLuca had sexually abused children prior to coming to St. Elizabeth's. So do you think that would have been something that would have been important to know so that you would be able to look out to see that your students would be protected from him?

A. I would answer yes.

Q. And your answer that day was, "No".

A. Was, "No." I must have misunderstood the question.

And then Mr. Crumplar, who was questioning you, his next question was, "No? Okay." And then he moved on, didn't he?

He did.

That was your answer that day, wasn't it, Father?

It's so recorded here.

Okay. And did you submit what you –

I did not submit an errata sheet, no.

And just for the – so that the jury knows, an errata sheet is a sheet which a person who gives a deposition is – the person who is deposed has an opportunity to review the transcript to correct any typographical errors or anything where you said "no" and you

-381-

meant to say "yes" or things of that nature?

That's correct.

And you didn't submit one for this, did you?

I did not.[552]

The fifth impeachment occurred when Cini identified just two families he could recall who had boys with whom DeLuca spent a great amount of time. But then he was forced to admit that earlier he had sworn that there were more than just two families, that he was "sure there were. The names don't come to me."[553]

[Cini then denied the testimony of John Doe Eighteen on the second day of the trial where John Doe Eighteen said Cini had confronted him and called him a temptation to DeLuca.]

Q. I think you previously testified that you would be surprised if a former student came forward and testified that he can recall you specifically warning him about Father DeLuca. Do you recall testifying that?

A. I read that in the transcript, yes.

And just so we're clear, Father, are you sure that you never warned or – or then just to use a different word – or chastised or cautioned any boy for spending too much time with Father DeLuca or maybe being in the car with Father DeLuca under some kind of troubling circumstances?

I think, as I testified before, I wouldn't have any basis to make that warning. I didn't perceive Frank as a danger.

You didn't perceive Frank as a danger?

To the – yes.

Okay. And is it your testimony that you don't recall ever having any misgivings about Frank DeLuca and kids?

That's my testimony, and that's what I believed.

Father, during your time at St. Elizabeth's in 1968 and 1969, when Father DeLuca was also stationed there, do you recall ever seeing Monsignor [John M.] Donohoe, the pastor, come running towards Father DeLuca, waving his arms?

No, I don't recall that.

Do you recall ever hearing Monsignor Donohoe tell Father DeLuca, "You told me you wouldn't do this anymore. What are they doing in the car?" And pointing to children?

I don't recall anything like that.

Did Monsignor Donohoe ever talk to you about any of those things?

No.

Do you ever recall telling a child in the high school that that child was partially responsible for getting Father DeLuca into trouble?

No.

Do you ever recall telling a child in the school that if they had anything that they needed to confess about Father DeLuca that they should do it exclusively, meaning confess exclusively to you and to no one else?

Never said it. I would have no reason to say that.

That's because, I think it's your testimony, that you never had – that you never knew that Father DeLuca was a danger to children in any way, shape or form, correct?

Not while we lived at St. Elizabeth's together or worked together, no.

Okay. I think you've – would it be your testimony that you're not aware that there

-383-

were any complaints about Father DeLuca while he was at St. Elizabeth's?

I wasn't aware of any complaints of that nature, no.

Now, can you presently recall ever seeing children on the second-floor bedroom area of the St. Elizabeth's rectory with Father DeLuca?

I do not recall seeing anyone – any children there.

Now, do you ever recall seeing children up there, period?

I'm presuming you mean children under the age of eighteen.

Yes.

No.

Okay. What's your definition of a child, Father?

Well, I just wanted to be sure.[554]

[Cini then was confronted with and denied the testimony of John Vai that Cini repeatedly knew that Vai was in that bedroom next door to Cini together with DeLuca who was abusing him.]

Now, you would agree that John Vai, the grown-man version of John Vai, has previously confronted you and questioned you about your knowledge about Father DeLuca, correct?

John did, yes.

And do you recall John saying to you that he was a victim of Father DeLuca at St. Elizabeth's Parish, and then asking you various questions about what you may or may not have known?

Yes. It was at the 341 meeting in November, I think. [Here Cini referred to testimony he had given in the bankruptcy court proceedings of the diocese.]

-384-

And do you recall him intensely questioning you under oath about whether you lived next door to Father DeLuca in the St. Elizabeth's rectory?

Yes.

And the answer you gave him was consistent with the answer you gave us today, correct?

Yes.

And do you recall John [Vai] asking you whether you remembered him walking by you as Father DeLuca made him walk up the stairs to the bedroom area of the rectory?

I recall him asking me, "Don't you remember seeing me come up the steps to count money with Father DeLuca?" And I answered, "No."

And do you recall John saying to you and asking you, as he was walking up the steps to count the Sunday – the Sunday givings – and I'm drawing a blank on the term.

Collection.

Thank you.

– the Sunday collections that John saying that he had to say to you, "Hello, Father." You know, "Thank you for stepping aside, Father. And have a nice day, Father"?

I remember his saying that, and I also read it in the transcript.

And do you recall John asking you, "How can you have no recollection that Father DeLuca was abusing me next door, and you were in the next room?"

I remember his asking the question, yes.

And do you recall John saying, "You know, I know who comes to my house. I know who comes to my parents' – when I was a kid, I knew who came to my parents' house. And, as a father, I knew who came to my house to see my kids"?

Yes, sir.

Do you recall him saying, just expressing exasperation that you didn't remember anything?

I think he said to me, "Look me straight in the eye."

And did you?

Yes, I did. [And the jury was left to assess these denials by Cini in light of the five times he had already been shown to have equivocated on his oath to tell the truth.][555]

Cini was impeached for the sixth time when he denied being aware of at least one instance of sexual abuse by a priest between the years 1969 and 1977. "I don't think so," he boldly told the jury, not having learned his lesson on five prior occasions that day. But after being shown the transcript of another deposition from the stacks on the podium he was forced to admit to the jury that he had sworn three years before that there was "an instance that I heard about."[556] When asked to declare who that one instance involved, Cini then claimed a total loss of memory about what he had been referring to in that sworn testimony three years earlier.[557]

Stephen then began a steady progression toward establishing that Cini was instrumental in covering-up DeLuca's crimes.

Now, Father, you're covering up for Father DeLuca, aren't you?

No, I'm not.

Now, Father, you turned a blind eye to Father DeLuca taking John Vai, John Doe Number Two, and other boys up into the rectory bedroom area, into the bedroom next door to you in 1968 and 1969, did you not?

No, I did not.

Father, you turned a blind eye to Father DeLuca taking Johnny Vai and other boys on overnight trips to New York City, did you not?

I didn't know that he took them to New York City. No, I did not know it.

Did you know that he was taking young boys any place?

When you say "any place," I don't recall him going to places with boys, no.

Do you recall him going to games with boys?

I – he was at games a lot. He could have taken some boys with him.

Do you recall him driving boys to games?

I don't recall that.

Do you recall hearing from Monsignor Donohoe that he was driving boys to games?

I don't recall monsignor ever telling me that.

Father, isn't it true that you're covering up for Father DeLuca when you turned a blind eye to his taking young Johnny Vai, Bobby Quill, and other boys, [including] Bobby Quill's brother, on overnight trips to the beach?

I didn't turn a blind eye, because I didn't know those things were happening.

Now, Father, you were covering up for Father DeLuca when you didn't call the Wilmington Police Department, didn't you?

I had no reason to call the Wilmington Police Department on Father.

Do you remember Lorenzo Vai?

I'm afraid I don't.

Do you recall Maria Vai or Mary Vai, to use the Americanized version?

Not at the moment, no.

Do you remember John Vai's parents?

I don't recall.

You don't recall. So it it's your testimony, just so we're clear, that you did not cover-up Father DeLuca's sexual abuse, correct? [Stephen had locked him in here just before pouncing.]

That's my clear testimony.

Okay. And you're not aware of there being a cover-up of Father DeLuca's sexual abuse, correct?

Personally aware of it, no.

[But] you apologized to Felix Flanigan for the cover-up of Father DeLuca's sexual abuse on September 13rd of 2004, did you not? [The reader will recall Felix Flanigan from chapter four where he took the stand in bankruptcy court and dramatically surrendered his anonymity. Felix was also in the last row of the gallery in court this day and now he actually stood up to be recognized as Stephen asked Cini this question and while Stephen dramatically pointed him out to the jury.]

And as I told the elder Mr. Neuberger, when he made the same question to me in the bankruptcy court, I was in the process of answering questions to Felix. Felix had come to see me at my invitation after I had heard that he had been abused. Through this third party, I sent the word to him, "Why don't you come and talk to us? And the diocese wants to, A, apologize to you for it; and if there's anything that we can do for you, like providing counseling and so forth, we would like to do that." Felix finally came. And towards the end of our conversation, which took place in the rectory at St. Ann's, he asked me several leading questions. After I had told him about our willingness to provide

counseling and gave him the name of the victim's assistance coordinator of the diocese,

he turned to me and said, "Father DeLuca violated me at St. John's, and then the diocese

pulled him out." I said, "That's what I've read." "And then they transferred him to St.

Elizabeth's." I said, "That's my understanding." "And they didn't tell the people at

St. Elizabeth's that he abused at St. John's." I said, "I'm not aware that they did."

"And then he transferred him to St. – to Holy Spirit. And they didn't tell the people at

Holy Spirit." I said, "Felix, I'm not aware that they told anybody at Holy Spirit." "And

then he transferred him to St. Matthews, and they didn't tell the people then." And I said,

"I'm not aware that the Diocese told them then." And he said, "That's a cover-up." To

which I said, "It certainly sounds like it." And yes, I wrote a memorandum to our

attorney

saying I apologized for what appeared to be a cover-up.

So you said you apologized for what appeared to be a cover-up in your

memorandum?

I said I apologized for the cover-up. I think that's what the memo says.

And so "cover-up" was your word; was it not?

It was John's word – pardon me – Felix's word to me, and I agreed. It appeared to

be a cover-up.

So "cover-up" was your word; was it not?

Yes. [He finally agreed.] That I was in a pastoral situation of trying to help out a

victim. And I wasn't about to start playing with words with the man or try to convince

him otherwise. He had told me of his abuse. He recounted the facts that he knew, and I was agreeing with those facts, that Father DeLuca was transferred from St. Elizabeth's to Holy Spirit, and he had other transfers as well. He specifically asked the question, or he made the statement, "I don't think the diocese – "something as to the effect," – told people at the parishes about what happened at St. John's." I said, "I don't think they did." "Sounds like cover-up." I said, "Yes, John (sic), and I'm sorry for it." And I repeat it today.

All right. And then Mr. Flanigan, he thanked you for your candor, did he not?

I believe he did, yes.[558]

[Stephen then concluded his questioning of this witness by presenting the jury with a Roman Catholic teaching which would justify Cini's six deviations from his prior sworn court testimony and even his denial of other accusations which had been lodged against him: that Cini could justify not telling the truth to serve a higher end, such as protecting the church from bad publicity.]

Q. Father, you would agree with me that you're familiar with the concept of mental reservation; are you not?

A. I am.

And your own personal definition of the concept of mental reservation is the idea of someone withholding facts and not describing everything about a particular situation or an event, correct?

I believe that's in my deposition.

Your November 18th, 2008, deposition, right, Father?

Yes.

And you would agree that mental reservation is a concept where you don't tell the truth, the whole truth, and nothing but the truth so help you God, correct? [Stephen pointed to the *Bible* on which Cini had taken his oath before testifying.]

That's part of it; yes, sir.

And you would agree that it's a concept that tries to justify lying by explaining that your own words, which said one thing, really mean something else?

I believe the formal definition is that you withhold certain aspects of the – of the – of the reality for a greater good to protect some other overriding interest. I believe that's the definition.

Right. So the greater good, that could be keeping a secret, right?

Yes.

It could be protecting a friend?

You shouldn't – yes, it could be.

Could be protecting your parish?

Could be.

Could be protecting the diocese, couldn't it be?

A mental reservation?

Mental reservations.

A person could use a mental reservation for a lot of a reasons.

Could be used to protect your church, correct?

I guess.

And you have been practicing the concept of mental reservation in your testimony here today, have you not?

No, I have not. No, I have not.

Father, you would agree that publically disclosing the sexual abuse of a child by a priest could have a negative impact on the image of the parish where that priest was sexually abusing the kid, correct?

It could have.

It could have. It could have a negative impact on the power that that parish is perceived to have in the community, could it not?

I think we've learned that it's very important, regardless of what negative impacts there are, that there be disclosure.

You believed in disclosure in 1968?

I believe I did.

Wouldn't you agree that disclosing the sexual abuse of a child by a priest in a parish could have a negative impact on the – on the offertory, as parents stop donating money because their child was sexually abused?

It could have an impact, yes.

And you wanted to avoid that negative impact, and that was why you didn't do anything about Father DeLuca at St. Elizabeth's in 1968 –

That's not correct.

– and 1969; is that true?

No, it's not true, and you know it.

I'm sorry?

It's not true.

What was that last part? Okay. Father, you were rewarded for your part in the cover-up, weren't you?

I can't believe you're asking that question. I wasn't rewarded for covering up anything.

So you went from being a rookie priest, freshly out of – freshly ordained in 1968, right? You were a freshly ordained priest in 1968?

I was ordained in 1968.

And just two years later you were made principal of St. Elizabeth's High School in 1970, correct?

I was.

And two years after that you were given responsibility for a larger diocesan high school, St. Mark's, my alma mater, in 1972, correct?

Yes.

Okay. And then you were the bishop's right-hand man just five years later, correct?

I was an episcopal vicar for administration. I was one of his staff people, yes.

You were in the bishop's inner circle, correct?

I was on the bishop's staff.

And all that in only nine years, correct?

Is that how many years it was?

Well, 1977 minus 1968, that's nine in my book.

Yes, sir.[559]

* * *

The next brief witness who Stephen called on the seventh day was priest Charles Dillingham, a diocese priest since 1973 and the pastor of St. Elizabeth's from 1997 to 2009. He also worked there from 1983 to 1987.[560] DeLuca helped mentor him as a young priest and they "became personal friends . . . [DeLuca's] closest priest friend."[561]

While Cini had denied being a friend of DeLuca, after being impeached Dillingham reluctantly contradicted Cini and Dillingham conceded that Thomas Cini could be biased in favor of DeLuca because they also were close priest friends. This cast still more doubt on the credibility of Cini.

MR. NEUBERGER: Q. You would agree that one of Father DeLuca's other close priest friends was Monsignor Thomas Cini.

WITNESS. A. Yes, I would agree to that, but I would say that that probably didn't happen in the very beginning when I first knew Father DeLuca.

Right. But he's one of his close priest friends now, right?

Well, it depends on how you define friend.

All right, Father, could you turn to page sixty-six of your deposition, please.

Of course.

And just tell me once you've found the page, Father.

Sure. I'm there.

I'll direct your attention to line eight.

Eight.

Line eight, does that say, "Question: Besides you being his closest priest friend, can you give me other close priest friends that Father DeLuca still would – that Father DeLuca still would claim?" . . . "Answer: Say, Father – Monsignor Lemon, Monsignor Cini." Was that your testimony that day?

Absolutely.[562]

-394-

Norman Carroll, a young priest who was just three years old in 1966 when DeLuca arrived at St. Elizabeth's and who the church used for trial as a sympathetic prop at the defense table, in contrast to the veteran diocesan priests who had to take the stand as hostile witnesses, then was called as another hostile witness to testify on collateral church corporate matters.[563] The day then concluded.

November 12

On day eight, it was John Vai's turn to face cross examination by the church's chief lawyer and to conclude his case. But first day eight began when his adult daughter Ryan testified briefly to explain how John behaved as a damaged father in his family circle. On cross examination by the church she then was attacked as an alleged drug addict.[564] This did not sit well with John Vai who, when he took the stand, explained that dark "stairway to hell" found in the rectory leading up to DeLuca's bedroom. As far as what he had endured at DeLuca's hands, that was addressed earlier in chapter four before Judge Sontchi. But when cross examination by the church lawyer began, John later said of himself, thinking of the church lawyer's vicious attack which his daughter had endured: "I hated her [the lawyer] more than anything in my life. I went into the zone. Game on, let's go." He was ready. The printed page cannot convey John's body language, his voice level or its inflection, the other ways in which he dominated the examination by the church's lawyer or how he challenged her every attempt to misdirect the jury.

CROSS-EXAMINATION[565]

BY CHURCH LAWYER [who began with the theme that his lawyers had put John Vai up to his false claims]:

Q. Good afternoon, Mr. Vai.

A. Good afternoon.

Mr. Vai, on direct examination, you looked to Father [Norman] Carroll and said, "You have me here on trial"; do you remember that?

Yes, I do.

Okay. Well, the fact of the matter is it was you who chose to consult a law firm and file a lawsuit in this case; isn't that true?

Yes, it is.

And, in fact, after you read the article in the Wilmington *News Journal* in July 2007 and testified to the jury that you felt suicidal, your first stop was not to a mental health care provider, but your first call was to the Neuberger-Crumplar law firm; isn't that true?

I don't understand your question, ma'am.

Well, is it your testimony that you went and sought some sort of mental health counseling, psychiatric or psychological counseling, before you consulted lawyers after reviewing *The News Journal* article?

The specific – well, what went first, what day it was, I am not sure of. I know that I read the [Robert] Quill article. I was outraged. I sent a e-mail, in shame, to somebody from this Catholic Diocese of Wilmington. Somewhere in a short period of time, I saw Maria Gregory [a counselor]. And in the same time frame, I sought legal counsel to help me understand what was happening to me.

Okay. Well, your e-mail indicated that you felt enraged and suicidal, and you told the jury that you felt either homicidal or suicidal, that you considered taking a gun over to the rectory. But – but again – and I'll ask you: You don't recall, at this time, whether or not, after that e-mail was sent, your next call was to the law firm, the Neuberger law firm?

Like I just said, ma'am, I remember the Quill article. I remember the shame, the outrage that I felt on that Sunday. I remember sending an e-mail to somebody at the Catholic Diocese of Wilmington expressing my shame and also the suicidal feelings. And I remember seeing a counselor not far from my house. And I remember finding a law firm that might help me find out what was happening, what was the truth.

Well, do you remember answering interrogatory answers in December of 2008 and signing an affidavit in connection with the responses that you provided to the interrogatory answers?

Ma'am, I'm not an attorney. At best, I'm a project manager and a father. Can you explain to me what an interrogatory is?

Did you write a narrative for your attorneys about the events that happened in this case and then sign a document, an affidavit, swearing under penalty of perjury that the information you included in the narrative was true and correct?

Yes, ma'am.

Okay.

What I'm handing you, Mr. Vai, is page eleven of your answers to interrogatories that had your affidavit, signed December 4th, 2008, attached to it. And there's a highlighted portion, and I'll ask you to read that highlighted portion that appears on page 11.

"The shock of the divorce has kept me drug free for over thirteen years."

No, sorry, sorry. There – I'm sorry. This one.

"After I contacted the Neuberger firm and had an intake interview with Raeann, I started seeing a mental health counselor here in Chadds Ford."

Thank you.

You're welcome.

Does that refresh your recollection, sir, that you contacted the Neuberger law firm and had an intake interview before you sought any mental health care as a result of the feelings and anger that reading *The News Journal* article started?

Like I said twice so far, is that I read the Quill article. I was outraged. I remember coming home by myself, sending an e-mail. Shortly after that, I sought counseling. I sought legal help to find out what was wrong with me, and also what was the truth, why was this happening? Why was I left out of the loop?

You testified that you wanted to find an honorable law firm. Was it the Neuberger-Crumplar full-page ads in the Wilmington *News Journal* regarding or seeking victims of clergy sexual abuse that drew you to them, as the honorable firm to handle your case?

I don't remember seeing any advertisements for any law firms in the Wilmington paper or any other papers associated with child sex abuse by a priest.

Now, you haven't sought any health care, mental health care, since you saw Maria Gregory back in 2007, four or five times; is that true?

Yes, ma'am. I have not sought any professional help during the last two, three years. Time is flying by. My take is I wanted to find out what the truth is, and the truth will take me to the next level where I can feel comfortable approaching a complete stranger, a mental health expert that can sit me down and walk me through part of what happened to me, because the truth will be revealed. Why I am so over-reactive, angry, depressive, sleep depravation, et cetera, et cetera, and help me come to a conclusion of how I'm going to get back to a true man that I should have been when I left St. Elizabeth's Parish.

Mr. Vai, when you sent the e-mail on Sunday, July 15, 2007, that Mr. Neuberger showed you earlier, you sent that to –

MR. CRUMPLAR: Mr. Crumplar.

BY CHURCH LAWYER:

– Mr. Crumplar showed you earlier, you sent that to someone at the Catholic Diocese of Wilmington, not to someone at St. Elizabeth's Parish; isn't that correct?

The e-mail will speak for itself.

Well, sir, do you remember?

Ma'am, on that Sunday, on the brink of committing suicide, on the edge of the sword of wanting to inflict serious harm on somebody else or myself, I cannot adequately address who I addressed it to. Somebody found the e-mail. I do not remember sending the e-mail. I was in complete outrage.

Well, Mr. Vai, just before lunch when Mr. Crumplar was asking you questions, didn't you answer to Mr. Crumplar that you located the name of someone at the Catholic Diocese of Wilmington? Are you telling the jury that over lunch you forgot who you sent the e-mail to?

No, ma'am. I don't remember the name of the person. I believe I found the e-mail address either in the newspaper or on the CDOW [Catholic Diocese of Wilmington]

-399-

website. I cannot recall. It's been two, three years.

But it was someone at the Catholic Diocese of Wilmington to whom you directed your anger over what happened to you, not someone at St. Elizabeth's Parish; is that correct?

Ma'am, when I contacted whoever, I believe it was a lady, and I sent the e-mail, and I was a parishioner at St. Elizabeth's parish from 1st grade to 12th grade, my idea of the Catholic Diocese of Wilmington was St. Elizabeth's, Ann's, all the parishes. So I cannot adequately sit here today and say I sent an e-mail to the bishop thinking that it wasn't going to St. Elizabeth's, St. John's, St. Matthew's. I thought it was all one big ball, all one big organization. But in the last month, year, I found out that everybody's separate. They're incorporated separate to whatever. So –

Okay. Well, sir, I understand. And if – it's perfectly natural and understandable that you feel very, very angry about what happened to you. You were a victim of Frank DeLuca, but do you leave no room for the possibility in this lawsuit that St. Elizabeth's was also victimized by DeLuca and the Diocese of Wilmington?

[Ma'am] I was and still am a victim, a survivor, I like to say, of gross abuse, numerous times, by a priest that was employed by St. Elizabeth's, Catholic Diocese of Wilmington, the Vatican. You guys can figure out the minutiae of this corporate entities. That is not my issue. I was abused by a priest that was employed by St. Elizabeth's, supervised by St. Elizabeth's, lived at St. Elizabeth's, invited me to his bedroom in the rectory at St. Elizabeth's, taught me at St. Elizabeth's, came to my house as a priest from St. Elizabeth's.

Well, sir, would you agree with me that if the bishop, as we've heard some

-400-

testimony suggesting that bishops sent priests who had been accused of victimizing children to unsuspecting parishes, if that's what happened here, wouldn't you agree with me that St. Elizabeth's was the victim of DeLuca and the Catholic Diocese of Wilmington?

[Ma'am], I have not heard any testimony, nor seen Bishop Malooly in this courtroom, so I'm not sure what your question is.

Well, Bishop Malooly – when – when was – when did Bishop Malooly – when was he the bishop?

Am I the historian for the diocese? You tell me.

Well, sir, are you talking about today, or are you talking about the bishop who assigned DeLuca to St. Elizabeth's Parish?

[Ma'am], in my limited knowledge of who's in charge, whoever is the bishop, because that's what they call the head of this organization, today, is in charge today. I don't know what your question is. Do you want me to bring up who the bishop was back in '66? I don't remember.

Well, do you know he's dead?

I'd heard he died, and I heard that they had a very big ceremony at St. Elizabeth's for him; that's correct.

Do you understand, sir, that the Catholic Diocese of Wilmington is not here as a party in this action, and that the party in this action that you're seeking, in addition to DeLuca, the party in this action that you're seeking money damages from, not – I understand you want truth, but you're also seeking money damages from a defendant; and the defendant in this courtroom today, do you understand, is St. Elizabeth's Parish and

-401-

school?

I believe you're wrong. Do you want me to explain?

Well, sir, you may – you may have some other understanding, but the defendant sitting here today is St. Elizabeth's Parish and school?

Well, let me answer the question.

Okay.

Do you want me to explain? I don't care what the organizational thing is. St. Elizabeth's Parish is here. DeLuca abused me time and time again at the rectory, on trips, while he was employed by St. Elizabeth's. He was supervised by St. Elizabeth's. I don't really care who the bishop was, if you don't think that the bishop is part of this. I heard testimony that the bishop sits on the board of St. Elizabeth's Parish, just like the chancellor, and now, Father Carroll. So, help me figure out what you're trying to ask me. If the bishop's not here, and he's a board member; the chancellor's not here, he's a board member; Father Carroll is here, he's a board member. And I don't have any issues with the bishop, even though he wears two hats? Catholic Diocese of Wilmington, the parish – I mean, even for a – a ten-year-old, I think he could figure this out, and I'm fifty-eight, and I think I'm just getting the rundown of the chute. Let's just mix it at all up and see how confusing we can make this corporate organization; who's in charge, who's not in charge, who's here. I want to know why the bishop's not here.

Well, sir, do you think that it's going to bring you healing to get an award of money damages against St. Elizabeth's Elementary School, High School and Parish?

[Ma'am] I'm not here – I did not file this lawsuit for money. Let me repeat that. I

-402-

did not file this lawsuit for money. What I want is my childhood back. I want the three years that St. Elizabeth's employee, DeLuca, stole, and that's all I want. If you can give me my three years back and give me some satisfaction that my brain will forget what happened to me time and time again in the rectory, on trips, while the priest is teaching me religion, we'll just call it even up.

Mr. Vai, we heard testimony from other victims that DeLuca acted in secrecy with regard to what he did to them. Is it your testimony that you don't think that DeLuca was acting to keep his – his dereliction a secret?

That's a soft word, "dereliction." No, I do not. I believe you are wrong. Do you want me to explain?

You believe the other victims who testified to that are wrong, too?

Do you want me to explain? I believe you're wrong.

Well, I'll let you explain, but how about you answer my question first?

Well, repeat the question, please.

Do you believe the other victims who testified to that were wrong?

Wrong to what? I'm losing you now.

Were wrong when they testified that DeLuca took great pains to keep what he was doing secret?

I cannot put words in other people's mouth, but I will tell you my feeling is that as Father Peterman, the principal and, at the time – we all know who Father Peterman is. He testified here. And Father Peterman – and I am convinced that what he said is so appropriate, that DeLuca was too chummy with young fellows, young boys. This is telling me that the secrecy that you're referring to is not that secret.

Well, Mr. Vai, let's talk about what Father Peterman said. Father Peterman said that DeLuca was very friendly. I think it was your attorney's words "too chummy," but Father Peterman said that by his observations, DeLuca was friendly with groups of boys and girls. Did you hear that testimony?

Yes, I did.

Okay. And did you hear him say that none of those boys or girls ever seemed to be in any duress or distress. Do you remember that?

I was one of those boys of the boys and girls. And yes, I did not walk around the hallway of St. Elizabeth's for three years, knowing that DeLuca was there, and look like I was in distress. If that was part of this secret society, I'm not sure what you're alluding to.

Well, was it your impression, as one of those boys, that the boys and girls that hung around DeLuca gravitated towards him, traveled with him, spent time with him, and appeared to be enjoying themselves to the outside world?

In hindsight, that sounds very nice. In reality, the grooming process for John Vai was ongoing. That's what chummy, hanging around with too many boys means in 2010. DeLuca was grooming me.

In 2010?

Well, I assume that the same word in Webster's dictionary was there in 1966, as the same explanation, as the same analogy that criminal activity in '66, a priest employed by St. Elizabeth's Parish can abuse me, abuse others. I don't know how he got away with it. I just can't – it's – it's beyond my comprehension. You can convince this jury whatever you want, but you're never going to convince John Vai that somebody did not know, even suspected, as Father Peterman said.

Well, Mr. Vai, your own parents didn't suspect; isn't that true? Father DeLuca was a charming guy. [Here the blame-the-parents theme was tried.]

My parents did – my parents did not hire Father DeLuca. My parents invited Father DeLuca into our family – into my house, their house, as a guest. They did not read his resume. They did not take him in and house him. Father DeLuca was a priest.

Well, Mr. Vai, didn't you tell – you remember who Dr. Tavani is; she's one of the psychiatrists your attorney sent you to?

One of many.

And do you remember telling Dr. Tavani that even today your own mother doesn't believe that DeLuca did these things to you?

I'm glad you brought up my eighty-seven-year-old mother. My mother is in denial. My mother was a saint with – my mother still supports this parish, because she cannot believe the scandal that is upon her. Now, because my mother cannot believe it, that doesn't negate what happened to me. I was abused by DeLuca. There's no doubt in my mind, and I believe there's no doubt in a lot of other people's minds. And to bring my mother into this, without having her here to defend herself, is insulting. She never got an apology.

Sir, no one's disputing that you were abused. The question was whether DeLuca acted in a manner in the 1960s that was secretive enough that he fooled your mother and convinced her that, to this day, she doesn't believe he did these things?

I believe there's a lot of people that got fooled. The problem I have –

Including St. Elizabeth's?

Well, the problem I have is that my mother did not employ DeLuca, did not check his background. She checked my background. She found out where I was sleeping. She found out who I brought into my house, along with my brothers. She made sure that she didn't leave a loaded pistol on the kitchen table for one of us to play with. And that's exactly what DeLuca was, was a loaded gun.

Well, she wanted to keep you safe, and if she thought DeLuca was a child molester, she wouldn't have endorsed you sleeping over at the rectory or going on trips with him, correct? He fooled people. Sir, do you remember being deposed, the attorney for the Diocese of Wilmington deposed you? Do you remember that?

Yes, I do.

And that was on May 26th 2009?

If you say so.

Have you reviewed your deposition transcript between May 2009 and today?

I looked through it. Quite painful.

Well, do you remember what you answered when the Diocesan attorney asked you, "During the time you were at St. Elizabeth's, either the high school or the grade school, do you remember any of the priests who were at the church other than DeLuca?" Do you remember your answer?

No, I don't.

How would you answer that today?

What I feel strongly today is that I tried to put Cini's face – seventy – I don't know, what is he, eighty years old? Into a period of sometime that's forty-five years back, through the memory of a thirteen, fourteen, fifteen, sixteen year-old, quite difficult, until I saw Cini's picture that was in the yearbook. And there was no doubt in my mind, with the glasses on, because I don't believe Father Peterman wore glasses back then, or DeLuca, that Father Cini, Monsignor Cini now, was in that rectory and visibly saw me, and I acknowledged and acted in a respectful manner to him before I went upstairs to DeLuca's room.

Well, so, sir, are you telling me and the jury today that you always remembered priests seeing you go to DeLuca's room, you just didn't remember who they were until you saw Monsignor Cini's photograph in the yearbook?

The unfortunate nature of being abused at an early age, and trying to stuff it in a box for forty-five years, and it explodes intermittently, and then it blows up beyond belief, and then you're asking me, "Well, Mr. Vai, why can't you remember something specific?" To me, it's a – I'm not – I don't have to justify my lack of ability to put pictures together from snippets. But I know what I saw. I know I was abused by Father DeLuca in that rectory. And I know I saw Father Cini in that rectory at a certain time when I was there with Father DeLuca.

Mr. Vai, when you were deposed by the Diocese's attorney in this case, did you try to tell the truth?

Always.

Okay.

I'm looking for the truth.

Can you read on page 151 – it's the page with the yellow tab on it, starting at line No. 15, can you read lines 15 through 17, please?

"Question: Do you recall entering other priests – encountering other priests when you slept over at the rectory?

"Answer: I don't recall.

"Question: Do you believe that aside from what you described as the Ambassador Hotel, your sexual interactions with DeLuca were limited to sleep-overs at the rectory?

"Answer: No."

That's fine. So your answer, when you were asked under oath by the diocesan attorney in May 2008 whether you recalled encountering other priests when you slept over in the rectory, your answer was then, "I don't recall," but your response and testimony today, for the jury, is that you have absolute, unquestionable memory of encountering Monsignor Cini; is that true?

As I just said, and I would repeat myself, I saw Father Cini one year ago, almost to the date, at another function. I had very strong feelings that Father Cini, even at his age, with the same, almost identical style glasses on, had something to do with some of my memory recall associated with the abuse at the parish rectory. When I got into this courtroom, and I believe it was last Wednesday, and I saw a picture of Father Cini, Monsignor Cini now, the dots connected. This is how it happens. I'm not pulling together some grand idea. I saw Cini's face. I know where I was at.

Well, are you saying that the first time your attorneys showed you that yearbook photograph was – was at this trial, and that you remember that? Because wasn't this case prepared to go to trial a year ago?

Which question should I answer first?

Wasn't this case prepared to go to trial a year ago?

I believe it was.

Okay. And are you telling the jury that the first time you saw the photograph of Monsignor Cini in the yearbook, the first time your attorney showed that to you to trigger that memory so you could come here into court to testify that monsignor Cini definitely saw you going into the rectory was just – just recently in connection with the trial that began a couple weeks ago?

My attorneys did not show me that picture. My attorneys did not show me a picture to try to trigger my memory. My attorneys are not psychiatrists or psychologists, they're legal. As I said before, and I'll say it again, I saw Father Cini at the Doubletree Hotel in Wilmington in the conference room, and I had bad feelings. And I confronted him that day, and I believe Father Cini testified to that. When I got into the court, and I don't know whose witness was on the stand, Father Cini's picture ended up on that wall. To me, it was crystal clear that day that my suspicions were now more than a suspicion.

So you developed a memory that you didn't have when you testified at the deposition?

I don't know what "develop a memory" means, ma'am. Can you explain that to me? What is your question?

When you were deposed at deposition, and you said you don't recall whether any priests at all saw you going in and out of the rectory, you had no memory at that point of any priests, and so this is a new memory about Father Cini?

I believe my answer in the deposition was I do not recall.

Because you could not recall any?

That is correct. But if you'll allow me, the longer I dabble in this abusive nightmare, the stronger the possibilities are that other issues are going to start coming up, other faces, other places, as painful as it may be.

Well, Mr. Vai, do you leave any possibility for the chance that, given your remembering painful things that happened over forty years ago, that some of your memories might not be a 100% accurate?

There's always that possibility.

Because, in fact, you were trying to be absolutely truthful, forthcoming and honest with Dr. Tavani, the psychiatrist your attorneys first sent you to, when you told her that the abuse – you met DeLuca in the fifth grade, and the abuse took place between the sixth and the eighth grade, weren't you?

I'm not sure what your question is; but let me answer it this way: I believe the complaint says 100 incidents, not sure what an incident is, but with that in mind, if I start opening up Pandora's box and letting it all out, just find the right psychiatrist, psychologist, whoever, and say, "We can help you; we can get you back to some level of normalcy," and the box opens up, and there's other priests in my mind, and there's other abuses, and a hundred doesn't count, 200 might be the number, as I originally thought it was, then what? Then I'm supposed to say, oh, well, I forgive everybody, I underestimated the abuse.

Sir, my question was: When you told Dr. Tavani that you met DeLuca in the fifth grade and the abuse took place between the sixth and the eighth grade, you thought that was right. You weren't trying to make something up for Dr. Tavani. You believed it was right, but it turned out that a memory from forty-some years ago was inaccurate; isn't that right?

My memory is inaccurate when it comes to looking at a picture of myself, wherever it may be, and seeing myself two, two and a half years younger. Yes, I was. naïve, I was immature; but my memory is not waffling that I was abused by Father DeLuca in the St. Elizabeth's rectory numerous times, numerous trips. That memory is not going to change. The specifics of when, what did I have on, what did he do, was the room green, was it in a bed, was he dry humping me, was he simulating sex [with] me, was it anal sex, was it oral sex, that will come to some kind of clarity with some serious help. But there's no doubt that the end result is I was abused numerous times.

Mr. Vai, you – you testified you have some strong memories about being abused in DeLuca's bedroom at the rectory. Where was DeLuca's bedroom at the rectory?

On the second-floor.

When did you remember that?

You ask me a day, I have no idea.

Well, when you were testifying under oath on May 26th, 2009, you couldn't recall where DeLuca's bedroom was in the rectory, could you?

That is a strong possibility, because as eerie as the stairs are, the second-floor is even darker; and I don't mean in color; I mean in spirit.

Well, isn't it true you couldn't recall, at the deposition, on May 26 of 2009, whether DeLuca's bedroom was even on the second-floor?

I don't recall.

Are you able to describe, for the jury, anything about DeLuca's bedroom? Because there are – your – your vivid memory of the event in New York, there are some very detailed descriptions about the color of the curtains and the radiator and how

-411-

the beds were situated and the neon sign out of the window. Are you able to give the jury any details about what DeLuca's bedroom at the rectory was like where you believe you were abused multiple times?

The upholstery in DeLuca's room does not draw any kind of memory, but what memory I do have, very current, is that DeLuca admitted violating me in the rectory.

Well, do you remember what he actually said? He said that he was tempted to say nothing happened, and that he could only recall one incident where you may have been overnight at the rectory?

I'll put it in my words: DeLuca admitted abusing me in the St. Elizabeth's rectory.

Okay. Well, would you agree with me, sir, that if you were in the bedroom at the rectory one time, there is far less possibility that any other priests that were residing at the rectory would have either seen you and/or suspected that anything inappropriate was going on as opposed to if you were there multiple times?

From what I've heard from testimony from the priests from that time, they have no recollection of, quite frankly, anything. So to answer your question, I don't know why they didn't see a flock of boys in and out of there. Once you got permission to go into the rectory, you could basically walk in, walk up the stairs. There was a housekeeper there. Where's she at? There was fifty nuns across the street. Where were they at? There was a half a dozen priests in and out of the – living in the rectory. Nobody saw anything except John Vai.

Sir, do you remember – well, I guess, let's talk about, first, the – the photographs and – and the grooming, the Hotel du Pont. Did all those things happen before the hotel incident in New York City?

I have a hard time putting things in chronological order. I'm basing my statements in all these different documents that you have that I said this and I said that under oath on my recollection, and it's piecemeal. Yes, I went to New York and was abused by

DeLuca. And, yes, I have more memory of that than other instances. What went first, second and third, I didn't keep a diary; DeLuca did.

Well, you've – you've told a number of health care providers and testified at your deposition that the incident in New York was the first time that he sexually assaulted you; is that accurate?

The first time that I remember that there are more than two pieces of the puzzle. If I can get four or five together, I can actually have some clarity.

Okay. Do you remember what you told the diocesan attorney at deposition about how old you were when the incident at the Ambassador Hotel occurred?

No, I don't.

Okay. Sir, do you recall telling the diocesan attorney that you were probably fifteen or sixteen years old when the New York City incident occurred?

MR. CRUMPLAR: I'm objecting. That's not what the testimony – I mean, if you would read his answer.

CHURCH LAWYER: Okay.

THE COURT: All right.

Okay. As I recall – can you take a look here, page 125, and start reading at line five and read through to line twelve?

A. "Question: Tell me what you recall about your abuse.

-413-

Answer: Start at the beginning?

Question: Yes, please.

Answer: My best recollection is a hotel in New York City.

Answer: I believe I was sixteen. Could have been fifteen. My birthday is in June."

Okay. Thank you, sir.

You're welcome.

Now, sir, not diminishing that even one instance of abuse is inexcusable, but to test your memory here, do you think it's possible that you are remembering more instances of abuse than actually occurred, that your memory is somewhat faulty because these are events occurring some forty years ago?

I apologize, but what's the question?

You don't understand it. Okay. Yeah. It was a long and bad question. Let me see if I can get – pare it down. How old were you when the abuse stopped?

I was a junior in high school.

So sixteen?

If you give me a piece of paper, I will do the math. I don't recall the specific day. I know my birthday is June 14th. I was born in 1952.

Sure.

So if you want to tell me.

Okay. So you were sixteen years old?

If you say so.

Your junior year, and seventeen your senior year, then you turn eighteen – no.

Did I calculate wrong?

You were seventeen years old – no.

Sir, in any event, you were sixteen or seventeen years old when the abuse stopped; is that your testimony?

On any event, seems like you're having a hard time telling me what I'm having a hard time with. Are we both having a hard time with my birthday or –

Well, sir, if the abuse started when you were sixteen years old and ended when you were sixteen [sic] years old, then there was a one-year period that abuse was occurring. And if there were a hundred episodes of abuse, that would be happening biweekly. And you told – I believe you've testified that the abuse took place at the rectory and on trips. And so if – and you've also testified that you were at the rectory between – or more than one time and less than twenty times. So if we subtract twenty from a hundred, then that means there were eighty instances that took place on trips. So during a one-year period, you were traveling with DeLuca eighty times?

I guess this is a math quiz here. Let me help you out. 1966, I was in the eighth grade. '67, I was in the ninth grade. '68, I was in the 10th grade. '69, I was in the eleventh grade. The abuse, from what I can piece together, based on DeLuca's admitting that he abused me, the birthday cards, other documents that I was fortunate that my mother saved, I was a friend of DeLuca for two and a half years, and DeLuca abused me over a two-and-a-half year period. If you want to do the math, it's real simple. My complaint says 100 times. If it's biweekly, it's closer to 150 to 200 times. I picked a safe number. I did not want to exaggerate the abuse, vile behavior of this evildoer.

And during that same period of time, you've heard other witnesses take the stand
-415-

and allege that they were also being abused up to two times a week during that same time period by DeLuca, so DeLuca was abusing upwards of four boys up to two times a week; is that – does that sound like you might be a little off in your numbers?

I believe you should have DeLuca down here, and maybe he can answer what his sexual prowess was. Maybe he could have been that sexually perverse.

Mr. Vai, when did you abandon the desire to become a priest?

Somewhere in the early part of my high school education at St. Elizabeth's when I realized that becoming a priest has nothing to do with sleeping with a priest.

Understood, sir. Well, what was the reason, then, the reason or excuse that you provided to your parents or anyone else for why, as a fifteen, sixteen or seventeen year-old you were sleeping at the rectory? Because didn't you live within walking distance of St. Elizabeth's?

That is correct. And as Tom Crumplar stated, and I believe I testified, we lived in a row house. It was a group of row houses, seven in a row. On the left-hand side of my parents' house was any Aunt Ginny and Carol. On the right-hand side was my Aunt Lucy and Bob. With four boys in my house, three boys and two girls in the house next door, and I believe my aunt had three girls, we basically could kind of just jump from house to house. With a grandmother there, it was very easy just to say, "I'm going to the church. I'm going to spend some time with Father D"; Come back in the morning, no one would have said a word. They trusted Father D, as I did. They thought he was part of the family. He broke bread with my parents. He drank wine at our house. He ate our polenta. He ate our Italian meals. And all of a sudden, now, Father DeLuca – I got to explain how I ended up with him? What's your question, Counselor?

I don't know. Did you say it was easy to go on those numbers of occasions to the rectory when you were being sexually abused?

It was easy to not let my parents know. And, no, when you're being sexually abused, as I was, there's nothing easy. You block it out. It's not like the guy shot me with a gun. He basically ruined my brain.

How many times, when you were fifteen, sixteen, seventeen, do you think you slept at the rectory?

I don't know. I didn't keep track. I didn't make a diary. I will have to use DeLuca's testimony that he admitted that I was there.

One time?

And I agree with you, one time is too many, and a hundred is off the Richter scale.

Mr. Vai, I saw somewhere – it might have been Dr. Springer's report – that you said, in addition to other drugs that you experimented with over the years, that LSD was one of them, and that you've done maybe a hundred or more hits of LSD; is that accurate?

I never really counted, but I know I was experimenting with substance abuse in my college years. It kind of progressed throughout some of my life, not all of it.

Have you ever had LSD flashbacks?

Never. I'm not even sure what an LSD flashback is.

Okay. Abused cocaine for a number of years, correct?

That is correct.

Okay. And were you – how frequently were you using cocaine at the height of your cocaine abuse?

I would say probably once a day.

Every day?

Yes.

Sir, did it ever occur to you that your sleep issues could be related to your abuse of illicit drugs?

I'm not the psychiatrist that's going to tie all the dots together that what happened to John Vai with drug abuse, painted at an early age with child-abuse, ending up through a divorce, trying to raise kids. I don't know. I don't know what came first, what came second. Is the volcano exploding half size? You tell me. I don't know what's happening to me.

Well, did you ever seek any kind of help, see a family doctor, anybody else, for something to help you with this inability to sleep more than two hours a night for – what did Dr. Springer say? Twenty years?

I'm not one to seek help. My – and this may – this probably is not the correct way to handle myself, but I just drew a line in the sand and said, look, you got issues. Deal with them. If you go to the doctor, that's admitting that there's something wrong with you. If you get cut, heal yourself. I wasn't one to run to professionals. I felt it was a weakness.

Well, sir, did it ever occur to you that use of illicit substances, abuse of illicit substances and lack of sleep could have contributed to some of the issues that you've experienced at work?

I was not able to connect the dots that, yes, I experimented with illegal drugs, yes, I did not sleep, I did not sleep for a long time; and yes, I was abused. So – which you're probably correct, yes, I should have seeked [sic] professional help a long time ago, but this man just couldn't put it together.

Because, I mean, using cocaine every day while you're working at a construction site, that could be an issue?

I never said that I used cocaine while I was working at a construction site. What I said was that I used cocaine daily. And you can come home from work. You can snort some cocaine. You can have some drinks.

Stay up all night and go to work?

I don't know about staying up all night, but most of it.

Sir, Mr. Crumplar asked you some questions about your divorce. Do you believe that the sexual abuse that you suffered at the hands of DeLuca contributed to your divorce?

I believe that Cindy and I would have gotten divorced no matter what; but, at the same time, I was not able to satisfy her emotional needs. I admit, I am like a rock, stoic. I have to control everything. I was experiencing issues before I met her. Those same issues went through our marriage, went through the divorce, and they are still here today.

But you've gone on to have a successful relationship with a woman that you care very much about, and your ex-wife has not had success in the relationships that she's pursued since the divorce; isn't that true?

I would like to say I have a successful relationship with Maria; but, at the same time, if success is predicated on me staying in Chadds Ford for two weeks and her staying in Virginia for two weeks, because I don't believe our longevity would have lasted for fifteen years if she was exposed to me on a day-to-day basis. As far as my ex-wife's success, you'll have to ask Cindy what she's doing.

Well, didn't you tell Dr. Tavani that she's had a series of failed relationships, and that you've often had to come to her assistance and bail her out?

Yeah. I'm a pretty good guy when it comes to people that got close to me.

Did I understand you to tell the jury your son was baptized in the Catholic church? Did you say you thought your daughter might have been baptized in a Baptist church? I'm not sure I heard –

I didn't say I think. I said that Ryan was baptized in a Baptist church. And I believe Jarred was baptized in a Catholic. And it might be vice versa, but one of them went to a Baptist church, one of them went to a Catholic church for the baptismal ceremony.

Did you do any kind of research after your deposition to determine whether your children were baptized? Because at your deposition, when the diocesan counsel asked you where your children were baptized, you said your son was at St. Cornelius Roman Catholic Church in the Chadds Ford area, and that you weren't sure about Ryan, but maybe even at St. Elizabeth's; do you remember that testimony?

No.

Did you do some research to find out that it was a Baptist church, not St. Elizabeth's, where you had Ryan baptized?

I asked my mother. I asked my ex-wife. And I asked Jarred and Ryan what they remember. Obviously they don't remember the baptism. Ryan remembered the CCD classes. And, yes, Cindy and my mother were helpful in refreshing my memory that my kids got baptized, and one of them made it to first holy communion.

You testified that after your divorce you had your kids sleep with you 'til your daughter was nine years old, and the divorce happened when they were – she was five; is that right?

That is correct.

And that was because you were worried what was going to happen?

What's the question?

Why did you have your children sleep with you for four or five years – four years?

I was paranoid. If they weren't close. I'm not sure.

Did they sleep with you and your wife before the divorce?

No. They had their own rooms.

Well, didn't you tell Dr. Tavani that after the divorce you were so blind-sided and emotionally distraught that you didn't want to sleep alone? And first you slept at your mom's house, and then at your brother's house. Was it maybe that you had your kids sleep with you because you were feeling so emotionally distraught over your divorce?

I don't know. You have to ask the psychiatrist about that one. I'm not self-analyzing myself, so I can't answer your question.

Mr. Vai, I know this is painful, and I don't want to belabor it, but I just have a couple more questions for you about the development of some of these memories. When was it that you believe you recall abuse taking place on trips to Rehoboth and trips to Wildwood and things like that?

Is your question when do I recall?

Yeah. When did you have those memories that you were abused on those kinds of trips?

[Ma'am] with all due respect, recollection of memories that are so compressed, so mixed up, and then to be asked a question, can you pull a piece of a thousand-piece puzzle out and say, Where does this go, and where is it taking you, is impossible. I wish I

had that type of clarity. I don't.

Okay. But when Mr. Crumplar asked you questions, you said that you recalled that Rehoboth was one of the places that you were abused, and that Wildwood was one of the places that you were abused. And I'm looking at your deposition transcript from May '09, when the Diocese attorney questioned you, and when she asked you whether you recall being abused on a trip to Washington, D.C., you didn't volunteer that. When she asked you about beach trips to the summer (sic), whether you were abused on any of those trips, you said, "I don't recall. I don't recall." So is it fair to say that you recalled that information since the time you were deposed on May 26, 2009?

I'm not sure, [ma'am]. Once again, to pull stuff out of my brain in a deposition, and then six months, whatever it is, go to a psychiatrist, and they have a different twist to a question, then go to another psychiatrist, they have a different twist, then St. Elizabeth's parish insists that I go to two more psychiatrists, and now you're asking me, "Well, which day did you remember Rehoboth Beach," I can't tell you.

But you're absolutely sure it was Monsignor Cini who you saw in the rectory? I don't have any more questions for you.

December 1

After the defense presented its witnesses on November 18, 22 and 23rd, closing arguments by Thomas Crumplar and the church's attorney were held on November 29th. On December 1st, 2010 the jury awarded compensatory damages to John Vai against Francis DeLuca in the amount of thirty million dollars. By a preponderance of the evidence the jury also found that St. Elizabeth's "was negligent in its retaining, supervising or controlling of Francis DeLuca in a manner which proximately caused injury to" John Vai. St. Elizabeth's conduct also was found to be grossly negligent. And then the jury awarded John Vai compensatory damages in the amount of three million dollars against St. Elizabeth's.[566]

In his press release that day, John Vai stated that "now that we have had the first of seven trials involving DeLuca and St. Elizabeth's, and next St. John the Beloved and then St. Matthews churches, stunning testimony is coming out which exposes to the light of day the rampant sexual abuse of innocent children. The cover-up continues and to this very day these churches refuse to accept responsibility for their actions but instead hire high priced lawyers to avoid the truth coming out. But their blame the victims and slash and burn defense did not fool this jury. The truth will come out. The State Courts in Delaware are open for survivors who are seeking justice and the truth. I thank the jury for doing justice for me and for all survivors and I thank President Judge Vaughn for a fair trial. The legal system in Delaware works and can render justice to all survivors of childhood sexual abuse."[567]

December 6, 7, and 8

Stephen Neuberger took the lead once again and an abbreviated three day trial was held next on December 6, 7 and 8th on the issue of punitive damages. The jury here learned about eleven more children who DeLuca had admitted abusing starting in the early 1960's and continuing until 2006.[568] Stephen Neuberger called five of those abuse survivors to the stand. Four of them – Michael Sowden, John Doe Number Three, John Doe Number Four and Felix Flanigan - had previously testified at the August 2010 hearing in bankruptcy court and so their testimony is omitted here.[569] The fifth survivor was DeLuca's own grandnephew, young Michael Dingle, who DeLuca admitted he had abused for years in Syracuse, New York. In 2006, young Mike's report of the abuse resulted in DeLuca's arrest by the Syracuse Police Department.[570] Michael and his mother Maria Dingle drove all night from Syracuse through a snowstorm in order to testify in Dover the morning of December 7.[571]

The jury learned that DeLuca arrived in Syracuse in 1993 after yet another survivor - Michael Schulte - came forward in Delaware and he, for the second time reported to the diocese that DeLuca had abused him in the early 1960's. After investigating, confirming and finding the report to be highly credible, the diocese publicly announced that DeLuca was retiring "for reasons of health" [a code word within the church] and was taken to Syracuse.[572] Also in 1993, secret restrictions were imposed on DeLuca which barred him from holding himself out as a priest, secret restrictions to which only the bishop and a select few diocese officials were privy.[573] Priest Charles Dillingham, DeLuca's close friend and the longtime pastor of St. Elizabeth's from 1997 to 2009, was one of those select few entrusted with that knowledge in 1993.[574]

But despite this knowledge, both Michael Dingle and his mother Maria testified that during Dillingham's many trips to visit DeLuca in Syracuse, Dillingham never warned them that DeLuca was a child molester despite knowing that young Mike and his even younger brother were spending the night frequently at DeLuca's New York apartment.[575] In Maria's anguished words after learning that Dillingham had known but he had not warned her that her children were

-424-

in danger, "I couldn't believe it. I just felt so betrayed that he would know something like that and he knew the closeness of their relationship and he wouldn't have at least warned me. I couldn't believe it."[576] In Michael's words, "I wish that he told my parents . . . about my uncle's history in Wilmington . . . It would have saved me from a lot and it would have brought – I believe it would have brought justice to others a lot sooner."[577]

The jury also learned that despite this knowledge, starting in 1997, then pastor Dillingham regularly invited his friend DeLuca to come to Delaware and stay at St. Elizabeth's for weeks at a time, on the same campus as the elementary and high schools.[578] And as former funeral director and DeLuca survivor Mike Sowden testified, as late as 2006, DeLuca officiated at funerals at St. Elizabeth's with Dillingham, all the while wearing full priestly regalia, in defiant open violation of any restrictions allegedly placed on DeLuca in his role as a priest.[579]

Against all this evidence, St. Elizabeth's threw itself on the mercy of the jury, pleaded poverty and begged the jury not to find that its actions were reckless in any way. Ironically, the church had shown no mercy to John Vai during his trial and the years leading up to it, but now the church begged the jury for mercy. In response Stephen argued that the jury should simply make a permanent historical record of the fact of the recklessness of St. Elizabeth's Church. He further argued that it was not the amount of an award which was at issue but that the general public should be informed that St. Elizabeth's was reckless and had deliberately endangered children.

After that, the Court instructed the jury that they could find the conduct of St. Elizabeth's merited further examination and even punishment if its conduct met any of four conditions which would permit an award of punitive damages:

THE COURT:

You may award punitive damages against St. Elizabeth's because of the conduct

of Francis DeLuca if one of the following conditions is met: One, St. Elizabeth's

authorized the doing and manner of Francis DeLuca's action; or two, Francis DeLuca

was unfit and St. Elizabeth's was reckless in retaining, supervising or controlling him; or

three, St. Elizabeth's ratified or approved Francis DeLuca's actions; or four, St.

Elizabeth's recklessly disregarded the health and safety of persons to whom Francis

DeLuca posed a risk of harm.

The law provides no fixed standard for the amount of punitive damages, but

leaves the amount to your sound discretion exercised without passion or prejudice.[580] . . .

After a brief period of deliberation, the jury awarded thirty million dollars in punitive

damages against DeLuca and in favor or John Vai. It then found that at least one of the four

above stated conditions set forth by the Court for an award against St. Elizabeth's had been

satisfied and that its misconduct met the higher standard required by the law. However, in its

discretion, the jury was merciful to the church, perhaps accepting its cry of poverty, and awarded

just one dollar in punitive damages against it and for John Vai.[581] But, as Stephen had requested,

for the historical record the jury found that the conduct of St. Elizabeth's was so far out of

bounds that this could not be denied.

Outside the courtroom, after his two victories in the verdicts against DeLuca and St.

Elizabeth's, John Vai explained that "St. Elizabeth's sole defense was a plea for mercy begging

the jury not to punish the current students in the schools for the wrongs of its priest employees.

[I] had no desire to punish or harm the people in the pews, but proceeded with his punitive

damages phase to send a message that kids must be protected and to expose additional evidence

of DeLuca's serial abuse and the recklessness of the priests at St. Elizabeth's."[582] He also explained that "the jury sent a clear and resounding message that if you put your head in the sand and allow children to be sexually abused, there will be consequences." In his opinion, here the consequences included a factual finding "that St. Elizabeth's recklessly disregarded the health and safety of numerous children."

As explained in chapter four, with this verdict the handwriting was on the wall for the diocese. Its attempts to fool and mislead twelve average citizens had failed. So the diocese, and eventually the Delaware religious orders, decided that there must be no more trials of survivors in Delaware which of necessity would result in exposing more of the church's dirty linen to public view. They all folded their tents and paid Delaware survivors some modicum of compensation for the crimes of the Roman Catholic Church against them.

Endnotes

1. The Boston Globe, "Church Allowed Abuse by Priest for Years" found at http://www.boston.com/globe/spotllight/abuse/stories/010602_geoghan.htm visited August 30, 2011.

2. See http://www.Bishopaccountability.org visited August 30, 2011.

3. Http://www.Bishop-accountability.org/pa_philadelphia/Philly_GJ_report.htm visited August 30, 2011.

4. Http://www.Bishop-accountability.org/reports/2011_01_21_Philadelphia_Grand_Jury_Final_Report_Clergy_Abuse_2.pdf visited August 30, 2011.

5. http://www.Bishop-accountability.org/reports/2011_07_13_Cloyne_Report/ visited August 30, 2011.

6. *Cox Broadcasting Corp. v. Cohn*, 420 U.S. 469, 491-92 (1975).

7. On January 25, 2012 virtually the entire public and private record of the decades long cover-up of childhood sexual abuse by priests of the Wilmington, Delaware diocese of the Roman Catholic Church was delivered to more than eleven individuals and law firms, as well as the Delaware federal bankruptcy court, in twenty-two CD's intended for eventual publication and posting on the internet or elsewhere, all in the interest of the public's right to know. *In re: Catholic Diocese of Wilmington, Inc.*, Chapter 11 case No. 09-13560 (CSS) (Bankr. D. Del.). The detailed references to the facts found within these records are located either in these CD's or in the public electronic dockets of the state and federal courts of the State of Delaware which are referenced throughout this book.

8. www.marines.com visited January 22, 2011.

9. Id.

10. *Delaware Today Magazine* (August 2006), at 56.

11. References are to the sworn deposition of Doug taken on January 7, 2009 in *McClure v. Catholic Diocese of Wilmington, Inc., et al.*, C.A.No., 06C-12-235 CLS, Delaware Superior

Court for New Castle County [hereinafter "McClure deposition"), at 125.

12. Johnny Cash, *Man In Black* (1971).   .

13. McClure deposition at 102.

14. Id. at 141.

15. Id. at 107.

16. Id. at 116.

17. Id. at 121.

18. Id. at 119.

19. Id. at 119-120.

20. *The Holy Bible* (New International Version, 1973).

21. McClure deposition at 45.

22. Id. at 9, 13.

23. Id. at 12.

24. Id. at 18.

25. Id. at 14.

26. Id. at 15-16.

27. Id. at 65.

28. Id.

29. Id. at 18.

30. Id. at 59.

31. Id. at 99.

32. Id. at 62.

33. Id. at 154.

34. Id. at 155.

35. Id. at 155-156.

36. Id. at 194.

37. Id. at 160.

38. Id. at 194.

39. Id. at 172.

40. Id. at 166.

41. Id. at 183.

42. Id. at 198.

43. Id. at 200.

44. Id. at 211.

45. Id at 224.

46. Id at 212

47. Id at 159.

48. *The News Journal* (November 21, 2005) found at
http://delawareonline.com/apps/pbcs.dll/article?AID=20051121/NEWS/511210353/1006.

49. Job 38:4, 12, 18, 32; 39:27; 40:8; 41:11 (New International Version, 1973).

50. Job 42:3.

51. Briggs-Green, Kara, *Forty Acres* (Arcadia Publishing 2008), at 11.

52. Id at 17.

53. Id at 57.

54. "Plaintiff's Fourth Revised Supplemental Answers to Defendant Catholic Diocese of
Wilmington, Inc's Revised First Set of Interrogatories Directed to Plaintiff," (hereinafter
"McClure Interrogatory"), served in the court case of *McClure v. Catholic Diocese of
Wilmington, Inc., et al.*, C.A.No., 06C-12-235 CLS, Delaware Superior Court for New Castle
County [hereafter "McClure case"].

55. Report of Carol A. Tavani, M.D. dated May 30, 2008 [hereafter "Tavani Report"].

56. McClure Interrogatory.

57. Tavani Report at 23-24.

58. McClure Interrogatory.

59. Dougherty Aff. in McClure case.¶¶ 3-5; Dougherty deposition dated January 28, 2009 in McClure case at 32.

60. Dougherty Aff. in McClure case at ¶ 6 and exhibit to aff. at p. 1; Dougherty deposition dated January 28, 2009 in McClure case at 33.

61. McClure deposition dated August 26, 2008 in McClure case at 34, 36; McClure Interrogatory, at pg. 7; McClure deposition dated 1/30/09 in McClure case at 275.

62. John Roe #1 deposition dated January 29, 2009 in McClure case. at 7, 9, 12, 14-15.

63. Id. at 12-15.

64. Id.

65. J. Taylor aff. dated January 22, 2009, filed in McClure case ¶¶ 4, 5.

66. Id. at 11.

67. Id. at 12.

68. McClure deposition dated August 26, 2008 in McClure case at 37-40; McClure deposition dated January 30, 2009 in McClure case at 236, 267, 271-76, 370.

69. Dougherty deposition dated January 28, 2009 in McClure case at 33-34; Dougherty aff. in McClure case at ¶ 11 and exhibit to aff. at p.4.

70. Rykiel Aff in McClure case dated November 18, 2008 at. ¶ 3-8.

71. J. Taylor Aff.in McClure case dated January 22, 2009, ¶ 15.

72. John Roe #1 deposition dated January 29, 2009 in McClure case at 7, 9, 12-15.

73. Dougherty deposition dated January 28, 2009 in McClure case at 17, 32; Dougherty Aff in McClure case at ¶ 9 and Ex. to Aff. at p. 1-4.

74. Gerres deposition dated November 14, 2008 in McClure case at 114, 66-67.

75. McClure deposition dated January 30, 2009 in McClure case at 267, 270, 276; McClure deposition dated August 26, 2008 in McClure case at 37).

76. John Roe #3 affidavit dated January 12, 2009 in McClure case ¶ 11-14.

77. John Roe #1 deposition dated January 29, 2009 in McClure case at 12-15, 7, 9.

78. Tavani Report at 3.

79. Tavani Report at 8, 13.

80. Tavani Report at 5, 10, 16, 21, 22, 27.

81. McClure case, Docket Item 376 (Redacted Statement of Facts), at 1.

82. Id. at 1-2.

83. Id. at 1.

84. Id. at 2.

85. Id.

86. Id.

87. Trial Transcript, testimony of Thomas J. Peterman, November 8, 2010 in *Vai v. Catholic Diocese of Wilmington, Inc, et al*, C.A. No. 08C-06-044 JTV (Del. Super.), at 50-52.

88. McClure case, Docket Item 376 (Redacted Statement of Facts), at 2 note 5.

89. Id.

90. Id.

91. Trial Transcript, testimony of Thomas Cini, November 9, 2010 in *Vai v. Catholic Diocese of Wilmington, Inc, et al*, C.A. No. 08C-06-044 JTV (Del. Superior Court), at 90.

92. McClure case, Docket Item 376 (Redacted Statement of Facts), at 9.

93. Id.

94. Id.

95. Redacted Appendix, dated October 3, 2009, filed in *Vai v. Catholic Diocese of Wilmington, Inc, et al*, C.A. No. 08C-06-044 JTV (Del. Super.), at A3267-69 (Mulvee Deposition at 293-296, 300-301).

96. Id. at A3678-79 (Saltarelli Deposition at 236-37).

97. McClure case, Docket Item 376 (Redacted Statement of Facts), at 3.

98. Trial Transcript, testimony of Thomas Cini, November 9, 2010 in *Vai v. Catholic Diocese of Wilmington, Inc, et al*, C.A. No. 08C-06-044 JTV (Del. Super.), at 94, 92-93.

99. McClure case, Docket Item 376 (Redacted Statement of Facts), at 3.

100. Id.

101. Id. at 9-10.

102. Id. at 10.

103. Id.

104. Id.

105. Id.

106. Id.

107. Id. at 10-11.

108. Id. at 11.

109. Id.

110. McClure deposition dated January 30, 2009 in McClure case at 305-306, 368.

111. McClure case, Docket Item 376 (Redacted Statement of Facts), at 12.

112. Id.

113. Id. at 11-12.

114. Id. at 12.

115. McClure deposition, at 234.

116. Id. at 238.

117. Id. at 236-37.

118. Id. at 240.

119. Id. at 241-42.

120. Dougherty Aff in McClure case at Ex. to Aff. at p. 1-6.

121. Id. at p. 1 (CDOW_EBC_00050).

122. Id. at p. 6 (CDOW_EBC_00055).

123. *The News Journal* (November 21, 2005) found at http://delawareonline.com/apps/pbcs.dll/article?AID=20051121/NEWS/511210353/1006.

124. Dougherty Press Release dated April 12, 2010.

125. Obituary, The News Journal dated March 30, 2011.

126. McClure deposition, at 246.

127. Id. at 248.

128. Id. at 250.

129. Id. at 253.

130. Id. at 287.

131. *The News Journal* (November 21, 2005).

132. McClure Press Release dated December 28, 2006.

133. Affidavit of Douglas McClure dated February 6, 2009.

134. McClure Press Release dated October 27, 2009.

135. Id.

136. McClure Press Release dated April 8, 2009.

137. McClure Press Release dated October 27, 2009.

138. McClure Press Release dated April 8, 2009.

139. *Whitwell v. Smith*, C.A. No. 05-796-SLR (D. Del. Jan. 31, 2007), D.I. 26.

140. Id. at D.I. 45 (March 30, 2007).

141. *The News Journal* (March 31, 2007), at A1.

142. Id.

143. Id.

144. Id.

145. Trial transcript in *Whitwell v. Smith*, C.A. No. 05-796 (SLR), D. Del. March 29-30, 2007, day 1 [hereinafter "Trial Transcript"], at 247.

146. Id. at 248.

147. Id. at 249.

148. Id. at 250.

149. Id.

150. Id. at 251.

151. Id. at 252.

152. Id. at 253.

153. Id.

154. Id. at 254.

155. Id.

156. Id. at 255.

157. Id. at 256.

158. Id.

159. Id. at 256-57.

160. Id. at 216.

161. Id. at 224.

162. Id. at 227

163. Id. at 234, 168.

164. Id. at 220.

165. Id. at 169.

166. Id. at 217.

167. Id. at 218.

168. Id. at 219.

169. Id. at 220.

170. Id. at 221.

171. Id. at 222.

172. Id. at 223.

173. Id. at 224.

174. Id. at 225.

175. Id. at 227

176. Id. at 228.

177. Id. at 225-26.

178. Id. at 226-27.

179. Id. at 228.

180. Id. at 229

181. Id. at 237.

182. Id. at 230-32.

183. Id. at 231.

184. Id. at 232.

185. Id. at 233.

186. Id. at 155.

187. Id. at 234.

188. Id. at 234-35.

189. Id. at 235, 176-177.

190. Id. at 236-37.

191. Id. at 239-40.

192. Id. at 240-41.

193. Id. at 244-46.

194. Id. at 173.

195. Id. at 176.

196. Http://en.wikipedia.org/wiki/United_States_Uniformed_Services_Oath_of_Office, viewed 8/24/11.

197. Trial Transcript at 192.

198. Http://www.navy.mil/navydata/navy_legacy_hr.asp?id=193, viewed 8/24/11.

199. Trial Transcript at 57.

200. Id. at 58.

201. Id. at 59-60.

202. Id. at 60-61.

203. Id. at 61.

204. Id. at 62-63.

205. Id. at 83.

206. Id. at 84-85.

207. Id. at 85-86.

208. Id. at 99-100.

209. Id. at 87-88.

210. *Whitwell v. Archmere Academy, et al.*, C.A. No. 07C-08-006 (RBY) (Del. Superior, December 20, 2007), D. I. 80, at A1184-1185, 1126-1127 (Bagnato).

211. Id. at 1128 (Bagnato).

212. Id. at 1142 (Bagnato).

213. Id. at 1174 (Bagnato).

214. Id. at A993-995 (Bagnato).

215. Id. at 1129 (Bagnato).

216. *Whitwell v. Archmere Academy, et al.*, C.A. No. 07C-08-006 (RBY) (Del. Superior, January 4, 2008), D. I. 88, at A1248-1249 (Collins).

217. Id. at A1264 (Collins).

218. Id. at 1265-1266 (Collins).

219. Id. at 1267 (Collins).

220. Id. at 1268-1269 (Collins).

221. Id. at 1277, 1279 (Collins).

222. Id. at 1283 (Collins).

223. *Whitwell v. Archmere Academy, et al.*, C.A. No. 07C-08-006 (RBY) (Del. Superior, January 4, 2008), D. I. 88, at A1314 (McLaughlin).

224. Id. at A1328 (McLaughlin).

225. Id. at A1333-35 (McLaughlin).

226. Id. at A1338, 1353 (McLaughlin).

227. Id. at A1374 (McLaughlin).

228. *Vai v. Catholic Diocese of Wilmington, Inc.,* C.A. No. 08C-06-044-JTV (Del. Super.), D.I. 296-299 - Redacted Appendix to Plaintiffs' Omnibus Answering Brief in Opposition to Defendants' Motions for Summary Judgment, at A000831.

229. Id. at A000868.

230. Id.

231. Id. at A000869.

232. Trial Transcript at 64.

233. Id. at 67.

234. Id. at 66-67.

235. Id. at 70-71.

236. Id. at 71.

237. Id. at 72.

238. Id. at 72-73.

239. Id. at 74.

240. Id. at 75.

241. Id. at 79-81.

242. Id. at 89-90.

243. Id. at 91.

244. Id. at 91-92.

245. Id. at 93.

246. Id. at 93-94.

247. Id. at 104-105.

248. Id. at 105-106.

249. Id. at 102-103.

250. Id. at 95.

251. Id. at 96-97.

252. Id. at 97.

253. Id. at 97-99.

254. Id. at 106.

255. Id. at 107-117.

256. Id. at 114, 116, 127.

257. Id. at 125, 129.

258. Id. at 131.

259. Id. at 133-136.

260. Id. at 138-139.

261. Id. at 190.

262. Id. at 190-191.

263. Id. at 191.

264. Id. at 191.

265. Id. at 195.

266. Id. at 197.

267. Id. at 198.

268. Id.

269. Id. at 199-200.

270. Id. at 200-201.

271. Id. at 201.

272. Id. at 203.

273. Id. at 203.

274. Id. at 204.

275. Id. at 205.

276. Id. at 209.

277. Id.

278. Id. at 210.

279. Id. at 213-214.

280. Id. at 215.

281. Trial transcript in *Whitwell v. Smith*, C.A. No. 05-796 (SLR), D. Del. March 29-30, 2007, day 2, at 6.

282. Id. at 7-49 contains the testimony of Dr. Tavani.

283. Id. at D.I. 45 (March 30, 2007).

284. *The News Journal* (March 31, 2007), at A1.

285. Http://www.oblates.org/ viewed September 13, 2011.

286. http://www.salesianum.org/about/index.asp viewed September 13, 2011.

287. *The News Journal*, Editorial, November 26, 2006.

288. *The News Journal*, Editorial, December 17, 2006.

289. *The News Journal*, reported by Sean O'Sullivan, August 4, 2011, found at http://www.Bishop-accountability.org/news2011/07_08/2011_08_04_Osullivan_OblatesSettle.htm viewed September 13, 2011; http://www.oblates.org/healing/healing_letter.htm, viewed March 15, 2012, contains the lists of these twelve priests and other relevant details.

290. Http://www.delawareonline.com/assets/pdf/BL17773484.PDF visited September 13, 2011; http://www.oblates.org/healing/healing_letter.htm viewed March 15, 2012.

291. Id. The statistics were calculated by the author.

292. Id.

293. Id.

294. Id.

295. *The Holy Bible* (New International Version, 1973), Matthew 23:27-28.

296. Id. at Matthew 23:33.

297. Id. at Matthew 18:5-6.

298. Dante Alighieri, *The Inferno*, translated by John Ciardi (Signet Classics 2001), Canto XVIII, verse 97, pg. 161.

299. Id. Canto XXX, verse 97, 114-15.

300. *Sheehan v. Oblates*, 15 A.3rd 1247, 1260 (Del. Supr. 2011)(en banc).

301. Id. at 1253.

302. Appendix to Appellant's Opening Brief in *Sheehan v. Oblates*, Docket Item 22, in No. 730, 2009 before the Supreme Court of the State of Delaware, dated April 26, 2010, Gambet A955; Keech A523 [Hereafter "D.I. 22, _____"]. D.I. 53, PX 42, AR435 [Hereafter "D.I. ___, PX ___"].

303. D.I. 22, DiFillipo A501-03.

304. D.I. 22, Gambet A955, 975, 985.

305. D.I. 22, Keech A523-24.

306. D.I. 53, PX31 at AR426.

307. D.I. 53, PX 28 at AR420; PX33, PX38-40, AR427, 432-34.

308. D.I. 53, PX31 at AR425.

309. D.I. 53, PX29 at AR211, AR429; PX30 at AR423-24; PX31 at AR4262; PX22 at A1430; Springer A430-37, 448-49.

310. D.I. 22, Springer A429.

311. D.I. 22, Sipe A575.

312. D.I. 22, Sipe A573-75.

313. D.I. 22, Sipe A615-17.

314. D.I. 22, Springer A433, 452, 455, 461.

315. D.I. 53, PX 27; AR418.

316. D.I. 22, Sipe 50-51; A615-16.

317. *Sheehan v. Oblates*, 15 A.3d 1247, 1252 (Del. Supr. 2011)(en banc).

318. D.I.22, Sipe A575-77, 585-88, 592, 595, 602, 610-11, 613-14; Springer A456-57, 459-60.

319. D.I. 22, Springer A414-20; D.I. 53 PX68 at AR438.

320. D.I. 22, Springer A433, 435.

321. D.I. 53, PX33 at AR428 (emphasis added).

322. D.I. 53, PX37 at AR431 (emphasis added).

323. D.I. 53, PX36, AR429.

324. D.I. 22, Jordan A403-405.

325. D.I. 22, Jordan A373-76.

326. D.I. 22, Doe A351-56.

327. Http://www.vlib.us/medieval/lectures/law.html, Lectures In Medieval History, visited September 19, 2011.

328. D.I. 22, Oblate Opening Statement, A213 line 18; A214 line 9.

329. D.I. 22, Sheehan A800.

330. D.I. 22, Oblate Closing Argument, A1418.

331. D.I. 22, Sheehan A730-731.

332. Id. at A789.

333. Id. at A730-731.

334. D.I. 22, Gambet A959.

335. D.I. 22, Sheehan A686, 687.

336. Id. at A668-89.

337. Id. at A689-91.

338. Id. at A691-93.

339. Id. at A693-94.

340. Id. at A694-96.

341. Id. at A696-98.

342. Id. at A740; *Sheehan v. Oblates*, 15 A.3d 1247, 1251 (Del. Supr. 2011)(en banc).

343. Id. at A740-42.

344. Id. at A698.

345. Id. at 699-700.

346. Id. at A703-05.

347. Id. at A708.

348. Id. at A751.

349. Id. at A709.

350. Id. at A710.

351. Id. at A710-711.

352. Id. at A808-809.

353. Id. at A748.

354. Id. at A749-750.

355. D.I. 22, verdict sheet A1569.

356. www.delawareonline.com/article/20091125/NEWS01/911250334/1006/NEWS?, Sean O'Sullivan, *The News Journal* (November 25, 2009).

357. Id.

358. Id.

359. James Sheehan, Press Release (November 24, 2009).

360. Id.

361. *The Philadelphia Inquirer*, Kristin E. Holmes, "Man Sues, Alleging Sex Abuse By Catholic School Principal" (January 9, 2004).

362. Id.

363. Http://www.delawareonline.com/assets/pdf/BL17773484.PDF visited September 13, 2011; http://www.oblates.org/healing/healing_letter.htm viewed March 15, 2012 contains the lists of these priests.

364. *The Philadelphia Inquirer*, Kristin E. Holmes (January 9, 2009).

365. *Eden v. Oblates of St. Francis de Sales, et al.* C.A. No. 04C-01-069 CLS (Delaware Superior Court), Hearing Transcript (March 22, 2005), Efiled May 24, 2005, at 29.

366. Http://www.oblates.org/chablais_mission_fund.php visited January 1, 2007, since removed from the world wide web.

367. *The News Journal*, Beth Miller (May 16, 2007).

368. Id.

369. Id.

370. *The News Journal*, Beth Miller (December 19, 2007).

371. Id.

372. Id.

373. Id.

374. *Associated Press*, Randall Chase (January 17, 2008).

375. *Associated Press*, Randall Chase (May 27, 2011).

376. Id.

377. Id.

378. Id.

379. Id.

380. Http://galvestondailynews.com/story/98338 quoting U.S. District Court Judge Samuel Kent, viewed September 24, 2011.

381. In Chapter two Dr. Carol Tavani briefly explained this emotional defense mechanism in the Ken Whitwell trial. In the John Vai trial found in Chapter five it is explained in even greater detail since John was a victim of this type of amnesia.

382. *Associated Press*, Randall Chase (January 18, 2008).

383. *Eden v. Oblates of St. Francis de Sales*, 2006 WL 3512482 (Del. Super. 2006) *5.

384. Id.

385. *Sheehan v. Oblates of St. Francis de Sales, et al*, No. 730, 2009 before the Supreme Court of the State of Delaware, D.I. 31 at 1-2, filed June 2, 2010 (Diocese Motion for Leave to File Brief).

386. Id. D.I. 32. at 6 (Diocese legal brief).

387. Id. at 20.

388. Id. D.I. 29 (Motion and Brief of the Brandywine, Capital, Christina, Colonial and Red Clay School Districts).

389. Http://www.stradley.com/firm-news.php?action=view&id=469 viewed September 26, 2011.

390. See chapter five below.

391. John A. Farrell, *Clarence Darrow: Attorney for the Damned*, 70-71 (Doubleday, 2011).

392. Http://www.law.temple.edu/Pages/Law_School/Law_School.aspx viewed September 25, 2011.

393. *Quill v. Catholic Diocese of Wilmington, Inc.*, 2008 WL 193000 (D.Del. Jan. 23, 2008) (recognizing the right of a federal court to hear lawsuits brought under the Delaware Child Victim's Act of 2007).

394. *E.g., Whitwell v. Archmere Academy*, C.A.No. 07C-08-006 (Del.Super. Feb. 22, 2008) (ordering a priest to answer deposition questions about his sexual abuse of a young boy in Delaware, Pennsylvania and New Jersey, despite the priest's efforts to hide behind the Fifth Amendment right against self-incrimination); *Eden v. Oblates of St. Francis DeSales*, 2007 WL 4722830 (Del.Super. Dec. 14,2007) (striking down a priest's efforts to hide behind the Fifth Amendment right against self-incrimination and instead requiring the priest to answer deposition questions about his sexual abuse of a young boy in Delaware and New Jersey).

395. *Whitwell v. Archmere Academy, Inc.*, 2008 WL 1735370 (Del.Super. April 16, 2008), and again in *Sheehan v. Oblates of St. Francis de Sales, et al.*, C.A.No. 07C-11-234 (Del.Super. Oct. 27, 2009) (slip. op. at 9).

396. 2010 *U.S. Chamber of Commerce State Liability Systems Ranking Study* (March 9, 2010) at 5,8 found at http://courts.delaware.gov/superior/pdf/harris_2010.pdf visited September 26, 2011.

397. Http://www.americanrhetoric.com/MovieSpeeches/moviespeechjudgmentatnuremberg3.html viewed September 27, 2011.

398. Id.

399. *Sheehan v. Oblates*, 15 A.3d 1247, 1259 (Del. Supr. 2011)(en banc).

400. Id.

401. Id.

402. Id. at 1260.

403. Id. at 1254, 1255.

404. Id. at 1255.

405. James Sheehan, Press Release (February 22, 2011).

406. James Sheehan, Press Release (February 22, 2011).

407. *Buckley v. Valeo*, 424 U.S. 1, 67 (1976)(quoting L. Brandeis, "Other People's Money" 62 (National Home Library Foundation ed. 1933)).

408. *Catholic Diocese of Wilmington, Inc.*, No. 09-13560-CSS (Bankr.D.Del.), hearing transcript (October 21, 2009), at 28-29; *Catholic Diocese of Wilmington, Inc.*, No. 09-13560-CSS (Bankr.D.Del.), hearing transcript (November 2, 2009), at 169-170.

409. *Catholic Diocese of Wilmington, Inc.*, No. 09-13560-CSS (Bankr.D.Del.), hearing transcript (October 21, 2009), at 26.

410. Id. at 28.

411. Id.

412. David O'Reilly, *The Philadelphia Inquirer* (October 20, 2009).

413. Id.

414. Brian Witte, *The Associated Press* (October 18, 2009).

415. *The Washington Post* (October 19, 2009).

416. Brian Witte, *The Associated Press* (October 18, 2009).

417. Ian Urbina, *The New York Times* (October 20, 2009).

418. Niall Stange, *The Irish Times* (October 20, 2009).

419. Press Release (October 18, 2009).

420. Editorial, *The Philadelphia Inquirer* (October 23, 2009).

421. *Catholic Diocese of Wilmington, Inc.*, No. 09-13560-CSS (Bankr.D.Del.), hearing transcript (October 21, 2009), at 31-32.

422. *Catholic Diocese of Wilmington, Inc.*, No. 09-13560-CSS (Bankr.D.Del.), hearing transcript (November 2, 2009), at 29.

423. Id. at 102-104.

424. *Catholic Diocese of Wilmington, Inc.*, No. 09-13560-CSS (Bankr.D.Del.), hearing transcript (August 12, 2010), at 14; Sean O'Sullivan, *The News Journal* (August 13, 2010, found at http://www.delawareonline.com/fdcp/?1281756075750.

425. *Catholic Diocese of Wilmington, Inc.*, No. 09-13560-CSS (Bankr.D.Del.), hearing transcript (August 12, 2010), at 16-21.

426. Id. at 82-97.

427. Id. at 98-112.

428. *Catholic Diocese of Wilmington, Inc.*, No. 09-13560-CSS (Bankr.D.Del.), hearing Exhibit 7, Michael Saltarelli deposition transcript (August 12, 2010), at 40.

429. Id. at 43.

430. Id. at 94.

431. Id. at 100-101.

432. Id. at 68.

433. Id. at 112-113, 125-127, 128, 129.

434. Id. at 71-72, 78, 81, 84, 85, 87.

435. *Catholic Diocese of Wilmington, Inc.*, No. 09-13560-CSS (Bankr.D.Del.), hearing transcript (August 12, 2010), at 115.

436. Id. at 117.

437. Id. at 120-121.

438. Id. at 122-135.

439. Sean O'Sullivan, *The News Journal* (August 13, 2010), found at http://www.delawareonline.com/fdcp/?1281756075750.

440. *Catholic Diocese of Wilmington, Inc.*, No. 09-13560-CSS (Bankr.D.Del.), hearing transcript (August 12, 2010), at 136-147.

441. Id. at 186-197.

442. Id. at 197-207.

443. Id. at 207-225.

444. *Catholic Diocese of Wilmington, Inc.*, No. 09-13560-CSS (Bankr.D.Del.), hearing transcript (August 13, 2010), at 20-21.

445. Id. at 64-69.

446. *The News Journal* (August 14, 2010) A1.

447. *The News Journal* (August 13, 2010) A1.

448. *The News Journal* (August 14, 2010) A1.

449. *The News Journal* (August 14, 2010), A1 found at http://www.delawareonline/fdcp/?1281788671453.

450. *Catholic Diocese of Wilmington, Inc.*, No. 09-13560-CSS (Bankr.D.Del.), D.I. 620 – Appendix to Defendants and the Abuse Survivors' Response in Opposition to the Debtor's Motion to Extend the Bankruptcy Stay.

451. Id. at B000417.

452. Id. at B000418.

453. Id.

454. Id. at B000416.

455. Id. at B000387-397.

456. Id. at B000388.

457. Id. at B000389-390.

458. Id. at B000391.

459. Id.

460. Id. at B000392.

461. Id. at B000393.

462. Id. at B000393, 394.

463. Id. at B000394.

464. Id. at B000395.

465. Id.

466. Id. at B000396.

467. Id. at B000156-194.

468. Id. at B000160.

469. Id. at B000164-166.

470. Http://www.archmereacademy.com/podium/default.aspx?t=125176 visited April 26, 2011.

471. *Catholic Diocese of Wilmington, Inc.*, No. 09-13560-CSS (Bankr.D.Del.), D.I. 620 – Appendix to Defendants and the Abuse Survivors' Response in Opposition to the Debtor's Motion to Extend the Bankruptcy Stay, at B000171-172.

472. Id. at B000405.

473. Id. at B000411-412.

474. Id. at B000413.

475. *Catholic Diocese of Wilmington, Inc.*, No. 09-13560-CSS (Bankr.D.Del.) (June 20, 2012), D.I. 2023.

476. *Catholic Diocese of Wilmington, Inc.*, No. 09-13560-CSS (Bankr.D.Del.), hearing transcript (May 20, 2011), at 9, 10.

477. Id. at 17-18.

478. *Catholic Diocese of Wilmington, Inc.*, No. 09-13560-CSS (Bankr.D.Del.), hearing transcript (July 14, 2011), at 141.

479. Id. at 175-180.

480. *Catholic Diocese of Wilmington, Inc.*, No. 09-13560-CSS (Bankr.D.Del.), hearing transcript (September 9, 2011), at 62-63.

481. Id. at 68.

482. *John Michael Vai v. Catholic Diocese of Wilmington, Inc, et al*, C.A. No. 08C-06-044 JTV (Del. Super.), trial transcript (October 26, 2010), at 2. The remainder of attorney Crumplar's opening statement set out in the text is found here at pages 2-50.

483. *John Michael Vai v. Catholic Diocese of Wilmington, Inc, et al*, C.A. No. 08C-06-044 JTV (Del. Super.), Jennings (March 10, 2009) video deposition transcript (trial October 27, 2010), at 4-41.

484. *John Michael Vai v. Catholic Diocese of Wilmington, Inc, et al*, C.A. No. 08C-06-044 JTV (Del. Super.), Saltarelli (August 12, 2010) video deposition transcript (trial October 27, 2010), at 40, 43, 94, 100-101, 68, 112-113, 125-127, 128, 129, 71-72, 78, 81, 84, 85, 87.

485. *John Michael Vai v. Catholic Diocese of Wilmington, Inc, et al*, C.A. No. 08C-06-044 JTV (Del. Super.), Mulvee (May 13, 2009) video deposition transcript (trial October 27, 2010), at 293-295.

486. *John Michael Vai v. Catholic Diocese of Wilmington, Inc, et al*, C.A. No. 08C-06-044 JTV (Del. Super.), trial transcript (November 1, 2010), at 10-34.

487. Id. at 35-49.

488. Id. at 50-65.

489. *John Michael Vai v. Catholic Diocese of Wilmington, Inc, et al*, C.A. No. 08C-06-044 JTV (Del. Super.), Nagle (October 28, 2010) video deposition transcript (trial November 1, 2010), at 3-38.

490. *John Michael Vai v. Catholic Diocese of Wilmington, Inc, et al*, C.A. No. 08C-06-044 JTV (Del. Super.), trial transcript (November 1, 2010), at 4.

491. Id. at 22.

492. Id. at 21-22.

493. Id. at 30-31.

494. Id. at 32-37, 41.

495. Id. at 38.

496. Id. at 85.

497. Id. at 40.

498. Id. at 85-86.

499. Id. at 87-89.

500. *John Michael Vai v. Catholic Diocese of Wilmington, Inc, et al*, C.A. No. 08C-06-044 JTV (Del. Super.), trial transcript (November 3, 2010, morning), at 9-74, 111-117.

501. Id. at 72.

502. Id. at 112-113.

503. Id. at 116.

504. *John Michael Vai v. Catholic Diocese of Wilmington, Inc, et al*, C.A. No. 08C-06-044 JTV (Del. Super.), trial transcript (November 3, 2010, afternoon), at 3-67.

505. Id. at 63-64.

506. *John Michael Vai v. Catholic Diocese of Wilmington, Inc, et al*, C.A. No. 08C-06-044 JTV (Del. Super.), trial transcript (November 8, 2010, morning), at 6-31.

507. *John Michael Vai v. Catholic Diocese of Wilmington, Inc, et al*, C.A. No. 08C-06-044 JTV (Del. Super.), Tavani (November 2, 2010) video deposition transcript (trial November 8, 2010, afternoon), at 6-52.

508. Id. at 22-29.

509. Id. at 32-34.

510. Id. at 42-45.

511. *John Michael Vai v. Catholic Diocese of Wilmington, Inc, et al*, C.A. No. 08C-06-044 JTV (Del. Super.), trial transcript (November 8, 2010, morning), at 40, 42.

512. Id. at 50.

513. Id. at 60.

514. Id. at 61-63.

515. Id. at 63-64, 67-68, 69.

516. *John Michael Vai v. Catholic Diocese of Wilmington, Inc, et al*, C.A. No. 08C-06-044 JTV (Del. Super.), trial transcript (November 8, 2010, afternoon), at 5-6.

517. Id. at 7.

518. Id. at 46.

519. Id. at 10.

520. Id. at 15.

521. Id. at 17.

522. Id. at 23.

523. Id. at 27.

524. Id. at 34.

525. Id. at 36-37.

526. Id. at 46-51.

527. Id. at 51-52.

528. *John Michael Vai v. Catholic Diocese of Wilmington, Inc, et al*, C.A. No. 08C-06-044 JTV (Del. Super.), trial transcript (November 9, 2010, morning), at 5-6.

529. Id. at 13-14.

530. *John Michael Vai v. Catholic Diocese of Wilmington, Inc, et al*, C.A. No. 08C-06-044 JTV (Del. Super.), trial transcript jury charge (November 30, 2010), at 43-44.

531. *John Michael Vai v. Catholic Diocese of Wilmington, Inc, et al*, C.A. No. 08C-06-044 JTV (Del. Super.), trial transcript (November 9, 2010, morning), at 17-18.

532. Id. at 26-27.

533. Id. at 27.

534. Id. at 27-28.

535. Id. at 30.

536. Id. at 32-35.

537. Id. at 60.

538. Id. at 66-67.

539. Id. at 73-74.

540. Id. at 74.

541. Id. at 75.

542. Id. at 76-82.

543. Id. at 83-84.

544. Id. at 88-90.

545. Id. at 91-92.

546. Id. at 93-94.

547. Id. at 96-97.

548. *John Michael Vai v. Catholic Diocese of Wilmington, Inc, et al*, C.A. No. 08C-06-044 JTV (Del. Super.), trial transcript (November 9, 2010, afternoon), at 2-3.

549. Id. at 7-8.

550. Id. at 11-14.

551. Id. at 16-17.

552. Id. at 18-21.

553. Id. at 30-31.

554. Id. at 33-36.

555. Id. at 36-39.

556. Id. at 39-42.

557. Id. at 49-51.

558. Id. at 52-57.

559. Id. at 59-64.

560. Id. at 95-96.

561. Id. at 98-99.

562. Id. at 107-109.

563. Id. at 115.

564. *John Michael Vai v. Catholic Diocese of Wilmington, Inc, et al*, C.A. No. 08C-06-044 JTV (Del. Super.), trial transcript (November 12, 2010, morning), at 37.

565. Id. at 4-45.

566. *John Michael Vai v. Catholic Diocese of Wilmington, Inc, et al*, C.A. No. 08C-06-044 JTV (Del. Super.), trial transcript (December 1, 2010) and completed Verdict Form.

567. John Vai, press release (December 1, 2010).

568. *John Michael Vai v. Catholic Diocese of Wilmington, Inc, et al*, C.A. No. 08C-06-044 JTV (Del. Super.), trial transcript (December 6, 2010, morning) at 89-90.

569. Id. at 71-89; *John Michael Vai v. Catholic Diocese of Wilmington, Inc, et al*, C.A. No. 08C-06-044 JTV (Del. Super.), trial transcript (December 6, 2010, afternoon) at 61-66; *John Michael Vai v. Catholic Diocese of Wilmington, Inc, et al*, C.A. No. 08C-06-044 JTV (Del. Super.), trial transcript (December 7, 2010, morning) at 4-12.

570. *John Michael Vai v. Catholic Diocese of Wilmington, Inc, et al*, C.A. No. 08C-06-044 JTV (Del. Super.), trial transcript (December 7, 2010, morning) at 13-18; *John Michael Vai v. Catholic Diocese of Wilmington, Inc, et al*, C.A. No. 08C-06-044 JTV (Del. Super.), trial transcript (December 6, 2010, afternoon) at 4-7; *John Michael Vai v. Catholic Diocese of Wilmington, Inc, et al*, C.A. No. 08C-06-044 JTV (Del. Super.), trial transcript (December 6, 2010, morning) at 51-57.

571. *John Michael Vai v. Catholic Diocese of Wilmington, Inc, et al*, C.A. No. 08C-06-044 JTV (Del. Super.), trial transcript (December 7, 2010, morning) at 19, 13.

572. *John Michael Vai v. Catholic Diocese of Wilmington, Inc, et al*, C.A. No. 08C-06-044 JTV (Del. Super.), trial transcript (December 6, 2010, morning) at 46-54.

573. Id. at 51-55; *John Michael Vai v. Catholic Diocese of Wilmington, Inc, et al*, C.A. No. 08C-06-044 JTV (Del. Super.), trial transcript (December 6, 2010, afternoon) at 37-39.

574. Id. at 38-39; *John Michael Vai v. Catholic Diocese of Wilmington, Inc, et al*, C.A. No. 08C-06-044 JTV (Del. Super.), trial transcript (December 6, 2010, morning) at 54.

575. *John Michael Vai v. Catholic Diocese of Wilmington, Inc, et al*, C.A. No. 08C-06-044 JTV (Del. Super.), trial transcript (December 7, 2010, morning) at 24-26, 15-16; *John Michael Vai v. Catholic Diocese of Wilmington, Inc, et al*, C.A. No. 08C-06-044 JTV (Del. Super.), trial transcript (December 6, 2010, afternoon) at 33.

576. *John Michael Vai v. Catholic Diocese of Wilmington, Inc, et al*, C.A. No. 08C-06-044 JTV (Del. Super.), trial transcript (December 7, 2010, morning) at 26.

577. Id. 17-18.

578. *John Michael Vai v. Catholic Diocese of Wilmington, Inc, et al*, C.A. No. 08C-06-044 JTV (Del. Super.), trial transcript (December 6, 2010, afternoon) at 39-41, 28-29.

579. Id. at 64-65.

580. *John Michael Vai v. Catholic Diocese of Wilmington, Inc, et al*, C.A. No. 08C-06-044 JTV (Del. Super.), trial transcript (December 8, 2010) at 55-56.

581. Id., Completed Verdict Form.

582. John Vai, handwritten press statement (December 8, 2010).

Master Index

A

Aberdeen, Maryland, 55
Agostini, Carl, 11
Agostini, Carrie, 36
alcoholism, 4, 12, 24, 114, 118, 126, 245, 338
Alighieri, Dante, 111
altar boy, 18, 19, 26, 36, 119, 146, 156, 157, 177, 179, 198, 222, 237, 241, 253, 259, 262, 270, 288, 295, 313, 320, 322, 323
Altar Society, 156
Alter Christus, 321
American Bandstand, 11
American Family Journal, 348
Americana Hotel, New York City, 179
amnesia, 5, 14, 38, 96, 134, 135, 137, 333, 340, 347, 353, 358, 453
amnesia, traumatic (related to post traumatic stress disorder), 96, 134, 333
anterograde amnesia, 358
anxiety attacks, 160
Archdiocese of Chicago, 317
Archdiocese of Philadelphia, 114, 147, 329
Archmere Academy, 61, 62, 65, 66, 83, 222
Associated Press, The, 132, 133, 144

B

Bagnato, James (priest), 63, 65, 83, 84
Bellevue-Stratford Hotel, Philadelphia, 199
Benedictines, 314
Benkert Ph.D, Marianne, 317
bingo, 194
The Bible, 20, 21, 66, 164, 261, 398
bipolar disorder, 185, 329, 330
Bolen, John J. (priest), 20, 26, 32
Book of Job, 14, 16, 17
Boston Globe, 436
Boyd Theater, 204
Brady, Jane (attorney general), 207
Brandeis, Louis (U S. Supreme Court Justice), 141, 454
Briggs-Green, Kara, 438
Buckley v. Valeo, 424 U.S. 1, 67 (1976), 454
Butler, Joe, 11

C

Camaro, 276, 278, 283

Canby Park, 238, 301

Canby Park Pool, 11

Canon Law, Code of, 315, 316, 320, 325, 364, 378

Capuchins, 2

Carley, Edward B. (priest), 8, 18, 19, 20, 21, 22, 23, 24, 25, 26, 27, 28, 29, 30, 31, 32, 33, 34, 35, 36, 37, 38, 39, 40, 41, 42, 44, 127, 309

Carroll, Norman B. (priest), 250, 258, 402, 403, 409, 410

Cartagena, Felix, 36

Cartwright, H. James (Bishop), 119, 218

Casey, Joyce, 48

Cash, Johnny, 8

Catholic Conference, 147

Catholic Diocese of Wilmington, 2, 22, 109, 224, 227, 404, 406, 407, 408, 409, 410

Catholic Theological Union, 317

Catholic Youth Organization (CYO), 36, 165, 166, 167, 288

celibacy, 261

Centers for Disease Control, 352

Central Park (New York City), 54

Chablais Mission Fund, 130

Chapter 11, 152

Chesapeake Bay, 16, 45

Child Victim's Act of 2007 (10 Del. C. § 8145), 1, 31, 38, 40, 42, 47, 65, 105, 128, 129, 131, 134, 135, 136, 137, 139, 140, 143, 203

chronic memories, 155

chronic obstructive pulmonary disease (COPD), 118

chronic post-traumatic stress disorder, 164, 197

Chuck Wagon Restaurant, 289, 290

Cini, J. Thomas (priest), 32, 33, 42, 44, 189, 208, 209, 213, 248, 255, 256, 258, 267, 274, 276, 284, 285, 309, 365, 370, 375, 377, 379, 381, 382, 383, 385, 386, 388, 389, 391, 393, 395, 397, 398, 401, 402, 414, 415, 416, 417, 431

Civil War, 17, 367

Clark, Dick, 11

Cloyne Report, 1

cocaine, 425, 426, 427

Collins, Michael (priest), 63, 64, 66, 83

Conex box, 10, 14

Confraternity of Christian Doctrine (CCD), 429

COPD (Chronic Obstructive Pulmonary Disease), 118

Cox Broadcasting Corp. v. Cohn, 420 U.S. 469 (1975), 3

Crumplar, Thomas C., 131, 137, 233, 234, 238, 239, 244, 246, 248, 250, 255, 260, 267, 272, 302, 308, 309, 310, 311, 313, 324, 326, 345, 356, 361, 368, 388, 406, 407, 421, 424, 427, 430, 431

Cuccia, Salvatore H. (priest), 63

Curry, Joseph, 41, 215

D

Darrow, Clarence, 136

David and Bathsheba, 261

Delaware Bankruptcy Court (see U.S. Bankruptcy Court – District of Delaware)

Delaware General Assembly, 1, 44, 137, 141

Delaware Psychiatric Center, 13

Delaware Rules of Evidence, 282

Delaware State Legislature, 47, 137, 203, 253

Delaware Superior Court, 43, 131, 133, 135, 142

Delaware Supreme Court, 111, 135, 137, 138, 139, 140, 141, 282

Delaware Today Magazine, 436

Delaware, Claymont, 62

Delaware, Montchanin, 28

Delaware, Rehoboth Beach, 180, 245, 279, 430

Delaware, Woodcrest, 307

DeLuca Eight, 142, 143, 151, 197, 203, 211, 423

DeLuca Seven, 215, 216

DeLuca, Francis J. (priest), 137, 142-43, 149, 150, 152, 155-57, 159-60, 175-80, 182-87, 190-94, 196-99, 202-207, 209, 211-13, 215-16, 219, 222, 238-60, 262-65, 267-68, 271, 273-81, 283-86, 293-98, 300, 309-11, 313, 320, 324-26, 332-33, 338-39, 345, 358-59, 362, 365, 371-75, 381, 383-96, 401-402, 407-15, 418-21, 423-25, 427, 431-35

Dempster, Douglas (priest), 206, 207

depression, 14, 24, 29, 40, 41, 88, 90, 97, 98, 114, 160, 161, 163, 170, 172, 176, 329, 330, 336

depressive disorder, 164, 193, 195, 197, 203, 210

Devine, Donn, 31

DeWane, Thomas E. (Abbot), 34, 68

DiFillipo, John (priest), 112

Dillingham, Charles C. (priest), 401, 432, 433

Dingle, Maria, 432, 433

Dingle, Michael, 208, 211, 432, 433

Diocese of Wilmington (see Catholic Diocese of Wilmington)

disassociation, 353

Doe Number One, John, (see Felix Flanigan), 184, 185, 188

Doe Number Two, John, 256, 257, 258, 293, 294, 393

Doe Number Three, John, 154, 155, 173, 432

Doe Number Four, John, 192, 432

Doe Number Seven, John, 116

Doe Number Eighteen, John, 257, 258

Doherty, John Holmes, 36

Dominican Order, 314

Donahue, Raymond, 154, 220

Donohoe, John M. (priest), 240, 255, 265, 267, 274, 280, 281, 282, 286, 309, 310, 365, 366, 367, 374, 383, 384, 385, 389, 390, 394

Doubletree Hotel, 417

Dougherty, John F., 8, 23, 25, 27, 32, 35, 37, 38, 39, 40, 41, 43, 203

Dougherty, Mary, 164, 173, 175, 215, 216, 219, 220
Doyle, Thomas Patrick (Dominican priest), 266, 272, 313, 324, 325, 326, 363
Drelich, Robert (priest), 110
Drexel University, 264
DSM-IV, 93, 97, 98
Dudzinski, Edward (priest), 222, 223

E
Eastern Shore of Maryland, 36, 45, 135
Eden, Eric, 129, 130, 132, 133, 134, 135
Elavil™ , 29
errata sheet, 388
excommunication, 206

F
Fallers, Paul (priest), 26, 32
Farrell, Lt. Amy (see Amy F. Whitwell), 52
Finch, Atticus, 233
FitzMaurice, Edmond John (Bishop), 30, 31
Flagg Brothers, 11
Flanigan, Felix (see John Doe Number One), 184, 189, 192, 215, 395, 397, 432
flashbacks, 97, 155, 160, 163, 186, 200, 264, 328, 354, 425
Florida, Jacksonville, 11
Forty Acres (in Wilmington, DE), 11, 17, 25, 27
Friends School, 276

G
Galilee, 145
Gambet, Daniel (Provincial), 112, 119
Gaylord's, 307
General Motors, 204, 259
Gerard, Sister, 295
Gerres, Daniel W. (priest), 27
Global Assessment of Functioning (GAF), 99, 100, 101, 155, 185, 193, 195, 197, 203
Gore (W. L. Gore & Associates, Inc.), 259
Governor Bacon Health Center, 12
Grady & Hurst, 11
Grant Hall (at St. Elizabeth's church), 280, 282
Grant, James M. (priest), 288
Grant, Richard N. (priest), 110, 130
Graves, T. Henley (Judge), 164, 171, 172
Gregory, Maria, 404, 406
grooming process, 239, 240, 243, 412
Groton, Connecticut, 51
Ground Zero, 340, 349

H

Hagendorf, Thomas (priest), 63
Hahn, John, 35
Harvey, John X. (priest), 110
Haywood, Dan, 139
Heaney, Kevin, 222
Heckle, John (priest), 110, 130
Heesters, Nicholas, 35
Hermley, Harold (priest), 110
Hernandez, Kay, 12
Highland Elementary School, 23
Holy Rosary Church, 171, 219
Holy Spirit Church, 396, 397
Hotel DuPont, 240, 420
Howard Johnson's, 198
Hudson, Representative Deborah D., 1
Hyle, Michael W. (Bishop), 119, 206, 218, 219, 220

I

illicit drugs, 426
Illinois, Chicago, 62, 315, 317
Indian River Inlet, 167
insomnia, 181, 354
The Inferno, 111
The Irish Times, 144
irreparable harm, 215, 216

J

Jacobs & Crumplar, 228, 229, 302, 345
Jacobs, Robert, 149, 150, 224
Jennings, William E. (priest), 33, 34, 268, 269, 326, 380
Jesus of Nazareth, 83, 110, 111, 237, 321, 364
Jordan, Michael, 115
Judgment at Nuremburg, 139

K

Keech, William (priest), 112
Kempski, Leonard (priest), 167, 168
Kent County, Delaware, 142
Kent County Courthouse, 232
Killion, Dennis W. (priest), 110, 130
King of Kings, 204
Kirkwood Detox, 13
Kirkwood Highway, 156, 289
To Kill A Mockingbird, 233

L

Lamb, Barry, 154, 222, 223
Langberg Ph.D, Diane, 263, 339, 340, 353, 356
Law, Bernard (Cardinal), 134
Leave it to Beaver, 17
Lee, Nelle Harper E., 233
Leinheiser, Edward M. (priest), 219
Lemon, Clement (priest), 31, 207, 308, 309, 310, 311, 362, 402
Lenderman, Donald, 35
Lind, John A. (priest), 41, 220, 221, 222, 257, 286, 288, 289, 290, 291, 292, 293, 301, 302, 304, 305, 307, 309, 313, 325, 326, 374
Loe Number Two, John, 257
Loe Number Six, John (see Saggione, Philip A.), 257, 286
Logan, John (priest), 63
LSD, 425
LSD flashbacks, 425

M

Mackiewicz, Leonard J. (priest), 164, 165, 167, 168, 219
Malooly, W. Francis (Bishop), 44, 145, 146, 408
Man in Black, The, 8
Mann, Brian, 11
Mardaga, Thomas (Bishop), 217
Marine Corps League, 13
Maryland, Aberdeen, 55
Maryland, Baltimore, 113, 325
Maryland, Galena, 28
Maryland, Ocean City, 19, 27, 37
Mass, Roman Catholic, 34, 49, 52, 156, 157, 177, 199, 237, 241, 248, 295, 321, 322
McClure, Douglas F., 7, 8, 28, 32, 36, 37, 39, 41, 42, 44, 119, 127, 130
McClure, Kevin, 13
McClure, Mark, 13
McClure, Marty, 13
McClure, Nancy, 11, 12, 15, 23, 24, 29, 38, 43
McClure, Natalie, 11
McDevitt, Jack (priest), 110, 130
McDonald, William A. (Captain), 57, 82, 91
McGovern, Harold J. (priest), 110
McLaughlin, Joseph (priest), 64, 67
mental reservation, 397, 398
Mexico, 27
Miller, Beth, 37, 252
Milltown™ , 29
MMPI, 344
Montreal, 27

P. S. DuPont High School, 121
panic attacks, 162, 328
panic disorder, 203
Parkinson's Disorder, 328
Pastoral Psychology, 317
Patio, The, 62
Paul, Henry (priest), 110
Peck, Gregory, 233
pedophile(s), 25, 43, 114, 152, 207, 241, 245, 258, 264, 328, 330, 335
pedophilia, 114, 239, 320, 330, 374
Pennsylvania Catholic Conference, 147
Pennsylvania, Chadds Ford, 405, 428
Pennsylvania, Downingtown, 329
Pennsylvania, Philadelphia Badlands of, 342
personality disorders, 155
Peterman, Thomas J. (priest), 31, 222, 248, 255, 256, 267, 277, 309, 310, 365, 368, 370, 371, 372, 373, 374, 377, 378, 385, 411, 412, 414
Peterson, Senator Karen, 1
Phi Beta Kappa, 12
Philadelphia Daily News, 65
The Philadelphia Inquirer, 129, 144, 145
Place of Refuge, The, 342
Poconos, 12
post traumatic stress disorder (PTSD), 9, 155, 159
Power, Walter D. (priest), 217, 218, 219, 274
primary cognitive deficit, 357
Priory, The, 49, 50, 62, 63, 64, 68, 72, 76, 83, 315
Prothonotary, 233
Psalms, 10
psychiatric medications, 198, 204
psychiatrist, 5, 23, 42, 57, 60, 81, 87, 91, 113, 160, 164, 193, 245, 250, 264, 266, 317, 319, 320, 327, 328, 330, 331, 412, 417, 418, 426, 429, 430, 471
psychosexual abuse, 325
psychotherapy, 155, 191, 193
PTSD (see posttraumatic stress disorder)

Q
Quill, Robert, 46, 246, 252, 253, 254, 258, 262, 394, 403, 404, 405

R
Radio City Music Hall, 27, 158
rape, 21, 23, 26, 27, 28, 39, 40, 42, 47, 63, 79, 80, 87, 148, 149, 178, 202, 219, 222, 243, 245, 256, 262, 265, 286, 296, 298, 344, 348, 352
Rebman, Joseph F. (priest), 259, 361, 362
repressed memory, 333, 334

U

U. S. Air Force, 266, 315

U. S. Conference of Catholic Bishops, 136

U. S. Marine Corps, 7, 9, 11, 37, 60, 186

U. S. Marine Corps League, 13

U. S. Navy , 46, 51, 52, 55, 60, 81

U. S. Navy Flight School, 55, 59

U. S. Navy MBA program, 54

U. S. Chamber of Commerce, 138

U. S. Bankruptcy Court – District of Delaware, 5, 142, 143, 149, 151, 152, 184, 220, 224, 225, 232, 271, 274, 391, 395, 432, 436

U. S. Supreme Court, 3, 140, 141

University of Delaware, 159, 250

V

Vai, Cindy, 251, 358, 427, 428, 429

Vai, John M. (Johnny), 5, 6, 31-33, 87, 118, 137, 139, 146, 153, 175, 184, 196, 215-18, 222, 224, 230, 232-35, 237, 239-58, 261-68, 271, 294, 320, 322-23, 327-28, 331-40, 345-46, 350-58, 361, 365, 377, 385, 391-94, 402-03, 405-07, 410-12, 415-17, 419-20, 424-26, 429, 431, 433-35

Vai, Lorenzo, 394

Vai, Maria, 394

Vai, Ryan, 402, 428, 429

Vatican, 267, 313, 318, 408

Vatican Embassy (Washington D.C.), 318, 319

Vaughn, James T. (President Judge), 142, 152, 161, 162, 163, 175, 182, 201, 232, 234, 370, 431

Vermont, 27, 53, 80

Veterans Administration Hospital, 13

Vietnam, 8, 9, 13, 14, 44, 184, 186, 335

Vietnam Memorial, 329

Vietnam War, 8, 103, 334

W

Warner, Raeann, 273, 274, 281, 282, 286, 294, 301, 339, 340, 356

Washington, D.C., 245, 313, 317, 318, 319, 329, 430

The Washington Post, 144

Wayne, John, 195, 264

Whitwell, Amy F., 48, 50, 51, 53, 55, 56, 81, 93

Whitwell, David, 61

Whitwell, Kenneth J. (Commander), 46, 47, 52, 67, 90, 97, 104, 327, 356

Wilmington High School, 11

Wilmington Police Department, 286, 287, 394

Wilmington Veterans Administration Nursing Home, 13

World Vision, 342

Wright and Simon, 178

Y
YMCA, 11, 23
YMCA, Jewish, 19, 23
Young, Robert B. (Judge), 153

About the Author

For nearly eight years, the author had primary responsibility, on a legal team of six lawyers, for over 110 of the Delaware court cases for victims of childhood sexual abuse who lost their childhood innocence and whose normal lives were derailed by crimes committed by priests of the Roman Catholic Church. He has first hand knowledge of the secret torment which these men and women have suffered and control of the documents upon which their court proceedings were founded. These records eventually made their way into public court filings, available under the First Amendment and the common law to any citizen, and into public sworn courtroom testimony before juries composed of ordinary citizens.

Biographical information on the author can be found at www.neubergerlaw.com. In 2003 he took up another cause for what he always called "the little man."[1] As one magazine explained – "If he's known for anything, it's being relentless. And for winning."[2] "He'll fight the devil for you," one client has said.[3] In the words of the editorial board of *The News Journal* – "He never gave up on his fight to receive justice for his abused clients" despite the fact that he was "stigmatized and ridiculed for his persistent and sometimes overly public pursuit of justice for his clients."[4] Philadelphia TV newsman Vernon Odom summed it all up when he described Tom as a "flame throwing lawyer."[5]

---

[1] *Delaware Today Magazine* (August 2006), at 56.

[2] *Pennsylvania Super Lawyers* (2007), at 28.

[3] Id.

[4] *The News Journal*, Editorial (February 4, 2011), at A10.

[5] WPVI-TV6 Philadelphia broadcast on February 3, 2011 accessed at http://abclocal.go.com/wpvi/story?section=news/local&id=7937473.

Reader's Notes